MIT/GNU Scheme Reference Manual

A catalogue record for this book is available from the Hong Kong Public Libraries.

Published in Hong Kong by Samurai Media Limited.

Email: info@samuraimedia.org

ISBN 978-988-8381-57-9

Short Contents

Table of Contents

Acknowledgements

While "a cast of thousands" may be an overstatement, it is certainly the case that this document represents the work of many people. First and foremost, thanks go to the authors of the *Revised^4 Report on the Algorithmic Language Scheme*, from which much of this document is derived. Thanks also to BBN Advanced Computers Inc. for the use of parts of their *Butterfly Scheme Reference*, and to Margaret O'Connell for translating it from BBN's text-formatting language to ours.

Special thanks to Richard Stallman, Bob Chassell, and Brian Fox, all of the Free Software Foundation, for creating and maintaining the Texinfo formatting language in which this document is written.

This report describes research done at the Artificial Intelligence Laboratory and the Laboratory for Computer Science, both of the Massachusetts Institute of Technology. Support for this research is provided in part by the Advanced Research Projects Agency of the Department of Defense and by the National Science Foundation.

1 Overview

This manual is a detailed description of the MIT/GNU Scheme runtime system. It is intended to be a reference document for programmers. It does not describe how to run Scheme or how to interact with it — that is the subject of the *MIT/GNU Scheme User's Manual*.

This chapter summarizes the semantics of Scheme, briefly describes the MIT/GNU Scheme programming environment, and explains the syntactic and lexical conventions of the language. Subsequent chapters describe special forms, numerous data abstractions, and facilities for input and output.

Throughout this manual, we will make frequent references to *standard Scheme*, which is the language defined by the document *Revised^4 Report on the Algorithmic Language Scheme*, by William Clinger, Jonathan Rees, et al., or by IEEE Std. 1178-1990, *IEEE Standard for the Scheme Programming Language* (in fact, several parts of this document are copied from the *Revised Report*). MIT/GNU Scheme is an extension of standard Scheme.

These are the significant semantic characteristics of the Scheme language:

Variables are statically scoped
> Scheme is a *statically scoped* programming language, which means that each use of a variable is associated with a lexically apparent binding of that variable. Algol is another statically scoped language.

Types are latent
> Scheme has *latent* types as opposed to *manifest* types, which means that Scheme associates types with values (or objects) rather than with variables. Other languages with latent types (also referred to as *weakly* typed or *dynamically* typed languages) include APL, Snobol, and other dialects of Lisp. Languages with manifest types (sometimes referred to as *strongly* typed or *statically* typed languages) include Algol 60, Pascal, and C.

Objects have unlimited extent
> All objects created during a Scheme computation, including procedures and continuations, have unlimited extent; no Scheme object is ever destroyed. The system doesn't run out of memory because the garbage collector reclaims the storage occupied by an object when the object cannot possibly be needed by a future computation. Other languages in which most objects have unlimited extent include APL and other Lisp dialects.

Proper tail recursion
> Scheme is *properly tail-recursive*, which means that iterative computation can occur in constant space, even if the iterative computation is described by a syntactically recursive procedure. With a tail-recursive implementation, you can express iteration using the ordinary procedure-call mechanics; special iteration expressions are provided only for syntactic convenience.

Procedures are objects
> Scheme procedures are objects, which means that you can create them dynamically, store them in data structures, return them as the results of other procedures, and so on. Other languages with such procedure objects include Common Lisp and ML.

Continuations are explicit

> In most other languages, continuations operate behind the scenes. In Scheme, continuations are objects; you can use continuations for implementing a variety of advanced control constructs, including non-local exits, backtracking, and coroutines.

Arguments are passed by value

> Arguments to Scheme procedures are passed by value, which means that Scheme evaluates the argument expressions before the procedure gains control, whether or not the procedure needs the result of the evaluations. ML, C, and APL are three other languages that pass arguments by value. In languages such as SASL and Algol 60, argument expressions are not evaluated unless the values are needed by the procedure.

Scheme uses a parenthesized-list Polish notation to describe programs and (other) data. The syntax of Scheme, like that of most Lisp dialects, provides for great expressive power, largely due to its simplicity. An important consequence of this simplicity is the susceptibility of Scheme programs and data to uniform treatment by other Scheme programs. As with other Lisp dialects, the `read` primitive parses its input; that is, it performs syntactic as well as lexical decomposition of what it reads.

1.1 Notational Conventions

This section details the notational conventions used throughout the rest of this document.

1.1.1 Errors

When this manual uses the phrase "an error will be signalled," it means that Scheme will call `error`, which normally halts execution of the program and prints an error message.

When this manual uses the phrase "it is an error," it means that the specified action is not valid in Scheme, but the system may or may not signal the error. When this manual says that something "must be," it means that violating the requirement is an error.

1.1.2 Examples

This manual gives many examples showing the evaluation of expressions. The examples have a common format that shows the expression being evaluated on the left hand side, an "arrow" in the middle, and the value of the expression written on the right. For example:

```
(+ 1 2)           ⇒  3
```

Sometimes the arrow and value will be moved under the expression, due to lack of space. Occasionally we will not care what the value is, in which case both the arrow and the value are omitted.

If an example shows an evaluation that results in an error, an error message is shown, prefaced by ' error ':

```
(+ 1 'foo)                        error   Illegal datum
```

An example that shows printed output marks it with ' ⊣ ':

```
(begin (write 'foo) 'bar)
      ⊣ foo
      ⇒ bar
```

When this manual indicates that the value returned by some expression is *unspecified*, it means that the expression will evaluate to some object without signalling an error, but that programs should not depend on the value in any way.

1.1.3 Entry Format

Each description of an MIT/GNU Scheme variable, special form, or procedure begins with one or more header lines in this format:

`template`   [*category*]

where *category* specifies the kind of item ("variable", "special form", or "procedure"). The form of *template* is interpreted depending on *category*.

Variable   *Template* consists of the variable's name.

Special Form

Template* starts with the syntactic keyword of the special form, followed by a description of the special form's syntax. The description is written using the following conventions.

Named components are italicized in the printed manual, and uppercase in the Info file. "Noise" keywords, such as the `else` keyword in the `cond` special form, are set in a fixed width font in the printed manual; in the Info file they are not distinguished. Parentheses indicate themselves.

A horizontal ellipsis (...) is describes repeated components. Specifically,

> *thing* ...

indicates *zero* or more occurrences of *thing*, while

> *thing thing* ...

indicates *one* or more occurrences of *thing*.

Brackets, [ ], enclose optional components.

Several special forms (e.g. `lambda`) have an internal component consisting of a series of expressions; usually these expressions are evaluated sequentially under conditions that are specified in the description of the special form. This sequence of expressions is commonly referred to as the *body* of the special form.

Procedure   *Template* starts with the name of the variable to which the procedure is bound, followed by a description of the procedure's arguments. The arguments are described using "lambda list" notation (see Section 2.1 [Lambda Expressions], page 15), except that brackets are used to denote optional arguments, and ellipses are used to denote "rest" arguments.

The names of the procedure's arguments are italicized in the printed manual, and uppercase in the Info file.

When an argument names a Scheme data type, it indicates that the argument must be that type of data object. For example,

`cdr` *pair*   [procedure]

indicates that the standard Scheme procedure `cdr` takes one argument, which must be a pair.

Many procedures signal an error when an argument is of the wrong type; usually this error is a condition of type `condition-type:wrong-type-argument`.

In addition to the standard data-type names (*pair*, *list*, *boolean*, *string*, etc.), the following names as arguments also imply type restrictions:

- *object*: any object
- *thunk*: a procedure of no arguments
- *x*, *y*: real numbers
- *q*, *n*: integers
- *k*: an exact non-negative integer

Some examples:

`list` *object* ...   [procedure]

indicates that the standard Scheme procedure `list` takes zero or more arguments, each of which may be any Scheme object.

`write-char` *char* [*output-port*]   [procedure]

indicates that the standard Scheme procedure `write-char` must be called with a character, *char*, and may also be called with a character and an output port.

1.2 Scheme Concepts

1.2.1 Variable Bindings

Any identifier that is not a syntactic keyword may be used as a variable (see Section 1.3.3 [Identifiers], page 10). A variable may name a location where a value can be stored. A variable that does so is said to be *bound* to the location. The value stored in the location to which a variable is bound is called the variable's *value*. (The variable is sometimes said to *name* the value or to be *bound to* the value.)

A variable may be bound but still not have a value; such a variable is said to be *unassigned*. Referencing an unassigned variable is an error. When this error is signalled, it is a condition of type `condition-type:unassigned-variable`; sometimes the compiler does not generate code to signal the error. Unassigned variables are useful only in combination with side effects (see Section 2.5 [Assignments], page 22).

1.2.2 Environment Concepts

An *environment* is a set of variable bindings. If an environment has no binding for a variable, that variable is said to be *unbound* in that environment. Referencing an unbound variable signals a condition of type `condition-type:unbound-variable`.

A new environment can be created by *extending* an existing environment with a set of new bindings. Note that "extending an environment" does **not** modify the environment; rather, it creates a new environment that contains the new bindings and the old ones. The new bindings *shadow* the old ones; that is, if an environment that contains a binding for `x` is extended with a new binding for `x`, then only the new binding is seen when `x` is looked up in the extended environment. Sometimes we say that the original environment is the *parent* of the new one, or that the new environment is a *child* of the old one, or that the new environment *inherits* the bindings in the old one.

Procedure calls extend an environment, as do `let`, `let*`, `letrec`, and `do` expressions. Internal definitions (see Section 2.4.2 [Internal Definitions], page 21) also extend an environment. (Actually, all the constructs that extend environments can be expressed in terms of procedure calls, so there is really just one fundamental mechanism for environment extension.) A top-level definition (see Section 2.4.1 [Top-Level Definitions], page 21) may add a binding to an existing environment.

1.2.3 Initial and Current Environments

MIT/GNU Scheme provides an *initial environment* that contains all of the variable bindings described in this manual. Most environments are ultimately extensions of this initial environment. In Scheme, the environment in which your programs execute is actually a child (extension) of the environment containing the system's bindings. Thus, system names are visible to your programs, but your names do not interfere with system programs.

The environment in effect at some point in a program is called the *current environment* at that point. In particular, every REP loop has a current environment. (REP stands for "read-eval-print"; the REP loop is the Scheme program that reads your input, evaluates it, and prints the result.) The environment of the top-level REP loop (the one you are in when Scheme starts up) starts as `user-initial-environment`, although it can be changed by the `ge` procedure. When a new REP loop is created, its environment is determined by the program that creates it.

1.2.4 Static Scoping

Scheme is a statically scoped language with block structure. In this respect, it is like Algol and Pascal, and unlike most other dialects of Lisp except for Common Lisp.

The fact that Scheme is statically scoped (rather than dynamically bound) means that the environment that is extended (and becomes current) when a procedure is called is the environment in which the procedure was created (i.e. in which the procedure's defining lambda expression was evaluated), not the environment in which the procedure is called. Because all the other Scheme *binding expressions* can be expressed in terms of procedures, this determines how all bindings behave.

Consider the following definitions, made at the top-level REP loop (in the initial environment):

```
(define x 1)
(define (f x) (g 2))
(define (g y) (+ x y))
(f 5)                                    ⇒   3 ; not 7
```

Here `f` and `g` are bound to procedures created in the initial environment. Because Scheme is statically scoped, the call to `g` from `f` extends the initial environment (the one in which `g` was created) with a binding of `y` to 2. In this extended environment, `y` is 2 and `x` is 1. (In a dynamically bound Lisp, the call to `g` would extend the environment in effect during the call to `f`, in which `x` is bound to 5 by the call to `f`, and the answer would be 7.)

Note that with static scoping, you can tell what binding a variable reference refers to just from looking at the text of the program; the referenced binding cannot depend on how the program is used. That is, the nesting of environments (their parent-child relationship) corresponds to the nesting of binding expressions in program text. (Because

of this connection to the text of the program, static scoping is also called *lexical* scoping.)
For each place where a variable is bound in a program there is a corresponding *region*
of the program text within which the binding is effective. For example, the region of a
binding established by a `lambda` expression is the entire body of the `lambda` expression.
The documentation of each binding expression explains what the region of the bindings it
makes is. A use of a variable (that is, a reference to or assignment of a variable) refers to
the innermost binding of that variable whose region contains the variable use. If there is no
such region, the use refers to the binding of the variable in the global environment (which
is an ancestor of all other environments, and can be thought of as a region in which all your
programs are contained).

1.2.5 True and False

In Scheme, the boolean values true and false are denoted by `#t` and `#f`. However, any
Scheme value can be treated as a boolean for the purpose of a conditional test. This
manual uses the word *true* to refer to any Scheme value that counts as true, and the word
false to refer to any Scheme value that counts as false. In conditional tests, all values count
as true except for `#f`, which counts as false (see Section 2.7 [Conditionals], page 24).

1.2.6 External Representations

An important concept in Scheme is that of the *external representation* of an object as
a sequence of characters. For example, an external representation of the integer 28 is the
sequence of characters '28', and an external representation of a list consisting of the integers
8 and 13 is the sequence of characters '(8 13)'.

The external representation of an object is not necessarily unique. The integer 28 also
has representations '#e28.000' and '#x1c', and the list in the previous paragraph also has
the representations '(08 13)' and '(8 . (13 . ( )))'.

Many objects have standard external representations, but some, such as procedures
and circular data structures, do not have standard representations (although particular
implementations may define representations for them).

An external representation may be written in a program to obtain the corresponding
object (see Section 2.6 [Quoting], page 22).

External representations can also be used for input and output. The procedure `read`
parses external representations, and the procedure `write` generates them. Together, they
provide an elegant and powerful input/output facility.

Note that the sequence of characters '(+ 2 6)' is *not* an external representation of the
integer 8, even though it *is* an expression that evaluates to the integer 8; rather, it is an
external representation of a three-element list, the elements of which are the symbol `+` and
the integers 2 and 6. Scheme's syntax has the property that any sequence of characters
that is an expression is also the external representation of some object. This can lead to
confusion, since it may not be obvious out of context whether a given sequence of characters
is intended to denote data or program, but it is also a source of power, since it facilitates
writing programs such as interpreters and compilers that treat programs as data or data as
programs.

1.2.7 Disjointness of Types

Every object satisfies at most one of the following predicates (but see Section 1.2.5 [True and False], page 8, for an exception):

```
bit-string?      environment?      port?          symbol?
boolean?         null?             procedure?     vector?
cell?            number?           promise?       weak-pair?
char?            pair?             string?
condition?
```

1.2.8 Storage Model

This section describes a model that can be used to understand Scheme's use of storage.

Variables and objects such as pairs, vectors, and strings implicitly denote locations or sequences of locations. A string, for example, denotes as many locations as there are characters in the string. (These locations need not correspond to a full machine word.) A new value may be stored into one of these locations using the `string-set!` procedure, but the string continues to denote the same locations as before.

An object fetched from a location, by a variable reference or by a procedure such as `car`, `vector-ref`, or `string-ref`, is equivalent in the sense of `eqv?` to the object last stored in the location before the fetch.

Every location is marked to show whether it is in use. No variable or object ever refers to a location that is not in use. Whenever this document speaks of storage being allocated for a variable or object, what is meant is that an appropriate number of locations are chosen from the set of locations that are not in use, and the chosen locations are marked to indicate that they are now in use before the variable or object is made to denote them.

In many systems it is desirable for constants (i.e. the values of literal expressions) to reside in read-only memory. To express this, it is convenient to imagine that every object that denotes locations is associated with a flag telling whether that object is mutable or immutable. The constants and the strings returned by `symbol->string` are then the immutable objects, while all objects created by other procedures are mutable. It is an error to attempt to store a new value into a location that is denoted by an immutable object. Note that the MIT/GNU Scheme compiler takes advantage of this property to share constants, but that these constants are not immutable. Instead, two constants that are `equal?` may be `eq?` in compiled code.

1.3 Lexical Conventions

This section describes Scheme's lexical conventions.

1.3.1 Whitespace

Whitespace characters are spaces, newlines, tabs, and page breaks. Whitespace is used to improve the readability of your programs and to separate tokens from each other, when necessary. (A *token* is an indivisible lexical unit such as an identifier or number.) Whitespace is otherwise insignificant. Whitespace may occur between any two tokens, but not within a token. Whitespace may also occur inside a string, where it is significant.

1.3.2 Delimiters

All whitespace characters are *delimiters*. In addition, the following characters act as delimiters:

```
( )  ;  "  ,  '  |
```

Finally, these next characters act as delimiters, despite the fact that Scheme does not define any special meaning for them:

```
[ ]  { }
```

For example, if the value of the variable `name` is `"max"`:

```
(list"Hi"name(+ 1 2))                    ⇒  ("Hi" "max" 3)
```

1.3.3 Identifiers

An *identifier* is a sequence of one or more non-delimiter characters. Identifiers are used in several ways in Scheme programs:

- An identifier can be used as a variable or as a syntactic keyword.
- When an identifier appears as a literal or within a literal, it denotes a symbol.

Scheme accepts most of the identifiers that other programming languages allow. MIT/GNU Scheme allows all of the identifiers that standard Scheme does, plus many more.

MIT/GNU Scheme defines a potential identifier to be a sequence of non-delimiter characters that does not begin with either of the characters '#' or ','. Any such sequence of characters that is not a syntactically valid number (see Chapter 4 [Numbers], page 61) is considered to be a valid identifier. Note that, although it is legal for '#' and ',' to appear in an identifier (other than in the first character position), it is poor programming practice.

Here are some examples of identifiers:

```
lambda              q
list->vector        soup
+                   V17a
<=?                 a34kTMNs
the-word-recursion-has-many-meanings
```

1.3.4 Uppercase and Lowercase

Scheme doesn't distinguish uppercase and lowercase forms of a letter except within character and string constants; in other words, Scheme is *case-insensitive*. For example, 'Foo' is the same identifier as 'FOO', and '#x1AB' is the same number as '#X1ab'. But '#\a' and '#\A' are different characters.

1.3.5 Naming Conventions

A *predicate* is a procedure that always returns a boolean value (`#t` or `#f`). By convention, predicates usually have names that end in '?'.

A *mutation procedure* is a procedure that alters a data structure. By convention, mutation procedures usually have names that end in '!'.

1.3.6 Comments

The beginning of a comment is indicated with a semicolon (;). Scheme ignores everything on a line in which a semicolon appears, from the semicolon until the end of the line. The entire comment, including the newline character that terminates it, is treated as whitespace.

An alternative form of comment (sometimes called an *extended comment*) begins with the characters '#|' and ends with the characters '|#'. This alternative form is an MIT/GNU Scheme extension. As with ordinary comments, all of the characters in an extended comment, including the leading '#|' and trailing '|#', are treated as whitespace. Comments of this form may extend over multiple lines, and additionally may be nested (unlike the comments of the programming language C, which have a similar syntax).

```
;;; This is a comment about the FACT procedure.  Scheme
;;; ignores all of this comment.  The FACT procedure computes
;;; the factorial of a non-negative integer.


#|
This is an extended comment.
Such comments are useful for commenting out code fragments.
|#


(define fact
  (lambda (n)
    (if (= n 0)                          ;This is another comment:
        1                                ;Base case: return 1
        (* n (fact (- n 1)))))))
```

1.3.7 Additional Notations

The following list describes additional notations used in Scheme. See Chapter 4 [Numbers], page 61, for a description of the notations used for numbers.

+ - .   The plus sign, minus sign, and period are used in numbers, and may also occur in an identifier. A delimited period (not occurring within a number or identifier) is used in the notation for pairs and to indicate a "rest" parameter in a formal parameter list (see Section 2.1 [Lambda Expressions], page 15).

( )   Parentheses are used for grouping and to notate lists (see Chapter 7 [Lists], page 109).

"   The double quote delimits strings (see Chapter 6 [Strings], page 91).

\   The backslash is used in the syntax for character constants (see Chapter 5 [Characters], page 79) and as an escape character within string constants (see Chapter 6 [Strings], page 91).

;   The semicolon starts a comment.

'   The single quote indicates literal data; it suppresses evaluation (see Section 2.6 [Quoting], page 22).

`   The backquote indicates almost-constant data (see Section 2.6 [Quoting], page 22).

,   The comma is used in conjunction with the backquote (see Section 2.6 [Quoting], page 22).

,@   A comma followed by an at-sign is used in conjunction with the backquote (see Section 2.6 [Quoting], page 22).

The sharp (or pound) sign has different uses, depending on the character that immediately follows it:

#t #f   These character sequences denote the boolean constants (see Section 10.1 [Booleans], page 133).

#\   This character sequence introduces a character constant (see Chapter 5 [Characters], page 79).

#(This character sequence introduces a vector constant (see Chapter 8 [Vectors], page 125). A close parenthesis, ')', terminates a vector constant.

#e #i #b #o #d #l #s #x

            These character sequences are used in the notation for numbers (see Chapter 4 [Numbers], page 61).

#| This character sequence introduces an extended comment. The comment is terminated by the sequence '|#'. This notation is an MIT/GNU Scheme extension.

#!   This character sequence is used to denote a small set of named constants. Currently there are only two of these, #!optional and #!rest, both of which are used in the lambda special form to mark certain parameters as being "optional" or "rest" parameters. This notation is an MIT/GNU Scheme extension.

#*   This character sequence introduces a bit string (see Chapter 9 [Bit Strings], page 129). This notation is an MIT/GNU Scheme extension.

#[This character sequence is used to denote objects that do not have a readable external representation (see Section 14.7 [Custom Output], page 200). A close bracket, ']', terminates the object's notation. This notation is an MIT/GNU Scheme extension.

#@   This character sequence is a convenient shorthand used to refer to objects by their hash number (see Section 14.7 [Custom Output], page 200). This notation is an MIT/GNU Scheme extension.

#=

These character sequences introduce a notation used to show circular structures in printed output, or to denote them in input. The notation works much like that in Common Lisp, and is an MIT/GNU Scheme extension.

1.4 Expressions

A Scheme *expression* is a construct that returns a value. An expression may be a *literal*, a *variable reference*, a *special form*, or a *procedure call*.

1.4.1 Literal Expressions

Literal constants may be written by using an external representation of the data. In general, the external representation must be *quoted* (see Section 2.6 [Quoting], page 22); but some external representations can be used without quotation.

```
"abc"                               ⇒   "abc"
145932                              ⇒   145932
#t                                  ⇒   #t
#\a                                 ⇒   #\a
```

The external representation of numeric constants, string constants, character constants, and boolean constants evaluate to the constants themselves. Symbols, pairs, lists, and vectors require quoting.

1.4.2 Variable References

An expression consisting of an identifier (see Section 1.3.3 [Identifiers], page 10) is a *variable reference*; the identifier is the name of the variable being referenced. The value of the variable reference is the value stored in the location to which the variable is bound. An error is signalled if the referenced variable is unbound or unassigned.

```
(define x 28)
x                                   ⇒   28
```

1.4.3 Special Form Syntax

```
(keyword component ...)
```

A parenthesized expression that starts with a *syntactic keyword* is a *special form*. Each special form has its own syntax, which is described later in the manual.

Note that syntactic keywords and variable bindings share the same namespace. A local variable binding may shadow a syntactic keyword, and a local syntactic-keyword definition may shadow a variable binding.

The following list contains all of the syntactic keywords that are defined when MIT/GNU Scheme is initialized:

access	and	begin
case	cond	cons-stream
declare	define	
define-integrable	define-structure	define-syntax
delay	do	er-macro-transformer
fluid-let	if	lambda
let	let*	let*-syntax
let-syntax	letrec	letrec-syntax
local-declare	named-lambda	non-hygienic-macro-transformer
or	quasiquote	quote
rsc-macro-transformer	sc-macro-transformer	set!
syntax-rules	the-environment	

1.4.4 Procedure Call Syntax

```
(operator operand ...)
```

A *procedure call* is written by simply enclosing in parentheses expressions for the procedure to be called (the *operator*) and the arguments to be passed to it (the *operands*). The *operator* and *operand* expressions are evaluated and the resulting procedure is passed the resulting arguments. See Section 2.1 [Lambda Expressions], page 15, for a more complete description of this.

Another name for the procedure call expression is *combination*. This word is more specific in that it always refers to the expression; "procedure call" sometimes refers to the *process* of calling a procedure.

Unlike some other dialects of Lisp, Scheme always evaluates the operator expression and the operand expressions with the same evaluation rules, and the order of evaluation is unspecified.

```
(+ 3 4)                              ⇒  7
((if #f = *) 3 4)                    ⇒  12
```

A number of procedures are available as the values of variables in the initial environment; for example, the addition and multiplication procedures in the above examples are the values of the variables + and *. New procedures are created by evaluating `lambda` expressions.

If the *operator* is a syntactic keyword, then the expression is not treated as a procedure call: it is a special form.

2 Special Forms

A special form is an expression that follows special evaluation rules. This chapter describes the basic Scheme special forms.

2.1 Lambda Expressions

`lambda` *formals expression expression* ...   [special form]

A `lambda` expression evaluates to a procedure. The environment in effect when the `lambda` expression is evaluated is remembered as part of the procedure; it is called the *closing environment*. When the procedure is later called with some arguments, the closing environment is extended by binding the variables in the formal parameter list to fresh locations, and the locations are filled with the arguments according to rules about to be given. The new environment created by this process is referred to as the *invocation environment*.

Once the invocation environment has been constructed, the *expressions* in the body of the `lambda` expression are evaluated sequentially in it. This means that the region of the variables bound by the `lambda` expression is all of the *expressions* in the body. The result of evaluating the last *expression* in the body is returned as the result of the procedure call.

Formals, the formal parameter list, is often referred to as a *lambda list*.

The process of matching up formal parameters with arguments is somewhat involved. There are three types of parameters, and the matching treats each in sequence:

Required   All of the *required* parameters are matched against the arguments first. If there are fewer arguments than required parameters, an error of type `condition-type:wrong-number-of-arguments` is signalled; this error is also signalled if there are more arguments than required parameters and there are no further parameters.

Optional   Once the required parameters have all been matched, the *optional* parameters are matched against the remaining arguments. If there are fewer arguments than optional parameters, the unmatched parameters are bound to special objects called *default objects*. If there are more arguments than optional parameters, and there are no further parameters, an error of type `condition-type:wrong-number-of-arguments` is signalled.

The predicate `default-object?`, which is true only of default objects, can be used to determine which optional parameters were supplied, and which were defaulted.

Rest   Finally, if there is a *rest* parameter (there can only be one), any remaining arguments are made into a list, and the list is bound to the rest parameter. (If there are no remaining arguments, the rest parameter is bound to the empty list.)

In Scheme, unlike some other Lisp implementations, the list to which a rest parameter is bound is always freshly allocated. It has infinite extent and may be modified without affecting the procedure's caller.

Specially recognized keywords divide the *formals* parameters into these three classes. The keywords used here are '`#!optional`', '`.`', and '`#!rest`'. Note that only '`.`' is defined by standard Scheme — the other keywords are MIT/GNU Scheme extensions. '`#!rest`' has the same meaning as '`.`' in *formals*.

The use of these keywords is best explained by means of examples. The following are typical lambda lists, followed by descriptions of which parameters are required, optional, and rest. We will use '`#!rest`' in these examples, but anywhere it appears '`.`' could be used instead.

`(a b c)`   a, b, and c are all required. The procedure must be passed exactly three arguments.

`(a b #!optional c)`

a and b are required, c is optional. The procedure may be passed either two or three arguments.

`(#!optional a b c)`

a, b, and c are all optional. The procedure may be passed any number of arguments between zero and three, inclusive.

`a`
`(#!rest a)`

These two examples are equivalent. a is a rest parameter. The procedure may be passed any number of arguments. Note: this is the only case in which '`.`' cannot be used in place of '`#!rest`'.

`(a b #!optional c d #!rest e)`

a and b are required, c and d are optional, and e is rest. The procedure may be passed two or more arguments.

Some examples of `lambda` expressions:

```
(lambda (x) (+ x x))              ⇒  #[compound-procedure 53]

((lambda (x) (+ x x)) 4)             ⇒  8

(define reverse-subtract
  (lambda (x y)
    (- y x)))
(reverse-subtract 7 10)              ⇒  3

(define foo
  (let ((x 4))
    (lambda (y) (+ x y))))
(foo 6)                              ⇒  10
```

`named-lambda` *formals expression expression . . .*   [special form]

The `named-lambda` special form is similar to `lambda`, except that the first "required parameter" in *formals* is not a parameter but the *name* of the resulting procedure; thus *formals* must have at least one required parameter. This name has no semantic meaning, but is included in the external representation of the procedure, making it useful for debugging. In MIT/GNU Scheme, `lambda` is implemented as `named-lambda`, with a special name that means "unnamed".

```
(named-lambda (f x) (+ x x))     ⇒   #[compound-procedure 53 f]
((named-lambda (f x) (+ x x)) 4)   ⇒   8
```

2.2 Lexical Binding

The three binding constructs `let`, `let*`, and `letrec`, give Scheme block structure. The syntax of the three constructs is identical, but they differ in the regions they establish for their variable bindings. In a `let` expression, the initial values are computed before any of the variables become bound. In a `let*` expression, the evaluations and bindings are sequentially interleaved. And in a `letrec` expression, all the bindings are in effect while the initial values are being computed (thus allowing mutually recursive definitions).

`let ((`*variable init*`) ...) ` *expression expression* ...   [special form]

> The *init*s are evaluated in the current environment (in some unspecified order), the *variable*s are bound to fresh locations holding the results, the *expression*s are evaluated sequentially in the extended environment, and the value of the last *expression* is returned. Each binding of a *variable* has the *expression*s as its region.

> MIT/GNU Scheme allows any of the *init*s to be omitted, in which case the corresponding *variable*s are unassigned.

> Note that the following are equivalent:

```
(let ((variable init) ...) expression expression ...)
((lambda (variable ...) expression expression ...) init ...)
```

> Some examples:

```
(let ((x 2) (y 3))
  (* x y))                        ⇒   6

(let ((x 2) (y 3))
  (let ((foo (lambda (z) (+ x y z)))
        (x 7))
    (foo 4)))                     ⇒   9
```

> See Section 2.9 [Iteration], page 27, for information on "named `let`".

`let* ((`*variable init*`) ...) ` *expression expression* ...   [special form]

> `let*` is similar to `let`, but the bindings are performed sequentially from left to right, and the region of a binding is that part of the `let*` expression to the right of the binding. Thus the second binding is done in an environment in which the first binding is visible, and so on.

> Note that the following are equivalent:

```
(let* ((variable1 init1)
       (variable2 init2)
       ...
       (variableN initN))
  expression
  expression ...)
```

```
(let ((variable1 init1))
  (let ((variable2 init2))
    ...
     (let ((variableN initN))
       expression
       expression ...)
   ...))
```

An example:

```
(let ((x 2) (y 3))
  (let* ((x 7)
         (z (+ x y)))
    (* z x)))                                    ⇒   70
```

letrec ((variable init) ...) expression expression ...   [special form]
The *variables* are bound to fresh locations holding unassigned values, the *inits* are
evaluated in the extended environment (in some unspecified order), each *variable* is
assigned to the result of the corresponding *init*, the *expressions* are evaluated sequentially in the extended environment, and the value of the last *expression* is returned.
Each binding of a *variable* has the entire letrec expression as its region, making it
possible to define mutually recursive procedures.

MIT/GNU Scheme allows any of the *inits* to be omitted, in which case the corresponding *variables* are unassigned.

```
(letrec ((even?
          (lambda (n)
            (if (zero? n)
                #t
                (odd? (- n 1)))))
         (odd?
          (lambda (n)
            (if (zero? n)
                #f
                (even? (- n 1))))))
  (even? 88))                                    ⇒   #t
```

One restriction on letrec is very important: it shall be possible to evaluated each
init without assigning or referring to the value of any *variable*. If this restriction
is violated, then it is an error. The restriction is necessary because Scheme passes
arguments by value rather than by name. In the most common uses of letrec, all the
inits are lambda or delay expressions and the restriction is satisfied automatically.

2.3 Dynamic Binding

fluid-let ((variable init) ...) expression expression ...   [special form]
The *inits* are evaluated in the current environment (in some unspecified order), the
current values of the *variables* are saved, the results are assigned to the *variables*, the

expressions are evaluated sequentially in the current environment, the *variables* are restored to their original values, and the value of the last *expression* is returned.

The syntax of this special form is similar to that of `let`, but `fluid-let` temporarily rebinds existing variables. Unlike `let`, `fluid-let` creates no new bindings; instead it *assigns* the value of each *init* to the binding (determined by the rules of lexical scoping) of its corresponding *variable*.

MIT/GNU Scheme allows any of the *init*s to be omitted, in which case the corresponding *variable*s are temporarily unassigned.

An error of type `condition-type:unbound-variable` is signalled if any of the *variables* are unbound. However, because `fluid-let` operates by means of side effects, it is valid for any *variable* to be unassigned when the form is entered.

Here is an example showing the difference between `fluid-let` and `let`. First see how `let` affects the binding of a variable:

```
(define variable #t)
(define (access-variable) variable)
variable                                    ⇒  #t
(let ((variable #f))
  (access-variable))                        ⇒  #t
variable                                    ⇒  #t
```

`access-variable` returns `#t` in this case because it is defined in an environment with `variable` bound to `#t`. `fluid-let`, on the other hand, temporarily reuses an existing variable:

```
variable                                    ⇒  #t
(fluid-let ((variable #f))                  ;reuses old binding
  (access-variable))                        ⇒  #f
variable                                    ⇒  #t
```

The *extent* of a dynamic binding is defined to be the time period during which the variable contains the new value. Normally this time period begins when the body is entered and ends when it is exited; on a sequential machine it is normally a contiguous time period. However, because Scheme has first-class continuations, it is possible to leave the body and then reenter it, as many times as desired. In this situation, the extent becomes non-contiguous.

When the body is exited by invoking a continuation, the new value is saved, and the variable is set to the old value. Then, if the body is reentered by invoking a continuation, the old value is saved, and the variable is set to the new value. In addition, side effects to the variable that occur both inside and outside of body are preserved, even if continuations are used to jump in and out of body repeatedly.

Here is a complicated example that shows the interaction between dynamic binding and continuations:

```
(define (complicated-dynamic-binding)
  (let ((variable 1)
        (inside-continuation))
    (write-line variable)
    (call-with-current-continuation
     (lambda (outside-continuation)
       (fluid-let ((variable 2))
         (write-line variable)
         (set! variable 3)
         (call-with-current-continuation
          (lambda (k)
            (set! inside-continuation k)
            (outside-continuation #t)))
         (write-line variable)
         (set! inside-continuation #f))))
    (write-line variable)
    (if inside-continuation
        (begin
          (set! variable 4)
          (inside-continuation #f)))))
```

Evaluating '(complicated-dynamic-binding)' writes the following on the console:

```
1
2
1
3
4
```

Commentary: the first two values written are the initial binding of variable and its new binding after the fluid-let's body is entered. Immediately after they are written, variable is set to '3', and then outside-continuation is invoked, causing us to exit the body. At this point, '1' is written, demonstrating that the original value of variable has been restored, because we have left the body. Then we set variable to '4' and reenter the body by invoking inside-continuation. At this point, '3' is written, indicating that the side effect that previously occurred within the body has been preserved. Finally, we exit body normally, and write '4', demonstrating that the side effect that occurred outside of the body was also preserved.

2.4 Definitions

define *variable* [*expression*]   [special form]
define *formals* *expression* *expression* ...   [special form]
  Definitions are valid in some but not all contexts where expressions are allowed. Definitions may only occur at the top level of a program and at the beginning of a lambda body (that is, the body of a lambda, let, let*, letrec, fluid-let, or "procedure define" expression). A definition that occurs at the top level of a program is called a *top-level definition*, and a definition that occurs at the beginning of a body is called an *internal definition*.

In the second form of `define` (called *"procedure* `define"`), the component *formals* is identical to the component of the same name in a `named-lambda` expression. In fact, these two expressions are equivalent:

```
(define (name1 name2 ...)
  expression
  expression ...)

(define name1
  (named-lambda (name1 name2 ...)
    expression
    expression ...))
```

2.4.1 Top-Level Definitions

A top-level definition,

```
(define variable expression)
```

has essentially the same effect as this assignment expression, if *variable* is bound:

```
(set! variable expression)
```

If *variable* is not bound, however, `define` binds *variable* to a new location in the current environment before performing the assignment (it is an error to perform a `set!` on an unbound variable). If you omit *expression*, the variable becomes unassigned; an attempt to reference such a variable is an error.

```
(define add3
  (lambda (x) (+ x 3)))          ⇒   unspecified
(add3 3)                         ⇒   6

(define first car)               ⇒   unspecified
(first '(1 2))                   ⇒   1

(define bar)                     ⇒   unspecified
bar                              error   Unassigned variable
```

2.4.2 Internal Definitions

An *internal definition* is a definition that occurs at the beginning of a *body* (that is, the body of a `lambda`, `let`, `let*`, `letrec`, `fluid-let`, or "procedure `define`" expression), rather than at the top level of a program. The variable defined by an internal definition is local to the *body*. That is, *variable* is bound rather than assigned, and the region of the binding is the entire *body*. For example,

```
(let ((x 5))
  (define foo (lambda (y) (bar x y)))
  (define bar (lambda (a b) (+ (* a b) a)))
  (foo (+ x 3)))                 ⇒   45
```

A *body* containing internal definitions can always be converted into a completely equivalent `letrec` expression. For example, the `let` expression in the above example is equivalent to

```
(let ((x 5))
  (letrec ((foo (lambda (y) (bar x y)))
           (bar (lambda (a b) (+ (* a b) a))))
    (foo (+ x 3))))
```

2.5 Assignments

set! *variable* [*expression*]   [special form]
> If *expression* is specified, evaluates *expression* and stores the resulting value in the
> location to which *variable* is bound. If *expression* is omitted, *variable* is altered to be
> unassigned; a subsequent reference to such a *variable* is an error. In either case, the
> value of the set! expression is unspecified.
>
> *Variable* must be bound either in some region enclosing the set! expression, or at
> the top level. However, *variable* is permitted to be unassigned when the set! form
> is entered.
>
> | | | |
> |---|---|---|
> | (define x 2) | ⇒ | unspecified |
> | (+ x 1) | ⇒ | 3 |
> | (set! x 4) | ⇒ | unspecified |
> | (+ x 1) | ⇒ | 5 |
>
> *Variable* may be an access expression (see Chapter 13 [Environments], page 183).
> This allows you to assign variables in an arbitrary environment. For example,
>
> | | | |
> |---|---|---|
> | (define x (let ((y 0)) (the-environment))) | | |
> | (define y 'a) | | |
> | y | ⇒ | a |
> | (access y x) | ⇒ | 0 |
> | (set! (access y x) 1) | ⇒ | unspecified |
> | y | ⇒ | a |
> | (access y x) | ⇒ | 1 |

2.6 Quoting

This section describes the expressions that are used to modify or prevent the evaluation of
objects.

quote *datum*   [special form]
> (quote *datum*) evaluates to *datum*. *Datum* may be any external representation of a
> Scheme object (see Section 1.2.6 [External Representations], page 8). Use quote to
> include literal constants in Scheme code.
>
> | | | |
> |---|---|---|
> | (quote a) | ⇒ | a |
> | (quote #(a b c)) | ⇒ | #(a b c) |
> | (quote (+ 1 2)) | ⇒ | (+ 1 2) |
>
> (quote *datum*) may be abbreviated as '*datum*. The two notations are equivalent in
> all respects.

```
'a                                    ⇒   a
'#(a b c)                             ⇒   #(a b c)
'(+ 1 2)                             ⇒   (+ 1 2)
'(quote a)                           ⇒   (quote a)
''a                                  ⇒   (quote a)
```

Numeric constants, string constants, character constants, and boolean constants evaluate to themselves, so they don't need to be quoted.

```
'"abc"                               ⇒   "abc"
"abc"                                ⇒   "abc"
'145932                              ⇒   145932
145932                               ⇒   145932
'#t                                  ⇒   #t
#t                                   ⇒   #t
'#\a                                 ⇒   #\a
#\a                                  ⇒   #\a
```

quasiquote *template*   [special form]

"Backquote" or "quasiquote" expressions are useful for constructing a list or vector structure when most but not all of the desired structure is known in advance. If no commas appear within the *template*, the result of evaluating `template is equivalent (in the sense of equal?) to the result of evaluating '*template*. If a comma appears within the *template*, however, the expression following the comma is evaluated ("unquoted") and its result is inserted into the structure instead of the comma and the expression. If a comma appears followed immediately by an at-sign (@), then the following expression shall evaluate to a list; the opening and closing parentheses of the list are then "stripped away" and the elements of the list are inserted in place of the comma at-sign expression sequence.

```
`(list ,(+ 1 2) 4)                   ⇒   (list 3 4)

(let ((name 'a)) `(list ,name ',name))   ⇒   (list a 'a)

`(a ,(+ 1 2) ,@(map abs '(4 -5 6)) b)   ⇒   (a 3 4 5 6 b)

`((foo ,(- 10 3)) ,@(cdr '(c)) . ,(car '(cons)))
                                     ⇒   ((foo 7) . cons)

`#(10 5 ,(sqrt 4) ,@(map sqrt '(16 9)) 8)
                                     ⇒   #(10 5 2 4 3 8)

`,(+ 2 3)                            ⇒   5
```

Quasiquote forms may be nested. Substitutions are made only for unquoted components appearing at the same nesting level as the outermost backquote. The nesting level increases by one inside each successive quasiquotation, and decreases by one inside each unquotation.

```
‘(a ‘(b ,(+ 1 2) ,(foo ,(+ 1 3) d) e) f)
     ⇒  (a ‘(b ,(+ 1 2) ,(foo 4 d) e) f)

(let ((name1 ’x)
      (name2 ’y))
  ‘(a ‘(b ,,name1 ,’,name2 d) e))
     ⇒  (a ‘(b ,x ,’y d) e)
```

The notations `‘template` and (`quasiquote template`) are identical in all respects.
`,expression` is identical to (`unquote expression`) and `,@expression` is identical
to (`unquote-splicing expression`).

```
(quasiquote (list (unquote (+ 1 2)) 4))
     ⇒  (list 3 4)

’(quasiquote (list (unquote (+ 1 2)) 4))
     ⇒  ‘(list ,(+ 1 2) 4)
   i.e., (quasiquote (list (unquote (+ 1 2)) 4))
```

Unpredictable behavior can result if any of the symbols `quasiquote`, `unquote`, or
`unquote-splicing` appear in a *template* in ways otherwise than as described above.

2.7 Conditionals

The behavior of the *conditional expressions* is determined by whether objects are true or
false. The conditional expressions count only `#f` as false. They count everything else,
including `#t`, pairs, symbols, numbers, strings, vectors, and procedures as true (but see
Section 1.2.5 [True and False], page 8).

In the descriptions that follow, we say that an object has "a true value" or "is true"
when the conditional expressions treat it as true, and we say that an object has "a false
value" or "is false" when the conditional expressions treat it as false.

if *predicate consequent* [*alternative*]   [special form]
    Predicate, *consequent*, and *alternative* are expressions. An `if` expression is evaluated
    as follows: first, *predicate* is evaluated. If it yields a true value, then *consequent* is
    evaluated and its value is returned. Otherwise *alternative* is evaluated and its value
    is returned. If *predicate* yields a false value and no *alternative* is specified, then the
    result of the expression is unspecified.

    An `if` expression evaluates either *consequent* or *alternative*, never both. Programs
    should not depend on the value of an `if` expression that has no *alternative*.

```
(if (> 3 2) ’yes ’no)                    ⇒   yes
(if (> 2 3) ’yes ’no)                    ⇒   no
(if (> 3 2)
    (- 3 2)
    (+ 3 2))                             ⇒   1
```

cond *clause clause . . .*   [special form]
    Each *clause* has this form:

        (*predicate expression . . .*)

where *predicate* is any expression. The last *clause* may be an **else** *clause*, which has the form:

```
(else expression expression ...)
```

A **cond** expression does the following:

1. Evaluates the *predicate* expressions of successive *clauses* in order, until one of the *predicates* evaluates to a true value.

2. When a *predicate* evaluates to a true value, **cond** evaluates the *expressions* in the associated *clause* in left to right order, and returns the result of evaluating the last *expression* in the *clause* as the result of the entire **cond** expression.

   If the selected *clause* contains only the *predicate* and no *expressions*, **cond** returns the value of the *predicate* as the result.

3. If all *predicates* evaluate to false values, and there is no **else** clause, the result of the conditional expression is unspecified; if there is an **else** clause, **cond** evaluates its *expressions* (left to right) and returns the value of the last one.

```
(cond ((> 3 2) 'greater)
      ((< 3 2) 'less))                    ⇒   greater

(cond ((> 3 3) 'greater)
      ((< 3 3) 'less)
      (else 'equal))                       ⇒   equal
```

Normally, programs should not depend on the value of a **cond** expression that has no **else** clause. However, some Scheme programmers prefer to write **cond** expressions in which at least one of the *predicates* is always true. In this style, the final *clause* is equivalent to an **else** clause.

Scheme supports an alternative *clause* syntax:

```
(predicate => recipient)
```

where *recipient* is an expression. If *predicate* evaluates to a true value, then *recipient* is evaluated. Its value must be a procedure of one argument; this procedure is then invoked on the value of the *predicate*.

```
(cond ((assv 'b '((a 1) (b 2))) => cadr)
      (else #f))                           ⇒   2
```

case *key clause clause ...*   [special form]

Key may be any expression. Each *clause* has this form:

```
((object ...) expression expression ...)
```

No *object* is evaluated, and all the *objects* must be distinct. The last *clause* may be an **else** *clause*, which has the form:

```
(else expression expression ...)
```

A **case** expression does the following:

1. Evaluates *key* and compares the result with each *object*.

2. If the result of evaluating *key* is equivalent (in the sense of **eqv?**; see Chapter 3 [Equivalence Predicates], page 55) to an *object*, **case** evaluates the *expressions* in the corresponding *clause* from left to right and returns the result of evaluating the last *expression* in the *clause* as the result of the **case** expression.

3. If the result of evaluating *key* is different from every *object*, and if there's an
   `else` clause, `case` evaluates its *expressions* and returns the result of the last one
   as the result of the `case` expression. If there's no `else` clause, `case` returns an
   unspecified result. Programs should not depend on the value of a `case` expression
   that has no `else` clause.

For example,

```
(case (* 2 3)
   ((2 3 5 7) 'prime)
   ((1 4 6 8 9) 'composite))          ⇒   composite

(case (car '(c d))
   ((a) 'a)
   ((b) 'b))                          ⇒   unspecified

(case (car '(c d))
   ((a e i o u) 'vowel)
   ((w y) 'semivowel)
   (else 'consonant))                 ⇒   consonant
```

and *expression* ...   [special form]
> The *expressions* are evaluated from left to right, and the value of the first *expression*
> that evaluates to a false value is returned. Any remaining *expressions* are not evalu-
> ated. If all the *expressions* evaluate to true values, the value of the last *expression* is
> returned. If there are no *expressions* then `#t` is returned.

```
(and (= 2 2) (> 2 1))          ⇒   #t
(and (= 2 2) (< 2 1))          ⇒   #f
(and 1 2 'c '(f g))            ⇒   (f g)
(and)                          ⇒   #t
```

or *expression* ...   [special form]
> The *expressions* are evaluated from left to right, and the value of the first *expression*
> that evaluates to a true value is returned. Any remaining *expressions* are not eval-
> uated. If all *expressions* evaluate to false values, the value of the last *expression* is
> returned. If there are no *expressions* then `#f` is returned.

```
(or (= 2 2) (> 2 1))           ⇒   #t
(or (= 2 2) (< 2 1))           ⇒   #t
(or #f #f #f)                  ⇒   #f
(or (memq 'b '(a b c)) (/ 3 0))   ⇒   (b c)
```

2.8 Sequencing

The `begin` special form is used to evaluate expressions in a particular order.

begin *expression expression* ...   [special form]
> The *expressions* are evaluated sequentially from left to right, and the value of the last
> *expression* is returned. This expression type is used to sequence side effects such as
> input and output.

```
(define x 0)
(begin (set! x 5)
       (+ x 1))                    ⇒  6

(begin (display "4 plus 1 equals ")
       (display (+ 4 1)))
                                   ⊣  4 plus 1 equals 5
                                   ⇒  unspecified
```

Often the use of **begin** is unnecessary, because many special forms already support sequences of expressions (that is, they have an implicit **begin**). Some of these special forms are:

```
case
cond
define                ;"procedure define" only
do
fluid-let
lambda
let
let*
letrec
named-lambda
```

The obsolete special form **sequence** is identical to **begin**. It should not be used in new code.

2.9 Iteration

The *iteration expressions* are: "named **let**" and **do**. They are also binding expressions, but are more commonly referred to as iteration expressions. Because Scheme is properly tail-recursive, you don't need to use these special forms to express iteration; you can simply use appropriately written "recursive" procedure calls.

let *name* ((`variable init`) ...) *expression expression* ...   [special form]
    MIT/GNU Scheme permits a variant on the syntax of **let** called "named **let**" which provides a more general looping construct than **do**, and may also be used to express recursions.

    Named **let** has the same syntax and semantics as ordinary **let** except that *name* is bound within the *expression*s to a procedure whose formal arguments are the *variable*s and whose body is the *expression*s. Thus the execution of the *expression*s may be repeated by invoking the procedure named by *name*.

    MIT/GNU Scheme allows any of the *init*s to be omitted, in which case the corresponding *variable*s are unassigned.

    Note: the following expressions are equivalent:

```
(let name ((variable init) ...)
  expression
  expression ...)

((letrec ((name
           (named-lambda (name variable ...)
             expression
             expression ...)))
   name)
 init ...)
```

Here is an example:

```
(let loop
    ((numbers '(3 -2 1 6 -5))
     (nonneg '())
     (neg '()))
  (cond ((null? numbers)
         (list nonneg neg))
        ((>= (car numbers) 0)
         (loop (cdr numbers)
               (cons (car numbers) nonneg)
               neg))
        (else
         (loop (cdr numbers)
               nonneg
               (cons (car numbers) neg)))))

    ⇒  ((6 1 3) (-5 -2))
```

do ((*variable init step*) ...) (*test expression* ...) *command*   [special form]
    ...

do is an iteration construct. It specifies a set of variables to be bound, how they are
to be initialized at the start, and how they are to be updated on each iteration. When
a termination condition is met, the loop exits with a specified result value.

do expressions are evaluated as follows: The *init* expressions are evaluated (in some
unspecified order), the *variable*s are bound to fresh locations, the results of the *init*
expressions are stored in the bindings of the *variable*s, and then the iteration phase
begins.

Each iteration begins by evaluating *test*; if the result is false, then the *command*
expressions are evaluated in order for effect, the *step* expressions are evaluated in
some unspecified order, the *variable*s are bound to fresh locations, the results of the
*step*s are stored in the bindings of the *variable*s, and the next iteration begins.

If *test* evaluates to a true value, then the *expression*s are evaluated from left to right
and the value of the last *expression* is returned as the value of the do expression. If no
*expression*s are present, then the value of the do expression is unspecified in standard
Scheme; in MIT/GNU Scheme, the value of *test* is returned.

The region of the binding of a *variable* consists of the entire do expression except for the *inits*. It is an error for a *variable* to appear more than once in the list of do variables.

A *step* may be omitted, in which case the effect is the same as if (`variable init variable`) had been written instead of (`variable init`).

```
(do ((vec (make-vector 5))
     (i 0 (+ i 1)))
    ((= i 5) vec)
  (vector-set! vec i i))              ⇒  #(0 1 2 3 4)

(let ((x '(1 3 5 7 9)))
  (do ((x x (cdr x))
       (sum 0 (+ sum (car x))))
      ((null? x) sum)))              ⇒   25
```

2.10 Structure Definitions

This section provides examples and describes the options and syntax of `define-structure`, an MIT/GNU Scheme macro that is very similar to `defstruct` in Common Lisp. The differences between them are summarized at the end of this section. For more information, see Steele's Common Lisp book.

define-structure (*name structure-option* ...) *slot-description* ...   [special form]
    Each *slot-description* takes one of the following forms:

> *slot-name*
> (*slot-name default-init* [*slot-option value*]*)

The fields *name* and *slot-name* must both be symbols. The field *default-init* is an expression for the initial value of the slot. It is evaluated each time a new instance is constructed. If it is not specified, the initial content of the slot is undefined. Default values are only useful with a BOA constructor with argument list or a keyword constructor (see below).

Evaluation of a `define-structure` expression defines a structure descriptor and a set of procedures to manipulate instances of the structure. These instances are represented as records by default (see Section 10.4 [Records], page 138) but may alternately be lists or vectors. The accessors and modifiers are marked with compiler declarations so that calls to them are automatically transformed into appropriate references. Often, no options are required, so a simple call to `define-structure` looks like:

```
(define-structure foo a b c)
```

This defines a type descriptor `rtd:foo`, a constructor `make-foo`, a predicate `foo?`, accessors `foo-a`, `foo-b`, and `foo-c`, and modifiers `set-foo-a!`, `set-foo-b!`, and `set-foo-c!`.

In general, if no options are specified, `define-structure` defines the following (using the simple call above as an example):

type descriptor

> The name of the type descriptor is `"rtd:"` followed by the name of
> the structure, e.g. 'rtd:foo'. The type descriptor satisfies the predicate
> `record-type?`.

constructor

> The name of the constructor is `"make-"` followed by the name of the
> structure, e.g. 'make-foo'. The number of arguments accepted by the
> constructor is the same as the number of slots; the arguments are the
> initial values for the slots, and the order of the arguments matches the
> order of the slot definitions.

predicate   The name of the predicate is the name of the structure followed by `"?"`,
> e.g. 'foo?'. The predicate is a procedure of one argument, which re-
> turns #t if its argument is a record of the type defined by this structure
> definition, and #f otherwise.

accessors   For each slot, an accessor is defined. The name of the accessor is formed
> by appending the name of the structure, a hyphen, and the name of the
> slot, e.g. 'foo-a'. The accessor is a procedure of one argument, which
> must be a record of the type defined by this structure definition. The
> accessor extracts the contents of the corresponding slot in that record
> and returns it.

modifiers   For each slot, a modifier is defined. The name of the modifier is formed by
> appending `"set-"`, the name of the accessor, and `"!"`, e.g. 'set-foo-a!'.
> The modifier is a procedure of two arguments, the first of which must
> be a record of the type defined by this structure definition, and the sec-
> ond of which may be any object. The modifier modifies the contents of
> the corresponding slot in that record to be that object, and returns an
> unspecified value.

When options are not supplied, (**name**) may be abbreviated to *name*. This convention
holds equally for *structure-options* and *slot-options*. Hence, these are equivalent:

```
(define-structure foo a b c)
(define-structure (foo) (a) b (c))
```

as are

```
(define-structure (foo keyword-constructor) a b c)
(define-structure (foo (keyword-constructor)) a b c)
```

When specified as option values, `false` and `nil` are equivalent to #f, and `true` and
`t` are equivalent to #t.

Possible *slot-options* are:

read-only *value*   [slot option]
> When given a *value* other than #f, this specifies that no modifier should be created
> for the slot.

type *type-descriptor*   [slot option]
> This is accepted but not presently used.

Possible *structure-options* are:

predicate [*name*]   [structure option]
> This option controls the definition of a predicate procedure for the structure. If *name* is not given, the predicate is defined with the default name (see above). If *name* is #f, the predicate is not defined at all. Otherwise, *name* must be a symbol, and the predicate is defined with that symbol as its name.

copier [*name*]   [structure option]
> This option controls the definition of a procedure to copy instances of the structure. This is a procedure of one argument, a structure instance, that makes a newly allocated copy of the structure and returns it. If *name* is not given, the copier is defined, and the name of the copier is "copy-" followed by the structure name (e.g. 'copy-foo'). If *name* is #f, the copier is not defined. Otherwise, *name* must be a symbol, and the copier is defined with that symbol as its name.

print-procedure *expression*   [structure option]
> Evaluating *expression* must yield a procedure of two arguments, which is used to print instances of the structure. The procedure is an *unparser method* (see Section 14.7 [Custom Output], page 200). If the structure instances are records, this option has the same effect as calling set-record-type-unparser-method!.

constructor [*name* [*argument-list*]]   [structure option]
> This option controls the definition of constructor procedures. These constructor procedures are called "BOA constructors", for "By Order of Arguments", because the arguments to the constructor specify the initial contents of the structure's slots by the order in which they are given. This is as opposed to "keyword constructors", which specify the initial contents using keywords, and in which the order of arguments is irrelevant.
>
> If *name* is not given, a constructor is defined with the default name and arguments (see above). If *name* is #f, no constructor is defined; *argument-list* may not be specified in this case. Otherwise, *name* must be a symbol, and a constructor is defined with that symbol as its name. If *name* is a symbol, *argument-list* is optionally allowed; if it is omitted, the constructor accepts one argument for each slot in the structure definition, in the same order in which the slots appear in the definition. Otherwise, *argument-list* must be a lambda list (see Section 2.1 [Lambda Expressions], page 15), and each of the parameters of the lambda list must be the name of a slot in the structure. The arguments accepted by the constructor are defined by this lambda list. Any slot that is not specified by the lambda list is initialized to the *default-init* as specified above; likewise for any slot specified as an optional parameter when the corresponding argument is not supplied.
>
> If the **constructor** option is specified, the default constructor is not defined. Additionally, the **constructor** option may be specified multiple times to define multiple constructors with different names and argument lists.
>
> ```
> (define-structure (foo
>                    (constructor make-foo (#!optional a b)))
>   (a 6 read-only #t)
>   (b 9))
> ```

keyword-constructor [*name*]   [structure option]

> This option controls the definition of keyword constructor procedures. A *keyword constructor* is a procedure that accepts arguments that are alternating slot names and values. If *name* is omitted, a keyword constructor is defined, and the name of the constructor is `"make-"` followed by the name of the structure (e.g. 'make-foo'). Otherwise, *name* must be a symbol, and a keyword constructor is defined with this symbol as its name.
>
> If the keyword-constructor option is specified, the default constructor is not defined. Additionally, the keyword-constructor option may be specified multiple times to define multiple keyword constructors; this is usually not done since such constructors would all be equivalent.
>
> ```
> (define-structure (foo (keyword-constructor make-bar)) a b)
> (foo-a (make-bar 'b 20 'a 19))            ⇒ 19
> ```

type-descriptor *name*   [structure option]

> This option cannot be used with the type or named options.
>
> By default, structures are implemented as records. The name of the structure is defined to hold the type descriptor of the record defined by the structure. The type-descriptor option specifies a different name to hold the type descriptor.
>
> ```
> (define-structure foo a b)
> foo                 ⇒ #[record-type 18]
> ```
>
> ```
> (define-structure (bar (type-descriptor <bar>)) a b)
> bar                 [error] Unbound variable: bar
> <bar>               ⇒ #[record-type 19]
> ```

conc-name [*name*]   [structure option]

> By default, the prefix for naming accessors and modifiers is the name of the structure followed by a hyphen. The conc-name option can be used to specify an alternative. If *name* is not given, the prefix is the name of the structure followed by a hyphen (the default). If *name* is #f, the slot names are used directly, without prefix. Otherwise, *name* must a symbol, and that symbol is used as the prefix.
>
> ```
> (define-structure (foo (conc-name moby/)) a b)
> ```
> defines accessors moby/a and moby/b, and modifiers set-moby/a! and set-moby/b!.
> ```
> (define-structure (foo (conc-name #f)) a b)
> ```
> defines accessors a and b, and modifiers set-a! and set-b!.

type *representation-type*   [structure option]

> This option cannot be used with the type-descriptor option.
>
> By default, structures are implemented as records. The type option overrides this default, allowing the programmer to specify that the structure be implemented using another data type. The option value *representation-type* specifies the alternate data type; it is allowed to be one of the symbols vector or list, and the data type used is the one corresponding to the symbol.
>
> If this option is given, and the named option is not specified, the representation will not be tagged, and neither a predicate nor a type descriptor will be defined; also, the print-procedure option may not be given.

```
(define-structure (foo (type list)) a b)
(make-foo 1 2)                              ⇒ (1 2)
```

named [*expression*]   [structure option]

This is valid only in conjunction with the **type** option and specifies that the structure instances be tagged to make them identifiable as instances of this structure type. This option cannot be used with the **type-descriptor** option.

In the usual case, where *expression* is not given, the **named** option causes a type descriptor and predicate to be defined for the structure (recall that the **type** option without **named** suppresses their definition), and also defines a default unparser method for the structure instances (which can be overridden by the **print-procedure** option). If the default unparser method is not wanted then the **print-procedure** option should be specified as **#F**. This causes the structure to be printed in its native representation, as a list or vector, which includes the type descriptor. The type descriptor is a unique object, *not* a record type, that describes the structure instances and is additionally stored in the structure instances to identify them: if the representation type is **vector**, the type descriptor is stored in the zero-th slot of the vector, and if the representation type is **list**, it is stored as the first element of the list.

```
(define-structure (foo (type vector) named) a b c)
(vector-ref (make-foo 1 2 3) 0) ⇒ #[structure-type 52]
```

If *expression* is specified, it is an expression that is evaluated to yield a tag object. The *expression* is evaluated once when the structure definition is evaluated (to specify the unparser method), and again whenever a predicate or constructor is called. Because of this, *expression* is normally a variable reference or a constant. The value yielded by *expression* may be any object at all. That object is stored in the structure instances in the same place that the type descriptor is normally stored, as described above. If *expression* is specified, no type descriptor is defined, only a predicate.

```
(define-structure (foo (type vector) (named 'foo)) a b c)
(vector-ref (make-foo 1 2 3) 0) ⇒ foo
```

safe-accessors [*boolean*]   [structure option]

This option allows the programmer to have some control over the safety of the slot accessors (and modifiers) generated by **define-structure**. If **safe-accessors** is not specified, or if *boolean* is **#f**, then the accessors are optimized for speed at the expense of safety; when compiled, the accessors will turn into very fast inline sequences, usually one to three machine instructions in length. However, if **safe-accessors** is specified and *boolean* is either omitted or **#t**, then the accessors are optimized for safety, will check the type and structure of their argument, and will be close-coded.

```
(define-structure (foo safe-accessors) a b c)
```

initial-offset *offset*   [structure option]

This is valid only in conjunction with the **type** option. *Offset* must be an exact non-negative integer and specifies the number of slots to leave open at the beginning of the structure instance before the specified slots are allocated. Specifying an *offset* of zero is equivalent to omitting the **initial-offset** option.

If the `named` option is specified, the structure tag appears in the first slot, followed by the "offset" slots, and then the regular slots. Otherwise, the "offset" slots come first, followed by the regular slots.

```
(define-structure (foo (type vector) (initial-offset 3))
  a b c)
(make-foo 1 2 3)                    ⇒ #(() () () 1 2 3)
```

The essential differences between MIT/GNU Scheme's `define-structure` and Common Lisp's `defstruct` are:

- The default constructor procedure takes positional arguments, in the same order as specified in the definition of the structure. A keyword constructor may be specified by giving the option `keyword-constructor`.

- BOA constructors are described using Scheme lambda lists. Since there is nothing corresponding to `&aux` in Scheme lambda lists, this functionality is not implemented.

- By default, no `copier` procedure is defined.

- The side-effect procedure corresponding to the accessor `foo` is given the name `set-foo!`.

- Keywords are ordinary symbols – use `foo` instead of `:foo`.

- The option values `false`, `nil`, `true`, and `t` are treated as if the appropriate boolean constant had been specified instead.

- The `print-function` option is named `print-procedure`. Its argument is a procedure of two arguments (the unparser state and the structure instance) rather than three as in Common Lisp.

- By default, named structures are tagged with a unique object of some kind. In Common Lisp, the structures are tagged with symbols. This depends on the Common Lisp package system to help generate unique tags; MIT/GNU Scheme has no such way to generate unique symbols.

- The `named` option may optionally take an argument, which is normally the name of a variable (any expression may be used, but it is evaluated whenever the tag name is needed). If used, structure instances will be tagged with that variable's value. The variable must be defined when `define-structure` is evaluated.

- The `type` option is restricted to the values `vector` and `list`.

- The `include` option is not implemented.

2.11 Macros

(This section is largely taken from the *Revised^4 Report on the Algorithmic Language Scheme*. The section on Syntactic Closures is derived from a document written by Chris Hanson. The section on Explicit Renaming is derived from a document written by William Clinger.)

Scheme programs can define and use new derived expression types, called *macros*. Program-defined expression types have the syntax

```
(keyword datum ...)
```

where *keyword* is an identifier that uniquely determines the expression type. This identifier is called the *syntactic keyword*, or simply *keyword*, of the macro. The number of the *datums*, and their syntax, depends on the expression type.

Each instance of a macro is called a *use* of the macro. The set of rules that specifies how a use of a macro is transcribed into a more primitive expression is called the *transformer* of the macro.

MIT/GNU Scheme also supports *anonymous syntactic keywords*. This means that it's not necessary to bind a macro transformer to a syntactic keyword before it is used. Instead, any macro-transformer expression can appear as the first element of a form, and the form will be expanded by the transformer.

The macro definition facility consists of these parts:

- A set of expressions used to establish that certain identifiers are macro keywords, associate them with macro transformers, and control the scope within which a macro is defined.

- A standard high-level pattern language for specifying macro transformers, introduced by the `syntax-rules` special form.

- Two non-standard low-level languages for specifying macro transformers, *syntactic closures* and *explicit renaming*.

The syntactic keyword of a macro may shadow variable bindings, and local variable bindings may shadow keyword bindings. All macros defined using the pattern language are "hygienic" and "referentially transparent" and thus preserve Scheme's lexical scoping:

- If a macro transformer inserts a binding for an identifier (variable or keyword), the identifier will in effect be renamed throughout its scope to avoid conflicts with other identifiers.

- If a macro transformer inserts a free reference to an identifier, the reference refers to the binding that was visible where the transformer was specified, regardless of any local bindings that may surround the use of the macro.

2.11.1 Binding Constructs for Syntactic Keywords

`let-syntax`, `letrec-syntax`, `let*-syntax` and `define-syntax` are analogous to `let`, `letrec`, `let*` and `define`, but they bind syntactic keywords to macro transformers instead of binding variables to locations that contain values.

Any argument named *transformer-spec* must be a macro-transformer expression, which is one of the following:

- A macro transformer defined by the pattern language and denoted by the syntactic keyword `syntax-rules`.

- A macro transformer defined by one of the low-level mechanisms and denoted by one of the syntactic keywords `sc-macro-transformer`, `rsc-macro-transformer`, or `er-macro-transformer`.

- A syntactic keyword bound in the enclosing environment. This is used to bind another name to an existing macro transformer.

`let-syntax` *bindings expression expression ...*   [special form]
    Bindings should have the form

```
((keyword transformer-spec) ...)
```

Each *keyword* is an identifier, each *transformer-spec* is a a macro-transformer expression, and the body is a sequence of one or more expressions. It is an error for a *keyword* to appear more than once in the list of keywords being bound.

The *expressions* are expanded in the syntactic environment obtained by extending the syntactic environment of the `let-syntax` expression with macros whose keywords are the *keyword*s, bound to the specified transformers. Each binding of a *keyword* has the *expressions* as its region.

```
(let-syntax ((when (syntax-rules ()
                     ((when test stmt1 stmt2 ...)
                      (if test
                          (begin stmt1
                                 stmt2 ...))))))
  (let ((if #t))
    (when if (set! if 'now))
    if))                                    ⇒  now

(let ((x 'outer))
  (let-syntax ((m (syntax-rules () ((m) x))))
    (let ((x 'inner))
      (m))))                                ⇒  outer
```

letrec-syntax *bindings expression expression ...*   [special form]
    The syntax of `letrec-syntax` is the same as for `let-syntax`.

The *expressions* are expanded in the syntactic environment obtained by extending the syntactic environment of the `letrec-syntax` expression with macros whose keywords are the *keyword*s, bound to the specified transformers. Each binding of a *keyword* has the *bindings* as well as the *expressions* within its region, so the transformers can transcribe expressions into uses of the macros introduced by the `letrec-syntax` expression.

```
(letrec-syntax
  ((my-or (syntax-rules ()
            ((my-or) #f)
            ((my-or e) e)
            ((my-or e1 e2 ...)
             (let ((temp e1))
               (if temp
                   temp
                   (my-or e2 ...)))))))
    (let ((x #f)
          (y 7)
          (temp 8)
          (let odd?)
          (if even?))
      (my-or x
             (let temp)
             (if y)
             y)))           ⇒  7
```

let*-syntax *bindings expression expression ...*   [special form]
   The syntax of **let*-syntax** is the same as for **let-syntax**.

   The *expressions* are expanded in the syntactic environment obtained by extending the
   syntactic environment of the **letrec-syntax** expression with macros whose keywords
   are the *keywords*, bound to the specified transformers. Each binding of a *keyword*
   has the subsequent *bindings* as well as the *expressions* within its region. Thus

```
(let*-syntax
  ((a (syntax-rules ...))
   (b (syntax-rules ...)))
  ...)
```

   is equivalent to

```
(let-syntax ((a (syntax-rules ...)))
  (let-syntax ((b (syntax-rules ...)))
    ...))
```

define-syntax *keyword transformer-spec*   [special form]
   Keyword is an identifier, and *transformer-spec* is a macro transformer expression.
   The syntactic environment is extended by binding the *keyword* to the specified trans-
   former.

   The region of the binding introduced by **define-syntax** is the entire block in which
   it appears. However, the *keyword* may only be used after it has been defined.

   MIT/GNU Scheme permits **define-syntax** to appear both at top level and within
   lambda bodies. The Revised^4 Report permits only top-level uses of **define-syntax**.

   When compiling a program, a top-level instance of **define-syntax** both defines the
   syntactic keyword and generates code that will redefine the keyword when the program
   is loaded. This means that the same syntax can be used for defining macros that will
   be used during compilation and for defining macros to be used at run time.

Although macros may expand into definitions and syntax definitions in any context that permits them, it is an error for a definition or syntax definition to shadow a syntactic keyword whose meaning is needed to determine whether some form in the group of forms that contains the shadowing definition is in fact a definition, or, for internal definitions, is needed to determine the boundary between the group and the expressions that follow the group. For example, the following are errors:

```
(define define 3)

(begin (define begin list))

(let-syntax
  ((foo (syntax-rules ()
          ((foo (proc args ...) body ...)
           (define proc
             (lambda (args ...)
               body ...))))))
  (let ((x 3))
    (foo (plus x y) (+ x y))
    (define foo x)
    (plus foo x)))
```

2.11.2 Pattern Language

MIT/GNU Scheme supports a high-level pattern language for specifying macro transformers. This pattern language is defined by the Revised^4 Report and is portable to other conforming Scheme implementations. To use the pattern language, specify a *transformer-spec* as a **syntax-rules** form:

syntax-rules *literals syntax-rule* . . .   [special form]
    Literals is a list of identifiers and each *syntax-rule* should be of the form

        `(pattern template)`

The *pattern* in a *syntax-rule* is a list *pattern* that begins with the keyword for the macro.

A *pattern* is either an identifier, a constant, or one of the following

        `(pattern ...)`
        `(pattern pattern ... . pattern)`
        `(pattern ... pattern ellipsis)`

and a template is either an identifier, a constant, or one of the following

        `(element ...)`
        `(element element ... . template)`

where an *element* is a *template* optionally followed by an *ellipsis* and an *ellipsis* is the identifier '...' (which cannot be used as an identifier in either a template or a pattern).

An instance of **syntax-rules** produces a new macro transformer by specifying a sequence of hygienic rewrite rules. A use of a macro whose keyword is associated with a transformer specified by **syntax-rules** is matched against the patterns contained in the *syntax-rule*s, beginning with the leftmost *syntax-rule*. When a match is found, the macro use is transcribed hygienically according to the template.

An identifier that appears in the pattern of a *syntax-rule* is a *pattern-variable*, unless it is the keyword that begins the pattern, is listed in *literals*, or is the identifier '...'. Pattern variables match arbitrary input elements and are used to refer to elements of the input in the template. It is an error for the same pattern variable to appear more than once in a *pattern*.

The keyword at the beginning of the pattern in a *syntax-rule* is not involved in the matching and is not considered a pattern variable or literal identifier.

Identifiers that appear in *literals* are interpreted as literal identifiers to be matched against corresponding subforms of the input. A subform in the input matches a literal identifier if and only if it is an identifier and either both its occurrence in the macro expression and its occurrence in the macro definition have the same lexical binding, or the two identifiers are equal and both have no lexical binding.

A subpattern followed by '...' can match zero or more elements of the input. It is an error for '...' to appear in *literals*. Within a pattern the identifier '...' must follow the last element of a nonempty sequence of subpatterns.

More formally, an input form F matches a pattern P if and only if:

- P is a non-literal identifier; or

- P is a literal identifier and F is an identifier with the same binding; or

- P is a list (`P_1 ... P_n`) and F is a list of n forms that match `P_1` through `P_n`, respectively; or

- P is an improper list (`P_1 P_2 ... P_n . P_n+1`) and F is a list or improper list of n or more forms that match `P_1` through `P_n`, respectively, and whose nth "cdr" matches `P_n+1`; or

- P is of the form (`P_1 ... P_n P_n+1 ellipsis`) where *ellipsis* is the identifier '...' and F is a proper list of at least n forms, the first n of which match `P_1` through `P_n`, respectively, and each remaining element of F matches `P_n+1`; or

- P is a datum and F is equal to P in the sense of the `equal?` procedure.

It is an error to use a macro keyword, within the scope of its binding, in an expression that does not match any of the patterns.

When a macro use is transcribed according to the template of the matching *syntax rule*, pattern variables that occur in the template are replaced by the subforms they match in the input. Pattern variables that occur in subpatterns followed by one or more instances of the identifier '...' are allowed only in subtemplates that are followed by as many instances of '...'. They are replaced in the output by all of the subforms they match in the input, distributed as indicated. It is an error if the output cannot be built up as specified.

Identifiers that appear in the template but are not pattern variables or the identifier '...' are inserted into the output as literal identifiers. If a literal identifier is inserted as a free identifier then it refers to the binding of that identifier within whose scope the instance of **syntax-rules** appears. If a literal identifier is inserted as a bound identifier then it is in effect renamed to prevent inadvertent captures of free identifiers.

```
(let ((=> #f))
  (cond (#t => 'ok)))              ⇒ ok
```

The macro transformer for `cond` recognizes `=>` as a local variable, and hence an expression, and not as the top-level identifier `=>`, which the macro transformer treats as a syntactic keyword. Thus the example expands into

```
(let ((=> #f))
  (if #t (begin => 'ok)))
```

instead of

```
(let ((=> #f))
  (let ((temp #t))
    (if temp
        ('ok temp))))
```

which would result in an invalid procedure call.

2.11.3 Syntactic Closures

MIT/GNU Scheme's syntax-transformation engine is an implementation of *syntactic closures*, a mechanism invented by Alan Bawden and Jonathan Rees. The main feature of the syntactic-closures mechanism is its simplicity and its close relationship to the environment models commonly used with Scheme. Using the mechanism to write macro transformers is somewhat cumbersome and can be confusing for the newly initiated, but it is easily mastered.

2.11.3.1 Syntax Terminology

This section defines the concepts and data types used by the syntactic closures facility.

- *Forms* are the syntactic entities out of which programs are recursively constructed. A form is any expression, any definition, any syntactic keyword, or any syntactic closure. The variable name that appears in a `set!` special form is also a form. Examples of forms:

  ```
  17
  #t
  car
  (+ x 4)
  (lambda (x) x)
  (define pi 3.14159)
  if
  define
  ```

- An *alias* is an alternate name for a given symbol. It can appear anywhere in a form that the symbol could be used, and when quoted it is replaced by the symbol; however, it does not satisfy the predicate `symbol?`. Macro transformers rarely distinguish symbols from aliases, referring to both as *identifiers*. Another name for an alias is *synthetic identifier*; this document uses both names.

- A *syntactic environment* maps identifiers to their meanings. More precisely, it determines whether an identifier is a syntactic keyword or a variable. If it is a keyword, the meaning is an interpretation for the form in which that keyword appears. If it is a variable, the meaning identifies which binding of that variable is referenced. In short, syntactic environments contain all of the contextual information necessary for interpreting the meaning of a particular form.

- A *syntactic closure* consists of a form, a syntactic environment, and a list of identifiers. All identifiers in the form take their meaning from the syntactic environment, except those in the given list. The identifiers in the list are to have their meanings determined later.

  A syntactic closure may be used in any context in which its form could have been used. Since a syntactic closure is also a form, it may not be used in contexts where a form would be illegal. For example, a form may not appear as a clause in the **cond** special form.

  A syntactic closure appearing in a quoted structure is replaced by its form.

2.11.3.2 Transformer Definition

This section describes the special forms for defining syntactic-closures macro transformers, and the associated procedures for manipulating syntactic closures and syntactic environments.

sc-macro-transformer *expression*   [special form]

  The *expression* is expanded in the syntactic environment of the **sc-macro-transformer** expression, and the expanded expression is evaluated in the transformer environment to yield a macro transformer as described below. This macro transformer is bound to a macro keyword by the special form in which the **transformer** expression appears (for example, **let-syntax**).

  In the syntactic closures facility, a *macro transformer* is a procedure that takes two arguments, a form and a syntactic environment, and returns a new form. The first argument, the *input form*, is the form in which the macro keyword occurred. The second argument, the *usage environment*, is the syntactic environment in which the input form occurred. The result of the transformer, the *output form*, is automatically closed in the *transformer environment*, which is the syntactic environment in which the **transformer** expression occurred.

  For example, here is a definition of a **push** macro using **syntax-rules**:

```
(define-syntax push
  (syntax-rules ()
    ((push item list)
     (set! list (cons item list)))))
```

  Here is an equivalent definition using **sc-macro-transformer**:

```
(define-syntax push
  (sc-macro-transformer
   (lambda (exp env)
     (let ((item (make-syntactic-closure env '() (cadr exp)))
           (list (make-syntactic-closure env '() (caddr exp))))
       `(set! ,list (cons ,item ,list))))))
```

  In this example, the identifiers **set!** and **cons** are closed in the transformer environment, and thus will not be affected by the meanings of those identifiers in the usage environment **env**.

Some macros may be non-hygienic by design. For example, the following defines a
`loop` macro that implicitly binds `exit` to an escape procedure. The binding of `exit`
is intended to capture free references to `exit` in the body of the loop, so `exit` must
be left free when the body is closed:

```
(define-syntax loop
  (sc-macro-transformer
   (lambda (exp env)
     (let ((body (cdr exp)))
       `(call-with-current-continuation
         (lambda (exit)
           (let f ()
             ,@(map (lambda (exp)
                      (make-syntactic-closure env '(exit)
                        exp))
                    body)
             (f)))))))))
```

`rsc-macro-transformer` *expression*   [special form]

This form is an alternative way to define a syntactic-closures macro transformer. Its
syntax and usage are identical to `sc-macro-transformer`, except that the roles of the
usage environment and transformer environment are reversed. (Hence RSC stands for
Reversed Syntactic Closures.) In other words, the procedure specified by *expression*
still accepts two arguments, but its second argument will be the transformer environment rather than the usage environment, and the returned expression is closed in the
usage environment rather than the transformer environment.

The advantage of this arrangement is that it allows a simpler definition style in some
situations. For example, here is the `push` macro from above, rewritten in this style:

```
(define-syntax push
  (rsc-macro-transformer
   (lambda (exp env)
     `(,(make-syntactic-closure env '() 'SET!)
       ,(caddr exp)
       (,(make-syntactic-closure env '() 'CONS)
        ,(cadr exp)
        ,(caddr exp))))))
```

In this style only the introduced keywords are closed, while everything else remains
open.

Note that `rsc-macro-transformer` and `sc-macro-transformer` are easily
interchangeable. Here is how to emulate `rsc-macro-transformer` using
`sc-macro-transformer`. (This technique can be used to effect the opposite
emulation as well.)

```
(define-syntax push
  (sc-macro-transformer
    (lambda (exp usage-env)
      (capture-syntactic-environment
        (lambda (env)
          (make-syntactic-closure usage-env '()
            `(,(make-syntactic-closure env '() 'SET!)
              ,(caddr exp)
              (,(make-syntactic-closure env '() 'CONS)
               ,(cadr exp)
               ,(caddr exp)))))))))
```

To assign meanings to the identifiers in a form, use `make-syntactic-closure` to close the form in a syntactic environment.

`make-syntactic-closure` *environment free-names form*   [procedure]

Environment must be a syntactic environment, *free-names* must be a list of identifiers, and *form* must be a form. `make-syntactic-closure` constructs and returns a syntactic closure of *form* in *environment*, which can be used anywhere that *form* could have been used. All the identifiers used in *form*, except those explicitly excepted by *free-names*, obtain their meanings from *environment*.

Here is an example where *free-names* is something other than the empty list. It is instructive to compare the use of *free-names* in this example with its use in the `loop` example above: the examples are similar except for the source of the identifier being left free.

```
(define-syntax let1
  (sc-macro-transformer
    (lambda (exp env)
      (let ((id (cadr exp))
            (init (caddr exp))
            (exp (cadddr exp)))
        `((lambda (,id)
            ,(make-syntactic-closure env (list id) exp))
          ,(make-syntactic-closure env '() init))))))
```

`let1` is a simplified version of `let` that only binds a single identifier, and whose body consists of a single expression. When the body expression is syntactically closed in its original syntactic environment, the identifier that is to be bound by `let1` must be left free, so that it can be properly captured by the `lambda` in the output form.

In most situations, the *free-names* argument to `make-syntactic-closure` is the empty list. In those cases, the more succinct `close-syntax` can be used:

`close-syntax` *form environment*   [procedure]

Environment must be a syntactic environment and *form* must be a form. Returns a new syntactic closure of *form* in *environment*, with no free names. Entirely equivalent to

```
(make-syntactic-closure environment '() form)
```

To obtain a syntactic environment other than the usage environment, use `capture-syntactic-environment`.

`capture-syntactic-environment` *procedure*   [procedure]

> `capture-syntactic-environment` returns a form that will, when transformed, call *procedure* on the current syntactic environment. *Procedure* should compute and return a new form to be transformed, in that same syntactic environment, in place of the form.

> An example will make this clear. Suppose we wanted to define a simple `loop-until` keyword equivalent to

```
(define-syntax loop-until
  (syntax-rules ()
    ((loop-until id init test return step)
     (letrec ((loop
               (lambda (id)
                 (if test return (loop step)))))
       (loop init)))))
```

> The following attempt at defining `loop-until` has a subtle bug:

```
(define-syntax loop-until
  (sc-macro-transformer
   (lambda (exp env)
     (let ((id (cadr exp))
           (init (caddr exp))
           (test (cadddr exp))
           (return (cadddr (cdr exp)))
           (step (cadddr (cddr exp)))
           (close
            (lambda (exp free)
              (make-syntactic-closure env free exp))))
       `(letrec ((loop
                  (lambda (,id)
                    (if ,(close test (list id))
                        ,(close return (list id))
                        (loop ,(close step (list id)))))))
          (loop ,(close init '())))))))
```

> This definition appears to take all of the proper precautions to prevent unintended captures. It carefully closes the subexpressions in their original syntactic environment and it leaves the `id` identifier free in the `test`, `return`, and `step` expressions, so that it will be captured by the binding introduced by the `lambda` expression. Unfortunately it uses the identifiers `if` and `loop` *within* that `lambda` expression, so if the user of `loop-until` just happens to use, say, `if` for the identifier, it will be inadvertently captured.

> The syntactic environment that `if` and `loop` want to be exposed to is the one just outside the `lambda` expression: before the user's identifier is added to the syntactic environment, but after the identifier `loop` has been added. `capture-syntactic-environment` captures exactly that environment as follows:

```
(define-syntax loop-until
  (sc-macro-transformer
   (lambda (exp env)
     (let ((id (cadr exp))
           (init (caddr exp))
           (test (cadddr exp))
           (return (cadddr (cdr exp)))
           (step (cadddr (cddr exp)))
           (close
            (lambda (exp free)
              (make-syntactic-closure env free exp))))
       `(letrec ((loop
                  ,(capture-syntactic-environment
                    (lambda (env)
                      `(lambda (,id)
                         (,(make-syntactic-closure env '() 'if)
                          ,(close test (list id))
                          ,(close return (list id))
                          (,(make-syntactic-closure env '() 'loop)
                           ,(close step (list id)))))))))
         (loop ,(close init '())))))))
```

In this case, having captured the desired syntactic environment, it is convenient to construct syntactic closures of the identifiers `if` and the `loop` and use them in the body of the `lambda`.

A common use of `capture-syntactic-environment` is to get the transformer environment of a macro transformer:

```
(sc-macro-transformer
 (lambda (exp env)
   (capture-syntactic-environment
    (lambda (transformer-env)
      ...))))
```

2.11.3.3 Identifiers

This section describes the procedures that create and manipulate identifiers. The identifier data type extends the syntactic closures facility to be compatible with the high-level `syntax-rules` facility.

As discussed earlier, an identifier is either a symbol or an *alias*. An alias is implemented as a syntactic closure whose *form* is an identifier:

```
(make-syntactic-closure env '() 'a) ⇒ an alias
```

Aliases are implemented as syntactic closures because they behave just like syntactic closures most of the time. The difference is that an alias may be bound to a new value (for example by `lambda` or `let-syntax`); other syntactic closures may not be used this way. If an alias is bound, then within the scope of that binding it is looked up in the syntactic environment just like any other identifier.

Aliases are used in the implementation of the high-level facility `syntax-rules`. A macro transformer created by `syntax-rules` uses a template to generate its output form, substituting subforms of the input form into the template. In a syntactic closures implementation, all of the symbols in the template are replaced by aliases closed in the transformer environment, while the output form itself is closed in the usage environment. This guarantees that the macro transformation is hygienic, without requiring the transformer to know the syntactic roles of the substituted input subforms.

`identifier?` *object*   [procedure]

Returns `#t` if *object* is an identifier, otherwise returns `#f`. Examples:

```
(identifier? 'a)          ⇒ #t
(identifier? (make-syntactic-closure env '() 'a))
                          ⇒ #t

(identifier? "a")         ⇒ #f
(identifier? #\a)         ⇒ #f
(identifier? 97)          ⇒ #f
(identifier? #f)          ⇒ #f
(identifier? '(a))        ⇒ #f
(identifier? '#(a))       ⇒ #f
```

The predicate `eq?` is used to determine if two identifers are "the same". Thus `eq?` can be used to compare identifiers exactly as it would be used to compare symbols. Often, though, it is useful to know whether two identifiers "mean the same thing". For example, the `cond` macro uses the symbol `else` to identify the final clause in the conditional. A macro transformer for `cond` cannot just look for the symbol `else`, because the `cond` form might be the output of another macro transformer that replaced the symbol `else` with an alias. Instead the transformer must look for an identifier that "means the same thing" in the usage environment as the symbol `else` means in the transformer environment.

`identifier=?` *environment1 identifier1 environment2 identifier2*   [procedure]

Environment1 and *environment2* must be syntactic environments, and *identifier1* and *identifier2* must be identifiers. `identifier=?` returns `#t` if the meaning of *identifier1* in *environment1* is the same as that of *identifier2* in *environment2*, otherwise it returns `#f`. Examples:

```
(let-syntax
    ((foo
      (sc-macro-transformer
       (lambda (form env)
         (capture-syntactic-environment
          (lambda (transformer-env)
            (identifier=? transformer-env 'x env 'x)))))))
  (list (foo)
        (let ((x 3))
          (foo))))
                          ⇒ (#t #f)
```

```
(let-syntax ((bar foo))
  (let-syntax
      ((foo
        (sc-macro-transformer
         (lambda (form env)
           (capture-syntactic-environment
            (lambda (transformer-env)
              (identifier=? transformer-env 'foo
                            env (cadr form)))))))))
    (list (foo foo)
          (foo bar))))
                        ⇒ (#f #t)
```

Sometimes it is useful to be able to introduce a new identifier that is guaranteed to be different from any existing identifier, similarly to the way that `generate-uninterned-symbol` is used.

`make-synthetic-identifier` *identifier*   [procedure]

Creates and returns and new synthetic identifier (alias) that is guaranteed to be different from all existing identifiers. *Identifier* is any existing identifier, which is used in deriving the name of the new identifier.

This is implemented by syntactically closing *identifier* in a special empty environment.

2.11.4 Explicit Renaming

Explicit renaming is an alternative facility for defining macro transformers. In the MIT/GNU Scheme implementation, explicit-renaming transformers are implemented as an abstraction layer on top of syntactic closures. An explicit-renaming macro transformer is defined by an instance of the `er-macro-transformer` keyword:

`er-macro-transformer` *expression*   [special form]

The *expression* is expanded in the syntactic environment of the `er-macro-transformer` expression, and the expanded expression is evaluated in the transformer environment to yield a macro transformer as described below. This macro transformer is bound to a macro keyword by the special form in which the `transformer` expression appears (for example, `let-syntax`).

In the explicit-renaming facility, a *macro transformer* is a procedure that takes three arguments, a form, a renaming procedure, and a comparison predicate, and returns a new form. The first argument, the *input form*, is the form in which the macro keyword occurred.

The second argument to a transformation procedure is a *renaming procedure* that takes the representation of an identifier as its argument and returns the representation of a fresh identifier that occurs nowhere else in the program. For example, the transformation procedure for a simplified version of the `let` macro might be written as

```
(lambda (exp rename compare)
  (let ((vars (map car (cadr exp)))
        (inits (map cadr (cadr exp)))
        (body (cddr exp)))
    '((lambda ,vars ,@body)
      ,@inits)))
```

This would not be hygienic, however. A hygienic `let` macro must rename the identifier `lambda` to protect it from being captured by a local binding. The renaming effectively creates an fresh alias for `lambda`, one that cannot be captured by any subsequent binding:

```
(lambda (exp rename compare)
  (let ((vars (map car (cadr exp)))
        (inits (map cadr (cadr exp)))
        (body (cddr exp)))
    '((,(rename 'lambda) ,vars ,@body)
      ,@inits)))
```

The expression returned by the transformation procedure will be expanded in the syntactic environment obtained from the syntactic environment of the macro application by binding any fresh identifiers generated by the renaming procedure to the denotations of the original identifiers in the syntactic environment in which the macro was defined. This means that a renamed identifier will denote the same thing as the original identifier unless the transformation procedure that renamed the identifier placed an occurrence of it in a binding position.

The renaming procedure acts as a mathematical function in the sense that the identifiers obtained from any two calls with the same argument will be the same in the sense of `eqv?`. It is an error if the renaming procedure is called after the transformation procedure has returned.

The third argument to a transformation procedure is a *comparison predicate* that takes the representations of two identifiers as its arguments and returns true if and only if they denote the same thing in the syntactic environment that will be used to expand the transformed macro application. For example, the transformation procedure for a simplified version of the `cond` macro can be written as

```
(lambda (exp rename compare)
  (let ((clauses (cdr exp)))
    (if (null? clauses)
        '(,(rename 'quote) unspecified)
        (let* ((first (car clauses))
               (rest (cdr clauses))
               (test (car first)))
          (cond ((and (identifier? test)
                      (compare test (rename 'else)))
                 '(,(rename 'begin) ,@(cdr first)))
                (else '(,(rename 'if)
                        ,test
                        (,(rename 'begin) ,@(cdr first))
                        (cond ,@rest)))))))))
```

In this example the identifier `else` is renamed before being passed to the comparison predicate, so the comparison will be true if and only if the test expression is an identifier that denotes the same thing in the syntactic environment of the expression being transformed as `else` denotes in the syntactic environment in which the `cond` macro was defined. If `else` were not renamed before being passed to the comparison predicate, then it would match a local variable that happened to be named `else`, and the macro would not be hygienic.

Some macros are non-hygienic by design. For example, the following defines a `loop` macro that implicitly binds `exit` to an escape procedure. The binding of `exit` is intended to capture free references to `exit` in the body of the loop, so `exit` is not renamed.

```
(define-syntax loop
  (er-macro-transformer
   (lambda (x r c)
     (let ((body (cdr x)))
       `(,(r 'call-with-current-continuation)
         (,(r 'lambda) (exit)
          (,(r 'let) ,(r 'f) () ,@body (,(r 'f)))))))))
```

Suppose a `while` macro is implemented using `loop`, with the intent that `exit` may be used to escape from the `while` loop. The `while` macro cannot be written as

```
(define-syntax while
  (syntax-rules ()
    ((while test body ...)
     (loop (if (not test) (exit #f))
           body ...))))
```

because the reference to `exit` that is inserted by the `while` macro is intended to be captured by the binding of `exit` that will be inserted by the `loop` macro. In other words, this `while` macro is not hygienic. Like `loop`, it must be written using the `er-macro-transformer` syntax:

```
(define-syntax while
  (er-macro-transformer
   (lambda (x r c)
     (let ((test (cadr x))
           (body (cddr x)))
       `(,(r 'loop)
         (,(r 'if) (,(r 'not) ,test) (exit #f))
         ,@body)))))
```

2.12 SRFI syntax

Several special forms have been introduced to support some of the Scheme Requests for Implementation (SRFI). Note that MIT/GNU Scheme has for some time supported SRFI 23 (error-reporting mechanism) and SRFI 30 (nested multi-line comments), since these SRFIs reflect existing practice rather than introducing new functionality.

2.12.1 cond-expand (SRFI 0)

SRFI 0 is a mechanism for portably determining the availability of SRFI *features*. The cond-expand special form conditionally expands according to the features available.

cond-expand *clause clause dots*   [special form]
    Each *clause* has the form

        (*feature-requirement* expression ...)

where *feature-requirement* can have one of the following forms:

        feature-identifier
        (and *feature-requirement* ...)
        (or *feature-requirement* ...)
        (not *feature-requirement*)
        else

(Note that at most one else clause may be present, and it must always be the last clause.)

The cond-expand special form tests for the existence of features at macro-expansion time. It either expands into the body of one of its *clauses* or signals an error during syntactic processing. cond-expand expands into the body of the first *clause* whose *feature-requirement* is currently satisfied (an else *clause*, if present, is selected if none of the previous *clauses* is selected).

A *feature-requirement* has an obvious interpretation as a logical formula, where the *feature-identifier* variables have meaning true if the feature corresponding to the *feature-identifier*, as specified in the SRFI registry, is in effect at the location of the cond-expand form, and false otherwise. A *feature-requirement* is satisfied if its formula is true under this interpretation.

```
(cond-expand
  ((and srfi-1 srfi-10)
   (write 1))
  ((or srfi-1 srfi-10)
   (write 2))
  (else))

(cond-expand
  (command-line
   (define (program-name) (car (argv)))))
```

The second example assumes that command-line is an alias for some feature which gives access to command line arguments. Note that an error will be signaled at macro-expansion time if this feature is not present.

Note that MIT/GNU Scheme allows cond-expand in any context where a special form is allowed. This is an extension of the semantics defined by SRFI 0, which only allows cond-expand at top level.

2.12.2 receive (SRFI 8)

SRFI 8 defines a convenient syntax to bind an identifier to each of the values of a multiple-valued expression and then evaluate an expression in the scope of the bindings. As an instance of this pattern, consider the following excerpt from a 'quicksort' procedure:

```
(call-with-values
  (lambda ()
    (partition (precedes pivot) others))
  (lambda (fore aft)
    (append (qsort fore) (cons pivot (qsort aft)))))
```

Here 'partition' is a multiple-valued procedure that takes two arguments, a predicate and a list, and returns two lists, one comprising the list elements that satisfy the predicate, the other those that do not. The purpose of the expression shown is to partition the list 'others', sort each of the sublists, and recombine the results into a sorted list.

For our purposes, the important step is the binding of the identifiers 'fore' and 'aft' to the values returned by 'partition'. Expressing the construction and use of these bindings with the call-by-values primitive is cumbersome: One must explicitly embed the expression that provides the values for the bindings in a parameterless procedure, and one must explicitly embed the expression to be evaluated in the scope of those bindings in another procedure, writing as its parameters the identifiers that are to be bound to the values received.

These embeddings are boilerplate, exposing the underlying binding mechanism but not revealing anything relevant to the particular program in which it occurs. So the use of a syntactic abstraction that exposes only the interesting parts – the identifiers to be bound, the multiple-valued expression that supplies the values, and the body of the receiving procedure – makes the code more concise and more readable:

```
(receive (fore aft) (partition (precedes pivot) others)
  (append (qsort fore) (cons pivot (qsort aft))))
```

The advantages are similar to those of a 'let' expression over a procedure call with a 'lambda' expression as its operator. In both cases, cleanly separating a "header" in which the bindings are established from a "body" in which they are used makes it easier to follow the code.

receive *formals expression body*   [special form]
> *Formals* and *body* are defined as for 'lambda' (see Section 2.1 [Lambda Expressions], page 15). Specifically, *formals* can have the following forms (the use of '#!optional' and '#!rest' is also allowed in *formals* but is omitted for brevity):

'(*ident1* ... *identN*)'
> The environment in which the 'receive' expression is evaluated is extended by binding *ident1*, ..., *identN* to fresh locations. The *expression* is evaluated, and its values are stored into those locations. (It is an error if *expression* does not have exactly N values.)

'*ident*'
> The environment in which the 'receive' expression is evaluated is extended by binding *ident* to a fresh location. The *expression* is evaluated, its values are converted into a newly allocated list, and the list is stored in the location bound to *ident*.

'(ident1 ... identN . identN+1)'

>   The environment in which the 'receive' expression is evaluated is ex-
>   tended by binding *ident1*, ..., *identN+1* to fresh locations. The *expres-*
>   *sion* is evaluated. Its first *N* values are stored into the locations bound
>   to *ident1 ... identN*. Any remaining values are converted into a newly
>   allocated list, which is stored into the location bound to *identN+1*. (It is
>   an error if *expression* does not have at least *N* values.)

In any case, the expressions in *body* are evaluated sequentially in the extended environment. The results of the last expression in the body are the values of the 'receive'
expression.

2.12.3 and-let* (SRFI 2)

SRFI 2 provides a form that combines 'and' and 'let*' for a logically short-circuiting sequential binding operator.

and-let* (*clause ...*) *body*   [special form]
>   Runs through each of the clauses left-to-right, short-circuiting like 'and' in that the
>   first false clause will result in the whole 'and-let*' form returning false. If a body is
>   supplied, and all of the clauses evaluate true, then the body is evaluated sequentially
>   as if in a 'begin' form, and the value of the 'and-let*' expression is the value of the
>   last body form, evaluated in a tail position with respect to the 'and-let*' expression.
>   If no body is supplied, the value of the last clause, also evaluated in a tail position
>   with respect to the 'and-let*' expression, is used instead.

Each *clause* should have one of the following forms:

'*identifier*'

>   in which case *identifier*'s value is tested.

'(*expression*)'

>   in which case the value of *expression* is tested.

'(*identifier expression*)'

>   in which case *expression* is evaluated, and, if its value is not false, *iden-*
>   *tifier* is bound to that value for the remainder of the clauses and the
>   optional body.

Example:

```
(and-let* ((list (compute-list))
           ((pair? list))
           (item (car list))
           ((integer? item)))
  (sqrt item))
```

2.12.4 define-record-type (SRFI 9)

The 'define-record-type' syntax described in SRFI 9 is a slight simplification of one
written for Scheme 48 by Jonathan Rees. Unlike many record-defining special forms, it does
not create any new identifiers. Instead, the names of the record type, predicate, constructor,
and so on are all listed explicitly in the source. This has the following advantages:

- It can be defined using a simple macro in Scheme implementations that provide a procedural interface for creating record types.

- It does not restrict users to a particular naming convention.

- Tools like `grep` and the GNU Emacs tag facility will see the defining occurance of each identifier.

`define-record-type` *type-name* (*constructor-name field-tag* . . .)   [special form]
   predicate-name field-spec . . .

Type-name, *contructor-name*, *field-tag*, and *predicate-name* are identifiers. *Field-spec* has one of these two forms:

```
(field-tag accessor-name)
(field-tag accessor-name modifier-name)
```

where *field-tag*, *accessor-name*, and *modifier-name* are each identifiers.

`define-record-type` is generative: each use creates a new record type that is distinct from all existing types, including other record types and Scheme's predefined types. Record-type definitions may only occur at top-level (there are two possible semantics for "internal" record-type definitions, generative and nongenerative, and no consensus as to which is better).

An instance of `define-record-type` is equivalent to the following definitions:

- *Type-name* is bound to a representation of the record type itself. Operations on record types, such as defining print methods, reflection, etc. are left to other SRFIs.

- *constructor-name* is bound to a procedure that takes as many arguments as there are *field-tag*s in the (*constructor-name* . . .) subform and returns a new *type-name* record. Fields whose tags are listed with *constructor-name* have the corresponding argument as their initial value. The initial values of all other fields are unspecified.

- *predicate-name* is a predicate that returns `#t` when given a value returned by *constructor-name* and `#f` for everything else.

- Each *accessor-name* is a procedure that takes a record of type *type-name* and returns the current value of the corresponding field. It is an error to pass an accessor a value which is not a record of the appropriate type.

- Each *modifier-name* is a procedure that takes a record of type *type-name* and a value which becomes the new value of the corresponding field; an unspecified value is returned. It is an error to pass a modifier a first argument which is not a record of the appropriate type.

Assigning the value of any of these identifiers has no effect on the behavior of any of their original values.

The following

```
(define-record-type :pare
  (kons x y)
  pare?
  (x kar set-kar!)
  (y kdr))
```

defines 'kons' to be a constructor, 'kar' and 'kdr' to be accessors, 'set-kar!' to be a modifier, and 'pare?' to be a predicate for objects of type ':pare'.

```
(pare? (kons 1 2))          ⇒ #t
(pare? (cons 1 2))          ⇒ #f
(kar (kons 1 2))            ⇒ 1
(kdr (kons 1 2))            ⇒ 2
(let ((k (kons 1 2)))
  (set-kar! k 3)
  (kar k))                  ⇒ 3
```

3 Equivalence Predicates

A *predicate* is a procedure that always returns a boolean value (#t or #f). An *equivalence predicate* is the computational analogue of a mathematical equivalence relation (it is symmetric, reflexive, and transitive). Of the equivalence predicates described in this section, eq? is the finest or most discriminating, and equal? is the coarsest. eqv? is slightly less discriminating than eq?.

eqv? *obj1 obj2*   [procedure]
    The eqv? procedure defines a useful equivalence relation on objects. Briefly, it returns #t if *obj1* and *obj2* should normally be regarded as the same object.

    The eqv? procedure returns #t if:

- *obj1* and *obj2* are both #t or both #f.
- *obj1* and *obj2* are both interned symbols and

  ```
  (string=? (symbol->string obj1)
            (symbol->string obj2))
      ⇒ #t
  ```

- *obj1* and *obj2* are both numbers, are numerically equal according to the = procedure, and are either both exact or both inexact (see Chapter 4 [Numbers], page 61).

- *obj1* and *obj2* are both characters and are the same character according to the char=? procedure (see Chapter 5 [Characters], page 79).

- both *obj1* and *obj2* are the empty list.

- *obj1* and *obj2* are procedures whose location tags are equal.

- *obj1* and *obj2* are pairs, vectors, strings, bit strings, records, cells, or weak pairs that denote the same locations in the store.

    The eqv? procedure returns #f if:

- *obj1* and *obj2* are of different types.
- one of *obj1* and *obj2* is #t but the other is #f.
- *obj1* and *obj2* are symbols but

  ```
  (string=? (symbol->string obj1)
            (symbol->string obj2))
      ⇒ #f
  ```

- one of *obj1* and *obj2* is an exact number but the other is an inexact number.

- *obj1* and *obj2* are numbers for which the = procedure returns #f.

- *obj1* and *obj2* are characters for which the char=? procedure returns #f.

- one of *obj1* and *obj2* is the empty list but the other is not.

- *obj1* and *obj2* are procedures that would behave differently (return a different value or have different side effects) for some arguments.

- *obj1* and *obj2* are pairs, vectors, strings, bit strings, records, cells, or weak pairs that denote distinct locations.

    Some examples:

```
(eqv? 'a 'a)                          ⇒   #t
(eqv? 'a 'b)                          ⇒   #f
(eqv? 2 2)                            ⇒   #t
(eqv? '() '())                        ⇒   #t
(eqv? 100000000 100000000)           ⇒   #t
(eqv? (cons 1 2) (cons 1 2))          ⇒   #f
(eqv? (lambda () 1)
      (lambda () 2))                  ⇒   #f
(eqv? #f 'nil)                        ⇒   #f
(let ((p (lambda (x) x)))
  (eqv? p p))                         ⇒   #t
```

The following examples illustrate cases in which the above rules do not fully specify the behavior of eqv?. All that can be said about such cases is that the value returned by eqv? must be a boolean.

```
(eqv? "" "")                          ⇒   unspecified
(eqv? '#() '#())                      ⇒   unspecified
(eqv? (lambda (x) x)
      (lambda (x) x))                 ⇒   unspecified
(eqv? (lambda (x) x)
      (lambda (y) y))                 ⇒   unspecified
```

The next set of examples shows the use of eqv? with procedures that have local state. gen-counter must return a distinct procedure every time, since each procedure has its own internal counter. gen-loser, however, returns equivalent procedures each time, since the local state does not affect the value or side effects of the procedures.

```
(define gen-counter
  (lambda ()
    (let ((n 0))
      (lambda () (set! n (+ n 1)) n))))
(let ((g (gen-counter)))
  (eqv? g g))                         ⇒   #t
(eqv? (gen-counter) (gen-counter))
                                      ⇒   #f

(define gen-loser
  (lambda ()
    (let ((n 0))
      (lambda () (set! n (+ n 1)) 27))))
(let ((g (gen-loser)))
  (eqv? g g))                         ⇒   #t
(eqv? (gen-loser) (gen-loser))
                                      ⇒   unspecified
```

```
(letrec ((f (lambda () (if (eqv? f g) 'both 'f)))
         (g (lambda () (if (eqv? f g) 'both 'g))))
  (eqv? f g))
```
$\Rightarrow$ unspecified

```
(letrec ((f (lambda () (if (eqv? f g) 'f 'both)))
         (g (lambda () (if (eqv? f g) 'g 'both))))
  (eqv? f g))
```
$\Rightarrow$ #f

Objects of distinct types must never be regarded as the same object.

Since it is an error to modify constant objects (those returned by literal expressions), the implementation may share structure between constants where appropriate. Thus the value of eqv? on constants is sometimes unspecified.

```
(let ((x '(a)))
  (eqv? x x))                             ⇒   #t
(eqv? '(a) '(a))                          ⇒   unspecified
(eqv? "a" "a")                            ⇒   unspecified
(eqv? '(b) (cdr '(a b)))                  ⇒   unspecified
```

Rationale: The above definition of eqv? allows implementations latitude in their treatment of procedures and literals: implementations are free either to detect or to fail to detect that two procedures or two literals are equivalent to each other, and can decide whether or not to merge representations of equivalent objects by using the same pointer or bit pattern to represent both.

eq? *obj1 obj2*   [procedure]

> eq? is similar to eqv? except that in some cases it is capable of discerning distinctions finer than those detectable by eqv?.
>
> eq? and eqv? are guaranteed to have the same behavior on symbols, booleans, the empty list, pairs, records, and non-empty strings and vectors. eq?'s behavior on numbers and characters is implementation-dependent, but it will always return either true or false, and will return true only when eqv? would also return true. eq? may also behave differently from eqv? on empty vectors and empty strings.
>
> ```
> (eq? 'a 'a)                        ⇒    #t
> (eq? '(a) '(a))                    ⇒    unspecified
> (eq? (list 'a) (list 'a))         ⇒    #f
> (eq? "a" "a")                      ⇒    unspecified
> (eq? "" "")                        ⇒    unspecified
> (eq? '() '())                      ⇒    #t
> (eq? 2 2)                          ⇒    unspecified
> (eq? #\A #\A)                      ⇒    unspecified
> (eq? car car)                      ⇒    #t
> (let ((n (+ 2 3)))
>   (eq? n n))                       ⇒    unspecified
> (let ((x '(a)))
>   (eq? x x))                       ⇒    #t
> (let ((x '#()))
>   (eq? x x))                       ⇒    #t
> (let ((p (lambda (x) x)))
>   (eq? p p))                       ⇒    #t
> ```

Rationale: It will usually be possible to implement eq? much more efficiently than eqv?, for example, as a simple pointer comparison instead of as some more complicated operation. One reason is that it may not be possible to compute eqv? of two numbers in constant time, whereas eq? implemented as pointer comparison will always finish in constant time. eq? may be used like eqv? in applications using procedures to implement objects with state since it obeys the same constraints as eqv?.

`equal?` *obj1 obj2*   [procedure]

    `equal?` recursively compares the contents of pairs, vectors, and strings, applying `eqv?` on other objects such as numbers, symbols, and records. A rule of thumb is that objects are generally `equal?` if they print the same. `equal?` may fail to terminate if its arguments are circular data structures.

```
(equal? 'a 'a)                      ⇒   #t
(equal? '(a) '(a))                  ⇒   #t
(equal? '(a (b) c)
        '(a (b) c))                 ⇒   #t
(equal? "abc" "abc")                ⇒   #t
(equal? 2 2)                        ⇒   #t
(equal? (make-vector 5 'a)
        (make-vector 5 'a))         ⇒   #t
(equal? (lambda (x) x)
        (lambda (y) y))             ⇒   unspecified
```

4 Numbers

(This section is largely taken from the *Revised^4 Report on the Algorithmic Language Scheme*.)

Numerical computation has traditionally been neglected by the Lisp community. Until Common Lisp there was no carefully thought out strategy for organizing numerical computation, and with the exception of the MacLisp system little effort was made to execute numerical code efficiently. This report recognizes the excellent work of the Common Lisp committee and accepts many of their recommendations. In some ways this report simplifies and generalizes their proposals in a manner consistent with the purposes of Scheme.

It is important to distinguish between the mathematical numbers, the Scheme numbers that attempt to model them, the machine representations used to implement the Scheme numbers, and notations used to write numbers. This report uses the types *number*, *complex*, *real*, *rational*, and *integer* to refer to both mathematical numbers and Scheme numbers. Machine representations such as fixed point and floating point are referred to by names such as *fixnum* and *flonum*.

4.1 Numerical types

Mathematically, numbers may be arranged into a tower of subtypes in which each level is a subset of the level above it:

> number
> complex
> real
> rational
> integer

For example, 3 is an integer. Therefore 3 is also a rational, a real, and a complex. The same is true of the Scheme numbers that model 3. For Scheme numbers, these types are defined by the predicates `number?`, `complex?`, `real?`, `rational?`, and `integer?`.

There is no simple relationship between a number's type and its representation inside a computer. Although most implementations of Scheme will offer at least two different representations of 3, these different representations denote the same integer.

Scheme's numerical operations treat numbers as abstract data, as independent of their representation as possible. Although an implementation of Scheme may use fixnum, flonum, and perhaps other representations for numbers, this should not be apparent to a casual programmer writing simple programs.

It is necessary, however, to distinguish between numbers that are represented exactly and those that may not be. For example, indexes into data structures must be known exactly, as must some polynomial coefficients in a symbolic algebra system. On the other hand, the results of measurements are inherently inexact, and irrational numbers may be approximated by rational and therefore inexact approximations. In order to catch uses of inexact numbers where exact numbers are required, Scheme explicitly distinguishes exact from inexact numbers. This distinction is orthogonal to the dimension of type.

4.2 Exactness

Scheme numbers are either *exact* or *inexact*. A number is exact if it was written as an exact constant or was derived from exact numbers using only exact operations. A number is inexact if it was written as an inexact constant, if it was derived using inexact ingredients, or if it was derived using inexact operations. Thus inexactness is a contagious property of a number.

If two implementations produce exact results for a computation that did not involve inexact intermediate results, the two ultimate results will be mathematically equivalent. This is generally not true of computations involving inexact numbers since approximate methods such as floating point arithmetic may be used, but it is the duty of each implementation to make the result as close as practical to the mathematically ideal result.

Rational operations such as + should always produce exact results when given exact arguments. If the operation is unable to produce an exact result, then it may either report the violation of an implementation restriction or it may silently coerce its result to an inexact value. See Section 4.3 [Implementation restrictions], page 62.

With the exception of `inexact->exact`, the operations described in this section must generally return inexact results when given any inexact arguments. An operation may, however, return an exact result if it can prove that the value of the result is unaffected by the inexactness of its arguments. For example, multiplication of any number by an exact zero may produce an exact zero result, even if the other argument is inexact.

4.3 Implementation restrictions

Implementations of Scheme are not required to implement the whole tower of subtypes (see Section 4.1 [Numerical types], page 61), but they must implement a coherent subset consistent with both the purposes of the implementation and the spirit of the Scheme language. For example, an implementation in which all numbers are real may still be quite useful.[1]

Implementations may also support only a limited range of numbers of any type, subject to the requirements of this section. The supported range for exact numbers of any type may be different from the supported range for inexact numbers of that type. For example, an implementation that uses flonums to represent all its inexact real numbers may support a practically unbounded range of exact integers and rationals while limiting the range of inexact reals (and therefore the range of inexact integers and rationals) to the dynamic range of the flonum format. Furthermore the gaps between the representable inexact integers and rationals are likely to be very large in such an implementation as the limits of this range are approached.

An implementation of Scheme must support exact integers throughout the range of numbers that may be used for indexes of lists, vectors, and strings or that may result from computing the length of a list, vector, or string. The `length`, `vector-length`, and `string-length` procedures must return an exact integer, and it is an error to use anything but an exact integer as an index. Furthermore any integer constant within the index range,

---

[1] MIT/GNU Scheme implements the whole tower of numerical types. It has unlimited-precision exact integers and exact rationals. Flonums are used to implement all inexact reals; on machines that support IEEE floating-point arithmetic these are double-precision floating-point numbers.

if expressed by an exact integer syntax, will indeed be read as an exact integer, regardless of any implementation restrictions that may apply outside this range. Finally, the procedures listed below will always return an exact integer result provided all their arguments are exact integers and the mathematically expected result is representable as an exact integer within the implementation:

```
*                 gcd               modulo
+                 imag-part         numerator
-                 inexact->exact    quotient
abs               lcm               rationalize
angle             magnitude         real-part
ceiling           make-polar        remainder
denominator       make-rectangular  round
expt              max               truncate
floor             min
```

Implementations are encouraged, but not required, to support exact integers and exact rationals of practically unlimited size and precision, and to implement the above procedures and the / procedure in such a way that they always return exact results when given exact arguments. If one of these procedures is unable to deliver an exact result when given exact arguments, then it may either report a violation of an implementation restriction or it may silently coerce its result to an inexact number. Such a coercion may cause an error later.

An implementation may use floating point and other approximate representation strategies for inexact numbers. This report recommends, but does not require, that the IEEE 32-bit and 64-bit floating point standards be followed by implementations that use flonum representations, and that implementations using other representations should match or exceed the precision achievable using these floating point standards.

In particular, implementations that use flonum representations must follow these rules: A flonum result must be represented with at least as much precision as is used to express any of the inexact arguments to that operation. It is desirable (but not required) for potentially inexact operations such as sqrt, when applied to exact arguments, to produce exact answers whenever possible (for example the square root of an exact 4 ought to be an exact 2). If, however, an exact number is operated upon so as to produce an inexact result (as by sqrt), and if the result is represented as a flonum, then the most precise flonum format available must be used; but if the result is represented in some other way then the representation must have at least as much precision as the most precise flonum format available.

Although Scheme allows a variety of written notations for numbers, any particular implementation may support only some of them.[2] For example, an implementation in which all numbers are real need not support the rectangular and polar notations for complex numbers. If an implementation encounters an exact numerical constant that it cannot represent as an exact number, then it may either report a violation of an implementation restriction or it may silently represent the constant by an inexact number.

---

[2] MIT/GNU Scheme implements all of the written notations for numbers.

4.4 Syntax of numerical constants

A number may be written in binary, octal, decimal, or hexadecimal by the use of a radix prefix. The radix prefixes are #b (binary), #o (octal), #d (decimal), and #x (hexadecimal). With no radix prefix, a number is assumed to be expressed in decimal.

A numerical constant may be specified to be either exact or inexact by a prefix. The prefixes are #e for exact, and #i for inexact. An exactness prefix may appear before or after any radix prefix that is used. If the written representation of a number has no exactness prefix, the constant may be either inexact or exact. It is inexact if it contains a decimal point, an exponent, or a # character in the place of a digit, otherwise it is exact.

In systems with inexact numbers of varying precisions it may be useful to specify the precision of a constant. For this purpose, numerical constants may be written with an *exponent marker* that indicates the desired precision of the inexact representation. The letters s, f, d, and l specify the use of *short, single, double,* and *long* precision, respectively. (When fewer than four internal inexact representations exist, the four size specifications are mapped onto those available. For example, an implementation with two internal representations may map short and single together and long and double together.) In addition, the exponent marker e specifies the default precision for the implementation. The default precision has at least as much precision as *double*, but implementations may wish to allow this default to be set by the user.

```
3.14159265358979F0
        Round to single — 3.141593
0.6L0
        Extend to long — .600000000000000
```

4.5 Numerical operations

See Section 1.1.3 [Entry Format], page 5, for a summary of the naming conventions used to specify restrictions on the types of arguments to numerical routines. The examples used in this section assume that any numerical constant written using an exact notation is indeed represented as an exact number. Some examples also assume that certain numerical constants written using an inexact notation can be represented without loss of accuracy; the inexact constants were chosen so that this is likely to be true in implementations that use flonums to represent inexact numbers.

number? *object*	[procedure]
complex? *object*	[procedure]
real? *object*	[procedure]
rational? *object*	[procedure]
integer? *object*	[procedure]

These numerical type predicates can be applied to any kind of argument, including non-numbers. They return #t if the object is of the named type, and otherwise they return #f. In general, if a type predicate is true of a number then all higher type predicates are also true of that number. Consequently, if a type predicate is false of a number, then all lower type predicates are also false of that number.[3]

---

[3] In MIT/GNU Scheme the **rational?** procedure is the same as **real?**, and the **complex?** procedure is the same as **number?**.

If z is an inexact complex number, then (real? z) is true if and only if (zero? (imag-part z)) is true. If x is an inexact real number, then (integer? x) is true if and only if (= x (round x)).

(complex? 3+4i)	⇒	#t
(complex? 3)	⇒	#t
(real? 3)	⇒	#t
(real? -2.5+0.0i)	⇒	#t
(real? #e1e10)	⇒	#t
(rational? 6/10)	⇒	#t
(rational? 6/3)	⇒	#t
(integer? 3+0i)	⇒	#t
(integer? 3.0)	⇒	#t
(integer? 8/4)	⇒	#t

Note: The behavior of these type predicates on inexact numbers is unreliable, since any inaccuracy may affect the result.

exact? z [procedure]

inexact? z [procedure]

These numerical predicates provide tests for the exactness of a quantity. For any Scheme number, precisely one of these predicates is true.

exact-integer? *object* [procedure]

exact-nonnegative-integer? *object* [procedure]

exact-rational? *object* [procedure]

These procedures test for some very common types of numbers. These tests could be written in terms of simpler predicates, but are more efficient.

= *z1 z2 z3* . . . [procedure]

< *x1 x2 x3* . . . [procedure]

> *x1 x2 x3* . . . [procedure]

<= *x1 x2 x3* . . . [procedure]

>= *x1 x2 x3* . . . [procedure]

These procedures return #t if their arguments are (respectively): equal, monotonically increasing, monotonically decreasing, monotonically nondecreasing, or monotonically nonincreasing.

These predicates are transitive. Note that the traditional implementations of these predicates in Lisp-like languages are not transitive.

Note: While it is not an error to compare inexact numbers using these predicates, the results may be unreliable because a small inaccuracy may affect the result; this is especially true of = and zero?. When in doubt, consult a numerical analyst.

zero? z [procedure]

positive? x [procedure]

negative? x [procedure]

odd? x [procedure]

even? x [procedure]

These numerical predicates test a number for a particular property, returning #t or #f. See note above regarding inexact numbers.

max *x1 x2* ...   [procedure]
min *x1 x2* ...   [procedure]
>   These procedures return the maximum or minimum of their arguments.

$$(\texttt{max 3 4}) \qquad \Rightarrow \quad 4 \qquad \texttt{; exact}$$
$$(\texttt{max 3.9 4}) \qquad \Rightarrow \quad 4.0 \quad \texttt{; inexact}$$

>   Note: If any argument is inexact, then the result will also be inexact (unless the
>   procedure can prove that the inaccuracy is not large enough to affect the result, which
>   is possible only in unusual implementations). If min or max is used to compare numbers
>   of mixed exactness, and the numerical value of the result cannot be represented as an
>   inexact number without loss of accuracy, then the procedure may report a violation
>   of an implementation restriction.[4]

+ *z1* ...   [procedure]
* *z1* ...   [procedure]
>   These procedures return the sum or product of their arguments.

```
(+ 3 4)        ⇒   7
(+ 3)          ⇒   3
(+)            ⇒   0
(* 4)          ⇒   4
(*)            ⇒   1
```

- *z1 z2* ...   [procedure]
/ *z1 z2* ...   [procedure]
>   With two or more arguments, these procedures return the difference or quotient of
>   their arguments, associating to the left. With one argument, however, they return
>   the additive or multiplicative inverse of their argument.

```
(- 3 4)        ⇒   -1
(- 3 4 5)      ⇒   -6
(- 3)          ⇒   -3
(/ 3 4 5)      ⇒   3/20
(/ 3)          ⇒   1/3
```

1+ *z*   [procedure]
-1+ *z*   [procedure]
>   (1+ z) is equivalent to (+ z 1); (-1+ z) is equivalent to (- z 1).

abs *x*   [procedure]
>   abs returns the magnitude of its argument.

```
(abs -7)       ⇒   7
```

quotient *n1 n2*   [procedure]
remainder *n1 n2*   [procedure]
modulo *n1 n2*   [procedure]
>   These procedures implement number-theoretic (integer) division: for positive integers
>   *n1* and *n2*, if *n3* and *n4* are integers such that

$$n_1 = n_2 n_3 + n_4$$

----

[4] MIT/GNU Scheme signals an error of type condition-type:bad-range-argument in this case.

$$0 \le n_4 < n_2$$

then

```
(quotient n1 n2)       ⇒   n3
(remainder n1 n2)      ⇒   n4
(modulo n1 n2)         ⇒   n4
```

For integers $n1$ and $n2$ with $n2$ not equal to 0,

```
(= n1
   (+ (* n2 (quotient n1 n2))
      (remainder n1 n2)))
```
$$\Rightarrow \quad \text{\#t}$$

provided all numbers involved in that computation are exact.

The value returned by `quotient` always has the sign of the product of its arguments. `remainder` and `modulo` differ on negative arguments — the `remainder` always has the sign of the dividend, the `modulo` always has the sign of the divisor:

```
(modulo 13 4)          ⇒   1
(remainder 13 4)       ⇒   1

(modulo -13 4)         ⇒   3
(remainder -13 4)      ⇒   -1

(modulo 13 -4)         ⇒   -3
(remainder 13 -4)      ⇒   1

(modulo -13 -4)        ⇒   -1
(remainder -13 -4)     ⇒   -1

(remainder -13 -4.0)   ⇒   -1.0   ; inexact
```

Note that `quotient` is the same as `integer-truncate`.

integer-floor *n1 n2*   [procedure]
integer-ceiling *n1 n2*   [procedure]
integer-truncate *n1 n2*   [procedure]
integer-round *n1 n2*   [procedure]

These procedures combine integer division with rounding. For example, the following are equivalent:

```
(integer-floor n1 n2)
(floor (/ n1 n2))
```

However, the former is faster and does not produce an intermediate result.

Note that `integer-truncate` is the same as `quotient`.

integer-divide *n1 n2*   [procedure]
integer-divide-quotient *qr*   [procedure]
integer-divide-remainder *qr*   [procedure]

`integer-divide` is equivalent to performing both `quotient` and `remainder` at once. The result of `integer-divide` is an object with two components; the procedures `integer-divide-quotient` and `integer-divide-remainder` select those components. These procedures are useful when both the quotient and remainder are needed; often computing both of these numbers simultaneously is much faster than computing them separately.

For example, the following are equivalent:

```
(lambda (n d)
  (cons (quotient n d)
        (remainder n d)))

(lambda (n d)
  (let ((qr (integer-divide n d)))
    (cons (integer-divide-quotient qr)
          (integer-divide-remainder qr))))
```

gcd *n1* ...   [procedure]
lcm *n1* ...   [procedure]
  These procedures return the greatest common divisor or least common multiple of their arguments. The result is always non-negative.

```
(gcd 32 -36)           ⇒   4
(gcd)                  ⇒   0

(lcm 32 -36)           ⇒   288
(lcm 32.0 -36)         ⇒   288.0   ; inexact
(lcm)                  ⇒   1
```

numerator *q*   [procedure]
denominator *q*   [procedure]
  These procedures return the numerator or denominator of their argument; the result is computed as if the argument was represented as a fraction in lowest terms. The denominator is always positive. The denominator of 0 is defined to be 1.

```
(numerator (/ 6 4))   ⇒   3
(denominator (/ 6 4))   ⇒   2
(denominator (exact->inexact (/ 6 4))) ⇒ 2.0
```

floor *x*   [procedure]
ceiling *x*   [procedure]
truncate *x*   [procedure]
round *x*   [procedure]
  These procedures return integers. `floor` returns the largest integer not larger than *x*. `ceiling` returns the smallest integer not smaller than *x*. `truncate` returns the integer closest to *x* whose absolute value is not larger than the absolute value of *x*. `round` returns the closest integer to *x*, rounding to even when *x* is halfway between two integers.

Rationale: `round` rounds to even for consistency with the rounding modes required by the IEEE floating point standard.

Note: If the argument to one of these procedures is inexact, then the result will also be inexact. If an exact value is needed, the result should be passed to the `inexact->exact` procedure (or use one of the procedures below).

```
(floor -4.3)        ⇒  -5.0
(ceiling -4.3)      ⇒  -4.0
(truncate -4.3)     ⇒  -4.0
(round -4.3)        ⇒  -4.0

(floor 3.5)         ⇒  3.0
(ceiling 3.5)       ⇒  4.0
(truncate 3.5)      ⇒  3.0
(round 3.5)         ⇒  4.0   ; inexact

(round 7/2)         ⇒  4     ; exact
(round 7)           ⇒  7
```

floor->exact *x*   [procedure]
ceiling->exact *x*   [procedure]
truncate->exact *x*   [procedure]
round->exact *x*   [procedure]
    These procedures are similar to the preceding procedures except that they always return an exact result. For example, the following are equivalent

```
(floor->exact x)
(inexact->exact (floor x))
```

except that the former is faster and has fewer range restrictions.

rationalize *x y*   [procedure]
rationalize->exact *x y*   [procedure]
    `rationalize` returns the *simplest* rational number differing from x by no more than y. A rational number *r1* is *simpler* than another rational number *r2* if *r1=p1/q1* and *r2=p2/q2* (both in lowest terms) and |*p1*|<=|*p2*| and |*q1*|<=|*q2*|. Thus 3/5 is simpler than 4/7. Although not all rationals are comparable in this ordering (consider 2/7 and 3/5) any interval contains a rational number that is simpler than every other rational number in that interval (the simpler 2/5 lies between 2/7 and 3/5). Note that 0=0/1 is the simplest rational of all.

```
(rationalize (inexact->exact .3) 1/10)  ⇒ 1/3      ; exact
(rationalize .3 1/10)                   ⇒ #i1/3  ; inexact
```

`rationalize->exact` is similar to `rationalize` except that it always returns an exact result.

simplest-rational *x y*   [procedure]
simplest-exact-rational *x y*   [procedure]
    `simplest-rational` returns the simplest rational number between x and y inclusive; `simplest-exact-rational` is similar except that it always returns an exact result.

    These procedures implement the same functionality as `rationalize` and `rationalize->exact`, except that they specify the input range by its endpoints; `rationalize` specifies the range by its center point and its (half-) width.

exp z	[procedure]
log z	[procedure]
sin z	[procedure]
cos z	[procedure]
tan z	[procedure]
asin z	[procedure]
acos z	[procedure]
atan z	[procedure]
atan y x	[procedure]

These procedures compute the usual transcendental functions. `log` computes the natural logarithm of z (not the base ten logarithm). `asin`, `acos`, and `atan` compute arcsine, arccosine, and arctangent, respectively. The two-argument variant of `atan` computes (angle (make-rectangular x y)) (see below).

In general, the mathematical functions log, arcsine, arccosine, and arctangent are multiply defined. For nonzero real x, the value of log x is defined to be the one whose imaginary part lies in the range minus *pi* (exclusive) to *pi* (inclusive). log 0 is undefined. The value of log z when z is complex is defined according to the formula

$$\log z = \log \text{magnitude}(z) + i\,\text{angle}(z)$$

With log defined this way, the values of arcsine, arccosine, and arctangent are according to the following formulae:

$$\sin^{-1} z = -i \log(iz + \sqrt{1 - z^2})$$

$$\cos^{-1} z = \pi/2 - \sin^{-1} z$$

$$\tan^{-1} z = (\log(1 + iz) - \log(1 - iz))/(2i)$$

The above specification follows *Common Lisp: the Language*, which in turn cites *Principal Values and Branch Cuts in Complex APL*; refer to these sources for more detailed discussion of branch cuts, boundary conditions, and implementation of these functions. When it is possible these procedures produce a real result from a real argument.

sqrt z	[procedure]

Returns the principal square root of z. The result will have either positive real part, or zero real part and non-negative imaginary part.

expt $z1$ $z2$	[procedure]

Returns $z1$ raised to the power $z2$:

$$z_1{}^{z_2} = e^{z_2 \log z_1}$$

0^0 is defined to be equal to 1.

make-rectangular $x1$ $x2$	[procedure]
make-polar $x3$ $x4$	[procedure]
real-part z	[procedure]
imag-part z	[procedure]

```
magnitude z                                                    [procedure]
angle z                                                        [procedure]
conjugate z                                                    [procedure]
```
Suppose *x1*, *x2*, *x3*, and *x4* are real numbers and *z* is a complex number such that

$$z = x_1 + x_2 i = x_3 \cdot e^{ix_4}$$

Then `make-rectangular` and `make-polar` return *z*, `real-part` returns *x1*, `imag-part` returns *x2*, `magnitude` returns *x3*, and `angle` returns *x4*. In the case of `angle`, whose value is not uniquely determined by the preceding rule, the value returned will be the one in the range minus *pi* (exclusive) to *pi* (inclusive).

`conjugate` returns the complex conjugate of *z*.

```
exact->inexact z                                               [procedure]
inexact->exact z                                               [procedure]
```
`exact->inexact` returns an inexact representation of *z*. The value returned is the inexact number that is numerically closest to the argument. If an exact argument has no reasonably close inexact equivalent, then a violation of an implementation restriction may be reported; MIT/GNU Scheme signals an error of type `condition-type:bad-range-argument` in this case.

`inexact->exact` returns an exact representation of *z*. The value returned is the exact number that is numerically closest to the argument. If an inexact argument has no reasonably close exact equivalent, then a violation of an implementation restriction may be reported; in MIT/GNU Scheme this case does not occur because all inexact numbers are representable as exact numbers.

These procedures implement the natural one-to-one correspondence between exact and inexact integers throughout an implementation-dependent range. See Section 4.3 [Implementation restrictions], page 62.

4.6 Numerical input and output

```
number->string number [radix]                                 [procedure]
```
Radix must be an exact integer, either 2, 8, 10, or 16. If omitted, *radix* defaults to 10. The procedure `number->string` takes a number and a radix and returns as a string an external representation of the given number in the given radix such that

```
(let ((number number)
      (radix radix))
  (eqv? number
        (string->number (number->string number radix)
                        radix)))
```
is true. It is an error if no possible result makes this expression true.

If *number* is inexact, the radix is 10, and the above expression can be satisfied by a result that contains a decimal point, then the result contains a decimal point and is expressed using the minimum number of digits (exclusive of exponent and trailing zeroes) needed to make the above expression true; otherwise the format of the result is unspecified.

The result returned by `number->string` never contains an explicit radix prefix.

Note: The error case can occur only when *number* is not a complex number or is a complex number with an non-rational real or imaginary part.

Rationale: If *number* is an inexact number represented using flonums, and the radix is 10, then the above expression is normally satisfied by a result containing a decimal point. The unspecified case allows for infinities, NaNs, and non-flonum representations.

`flonum-parser-fast?`   [variable]

This variable controls the behavior of `string->number` when parsing inexact numbers. Specifically, it allows the user to trade off accuracy against speed.

When set to its default value, `#f`, the parser provides maximal accuracy, as required by the Scheme standard. If set to `#t`, the parser uses faster algorithms that will sometimes introduce small errors in the result. The errors affect a few of the least-significant bits of the result, and consequently can be tolerated by many applications.

`flonum-unparser-cutoff`   [variable]

This variable controls the action of `number->string` when *number* is a flonum (and consequently controls all printing of flonums). The value of this variable is normally a list of three items:

rounding-type

> One of the following symbols: `normal`, `relative`, or `absolute`. The symbol `normal` means that the number should be printed with full precision. The symbol `relative` means that the number should be rounded to a specific number of digits. The symbol `absolute` means that the number should be rounded so that there are a specific number of digits to the right of the decimal point.

precision   An exact integer. If *rounding-type* is `normal`, *precision* is ignored. If *rounding-type* is `relative`, *precision* must be positive, and it specifies the number of digits to which the printed representation will be rounded. If *rounding-type* is `absolute`, the printed representation will be rounded *precision* digits to the right of the decimal point; if *precision* is negative, the representation is rounded (- *precision*) digits to the left of the decimal point.

format-type

> One of the symbols: `normal`, `scientific`, or `engineering`. This specifies the format in which the number will be printed.
> `scientific` specifies that the number will be printed using scientific notation: *x.xxxeyyy*. In other words, the number is printed as a significand between zero inclusive and ten exclusive, and an exponent. `engineering` is like `scientific`, except that the exponent is always a power of three, and the significand is constrained to be between zero inclusive and 1000 exclusive. If `normal` is specified, the number will be printed in positional notation if it is "small enough", otherwise it is printed in scientific notation. A number is "small enough" when the number of digits that would be printed using positional notation does not exceed the number of digits

of precision in the underlying floating-point number representation; IEEE double-precision floating-point numbers have 17 digits of precision.

This three-element list may be abbreviated in two ways. First, the symbol `normal` may be used, which is equivalent to the list `(normal 0 normal)`. Second, the third element of the list, *format-type*, may be omitted, in which case it defaults to `normal`.

The default value for `flonum-unparser-cutoff` is `normal`. If it is bound to a value different from those described here, `number->string` issues a warning and acts as though the value had been `normal`.

Some examples of `flonum-unparser-cutoff`:

```
(number->string (* 4 (atan 1 1)))
                                    ⇒ "3.141592653589793"
(fluid-let ((flonum-unparser-cutoff '(relative 5)))
  (number->string (* 4 (atan 1 1))))
                                    ⇒ "3.1416"
(fluid-let ((flonum-unparser-cutoff '(relative 5)))
  (number->string (* 4000 (atan 1 1))))
                                    ⇒ "3141.6"
(fluid-let ((flonum-unparser-cutoff '(relative 5 scientific)))
  (number->string (* 4000 (atan 1 1))))
                                    ⇒ "3.1416e3"
(fluid-let ((flonum-unparser-cutoff '(relative 5 scientific)))
  (number->string (* 40000 (atan 1 1))))
                                    ⇒ "3.1416e4"
(fluid-let ((flonum-unparser-cutoff '(relative 5 engineering)))
  (number->string (* 40000 (atan 1 1))))
                                    ⇒ "31.416e3"
(fluid-let ((flonum-unparser-cutoff '(absolute 5)))
  (number->string (* 4 (atan 1 1))))
                                    ⇒ "3.14159"
(fluid-let ((flonum-unparser-cutoff '(absolute 5)))
  (number->string (* 4000 (atan 1 1))))
                                    ⇒ "3141.59265"
(fluid-let ((flonum-unparser-cutoff '(absolute -4)))
  (number->string (* 4e10 (atan 1 1))))
                                    ⇒ "31415930000."
(fluid-let ((flonum-unparser-cutoff '(absolute -4 scientific)))
  (number->string (* 4e10 (atan 1 1))))
                                    ⇒ "3.141593e10"
(fluid-let ((flonum-unparser-cutoff '(absolute -4 engineering)))
  (number->string (* 4e10 (atan 1 1))))
                                    ⇒ "31.41593e9"
(fluid-let ((flonum-unparser-cutoff '(absolute -5)))
  (number->string (* 4e10 (atan 1 1))))
                                    ⇒ "31415900000."
```

string->number *string* [*radix*]   [procedure]
>   Returns a number of the maximally precise representation expressed by the given
>   *string*. *Radix* must be an exact integer, either 2, 8, 10, or 16. If supplied, *radix*
>   is a default radix that may be overridden by an explicit radix prefix in *string* (e.g.
>   "#o177"). If *radix* is not supplied, then the default radix is 10. If *string* is not a
>   syntactically valid notation for a number, then `string->number` returns #f.

(string->number "100")	$\Rightarrow$	100
(string->number "100" 16)	$\Rightarrow$	256
(string->number "1e2")	$\Rightarrow$	100.0
(string->number "15##")	$\Rightarrow$	1500.0

Note that a numeric representation using a decimal point or an exponent marker is
not recognized unless *radix* is 10.

4.7 Fixnum and Flonum Operations

This section describes numerical operations that are restricted forms of the operations
described above. These operations are useful because they compile very efficiently. However,
care should be exercised: if used improperly, these operations can return incorrect answers,
or even malformed objects that confuse the garbage collector.

4.7.1 Fixnum Operations

A *fixnum* is an exact integer that is small enough to fit in a machine word. In MIT/GNU
Scheme, fixnums are typically 24 or 26 bits, depending on the machine; it is reasonable to
assume that fixnums are at least 24 bits. Fixnums are signed; they are encoded using 2's
complement.

All exact integers that are small enough to be encoded as fixnums are always encoded as
fixnums — in other words, any exact integer that is not a fixnum is too big to be encoded
as such. For this reason, small constants such as 0 or 1 are guaranteed to be fixnums.

fix:fixnum? *object*   [procedure]
>   Returns #t if *object* is a fixnum; otherwise returns #f.

Here is an expression that determines the largest fixnum:

```
(let loop ((n 1))
  (if (fix:fixnum? n)
      (loop (* n 2))
      (- n 1)))
```

A similar expression determines the smallest fixnum.

fix:= *fixnum fixnum*   [procedure]
fix:< *fixnum fixnum*   [procedure]
fix:> *fixnum fixnum*   [procedure]
fix:<= *fixnum fixnum*   [procedure]
fix:>= *fixnum fixnum*   [procedure]
>   These are the standard order and equality predicates on fixnums. When compiled,
>   they do not check the types of their arguments.

`fix:zero?` *fixnum*   [procedure]
`fix:positive?` *fixnum*   [procedure]
`fix:negative?` *fixnum*   [procedure]

These procedures compare their argument to zero. When compiled, they do not check the type of their argument. The code produced by the following expressions is identical:

```
(fix:zero? fixnum)
(fix:= fixnum 0)
```

Similarly, `fix:positive?` and `fix:negative?` produce code identical to equivalent expressions using `fix:>` and `fix:<`.

`fix:+` *fixnum fixnum*   [procedure]
`fix:-` *fixnum fixnum*   [procedure]
`fix:*` *fixnum fixnum*   [procedure]
`fix:quotient` *fixnum fixnum*   [procedure]
`fix:remainder` *fixnum fixnum*   [procedure]
`fix:gcd` *fixnum fixnum*   [procedure]
`fix:1+` *fixnum*   [procedure]
`fix:-1+` *fixnum*   [procedure]

These procedures are the standard arithmetic operations on fixnums. When compiled, they do not check the types of their arguments. Furthermore, they do not check to see if the result can be encoded as a fixnum. If the result is too large to be encoded as a fixnum, a malformed object is returned, with potentially disastrous effect on the garbage collector.

`fix:divide` *fixnum fixnum*   [procedure]

This procedure is like `integer-divide`, except that its arguments and its results must be fixnums. It should be used in conjunction with `integer-divide-quotient` and `integer-divide-remainder`.

The following are *bitwise-logical* operations on fixnums.

`fix:not` *fixnum*   [procedure]

This returns the bitwise-logical inverse of its argument. When compiled, it does not check the type of its argument.

`(fix:not 0)`	$\Rightarrow$	-1
`(fix:not -1)`	$\Rightarrow$	0
`(fix:not 1)`	$\Rightarrow$	-2
`(fix:not -34)`	$\Rightarrow$	33

`fix:and` *fixnum fixnum*   [procedure]

This returns the bitwise-logical "and" of its arguments. When compiled, it does not check the types of its arguments.

`(fix:and #x43 #x0f)`	$\Rightarrow$	3
`(fix:and #x43 #xf0)`	$\Rightarrow$	#x40

`fix:andc` *fixnum fixnum*   [procedure]

Returns the bitwise-logical "and" of the first argument with the bitwise-logical inverse of the second argument. When compiled, it does not check the types of its arguments.

```
        (fix:andc #x43 #x0f)                      ⇒   #x40
        (fix:andc #x43 #xf0)                      ⇒   3
```

`fix:or` *fixnum fixnum*   [procedure]

    This returns the bitwise-logical "inclusive or" of its arguments. When compiled, it does not check the types of its arguments.

```
        (fix:or #x40 3)                           ⇒   #x43
        (fix:or #x41 3)                           ⇒   #x43
```

`fix:xor` *fixnum fixnum*   [procedure]

    This returns the bitwise-logical "exclusive or" of its arguments. When compiled, it does not check the types of its arguments.

```
        (fix:xor #x40 3)                          ⇒   #x43
        (fix:xor #x41 3)                          ⇒   #x42
```

`fix:lsh` *fixnum1 fixnum2*   [procedure]

    This procedure returns the result of logically shifting *fixnum1* by *fixnum2* bits. If *fixnum2* is positive, *fixnum1* is shifted left; if negative, it is shifted right. When compiled, it does not check the types of its arguments, nor the validity of its result.

```
        (fix:lsh 1 10)                            ⇒   #x400
        (fix:lsh #x432 -10)                       ⇒   1
        (fix:lsh -1 3)                            ⇒   -8
        (fix:lsh -128 -4)                         ⇒   #x3FFFF8
```

4.7.2 Flonum Operations

A *flonum* is an inexact real number that is implemented as a floating-point number. In MIT/GNU Scheme, all inexact real numbers are flonums. For this reason, constants such as `0.` and `2.3` are guaranteed to be flonums.

`flo:flonum?` *object*   [procedure]

    Returns `#t` if *object* is a flonum; otherwise returns `#f`.

`flo:=` *flonum1 flonum2*   [procedure]
`flo:<` *flonum1 flonum2*   [procedure]
`flo:>` *flonum1 flonum2*   [procedure]

    These procedures are the standard order and equality predicates on flonums. When compiled, they do not check the types of their arguments.

`flo:zero?` *flonum*   [procedure]
`flo:positive?` *flonum*   [procedure]
`flo:negative?` *flonum*   [procedure]

    Each of these procedures compares its argument to zero. When compiled, they do not check the type of their argument.

`flo:+` *flonum1 flonum2*   [procedure]
`flo:-` *flonum1 flonum2*   [procedure]
`flo:*` *flonum1 flonum2*   [procedure]
`flo:/` *flonum1 flonum2*   [procedure]

    These procedures are the standard arithmetic operations on flonums. When compiled, they do not check the types of their arguments.

`flo:finite?` *flonum*   [procedure]

> The IEEE floating-point number specification supports three special "numbers": positive infinity (`+inf`), negative infinity (`-inf`), and not-a-number (`NaN`). This predicate returns `#f` if *flonum* is one of these objects, and `#t` if it is any other floating-point number.

`flo:negate` *flonum*   [procedure]

> This procedure returns the negation of its argument. When compiled, it does not check the type of its argument. Equivalent to (`flo:- 0.` *flonum*).

`flo:abs` *flonum*   [procedure]
`flo:exp` *flonum*   [procedure]
`flo:log` *flonum*   [procedure]
`flo:sin` *flonum*   [procedure]
`flo:cos` *flonum*   [procedure]
`flo:tan` *flonum*   [procedure]
`flo:asin` *flonum*   [procedure]
`flo:acos` *flonum*   [procedure]
`flo:atan` *flonum*   [procedure]
`flo:sqrt` *flonum*   [procedure]
`flo:expt` *flonum1 flonum2*   [procedure]
`flo:floor` *flonum*   [procedure]
`flo:ceiling` *flonum*   [procedure]
`flo:truncate` *flonum*   [procedure]
`flo:round` *flonum*   [procedure]
`flo:floor->exact` *flonum*   [procedure]
`flo:ceiling->exact` *flonum*   [procedure]
`flo:truncate->exact` *flonum*   [procedure]
`flo:round->exact` *flonum*   [procedure]

> These procedures are flonum versions of the corresponding procedures. When compiled, they do not check the types of their arguments.

`flo:atan2` *flonum1 flonum2*   [procedure]

> This is the flonum version of `atan` with two arguments. When compiled, it does not check the types of its arguments.

4.8 Random Numbers

MIT/GNU Scheme provides a facility for generating pseudo-random numbers. The current implementation is a "subtract-with-carry" random-number generator, based on the algorithm from *A New Class of Random Number Generators*, George Marsaglia and Arif Zaman, *The Annals of Applied Probability*, Vol. 1, No. 3, 1991. At the time it was implemented, this was a good algorithm for general purposes, but the state of the art in random-number generation is constantly changing. If necessary, the implementation will be updated to use a new algorithm while retaining the same interface.

The interface described here is very similar to that of Common Lisp.

random *modulus* [*state*]   [procedure]

 Modulus must be a positive real number. **random** returns a pseudo-random number
between zero (inclusive) and *modulus* (exclusive). The exactness of the returned
number is the same as the exactness of *modulus*. Additionally, if *modulus* is an exact
integer, the returned number will be also. Usually, *modulus* is either an exact integer
or an inexact real; the current implementation has been tuned to make these two
cases fast.

 If *state* is given and not **#f**, it must be a random-state object; otherwise, it defaults
to the value of the variable ***random-state***. This object is used to maintain the
state of the pseudo-random-number generator and is altered as a side effect of the
random procedure.

```
(random 1.0)     ⇒ .32744744667719056
(random 1.0)     ⇒ .01668326768172354
(random 10)      ⇒ 3
(random 10)      ⇒ 8
(random 100)     ⇒ 38
(random 100)     ⇒ 63
(random 100/3)   ⇒ 130501475769920525/6755399441055744
(random 100/3)   ⇒ 170571694016427575/13510798882111488
```

flo:random-unit *state*   [procedure]

 State must be a random-state object. **flo:random-unit** returns a pseudo-random
number between zero inclusive and one exclusive; the returned number is always
a flonum and therefore an inexact real number. **flo:random-unit** is equivalent to
random with a *modulus* of **1.0**, except that it is faster.

 The next three definitions concern random-state objects. In addition to these definitions,
it is important to know that random-state objects are specifically designed so that they
can be saved to disk using the **fasdump** procedure, and later restored using the **fasload**
procedure. This allows a particular random-state object to be saved in order to replay a
particular pseudo-random sequence.

random-state   [variable]

 This variable holds a data structure, a random-state object, that encodes the internal
state of the random-number generator that **random** uses by default. A call to **random**
will perform a side effect on this data structure. This variable may be changed, using
set! or **fluid-let**, to hold a new random-state object.

make-random-state [*state*]   [procedure]

 This procedure returns a new random-state object, suitable for use as the value of the
variable ***random-state***, or as the *state* argument to **random**. If *state* is not given
or **#f**, **make-random-state** returns a *copy* of the current random-number state object
(the value of the variable ***random-state***). If *state* is a random-state object, a copy
of that object is returned. If *state* is **#t**, then a new random-state object is returned
that has been "randomly" initialized by some means (such as by a time-of-day clock).

random-state? *object*   [procedure]

 Returns **#t** if *object* is a random-state object, otherwise returns **#f**.

5 Characters

Characters are objects that represent printed characters, such as letters and digits.

5.1 External Representation of Characters

Characters are written using the notation `#\`*character* or `#\`*character-name*. For example:

```
#\a                     ; lowercase letter
#\A                     ; uppercase letter
#\(                     ; left parenthesis
#\space                 ; the space character
#\newline               ; the newline character
```

Case is significant in `#\`*character*, but not in `#\`*character-name*. If *character* in `#\`*character* is a letter, *character* must be followed by a delimiter character such as a space or parenthesis. Characters written in the `#\` notation are self-evaluating; you don't need to quote them.

In addition to the standard character syntax, MIT Scheme also supports a general syntax that denotes any Unicode character by its scalar value. This notation is `#\U+`*scalar-value*, where *scalar-value* is a sequence of hexadecimal digits for a valid scalar value. So the above examples could also be written like this:

```
#\U+61                  ; lowercase letter
#\U+41                  ; uppercase letter
#\U+28                  ; left parenthesis
#\U+20                  ; the space character
#\U+0A                  ; the newline character
```

A character name may include one or more *bucky bit* prefixes to indicate that the character includes one or more of the keyboard shift keys Control, Meta, Super, or Hyper (note that the Control bucky bit prefix is not the same as the ASCII control key). The bucky bit prefixes and their meanings are as follows (case is not significant):

```
Key             Bucky bit prefix        Bucky bit
---             ----------------        ---------

Meta            M- or Meta-             1
Control         C- or Control-          2
Super           S- or Super-            4
Hyper           H- or Hyper-            8
```

For example,

```
#\c-a                   ; Control-a
#\meta-b                ; Meta-b
#\c-s-m-h-a             ; Control-Meta-Super-Hyper-A
```

The following *character-names* are supported, shown here with their ASCII equivalents:

```
Character Name                ASCII Name
--------------                ----------

altmode                       ESC
backnext                      US
backspace                     BS
call                          SUB
linefeed                      LF
page                          FF
return                        CR
rubout                        DEL
space
tab                           HT
```

In addition, `#\newline` is the same as `#\linefeed` (but this may change in the future, so you should not depend on it). All of the standard ASCII names for non-printing characters are supported:

```
NUL     SOH     STX     ETX     EOT     ENQ     ACK     BEL
BS      HT      LF      VT      FF      CR      SO      SI
DLE     DC1     DC2     DC3     DC4     NAK     SYN     ETB
CAN     EM      SUB     ESC     FS      GS      RS      US
DEL
```

`char->name` *char* [*slashify?*]   [procedure]

Returns a string corresponding to the printed representation of *char*. This is the *character* or *character-name* component of the external representation, combined with the appropriate bucky bit prefixes.

```
(char->name #\a)              ⇒   "a"
(char->name #\space)          ⇒   "Space"
(char->name #\c-a)            ⇒   "C-a"
(char->name #\control-a)      ⇒   "C-a"
```

Slashify?, if specified and true, says to insert the necessary backslash characters in the result so that `read` will parse it correctly. In other words, the following generates the external representation of *char*:

```
(string-append "#\\" (char->name char #t))
```

If *slashify?* is not specified, it defaults to `#f`.

`name->char` *string*   [procedure]

Converts a string that names a character into the character specified. If *string* does not name any character, `name->char` signals an error.

```
(name->char "a")             ⇒   #\a
(name->char "space")         ⇒   #\Space
(name->char "c-a")           ⇒   #\C-a
(name->char "control-a")     ⇒   #\C-a
```

5.2 Comparison of Characters

char=? *char1 char2*   [procedure]
char<? *char1 char2*   [procedure]
char>? *char1 char2*   [procedure]
char<=? *char1 char2*   [procedure]
char>=? *char1 char2*   [procedure]
char-ci=? *char1 char2*   [procedure]
char-ci<? *char1 char2*   [procedure]
char-ci>? *char1 char2*   [procedure]
char-ci<=? *char1 char2*   [procedure]
char-ci>=? *char1 char2*   [procedure]

> Returns #t if the specified characters are have the appropriate order relationship to
> one another; otherwise returns #f. The -ci procedures don't distinguish uppercase
> and lowercase letters.
>
> Character ordering follows these portability rules:
>
> - The digits are in order; for example, (char<? #\0 #\9) returns #t.
> - The uppercase characters are in order; for example, (char<? #\A #\B) returns
>   #t.
> - The lowercase characters are in order; for example, (char<? #\a #\b) returns
>   #t.
>
> MIT/GNU Scheme uses a specific character ordering, in which characters have the
> same order as their corresponding integers. See the documentation for char->integer
> for further details.
>
> **Note**: Although character objects can represent all of Unicode, the model of alpha-
> betic case used covers only ASCII letters, which means that case-insensitive compar-
> isons and case conversions are incorrect for non-ASCII letters. This will eventually be
> fixed.

5.3 Miscellaneous Character Operations

char? *object*   [procedure]

> Returns #t if *object* is a character; otherwise returns #f.

char-upcase *char*   [procedure]
char-downcase *char*   [procedure]

> Returns the uppercase or lowercase equivalent of *char* if *char* is a letter; otherwise
> returns *char*. These procedures return a character *char2* such that (char-ci=? *char*
> *char2*).
>
> **Note**: Although character objects can represent all of Unicode, the model of alpha-
> betic case used covers only ASCII letters, which means that case-insensitive compar-
> isons and case conversions are incorrect for non-ASCII letters. This will eventually be
> fixed.

char->digit *char* [*radix*]   [procedure]

> If *char* is a character representing a digit in the given *radix*, returns the corresponding
> integer value. If you specify *radix* (which must be an exact integer between 2 and 36

inclusive), the conversion is done in that base, otherwise it is done in base 10. If *char* doesn't represent a digit in base *radix*, `char->digit` returns `#f`.

Note that this procedure is insensitive to the alphabetic case of *char*.

`(char->digit #\8)`	$\Rightarrow$	`8`
`(char->digit #\e 16)`	$\Rightarrow$	`14`
`(char->digit #\e)`	$\Rightarrow$	`#f`

`digit->char` *digit* [*radix*]   [procedure]
> Returns a character that represents *digit* in the radix given by *radix*. *Radix* must be an exact integer between 2 and 36 (inclusive), and defaults to 10. *Digit*, which must be an exact non-negative integer, should be less than *radix*; if *digit* is greater than or equal to *radix*, `digit->char` returns `#f`.

`(digit->char 8)`	$\Rightarrow$	`#\8`
`(digit->char 14 16)`	$\Rightarrow$	`#\E`

5.4 Internal Representation of Characters

An MIT/GNU Scheme character consists of a *code* part and a *bucky bits* part. The MIT/GNU Scheme set of characters can represent more characters than ASCII can; it includes characters with Super and Hyper bucky bits, as well as Control and Meta. Every ASCII character corresponds to some MIT/GNU Scheme character, but not vice versa.[1]

MIT/GNU Scheme uses a 21-bit character code with 4 bucky bits. The character code contains the Unicode scalar value for the character. This is a change from earlier versions of the system, which used the ISO-8859-1 scalar value, but it is upwards compatible with previous usage, since ISO-8859-1 is a proper subset of Unicode.

`make-char` *code bucky-bits*   [procedure]
> Builds a character from *code* and *bucky-bits*. Both *code* and *bucky-bits* must be exact non-negative integers in the appropriate range. Use `char-code` and `char-bits` to extract the code and bucky bits from the character. If 0 is specified for *bucky-bits*, `make-char` produces an ordinary character; otherwise, the appropriate bits are turned on as follows:

> | | |
> |---|---|
> | 1 | Meta |
> | 2 | Control |
> | 4 | Super |
> | 8 | Hyper |

For example,

`(make-char 97 0)`	$\Rightarrow$	`#\a`
`(make-char 97 1)`	$\Rightarrow$	`#\M-a`
`(make-char 97 2)`	$\Rightarrow$	`#\C-a`
`(make-char 97 3)`	$\Rightarrow$	`#\C-M-a`

`char-bits` *char*   [procedure]
> Returns the exact integer representation of *char*'s bucky bits. For example,

---

[1] Note that the Control bucky bit is different from the ASCII control key. This means that `#\SOH` (ASCII ctrl-A) is different from `#\C-A`. In fact, the Control bucky bit is completely orthogonal to the ASCII control key, making possible such characters as `#\C-SOH`.

```
(char-bits #\a)                            ⇒   0
(char-bits #\m-a)                          ⇒   1
(char-bits #\c-a)                          ⇒   2
(char-bits #\c-m-a)                        ⇒   3
```

char-code *char*   [procedure]

Returns the character code of *char*, an exact integer. For example,

```
(char-code #\a)                            ⇒   97
(char-code #\c-a)                          ⇒   97
```

Note that in MIT/GNU Scheme, the value of `char-code` is the Unicode scalar value for *char*.

char-code-limit   [variable]
char-bits-limit   [variable]

These variables define the (exclusive) upper limits for the character code and bucky bits (respectively). The character code and bucky bits are always exact non-negative integers, and are strictly less than the value of their respective limit variable.

char->integer *char*   [procedure]
integer->char *k*   [procedure]

`char->integer` returns the character code representation for *char*. `integer->char` returns the character whose character code representation is *k*.

In MIT/GNU Scheme, if (`char-ascii?` *char*) is true, then

> (eqv? (char->ascii *char*) (char->integer *char*))

However, this behavior is not required by the Scheme standard, and code that depends on it is not portable to other implementations.

These procedures implement order isomorphisms between the set of characters under the `char<=?` ordering and some subset of the integers under the `<=` ordering. That is, if

> (char<=? a b) ⇒ #t   and   (<= x y) ⇒ #t

and x and y are in the range of `char->integer`, then

```
(<= (char->integer a)
    (char->integer b))                     ⇒   #t
(char<=? (integer->char x)
         (integer->char y))                ⇒   #t
```

In MIT/GNU Scheme, the specific relationship implemented by these procedures is as follows:

```
(define (char->integer c)
  (+ (* (char-bits c) #x200000)
     (char-code c)))

(define (integer->char n)
  (make-char (remainder n #x200000)
             (quotient n #x200000)))
```

This implies that `char->integer` and `char-code` produce identical results for characters that have no bucky bits set, and that characters are ordered according to their Unicode scalar values.

Note: If the argument to `char->integer` or `integer->char` is a constant, the compiler will constant-fold the call, replacing it with the corresponding result. This is a very useful way to denote unusual character constants or ASCII codes.

`char-integer-limit`   [variable]

> The range of `char->integer` is defined to be the exact non-negative integers that are less than the value of this variable (exclusive). Note, however, that there are some holes in this range, because the character code must be a valid Unicode scalar value.

5.5 ISO-8859-1 Characters

MIT/GNU Scheme internally uses ISO-8859-1 codes for I/O, and stores character objects in a fashion that makes it convenient to convert between ISO-8859-1 codes and characters. Also, character strings are implemented as byte vectors whose elements are ISO-8859-1 codes; these codes are converted to character objects when accessed. For these reasons it is sometimes desirable to be able to convert between ISO-8859-1 codes and characters.

Not all characters can be represented as ISO-8859-1 codes. A character that has an equivalent ISO-8859-1 representation is called an *ISO-8859-1 character*.

For historical reasons, the procedures that manipulate ISO-8859-1 characters use the word "ASCII" rather than "ISO-8859-1".

`char-ascii?` *char*   [procedure]

> Returns the ISO-8859-1 code for *char* if *char* has an ISO-8859-1 representation; otherwise returns `#f`.

> In the current implementation, the characters that satisfy this predicate are those in which the bucky bits are turned off, and for which the character code is less than 256.

`char->ascii` *char*   [procedure]

> Returns the ISO-8859-1 code for *char*. An error `condition-type:bad-range-argument` is signalled if *char* doesn't have an ISO-8859-1 representation.

`ascii->char` *code*   [procedure]

> *Code* must be the exact integer representation of an ISO-8859-1 code. This procedure returns the character corresponding to *code*.

5.6 Character Sets

MIT/GNU Scheme's character-set abstraction is used to represent groups of characters, such as the letters or digits. A character set may contain any Unicode character.

`char-set?` *object*   [procedure]

> Returns `#t` if *object* is a character set; otherwise returns `#f`.

```
char-set:upper-case                                                    [variable]
char-set:lower-case                                                    [variable]
char-set:alphabetic                                                    [variable]
char-set:numeric                                                       [variable]
char-set:alphanumeric                                                  [variable]
char-set:whitespace                                                    [variable]
char-set:not-whitespace                                                [variable]
char-set:graphic                                                       [variable]
char-set:not-graphic                                                   [variable]
char-set:standard                                                      [variable]
```

These variables contain predefined character sets. At present, these character sets contain only ISO-8859-1 characters; in the future they will contain all the relevant Unicode characters. To see the contents of one of these sets, use `char-set->scalar-values`.

Alphabetic characters are the 52 upper and lower case letters. *Numeric* characters are the 10 decimal digits. *Alphanumeric* characters are those in the union of these two sets. *Whitespace* characters are `#\space`, `#\tab`, `#\page`, `#\linefeed`, and `#\return`. *Graphic* characters are the printing characters and `#\space`. *Standard* characters are the printing characters, `#\space`, and `#\newline`. These are the printing characters:

```
! " # $ % & ' ( ) * + , - . /
0 1 2 3 4 5 6 7 8 9
: ; < = > ? @
A B C D E F G H I J K L M N O P Q R S T U V W X Y Z
[ \ ] ^ _ `
a b c d e f g h i j k l m n o p q r s t u v w x y z
{ | } ~
```

char-upper-case? *char*   [procedure]
char-lower-case? *char*   [procedure]
char-alphabetic? *char*   [procedure]
char-numeric? *char*   [procedure]
char-alphanumeric? *char*   [procedure]
char-whitespace? *char*   [procedure]
char-graphic? *char*   [procedure]
char-standard? *object*   [procedure]

These predicates are defined in terms of the respective character sets defined above.

char-set-member? *char-set char*   [procedure]

Returns `#t` if *char* is in *char-set*; otherwise returns `#f`.

char-set=? *char-set-1 char-set-2*   [procedure]

Returns `#t` if *char-set-1* and *char-set-2* contain exactly the same characters; otherwise returns `#f`.

char-set *char* ...   [procedure]

Returns a character set consisting of the specified characters. With no arguments, `char-set` returns an empty character set.

chars->char-set *chars*   [procedure]
>   Returns a character set consisting of *chars*, which must be a list of characters. This
>   is equivalent to (apply char-set *chars*).

string->char-set *string*   [procedure]
>   Returns a character set consisting of all the characters that occur in *string*.

scalar-values->char-set *items*   [procedure]
>   Returns a character set containing the Unicode scalar values described by *items*.
>   *Items* must satisfy well-formed-scalar-values-list?.

char-set->scalar-values *char-set*   [procedure]
>   Returns a well-formed scalar-values list that describes the Unicode scalar values rep-
>   resented by *char-set*.

well-formed-scalar-values-list? *object*   [procedure]
>   Returns #t if *object* is a well-formed scalar-values list, otherwise returns #f. A well-
>   formed scalar-values list is a proper list, each element of which is either a Unicode
>   scalar value or a pair of Unicode scalar values. A pair of Unicode scalar values
>   represents a contiguous range of Unicode scalar values. The CAR of the pair is the
>   inclusive lower limit, and the CDR is the exclusive upper limit. The lower limit must
>   be less than or equal to the upper limit.

char-set-invert *char-set*   [procedure]
>   Returns a character set consisting of the characters that are not in *char-set*.

char-set-difference *char-set1 char-set* ...   [procedure]
>   Returns a character set consisting of the characters that are in *char-set1* but aren't
>   in any of the *char-sets*.

char-set-intersection *char-set* ...   [procedure]
>   Returns a character set consisting of the characters that are in all of the *char-sets*.

char-set-union *char-set* ...   [procedure]
>   Returns a character set consisting of the characters that are in at least one o the
>   *char-sets*.

8-bit-char-set? *char-set*   [procedure]
>   Returns #t if *char-set* contains only 8-bit scalar values (i.e.. ISO-8859-1 characters),
>   otherwise returns #f.

ascii-range->char-set *lower upper*   [procedure]
>   This procedure is obsolete. Instead use
>
>   (scalar-values->char-set (list (cons *lower upper*)))

char-set-members *char-set*   [procedure]
>   This procedure is obsolete; instead use char-set->scalar-values.
>
>   Returns a newly allocated list of the ISO-8859-1 characters in *char-set*. If *char-set* con-
>   tains any characters outside of the ISO-8859-1 range, they will not be in the returned
>   list.

5.7 Unicode

MIT/GNU Scheme provides rudimentary support for Unicode characters. In an ideal world, Unicode would be the base character set for MIT/GNU Scheme. But MIT/GNU Scheme predates the invention of Unicode, and converting an application of this size is a considerable undertaking. So for the time being, the base character set for strings is ISO-8859-1, and Unicode support is grafted on.

This Unicode support was implemented as a part of the XML parser (see Section 14.12 [XML Support], page 223) implementation. XML uses Unicode as its base character set, and any XML implementation *must* support Unicode.

The basic unit in a Unicode implementation is the *scalar value*. The character equivalent of a scalar value is a *Unicode character*.

unicode-scalar-value? *object*   [procedure]
> Returns #t if *object* is a Unicode scalar value. Scalar values are implemented as exact non-negative integers. They are further limited, by the Unicode standard, to be strictly less than #x110000, with the values #xD800 through #xDFFF, #xFFFE, and #xFFFF excluded.

unicode-char? *object*   [procedure]
> Returns #t if *object* is a Unicode character, specifically if *object* is a character with no bucky bits and whose code satisfies **unicode-scalar-value?**.

The Unicode implementation consists of these parts:

- An implementation of *wide strings*, which are character strings that support the full Unicode character set with constant-time access.
- I/O procedures that read and write Unicode characters in several external representations, specifically UTF-8, UTF-16, and UTF-32.

5.7.1 Wide Strings

Wide characters can be combined into *wide strings*, which are similar to strings but can contain any Unicode character sequence. The implementation used for wide strings is guaranteed to provide constant-time access to each character in the string.

wide-string? *object*   [procedure]
> Returns #t if *object* is a wide string.

make-wide-string *k* [*unicode-char*]   [procedure]
> Returns a newly allocated wide string of length *k*. If *char* is specified, all elements of the returned string are initialized to *char*; otherwise the contents of the string are unspecified.

wide-string *unicode-char* ...   [procedure]
> Returns a newly allocated wide string consisting of the specified characters.

wide-string-length *wide-string*   [procedure]
> Returns the length of *wide-string* as an exact non-negative integer.

wide-string-ref *wide-string k*   [procedure]
> Returns character *k* of *wide-string*. *K* must be a valid index of *string*.

`wide-string-set!` *wide-string k unicode-char*   [procedure]
> Stores *char* in element *k* of *wide-string* and returns an unspecified value. *K* must be
> a valid index of *wide-string*.

`string->wide-string` *string* [*start* [*end*]]   [procedure]
> Returns a newly allocated wide string with the same contents as *string*. If *start* and
> *end* are supplied, they specify a substring of *string* that is to be converted. *Start*
> defaults to '0', and *end* defaults to '(`string-length` *string*)'.

`wide-string->string` *wide-string* [*start* [*end*]]   [procedure]
> Returns a newly allocated string with the same contents as *wide-string*. The argument
> *wide-string* must satisfy `wide-string?`. If *start* and *end* are supplied, they specify a
> substring of *wide-string* that is to be converted. *Start* defaults to '0', and *end* defaults
> to '(`wide-string-length` *wide-string*)'.
>
> It is an error if any character in *wide-string* fails to satisfy `char-ascii?`.

`open-wide-input-string` *wide-string* [*start* [*end*]]   [procedure]
> Returns a new input port that sources the characters of *wide-string*. The optional
> arguments *start* and *end* may be used to specify that the port delivers characters
> from a substring of *wide-string*; if not given, *start* defaults to '0' and *end* defaults to
> '(`wide-string-length` *wide-string*)'.

`open-wide-output-string`   [procedure]
> Returns an output port that accepts Unicode characters and strings and accumulates
> them in a buffer. Call `get-output-string` on the returned port to get a wide string
> containing the accumulated characters.

`call-with-wide-output-string` *procedure*   [procedure]
> Creates a wide-string output port and calls *procedure* on that port. The value re-
> turned by *procedure* is ignored, and the accumulated output is returned as a wide
> string. This is equivalent to:
>
> ```
> (define (call-with-wide-output-string procedure)
>   (let ((port (open-wide-output-string)))
>     (procedure port)
>     (get-output-string port)))
> ```

5.7.2 Unicode Representations

The procedures in this section implement transformations that convert between the internal
representation of Unicode characters and several standard external representations. These
external representations are all implemented as sequences of bytes, but they differ in their
intended usage.

UTF-8   Each character is written as a sequence of one to four bytes.

UTF-16   Each character is written as a sequence of one or two 16-bit integers.

UTF-32   Each character is written as a single 32-bit integer.

The UTF-16 and UTF-32 representations may be serialized to and from a byte stream in
either *big-endian* or *little-endian* order. In big-endian order, the most significant byte is first,

the next most significant byte is second, etc. In little-endian order, the least significant byte is first, etc. All of the UTF-16 and UTF-32 representation procedures are available in both orders, which are indicated by names containing 'utfNN-be' and 'utfNN-le', respectively. There are also procedures that implement *host-endian* order, which is either big-endian or little-endian depending on the underlying computer architecture.

`utf8-string->wide-string` *string* [*start* [*end*]]	[procedure]
`utf16-be-string->wide-string` *string* [*start* [*end*]]	[procedure]
`utf16-le-string->wide-string` *string* [*start* [*end*]]	[procedure]
`utf16-string->wide-string` *string* [*start* [*end*]]	[procedure]
`utf32-be-string->wide-string` *string* [*start* [*end*]]	[procedure]
`utf32-le-string->wide-string` *string* [*start* [*end*]]	[procedure]
`utf32-string->wide-string` *string* [*start* [*end*]]	[procedure]

> Each of these procedures converts a byte vector to a wide string, treating *string* as a stream of bytes encoded in the corresponding 'utfNN' representation. The arguments *start* and *end* allow specification of a substring; they default to zero and *string*'s length, respectively.

`utf8-string-length` *string* [*start* [*end*]]	[procedure]
`utf16-be-string-length` *string* [*start* [*end*]]	[procedure]
`utf16-le-string-length` *string* [*start* [*end*]]	[procedure]
`utf16-string-length` *string* [*start* [*end*]]	[procedure]
`utf32-be-string-length` *string* [*start* [*end*]]	[procedure]
`utf32-le-string-length` *string* [*start* [*end*]]	[procedure]
`utf32-string-length` *string* [*start* [*end*]]	[procedure]

> Each of these procedures counts the number of Unicode characters in a byte vector, treating *string* as a stream of bytes encoded in the corresponding 'utfNN' representation. The arguments *start* and *end* allow specification of a substring; they default to zero and *string*'s length, respectively.

`wide-string->utf8-string` *string* [*start* [*end*]]	[procedure]
`wide-string->utf16-be-string` *string* [*start* [*end*]]	[procedure]
`wide-string->utf16-le-string` *string* [*start* [*end*]]	[procedure]
`wide-string->utf16-string` *string* [*start* [*end*]]	[procedure]
`wide-string->utf32-be-string` *string* [*start* [*end*]]	[procedure]
`wide-string->utf32-le-string` *string* [*start* [*end*]]	[procedure]
`wide-string->utf32-string` *string* [*start* [*end*]]	[procedure]

> Each of these procedures converts a wide string to a stream of bytes encoded in the corresponding 'utfNN' representation, and returns that stream as a byte vector. The arguments *start* and *end* allow specification of a substring; they default to zero and *string*'s length, respectively.

6 Strings

A *string* is a mutable sequence of characters. In the current implementation of MIT/GNU Scheme, the elements of a string must all satisfy the predicate `char-ascii?`; if someone ports MIT/GNU Scheme to a non-ASCII operating system this requirement will change.

A string is written as a sequence of characters enclosed within double quotes " ". To include a double quote inside a string, precede the double quote with a backslash \ (escape it), as in

    "The word \"recursion\" has many meanings."

The printed representation of this string is

    The word "recursion" has many meanings.

To include a backslash inside a string, precede it with another backslash; for example,

    "Use #\\Control-q to quit."

The printed representation of this string is

    Use #\Control-q to quit.

The effect of a backslash that doesn't precede a double quote or backslash is unspecified in standard Scheme, but MIT/GNU Scheme specifies the effect for three other characters: `\t`, `\n`, and `\f`. These escape sequences are respectively translated into the following characters: `#\tab`, `#\newline`, and `#\page`. Finally, a backslash followed by exactly three octal digits is translated into the character whose ISO-8859-1 code is those digits.

If a string literal is continued from one line to another, the string will contain the newline character (`#\newline`) at the line break. Standard Scheme does not specify what appears in a string literal at a line break.

The *length* of a string is the number of characters that it contains. This number is an exact non-negative integer that is established when the string is created (but see Section 6.10 [Variable-Length Strings], page 106). Each character in a string has an *index*, which is a number that indicates the character's position in the string. The index of the first (leftmost) character in a string is 0, and the index of the last character is one less than the length of the string. The *valid indexes* of a string are the exact non-negative integers less than the length of the string.

A number of the string procedures operate on substrings. A *substring* is a segment of a *string*, which is specified by two integers *start* and *end* satisfying these relationships:

    0 <= *start* <= *end* <= (string-length *string*)

Start is the index of the first character in the substring, and *end* is one greater than the index of the last character in the substring. Thus if *start* and *end* are equal, they refer to an empty substring, and if *start* is zero and *end* is the length of *string*, they refer to all of *string*.

Some of the procedures that operate on strings ignore the difference between uppercase and lowercase. The versions that ignore case include '`-ci`' (for "case insensitive") in their names.

6.1 Construction of Strings

make-string *k* [*char*]   [procedure]
>   Returns a newly allocated string of length *k*. If you specify *char*, all elements of
>   the string are initialized to *char*, otherwise the contents of the string are unspecified.
>   *Char* must satisfy the predicate char-ascii?.
>
>   (make-string 10 #\x)   ⇒   "xxxxxxxxxx"

string *char* ...   [procedure]
>   Returns a newly allocated string consisting of the specified characters. The arguments
>   must all satisfy char-ascii?.
>
>   (string #\a)   ⇒   "a"
>   (string #\a #\b #\c)   ⇒   "abc"
>   (string #\a #\space #\b #\space #\c) ⇒   "a b c"
>   (string)   ⇒   ""

list->string *char-list*   [procedure]
>   *Char-list* must be a list of ISO-8859-1 characters. list->string returns a newly
>   allocated string formed from the elements of *char-list*. This is equivalent to (apply
>   string *char-list*). The inverse of this operation is string->list.
>
>   (list->string '(#\a #\b))   ⇒   "ab"
>   (string->list "Hello")   ⇒   (#\H #\e #\l #\l #\o)

string-copy *string*   [procedure]
>   Returns a newly allocated copy of *string*.
>
>   Note regarding variable-length strings: the maximum length of the result depends
>   only on the length of *string*, not its maximum length. If you wish to copy a string
>   and preserve its maximum length, do the following:

```
(define (string-copy-preserving-max-length string)
  (let ((length))
    (dynamic-wind
      (lambda ()
        (set! length (string-length string))
        (set-string-length! string
                            (string-maximum-length string)))
      (lambda ()
        (string-copy string))
      (lambda ()
        (set-string-length! string length)))))
```

6.2 Selecting String Components

string? *object*   [procedure]
>   Returns #t if *object* is a string; otherwise returns #f.
>
>   (string? "Hi")   ⇒   #t
>   (string? 'Hi)   ⇒   #f

`string-length` *string*   [procedure]

    Returns the length of *string* as an exact non-negative integer.

```
(string-length "")          ⇒   0
(string-length "The length")  ⇒  10
```

`string-null?` *string*   [procedure]

    Returns #t if *string* has zero length; otherwise returns #f.

```
(string-null? "")           ⇒   #t
(string-null? "Hi")         ⇒   #f
```

`string-ref` *string k*   [procedure]

    Returns character *k* of *string*. *K* must be a valid index of *string*.

```
(string-ref "Hello" 1)      ⇒   #\e
(string-ref "Hello" 5)      error  5 not in correct range
```

`string-set!` *string k char*   [procedure]

    Stores *char* in element *k* of *string* and returns an unspecified value. *K* must be a valid index of *string*, and *char* must satisfy the predicate `char-ascii?`.

```
(define str "Dog")          ⇒   unspecified
(string-set! str 0 #\L)     ⇒   unspecified
str                         ⇒   "Log"
(string-set! str 3 #\t)     error  3 not in correct range
```

6.3 Comparison of Strings

`string=?` *string1 string2*   [procedure]
`substring=?` *string1 start end string2 start end*   [procedure]
`string-ci=?` *string1 string2*   [procedure]
`substring-ci=?` *string1 start end string2 start end*   [procedure]

    Returns #t if the two strings (substrings) are the same length and contain the same characters in the same (relative) positions; otherwise returns #f. `string-ci=?` and `substring-ci=?` don't distinguish uppercase and lowercase letters, but `string=?` and `substring=?` do.

```
(string=? "PIE" "PIE")              ⇒   #t
(string=? "PIE" "pie")              ⇒   #f
(string-ci=? "PIE" "pie")           ⇒   #t
(substring=? "Alamo" 1 3 "cola" 2 4)  ⇒   #t ; compares "la"
```

`string<?` *string1 string2*   [procedure]
`substring<?` *string1 start1 end1 string2 start2 end2*   [procedure]
`string>?` *string1 string2*   [procedure]
`string<=?` *string1 string2*   [procedure]
`string>=?` *string1 string2*   [procedure]
`string-ci<?` *string1 string2*   [procedure]
`substring-ci<?` *string1 start1 end1 string2 start2 end2*   [procedure]
`string-ci>?` *string1 string2*   [procedure]
`string-ci<=?` *string1 string2*   [procedure]

`string-ci>=?` *string1 string2*   [procedure]

These procedures compare strings (substrings) according to the order of the characters they contain (also see Section 5.2 [Comparison of Characters], page 81). The arguments are compared using a lexicographic (or dictionary) order. If two strings differ in length but are the same up to the length of the shorter string, the shorter string is considered to be less than the longer string.

```
(string<? "cat" "dog")        ⇒   #t
(string<? "cat" "DOG")        ⇒   #f
(string-ci<? "cat" "DOG")     ⇒   #t
(string>? "catkin" "cat")     ⇒   #t  ; shorter is lesser
```

`string-compare` *string1 string2 if-eq if-lt if-gt*   [procedure]
`string-compare-ci` *string1 string2 if-eq if-lt if-gt*   [procedure]

If-eq, *if-lt*, and *if-gt* are procedures of no arguments (thunks). The two strings are compared; if they are equal, *if-eq* is applied, if *string1* is less than *string2*, *if-lt* is applied, else if *string1* is greater than *string2*, *if-gt* is applied. The value of the procedure is the value of the thunk that is applied.

`string-compare` distinguishes uppercase and lowercase letters;
`string-compare-ci` does not.

```
(define (cheer) (display "Hooray!"))
(define (boo)   (display "Boo-hiss!"))
(string-compare "a" "b"  cheer  (lambda() 'ignore)  boo)
        ⊣  Hooray!
        ⇒  unspecified
```

`string-hash` *string*   [procedure]
`string-hash-mod` *string k*   [procedure]

`string-hash` returns an exact non-negative integer that can be used for storing the specified *string* in a hash table. Equal strings (in the sense of `string=?`) return equal (=) hash codes, and non-equal but similar strings are usually mapped to distinct hash codes.

`string-hash-mod` is like `string-hash`, except that it limits the result to a particular range based on the exact non-negative integer *k*. The following are equivalent:

```
(string-hash-mod string k)
(modulo (string-hash string) k)
```

6.4 Alphabetic Case in Strings

`string-capitalized?` *string*   [procedure]
`substring-capitalized?` *string start end*   [procedure]

These procedures return #t if the first word in the string (substring) is capitalized, and any subsequent words are either lower case or capitalized. Otherwise, they return #f. A word is defined as a non-null contiguous sequence of alphabetic characters, delimited by non-alphabetic characters or the limits of the string (substring). A word is capitalized if its first letter is upper case and all its remaining letters are lower case.

```
(map string-capitalized? '(""    "A"    "art"  "Art"  "ART"))
                ⇒ (#f    #t    #f    #t    #f)
```

```
string-upper-case? string                                     [procedure]
substring-upper-case? string start end                        [procedure]
string-lower-case? string                                     [procedure]
substring-lower-case? string start end                        [procedure]
```
>   These procedures return #t if all the letters in the string (substring) are of the correct
>   case, otherwise they return #f. The string (substring) must contain at least one letter
>   or the procedures return #f.

```
        (map string-upper-case? '(""     "A"     "art"   "Art"   "ART"))
                            ⇒ (#f      #t      #f      #f      #t)
```

```
string-capitalize string                                      [procedure]
string-capitalize! string                                     [procedure]
substring-capitalize! string start end                        [procedure]
```
>   string-capitalize returns a newly allocated copy of *string* in which the first alpha-
>   betic character is uppercase and the remaining alphabetic characters are lowercase.
>   For example, "abcDEF" becomes "Abcdef". string-capitalize! is the destructive
>   version of string-capitalize: it alters *string* and returns an unspecified value.
>   substring-capitalize! destructively capitalizes the specified part of *string*.

```
string-downcase string                                        [procedure]
string-downcase! string                                       [procedure]
substring-downcase! string start end                          [procedure]
```
>   string-downcase returns a newly allocated copy of *string* in which all upper-
>   case letters are changed to lowercase. string-downcase! is the destructive
>   version of string-downcase: it alters *string* and returns an unspecified value.
>   substring-downcase! destructively changes the case of the specified part of *string*.

```
        (define str "ABCDEFG")           ⇒   unspecified
        (substring-downcase! str 3 5)    ⇒   unspecified
        str                              ⇒   "ABCdeFG"
```

```
string-upcase string                                          [procedure]
string-upcase! string                                         [procedure]
substring-upcase! string start end                            [procedure]
```
>   string-upcase returns a newly allocated copy of *string* in which all lower-
>   case letters are changed to uppercase. string-upcase! is the destructive
>   version of string-upcase: it alters *string* and returns an unspecified value.
>   substring-upcase! destructively changes the case of the specified part of *string*.

6.5 Cutting and Pasting Strings

```
string-append string ...                                      [procedure]
```
>   Returns a newly allocated string made from the concatenation of the given strings.
>   With no arguments, string-append returns the empty string ("").

```
        (string-append)                      ⇒   ""
        (string-append "*" "ace" "*")        ⇒   "*ace*"
        (string-append "" "" "")             ⇒   ""
        (eq? str (string-append str))        ⇒   #f  ; newly allocated
```

substring *string start end*   [procedure]

Returns a newly allocated string formed from the characters of *string* beginning with index *start* (inclusive) and ending with *end* (exclusive).

```
(substring "" 0 0)                ⇒  ""
(substring "arduous" 2 5)         ⇒  "duo"
(substring "arduous" 2 8)         error  8 not in correct range

(define (string-copy s)
  (substring s 0 (string-length s)))
```

string-head *string end*   [procedure]

Returns a newly allocated copy of the initial substring of *string*, up to but excluding *end*. It could have been defined by:

```
(define (string-head string end)
  (substring string 0 end))
```

string-tail *string start*   [procedure]

Returns a newly allocated copy of the final substring of *string*, starting at index *start* and going to the end of *string*. It could have been defined by:

```
(define (string-tail string start)
  (substring string start (string-length string)))

(string-tail "uncommon" 2)       ⇒  "common"
```

string-pad-left *string k [char]*   [procedure]
string-pad-right *string k [char]*   [procedure]

These procedures return a newly allocated string created by padding *string* out to length *k*, using *char*. If *char* is not given, it defaults to #\space. If *k* is less than the length of *string*, the resulting string is a truncated form of *string*. **string-pad-left** adds padding characters or truncates from the beginning of the string (lowest indices), while **string-pad-right** does so at the end of the string (highest indices).

```
(string-pad-left "hello" 4)       ⇒  "ello"
(string-pad-left "hello" 8)       ⇒  "   hello"
(string-pad-left "hello" 8 #\*)   ⇒  "***hello"
(string-pad-right "hello" 4)      ⇒  "hell"
(string-pad-right "hello" 8)      ⇒  "hello   "
```

string-trim *string [char-set]*   [procedure]
string-trim-left *string [char-set]*   [procedure]
string-trim-right *string [char-set]*   [procedure]

Returns a newly allocated string created by removing all characters that are not in *char-set* from: (**string-trim**) both ends of *string*; (**string-trim-left**) the beginning of *string*; or (**string-trim-right**) the end of *string*. *Char-set* defaults to char-set:not-whitespace.

```
(string-trim "  in the end   ")          ⇒   "in the end"
(string-trim "               ")          ⇒   ""
(string-trim "100th" char-set:numeric)   ⇒   "100"
(string-trim-left "-.-+-=-" (char-set #\+))
                                         ⇒   "+-=-"
(string-trim "but (+ x y) is" (char-set #\( #\)))
                                         ⇒   "(+ x y)"
```

6.6 Searching Strings

The first few procedures in this section perform *string search*, in which a given string (the *text*) is searched to see if it contains another given string (the *pattern*) as a proper substring. At present these procedures are implemented using a hybrid strategy. For short patterns of less than 4 characters, the naive string-search algorithm is used. For longer patterns, the Boyer-Moore string-search algorithm is used.

string-search-forward *pattern string*   [procedure]
substring-search-forward *pattern string start end*   [procedure]

    Pattern must be a string. Searches *string* for the leftmost occurrence of the substring *pattern*. If successful, the index of the first character of the matched substring is returned; otherwise, #f is returned.

    substring-search-forward limits its search to the specified substring of *string*; string-search-forward searches all of *string*.

```
(string-search-forward "rat" "pirate")
    ⇒ 2
(string-search-forward "rat" "pirate rating")
    ⇒ 2
(substring-search-forward "rat" "pirate rating" 4 13)
    ⇒ 7
(substring-search-forward "rat" "pirate rating" 9 13)
    ⇒ #f
```

string-search-backward *pattern string*   [procedure]
substring-search-backward *pattern string start end*   [procedure]

    Pattern must be a string. Searches *string* for the rightmost occurrence of the substring *pattern*. If successful, the index to the right of the last character of the matched substring is returned; otherwise, #f is returned.

    substring-search-backward limits its search to the specified substring of *string*; string-search-backward searches all of *string*.

```
(string-search-backward "rat" "pirate")
    ⇒ 5
(string-search-backward "rat" "pirate rating")
    ⇒ 10
(substring-search-backward "rat" "pirate rating" 1 8)
    ⇒ 5
(substring-search-backward "rat" "pirate rating" 9 13)
    ⇒ #f
```

string-search-all *pattern string*   [procedure]
substring-search-all *pattern string start end*   [procedure]

Pattern must be a string. Searches *string* to find all occurrences of the substring *pattern*. Returns a list of the occurrences; each element of the list is an index pointing to the first character of an occurrence.

substring-search-all limits its search to the specified substring of *string*; **string-search-all** searches all of *string*.

```
(string-search-all "rat" "pirate")
    ⇒ (2)
(string-search-all "rat" "pirate rating")
    ⇒ (2 7)
(substring-search-all "rat" "pirate rating" 4 13)
    ⇒ (7)
(substring-search-all "rat" "pirate rating" 9 13)
    ⇒ ()
```

substring? *pattern string*   [procedure]

Pattern must be a string. Searches *string* to see if it contains the substring *pattern*. Returns #t if *pattern* is a substring of *string*, otherwise returns #f.

```
(substring? "rat" "pirate")          ⇒  #t
(substring? "rat" "outrage")         ⇒  #f
(substring? "" any-string)           ⇒  #t
(if (substring? "moon" text)
    (process-lunar text)
    'no-moon)
```

string-find-next-char *string char*   [procedure]
substring-find-next-char *string start end char*   [procedure]
string-find-next-char-ci *string char*   [procedure]
substring-find-next-char-ci *string start end char*   [procedure]

Returns the index of the first occurrence of *char* in the string (substring); returns #f if *char* does not appear in the string. For the substring procedures, the index returned is relative to the entire string, not just the substring. The -ci procedures don't distinguish uppercase and lowercase letters.

```
(string-find-next-char "Adam" #\A)              ⇒  0
(substring-find-next-char "Adam" 1 4 #\A)       ⇒  #f
(substring-find-next-char-ci "Adam" 1 4 #\A)    ⇒  2
```

string-find-next-char-in-set *string char-set*   [procedure]
substring-find-next-char-in-set *string start end char-set*   [procedure]

Returns the index of the first character in the string (or substring) that is also in *char-set*, or returns #f if none of the characters in *char-set* occur in *string*. For the substring procedure, only the substring is searched, but the index returned is relative to the entire string, not just the substring.

```
(string-find-next-char-in-set my-string char-set:alphabetic)
    ⇒   start position of the first word in my-string
; Can be used as a predicate:
(if (string-find-next-char-in-set my-string
                                  (char-set #\( #\) ))
    'contains-parentheses
    'no-parentheses)
```

string-find-previous-char *string char*   [procedure]
substring-find-previous-char *string start end char*   [procedure]
string-find-previous-char-ci *string char*   [procedure]
substring-find-previous-char-ci *string start end char*   [procedure]

Returns the index of the last occurrence of *char* in the string (substring); returns **#f** if *char* doesn't appear in the string. For the substring procedures, the index returned is relative to the entire string, not just the substring. The **-ci** procedures don't distinguish uppercase and lowercase letters.

string-find-previous-char-in-set *string char-set*   [procedure]
substring-find-previous-char-in-set *string start end char-set*   [procedure]

Returns the index of the last character in the string (substring) that is also in *char-set*. For the substring procedure, the index returned is relative to the entire string, not just the substring.

6.7 Matching Strings

string-match-forward *string1 string2*   [procedure]
substring-match-forward *string1 start end string2 start end*   [procedure]
string-match-forward-ci *string1 string2*   [procedure]
substring-match-forward-ci *string1 start end string2 start end*   [procedure]

Compares the two strings (substrings), starting from the beginning, and returns the number of characters that are the same. If the two strings (substrings) start differently, returns 0. The **-ci** procedures don't distinguish uppercase and lowercase letters.

```
(string-match-forward "mirror" "micro") ⇒  2  ; matches "mi"
(string-match-forward "a" "b")          ⇒  0  ; no match
```

string-match-backward *string1 string2*   [procedure]
substring-match-backward *string1 start end string2 start end*   [procedure]
string-match-backward-ci *string1 string2*   [procedure]
substring-match-backward-ci *string1 start end string2 start end*   [procedure]

Compares the two strings (substrings), starting from the end and matching toward the front, returning the number of characters that are the same. If the two strings (substrings) end differently, returns 0. The **-ci** procedures don't distinguish uppercase and lowercase letters.

```
(string-match-backward-ci "BULBOUS" "fractious")
                                     ⇒  3  ; matches "ous"
```

`string-prefix?` *string1 string2*   [procedure]
`substring-prefix?` *string1 start1 end1 string2 start2 end2*   [procedure]
`string-prefix-ci?` *string1 string2*   [procedure]
`substring-prefix-ci?` *string1 start1 end1 string2 start2 end2*   [procedure]

> These procedures return `#t` if the first string (substring) forms the prefix of the second; otherwise returns `#f`. The `-ci` procedures don't distinguish uppercase and lowercase letters.

> ```
> (string-prefix? "abc" "abcdef")      ⇒   #t
> (string-prefix? "" any-string)       ⇒   #t
> ```

`string-suffix?` *string1 string2*   [procedure]
`substring-suffix?` *string1 start1 end1 string2 start2 end2*   [procedure]
`string-suffix-ci?` *string1 string2*   [procedure]
`substring-suffix-ci?` *string1 start1 end1 string2 start2 end2*   [procedure]

> These procedures return `#t` if the first string (substring) forms the suffix of the second; otherwise returns `#f`. The `-ci` procedures don't distinguish uppercase and lowercase letters.

> ```
> (string-suffix? "ous" "bulbous")     ⇒   #t
> (string-suffix? "" any-string)       ⇒   #t
> ```

6.8 Regular Expressions

MIT/GNU Scheme provides support for using regular expressions to search and match strings. This manual does not define regular expressions; instead see Section "Syntax of Regular Expressions" in *The Emacs Editor*.

In addition to providing standard regular-expression support, MIT/GNU Scheme also provides the REXP abstraction. This is an alternative way to write regular expressions that is easier to read and understand than the standard notation. Regular expressions written in this notation can be translated into the standard notation.

The regular-expression support is a run-time-loadable option. To use it, execute

```
(load-option 'regular-expression)
```

once before calling any of the procedures defined here.

6.8.1 Regular-expression procedures

Procedures that perform regular-expression match and search accept standardized arguments. *Regexp* is the regular expression; it is either a string representation of a regular expression, or a compiled regular expression object. *String* is the string being matched or searched. Procedures that operate on substrings also accept *start* and *end* index arguments with the usual meaning. The optional argument *case-fold?* says whether the match/search is case-sensitive; if *case-fold?* is `#f`, it is case-sensitive, otherwise it is case-insensitive. The optional argument *syntax-table* is a character syntax table that defines the character syntax, such as which characters are legal word constituents. This feature is primarily for Edwin, so character syntax tables will not be documented here. Supplying `#f` for (or omitting) *syntax-table* will select the default character syntax, equivalent to Edwin's `fundamental` mode.

`re-string-match` *regexp string* [*case-fold?* [*syntax-table*]]   [procedure]
`re-substring-match` *regexp string start end* [*case-fold?* [*syntax-table*]]   [procedure]

> These procedures match *regexp* against the respective string or substring, returning
> `#f` for no match, or a set of match registers (see below) if the match succeeds. Here
> is an example showing how to extract the matched substring:

```
(let ((r (re-substring-match regexp string start end)))
  (and r
       (substring string start (re-match-end-index 0 r))))
```

`re-string-search-forward` *regexp string* [*case-fold?* [*syntax-table*]]   [procedure]
`re-substring-search-forward` *regexp string start end* [*case-fold?*   [procedure]
    [*syntax-table*]]

> Searches *string* for the leftmost substring matching *regexp*. Returns a set of match
> registers (see below) if the search is successful, or `#f` if it is unsuccessful.

> `re-substring-search-forward` limits its search to the specified substring of *string*;
> `re-string-search-forward` searches all of *string*.

`re-string-search-backward` *regexp string* [*case-fold?* [*syntax-table*]]   [procedure]
`re-substring-search-backward` *regexp string start end* [*case-fold?*   [procedure]
    [*syntax-table*]]

> Searches *string* for the rightmost substring matching *regexp*. Returns a set of match
> registers (see below) if the search is successful, or `#f` if it is unsuccessful.

> `re-substring-search-backward` limits its search to the specified substring of *string*;
> `re-string-search-backward` searches all of *string*.

When a successful match or search occurs, the above procedures return a set of *match
registers*. The match registers are a set of index registers that record indexes into the
matched string. Each index register corresponds to an instance of the regular-expression
grouping operator '\(', and records the start index (inclusive) and end index (exclusive) of
the matched group. These registers are numbered from 1 to 9, corresponding left-to-right to
the grouping operators in the expression. Additionally, register 0 corresponds to the entire
substring matching the regular expression.

`re-match-start-index` *n registers*   [procedure]
`re-match-end-index` *n registers*   [procedure]

> *N* must be an exact integer between 0 and 9 inclusive. *Registers* must be a match-
> registers object as returned by one of the regular-expression match or search proce-
> dures above. `re-match-start-index` returns the start index of the corresponding
> regular-expression register, and `re-match-end-index` returns the corresponding end
> index.

`re-match-extract` *string registers n*   [procedure]

> *Registers* must be a match-registers object as returned by one of the regular-expression
> match or search procedures above. *String* must be the string that was passed as an
> argument to the procedure that returned *registers*. *N* must be an exact integer
> between 0 and 9 inclusive. If the matched regular expression contained *m* grouping
> operators, then the value of this procedure is undefined for *n* strictly greater than *m*.

This procedure extracts the substring corresponding to the match register specified
by *registers* and *n*. This is equivalent to the following expression:

```
(substring string
            (re-match-start-index n registers)
            (re-match-end-index n registers))
```

regexp-group *alternative . . .*   [procedure]

Each *alternative* must be a string representation of a regular expression. The returned value is a new string representation of a regular expression that consists of the
alternatives combined by a grouping operator. For example:

```
(regexp-group "foo" "bar" "baz")
  ⇒ "\\(foo\\|bar\\|baz\\)"
```

re-compile-pattern *regexp-string*   [procedure]

Regexp-string must be the string representation of a regular expression. Returns a
compiled regular expression object of the represented regular expression.

Procedures that apply regular expressions, such as **re-string-search-forward**, are
sometimes faster when used with compiled regular expression objects than when used
with the string representations of regular expressions, so applications that reuse regular expressions may speed up matching and searching by caching the compiled regular
expression objects. However, the regular expression procedures have some internal
caches as well, so this is likely to improve performance only for applications that use
a large number of different regular expressions before cycling through the same ones
again.

6.8.2 REXP abstraction

In addition to providing standard regular-expression support, MIT/GNU Scheme also provides the REXP abstraction. This is an alternative way to write regular expressions that is
easier to read and understand than the standard notation. Regular expressions written in
this notation can be translated into the standard notation.

The REXP abstraction is a set of combinators that are composed into a complete regular
expression. Each combinator directly corresponds to a particular piece of regular-expression
notation. For example, the expression (**rexp-any-char**) corresponds to the . character in
standard regular-expression notation, while (**rexp*** *rexp*) corresponds to the * character.

The primary advantages of REXP are that it makes the nesting structure of regular
expressions explicit, and that it simplifies the description of complex regular expressions by
allowing them to be built up using straightforward combinators.

rexp? *object*   [procedure]

Returns **#t** if *object* is a REXP expression, or **#f** otherwise. A REXP is one of: a string,
which represents the pattern matching that string; a character set, which represents
the pattern matching a character in that set; or an object returned by calling one of
the procedures defined here.

rexp->regexp *rexp*   [procedure]

Converts *rexp* to standard regular-expression notation, returning a newly-allocated
string.

`rexp-compile` *rexp*   [procedure]

  Converts *rexp* to standard regular-expression notation, then compiles it and returns
  the compiled result. Equivalent to

    `(re-compile-pattern (rexp->regexp rexp) #f)`

`rexp-any-char`   [procedure]

  Returns a REXP that matches any single character except a newline. This is equivalent
  to the . construct.

`rexp-line-start`   [procedure]

  Returns a REXP that matches the start of a line. This is equivalent to the ^ construct.

`rexp-line-end`   [procedure]

  Returns a REXP that matches the end of a line. This is equivalent to the $ construct.

`rexp-string-start`   [procedure]

  Returns a REXP that matches the start of the text being matched. This is equivalent
  to the \' construct.

`rexp-string-end`   [procedure]

  Returns a REXP that matches the end of the text being matched. This is equivalent
  to the \' construct.

`rexp-word-edge`   [procedure]

  Returns a REXP that matches the start or end of a word. This is equivalent to the
  \b construct.

`rexp-not-word-edge`   [procedure]

  Returns a REXP that matches anywhere that is not the start or end of a word. This
  is equivalent to the \B construct.

`rexp-word-start`   [procedure]

  Returns a REXP that matches the start of a word. This is equivalent to the \<
  construct.

`rexp-word-end`   [procedure]

  Returns a REXP that matches the end of a word. This is equivalent to the \> construct.

`rexp-word-char`   [procedure]

  Returns a REXP that matches any word-constituent character. This is equivalent to
  the \w construct.

`rexp-not-word-char`   [procedure]

  Returns a REXP that matches any character that isn't a word constituent. This is
  equivalent to the \W construct.

The next two procedures accept a *syntax-type* argument specifying the syntax class
to be matched against. This argument is a symbol selected from the following list. Each
symbol is followed by the equivalent character used in standard regular-expression notation.
`whitespace` (space character), `punctuation` (.), `word` (w), `symbol` (_), `open` ((), `close`
()), `quote` ('), `string-delimiter` ("), `math-delimiter` ($), `escape` (\), `char-quote` (/),
`comment-start` (<), `comment-end` (>).

rexp-syntax-char *syntax-type*   [procedure]
> Returns a REXP that matches any character of type *syntax-type*. This is equivalent to the \s construct.

rexp-not-syntax-char *syntax-type*   [procedure]
> Returns a REXP that matches any character not of type *syntax-type*. This is equivalent to the \S construct.

rexp-sequence *rexp ...*   [procedure]
> Returns a REXP that matches each *rexp* argument in sequence. If no *rexp* argument is supplied, the result matches the null string. This is equivalent to concatenating the regular expressions corresponding to each *rexp* argument.

rexp-alternatives *rexp ...*   [procedure]
> Returns a REXP that matches any of the *rexp* arguments. This is equivalent to concatenating the regular expressions corresponding to each *rexp* argument, separating them by the \| construct.

rexp-group *rexp ...*   [procedure]
> **rexp-group** is like **rexp-sequence**, except that the result is marked as a match group. This is equivalent to the \(... \) construct.

The next three procedures in principal accept a single REXP argument. For convenience, they accept multiple arguments, which are converted into a single argument by **rexp-group**. Note, however, that if only one REXP argument is supplied, and it's very simple, no grouping occurs.

rexp* *rexp ...*   [procedure]
> Returns a REXP that matches zero or more instances of the pattern matched by the *rexp* arguments. This is equivalent to the * construct.

rexp+ *rexp ...*   [procedure]
> Returns a REXP that matches one or more instances of the pattern matched by the *rexp* arguments. This is equivalent to the + construct.

rexp-optional *rexp ...*   [procedure]
> Returns a REXP that matches zero or one instances of the pattern matched by the *rexp* arguments. This is equivalent to the ? construct.

rexp-case-fold *rexp*   [procedure]
> Returns a REXP that matches the same pattern as *rexp*, but is insensitive to character case. This has no equivalent in standard regular-expression notation.

6.9 Modification of Strings

string-replace *string char1 char2*   [procedure]
substring-replace *string start end char1 char2*   [procedure]
string-replace! *string char1 char2*   [procedure]
substring-replace! *string start end char1 char2*   [procedure]
> These procedures replace all occurrences of *char1* with *char2* in the original string (substring). **string-replace** and **substring-replace** return a newly allocated

string containing the result. `string-replace!` and `substring-replace!` destructively modify *string* and return an unspecified value.

```
(define str "a few words")            ⇒  unspecified
(string-replace str #\space #\-)      ⇒  "a-few-words"
(substring-replace str 2 9 #\space #\-) ⇒ "a few-words"
str                                   ⇒  "a few words"
(string-replace! str #\space #\-)     ⇒  unspecified
str                                   ⇒  "a-few-words"
```

string-fill! *string char*   [procedure]
    Stores *char* in every element of *string* and returns an unspecified value.

substring-fill! *string start end char*   [procedure]
    Stores *char* in elements *start* (inclusive) to *end* (exclusive) of *string* and returns an unspecified value.

```
(define s (make-string 10 #\space))   ⇒  unspecified
(substring-fill! s 2 8 #\*)           ⇒  unspecified
s                                     ⇒  "  ******  "
```

substring-move-left! *string1 start1 end1 string2 start2*   [procedure]
substring-move-right! *string1 start1 end1 string2 start2*   [procedure]
    Copies the characters from *start1* to *end1* of *string1* into *string2* at the *start2*-th position. The characters are copied as follows (note that this is only important when *string1* and *string2* are `eqv?`):

    `substring-move-left!`
        The copy starts at the left end and moves toward the right (from smaller indices to larger). Thus if *string1* and *string2* are the same, this procedure moves the characters toward the left inside the string.

    `substring-move-right!`
        The copy starts at the right end and moves toward the left (from larger indices to smaller). Thus if *string1* and *string2* are the same, this procedure moves the characters toward the right inside the string.

The following example shows how these procedures can be used to build up a string (it would have been easier to use `string-append`):

```
(define answer (make-string 9 #\*))   ⇒  unspecified
answer                                ⇒  "*********"
(substring-move-left! "start" 0 5 answer 0) ⇒ unspecified
answer                                ⇒  "start****"
(substring-move-left! "-end" 0 4 answer 5) ⇒ unspecified
answer                                ⇒  "start-end"
```

reverse-string *string*   [procedure]
reverse-substring *string start end*   [procedure]
reverse-string! *string*   [procedure]

reverse-substring! *string start end*   [procedure]
    Reverses the order of the characters in the given string or substring. `reverse-string`
    and `reverse-substring` return newly allocated strings; `reverse-string!` and
    `reverse-substring!` modify their argument strings and return an unspecified value.

```
(reverse-string "foo bar baz")        ⇒ "zab rab oof"
(reverse-substring "foo bar baz" 4 7) ⇒ "rab"
(let ((foo "foo bar baz"))
  (reverse-string! foo)
  foo)                                ⇒ "zab rab oof"
(let ((foo "foo bar baz"))
  (reverse-substring! foo 4 7)
  foo)                                ⇒ "foo rab baz"
```

6.10 Variable-Length Strings

MIT/GNU Scheme allows the length of a string to be dynamically adjusted in a limited
way. When a new string is allocated, by whatever method, it has a specific length. At the
time of allocation, it is also given a *maximum length*, which is guaranteed to be at least as
large as the string's length. (Sometimes the maximum length will be slightly larger than the
length, but it is a bad idea to count on this. Programs should assume that the maximum
length is the same as the length at the time of the string's allocation.) After the string is
allocated, the operation `set-string-length!` can be used to alter the string's length to
any value between 0 and the string's maximum length, inclusive.

string-maximum-length *string*   [procedure]
    Returns the maximum length of *string*. The following is guaranteed:

```
(<= (string-length string)
    (string-maximum-length string))   ⇒  #t
```

    The maximum length of a string never changes.

set-string-length! *string k*   [procedure]
    Alters the length of *string* to be *k*, and returns an unspecified value. *K* must be
    less than or equal to the maximum length of *string*. `set-string-length!` does not
    change the maximum length of *string*.

6.11 Byte Vectors

MIT/GNU Scheme implements strings as packed vectors of 8-bit ISO-8859-1 bytes. Most of
the string operations, such as `string-ref`, coerce these 8-bit codes into character objects.
However, some lower-level operations are made available for use.

vector-8b-ref *string k*   [procedure]
    Returns character *k* of *string* as an ISO-8859-1 code. *K* must be a valid index of
    string.

```
(vector-8b-ref "abcde" 2)             ⇒  99 ;c
```

vector-8b-set! *string k code*   [procedure]
    Stores *code* in element *k* of *string* and returns an unspecified value. *K* must be a
    valid index of *string*, and *code* must be a valid ISO-8859-1 code.

`vector-8b-fill!` *string start end code*   [procedure]

> Stores *code* in elements *start* (inclusive) to *end* (exclusive) of *string* and returns an unspecified value. *Code* must be a valid ISO-8859-1 code.

`vector-8b-find-next-char` *string start end code*   [procedure]
`vector-8b-find-next-char-ci` *string start end code*   [procedure]

> Returns the index of the first occurrence of *code* in the given substring; returns `#f` if *code* does not appear. The index returned is relative to the entire string, not just the substring. *Code* must be a valid ISO-8859-1 code.

> `vector-8b-find-next-char-ci` doesn't distinguish uppercase and lowercase letters.

`vector-8b-find-previous-char` *string start end code*   [procedure]
`vector-8b-find-previous-char-ci` *string start end code*   [procedure]

> Returns the index of the last occurrence of *code* in the given substring; returns `#f` if *code* does not appear. The index returned is relative to the entire string, not just the substring. *Code* must be a valid ISO-8859-1 code.

> `vector-8b-find-previous-char-ci` doesn't distinguish uppercase and lowercase letters.

7 Lists

A *pair* (sometimes called a *dotted pair*) is a data structure with two fields called the *car* and *cdr* fields (for historical reasons). Pairs are created by the procedure cons. The car and cdr fields are accessed by the procedures car and cdr. The car and cdr fields are assigned by the procedures set-car! and set-cdr!.

Pairs are used primarily to represent *lists*. A list can be defined recursively as either the empty list or a pair whose cdr is a list. More precisely, the set of lists is defined as the smallest set X such that

- The empty list is in X.
- If *list* is in X, then any pair whose cdr field contains *list* is also in X.

The objects in the car fields of successive pairs of a list are the *elements* of the list. For example, a two-element list is a pair whose car is the first element and whose cdr is a pair whose car is the second element and whose cdr is the empty list. The *length* of a list is the number of elements, which is the same as the number of pairs. The *empty list* is a special object of its own type (it is not a pair); it has no elements and its length is zero.[1]

The most general notation (external representation) for Scheme pairs is the "dotted" notation (*c1* . *c2*) where *c1* is the value of the car field and *c2* is the value of the cdr field. For example, (4 . 5) is a pair whose car is 4 and whose cdr is 5. Note that (4 . 5) is the external representation of a pair, not an expression that evaluates to a pair.

A more streamlined notation can be used for lists: the elements of the list are simply enclosed in parentheses and separated by spaces. The empty list is written (). For example, the following are equivalent notations for a list of symbols:

```
(a b c d e)
(a . (b . (c . (d . (e . ())))))
```

Whether a given pair is a list depends upon what is stored in the cdr field. When the set-cdr! procedure is used, an object can be a list one moment and not the next:

```
(define x (list 'a 'b 'c))
(define y x)
y                              ⇒ (a b c)
(list? y)                      ⇒ #t
(set-cdr! x 4)                 ⇒ unspecified
x                              ⇒ (a . 4)
(eqv? x y)                     ⇒ #t
y                              ⇒ (a . 4)
(list? y)                      ⇒ #f
(set-cdr! x x)                 ⇒ unspecified
(list? y)                      ⇒ #f
```

A chain of pairs that doesn't end in the empty list is called an *improper list*. Note that an improper list is not a list. The list and dotted notations can be combined to represent improper lists, as the following equivalent notations show:

---

[1] The above definitions imply that all lists have finite length and are terminated by the empty list.

```
(a b c . d)
(a . (b . (c . d)))
```

Within literal expressions and representations of objects read by the `read` procedure, the forms `'datum`, `‘datum`, `,datum`, and `,@datum` denote two-element lists whose first elements are the symbols `quote`, `quasiquote`, `unquote`, and `unquote-splicing`, respectively. The second element in each case is *datum*. This convention is supported so that arbitrary Scheme programs may be represented as lists. Among other things, this permits the use of the `read` procedure to parse Scheme programs.

7.1 Pairs

This section describes the simple operations that are available for constructing and manipulating arbitrary graphs constructed from pairs.

pair? *object*   [procedure]
> Returns `#t` if *object* is a pair; otherwise returns `#f`.
>
> | | |
> |---|---|
> | `(pair? '(a . b))` | $\Rightarrow$ `#t` |
> | `(pair? '(a b c))` | $\Rightarrow$ `#t` |
> | `(pair? '())` | $\Rightarrow$ `#f` |
> | `(pair? '#(a b))` | $\Rightarrow$ `#f` |

cons *obj1 obj2*   [procedure]
> Returns a newly allocated pair whose car is *obj1* and whose cdr is *obj2*. The pair is guaranteed to be different (in the sense of `eqv?`) from every previously existing object.
>
> | | |
> |---|---|
> | `(cons 'a '())` | $\Rightarrow$ `(a)` |
> | `(cons '(a) '(b c d))` | $\Rightarrow$ `((a) b c d)` |
> | `(cons "a" '(b c))` | $\Rightarrow$ `("a" b c)` |
> | `(cons 'a 3)` | $\Rightarrow$ `(a . 3)` |
> | `(cons '(a b) 'c)` | $\Rightarrow$ `((a b) . c)` |

xcons *obj1 obj2*   [procedure]
> (SRFI 1) Returns a newly allocated pair whose car is *obj2* and whose cdr is *obj1*.
>
> | | |
> |---|---|
> | `(xcons '(b c) 'a)` | $\Rightarrow$ `(a b c)` |

car *pair*   [procedure]
> Returns the contents of the car field of *pair*. Note that it is an error to take the `car` of the empty list.
>
> | | |
> |---|---|
> | `(car '(a b c))` | $\Rightarrow$ `a` |
> | `(car '((a) b c d))` | $\Rightarrow$ `(a)` |
> | `(car '(1 . 2))` | $\Rightarrow$ `1` |
> | `(car '())` | error Illegal datum |

cdr *pair*   [procedure]
> Returns the contents of the cdr field of *pair*. Note that it is an error to take the `cdr` of the empty list.
>
> | | |
> |---|---|
> | `(cdr '((a) b c d))` | $\Rightarrow$ `(b c d)` |
> | `(cdr '(1 . 2))` | $\Rightarrow$ `2` |
> | `(cdr '())` | error Illegal datum |

car+cdr *pair*   [procedure]

    (SRFI 1) The fundamental pair deconstructor:

```
(lambda (p) (values (car p) (cdr p)))

(receive (a b) (car+cdr (cons 1 2))
  (write-line a)
  (write-line b))
⊣ 1
⊣ 2
```

set-car! *pair object*   [procedure]

    Stores *object* in the car field of *pair*. The value returned by set-car! is unspecified.

```
(define (f) (list 'not-a-constant-list))
(define (g) '(constant-list))
(set-car! (f) 3)                    ⇒ unspecified
(set-car! (g) 3)                    error  Illegal datum
```

set-cdr! *pair object*   [procedure]

    Stores *object* in the cdr field of *pair*. The value returned by set-cdr! is unspecified.

caar *pair*	[procedure]
cadr *pair*	[procedure]
cdar *pair*	[procedure]
cddr *pair*	[procedure]
caaar *pair*	[procedure]
caadr *pair*	[procedure]
cadar *pair*	[procedure]
caddr *pair*	[procedure]
cdaar *pair*	[procedure]
cdadr *pair*	[procedure]
cddar *pair*	[procedure]
cdddr *pair*	[procedure]
caaaar *pair*	[procedure]
caaadr *pair*	[procedure]
caadar *pair*	[procedure]
caaddr *pair*	[procedure]
cadaar *pair*	[procedure]
cadadr *pair*	[procedure]
caddar *pair*	[procedure]
cadddr *pair*	[procedure]
cdaaar *pair*	[procedure]
cdaadr *pair*	[procedure]
cdadar *pair*	[procedure]
cdaddr *pair*	[procedure]
cddaar *pair*	[procedure]
cddadr *pair*	[procedure]
cdddar *pair*	[procedure]

cddddr *pair*   [procedure]

These procedures are compositions of `car` and `cdr`; for example, `caddr` could be defined by

```
(define caddr (lambda (x) (car (cdr (cdr x)))))
```

general-car-cdr *object path*   [procedure]

This procedure is a generalization of `car` and `cdr`. *Path* encodes a particular sequence of `car` and `cdr` operations, which `general-car-cdr` executes on *object*. *Path* is an exact non-negative integer that encodes the operations in a bitwise fashion: a zero bit represents a `cdr` operation, and a one bit represents a `car`. The bits are executed LSB to MSB, and the most significant one bit, rather than being interpreted as an operation, signals the end of the sequence.[2]

For example, the following are equivalent:

```
(general-car-cdr object #b1011)
(cdr (car (car object)))
```

Here is a partial table of path/operation equivalents:

```
#b10      cdr
#b11      car
#b100     cddr
#b101     cdar
#b110     cadr
#b111     caar
#b1000    cdddr
```

tree-copy *tree*   [procedure]

(SRFI 1) This copies an arbitrary *tree* constructed from pairs, copying both the car and cdr elements of every pair. This could have been defined by

```
(define (tree-copy tree)
  (let loop ((tree tree))
    (if (pair? tree)
        (cons (loop (car tree)) (loop (cdr tree)))
        tree)))
```

7.2 Construction of Lists

list *object* . . .   [procedure]

Returns a list of its arguments.

```
(list 'a (+ 3 4) 'c)                      ⇒ (a 7 c)
(list)                                    ⇒ ()
```

These expressions are equivalent:

```
(list obj1 obj2 ... objN)
(cons obj1 (cons obj2 ... (cons objN '()) ...))
```

---

[2] Note that *path* is restricted to a machine-dependent range, usually the size of a machine word. On many machines, this means that the maximum length of *path* will be 30 operations (32 bits, less the sign bit and the "end-of-sequence" bit).

make-list *k* [*element*]   [procedure]

> (SRFI 1) This procedure returns a newly allocated list of length *k*, whose elements are all *element*. If *element* is not supplied, it defaults to the empty list.
>
>   (make-list 4 'c)   ⇒ (c c c c)

cons* *object object ...*   [procedure]

> (SRFI 1) cons* is similar to list, except that cons* conses together the last two arguments rather than consing the last argument with the empty list. If the last argument is not a list the result is an improper list. If the last argument is a list, the result is a list consisting of the initial arguments and all of the items in the final argument. If there is only one argument, the result is the argument.
>
>   (cons* 'a 'b 'c)   ⇒ (a b . c)
>   (cons* 'a 'b '(c d))   ⇒ (a b c d)
>   (cons* 'a)   ⇒ a
>
> These expressions are equivalent:
>
>   (cons* obj1 obj2 ... objN-1 objN)
>   (cons obj1 (cons obj2 ... (cons objN-1 objN) ...))

list-tabulate *k init-proc*   [procedure]
make-initialized-list *k init-proc*   [procedure]

> Returns a *k*-element list. Element *i* of the list, where 0 <= *i* < *k*, is produced by (*init-proc i*). No guarantee is made about the dynamic order in which *init-proc* is applied to these indices.
>
>   (list-tabulate 4 values) => (0 1 2 3)
>
> list-tabulate is defined by SRFI 1.

list-copy *list*   [procedure]

> (SRFI 1) Returns a newly allocated copy of *list*. This copies each of the pairs comprising *list*. This could have been defined by
>
>   (define (list-copy list)
>   (if (null? list)
>   '()
>   (cons (car list)
>   (list-copy (cdr list)))))

iota *count* [*start* [*step*]]   [procedure]

> (SRFI 1) Returns a list containing the elements
>
>   (start start+step ... start+(count-1)*step)
>
> *Count* must be an exact non-negative integer, while *start* and *step* can be any numbers. The *start* and *step* parameters default to 0 and 1, respectively.
>
>   (iota 5) ⇒ (0 1 2 3 4)
>   (iota 5 0 -0.1) ⇒ (0 -0.1 -0.2 -0.3 -0.4)

vector->list *vector*   [procedure]
subvector->list *vector start end*   [procedure]

> vector->list returns a newly allocated list of the elements of *vector*.
>
> subvector->list returns a newly allocated list of the elements of the given subvector.
>
> The inverse of vector->list is list->vector.

```
(vector->list '#(dah dah didah))        ⇒ (dah dah didah)
```

string->list *string*   [procedure]
substring->list *string start end*   [procedure]

    string->list returns a newly allocated list of the character elements of *string*.
substring->list returns a newly allocated list of the character elements of the given
substring. The inverse of string->list is list->string.

```
(string->list "abcd")              ⇒ (#\a #\b #\c #\d)
(substring->list "abcdef" 1 3)     ⇒ (#\b #\c)
```

7.3 Selecting List Components

list? *object*   [procedure]

    Returns #t if *object* is a list, otherwise returns #f. By definition, all lists have finite
length and are terminated by the empty list. This procedure returns an answer even
for circular structures.

    Any *object* satisfying this predicate will also satisfy exactly one of pair? or null?.

```
(list? '(a b c))               ⇒ #t
(list? '())                    ⇒ #t
(list? '(a . b))               ⇒ #f
(let ((x (list 'a)))
  (set-cdr! x x)
  (list? x))                   ⇒ #f
```

circular-list? *object*   [procedure]

    (SRFI 1) Returns #t if *object* is a circular list, otherwise returns #f.

```
(dotted-list? (list 'a 'b 'c))        ⇒ #f
(dotted-list? (cons* 'a 'b 'c))       ⇒ #t
(dotted-list? (circular-list 'a 'b 'c)) ⇒ #f
```

dotted-list? *object*   [procedure]

    (SRFI 1) Returns #t if *object* is an improper list, otherwise returns #f.

```
(circular-list? (list 'a 'b 'c))        ⇒ #f
(circular-list? (cons* 'a 'b 'c))       ⇒ #f
(circular-list? (circular-list 'a 'b 'c)) ⇒ #t
```

length *list*   [procedure]

    Returns the length of *list*. Signals an error if *list* isn't a proper list.

```
(length '(a b c))              ⇒ 3
(length '(a (b) (c d e)))      ⇒ 3
(length '())                   ⇒ 0
(length (circular-list 'a 'b 'c))    error
```

length+ *clist*   [procedure]

    (SRFI 1) Returns the length of *clist*, if it is a proper list. Returns #f if *clist* is a
circular list. Otherwise signals an error.

```
(length+ (list 'a 'b 'c))              ⇒ 3
(length+ (cons* 'a 'b 'c))             error
(length+ (circular-list 'a 'b 'c))     ⇒ #f
```

null? *object*   [procedure]

Returns #t if *object* is the empty list; otherwise returns #f.

```
(null? '(a . b))                       ⇒ #f
(null? '(a b c))                       ⇒ #f
(null? '())                            ⇒ #t
```

list-ref *list k*   [procedure]

Returns the *k*th element of *list*, using zero-origin indexing. The *valid indexes* of a list are the exact non-negative integers less than the length of the list. The first element of a list has index 0, the second has index 1, and so on.

```
(list-ref '(a b c d) 2)                ⇒ c
(list-ref '(a b c d)
          (inexact->exact (round 1.8)))
      ⇒ c
```

(list-ref *list k*) is equivalent to (car (list-tail *list k*)).

first *list*   [procedure]
second *list*   [procedure]
third *list*   [procedure]
fourth *list*   [procedure]
fifth *list*   [procedure]
sixth *list*   [procedure]
seventh *list*   [procedure]
eighth *list*   [procedure]
ninth *list*   [procedure]
tenth *list*   [procedure]

Returns the specified element of *list*. It is an error if *list* is not long enough to contain the specified element (for example, if the argument to seventh is a list that contains only six elements).

7.4 Cutting and Pasting Lists

sublist *list start end*   [procedure]

Start and *end* must be exact integers satisfying

```
0 <= start <= end <= (length list)
```

sublist returns a newly allocated list formed from the elements of *list* beginning at index *start* (inclusive) and ending at *end* (exclusive).

list-head *list k*   [procedure]

Returns a newly allocated list consisting of the first *k* elements of *list*. *K* must not be greater than the length of *list*.

We could have defined list-head this way:

```
(define (list-head list k)
  (sublist list 0 k))
```

`list-tail` *list k*   [procedure]

Returns the sublist of *list* obtained by omitting the first *k* elements. The result, if it is not the empty list, shares structure with *list*. *K* must not be greater than the length of *list*.

`append` *list* ...   [procedure]

Returns a list consisting of the elements of the first *list* followed by the elements of the other *lists*.

```
(append '(x) '(y))                      ⇒ (x y)
(append '(a) '(b c d))                  ⇒ (a b c d)
(append '(a (b)) '((c)))                ⇒ (a (b) (c))
(append)                                ⇒ ()
```

The resulting list is always newly allocated, except that it shares structure with the last *list* argument. The last argument may actually be any object; an improper list results if the last argument is not a proper list.

```
(append '(a b) '(c . d))                ⇒ (a b c . d)
(append '() 'a)                         ⇒ a
```

`append!` *list* ...   [procedure]

Returns a list that is the argument *lists* concatenated together. The arguments are changed rather than copied. (Compare this with `append`, which copies arguments rather than destroying them.) For example:

```
(define x '(a b c))
(define y '(d e f))
(define z '(g h))
(append! x y z)                         ⇒ (a b c d e f g h)
x                                       ⇒ (a b c d e f g h)
y                                       ⇒ (d e f g h)
z                                       ⇒ (g h)
```

`last-pair` *list*   [procedure]

Returns the last pair in *list*, which may be an improper list. `last-pair` could have been defined this way:

```
(define last-pair
  (lambda (x)
    (if (pair? (cdr x))
        (last-pair (cdr x))
        x)))
```

`except-last-pair` *list*   [procedure]
`except-last-pair!` *list*   [procedure]

These procedures remove the last pair from *list*. *List* may be an improper list, except that it must consist of at least one pair. `except-last-pair` returns a newly allocated copy of *list* that omits the last pair. `except-last-pair!` destructively removes the last pair from *list* and returns *list*. If the cdr of *list* is not a pair, the empty list is returned by either procedure.

7.5 Filtering Lists

filter *predicate list*   [procedure]

> (SRFI 1) Returns a newly allocated copy of *list* containing only the elements satisfying *predicate*. *Predicate* must be a procedure of one argument.
>
>> (filter odd? '(1 2 3 4 5)) ⇒ (1 3 5)
>
> The non-standard procedure `keep-matching-items` (and its alias `list-transform-positive`) are the same except that its arguments are reversed.

remove *predicate list*   [procedure]

> (SRFI 1) Like `filter`, except that the returned list contains only those elements *not* satisfying *predicate*.
>
>> (remove odd? '(1 2 3 4 5)) ⇒ (2 4)
>
> The non-standard procedure `delete-matching-items` (and its alias `list-transform-negative`) are the same except that its arguments are reversed.

partition *predicate list*   [procedure]

> (SRFI 1) Partitions the elements of *list* with *predicate*, and returns two values: the list of in-elements and the list of out-elements. The *list* is not disordered—elements occur in the result lists in the same order as they occur in the argument *list*. The dynamic order in which the various applications of `predicate` are made is not specified. One of the returned lists may share a common tail with the argument *list*.
>
>> (partition symbol? '(one 2 3 four five 6)) =>
>>   (one four five)
>>   (2 3 6)

filter! *predicate list*   [procedure]
remove! *predicate list*   [procedure]
partition! *predicate list*   [procedure]

> (SRFI 1) Linear-update variants of `filter`, `remove` and `partition`. These procedures are allowed, but not required, to alter the cons cells in the argument `list` to construct the result lists.
>
> The non-standard procedures `keep-matching-items!` and `delete-matching-items!` bear a similar relationship to `keep-matching-items` and `delete-matching-items`, respectively.

delq *element list*   [procedure]
delv *element list*   [procedure]
delete *element list*   [procedure]

> Returns a newly allocated copy of *list* with all entries equal to *element* removed. `delq` uses `eq?` to compare *element* with the entries in *list*, `delv` uses `eqv?`, and `delete` uses `equal?`.

delq! *element list*   [procedure]
delv! *element list*   [procedure]

`delete!` *element list*   [procedure]

Returns a list consisting of the top-level elements of *list* with all entries equal to *element* removed. These procedures are like `delq`, `delv`, and `delete` except that they destructively modify *list*. `delq!` uses `eq?` to compare element with the entries in *list*, `delv!` uses `eqv?`, and `delete!` uses `equal?`. Because the result may not be `eq?` to *list*, it is desirable to do something like `(set! x (delete! x))`.

```
(define x '(a b c b))
(delete 'b x)                           ⇒ (a c)
x                                       ⇒ (a b c b)


(define x '(a b c b))
(delete! 'b x)                          ⇒ (a c)
x                                       ⇒ (a c)
;; Returns correct result:
(delete! 'a x)                          ⇒ (c)


;; Didn't modify what x points to:
x                                       ⇒ (a c)
```

`delete-member-procedure` *deletor predicate*   [procedure]

Returns a deletion procedure similar to `delv` or `delete!`. *Deletor* should be one of the procedures `list-deletor` or `list-deletor!`. *Predicate* must be an equivalence predicate. The returned procedure accepts exactly two arguments: first, an object to be deleted, and second, a list of objects from which it is to be deleted. If *deletor* is `list-deletor`, the procedure returns a newly allocated copy of the given list in which all entries equal to the given object have been removed. If *deletor* is `list-deletor!`, the procedure returns a list consisting of the top-level elements of the given list with all entries equal to the given object removed; the given list is destructively modified to produce the result. In either case *predicate* is used to compare the given object to the elements of the given list.

Here are some examples that demonstrate how `delete-member-procedure` could have been used to implement `delv` and `delete!`:

```
(define delv
  (delete-member-procedure list-deletor eqv?))
(define delete!
  (delete-member-procedure list-deletor! equal?))
```

`list-deletor` *predicate*   [procedure]
`list-deletor!` *predicate*   [procedure]

These procedures each return a procedure that deletes elements from lists. *Predicate* must be a procedure of one argument. The returned procedure accepts exactly one argument, which must be a proper list, and applies *predicate* to each of the elements of the argument, deleting those for which it is true.

The procedure returned by `list-deletor` deletes elements non-destructively, by returning a newly allocated copy of the argument with the appropriate elements removed. The procedure returned by `list-deletor!` performs a destructive deletion.

7.6 Searching Lists

find *predicate list*   [procedure]

    (SRFI 1) Returns the first element in *list* for which *predicate* is true; returns **#f** if it doesn't find such an element. *Predicate* must be a procedure of one argument.

```
(find even? '(3 1 4 1 5 9)) => 4
```

Note that **find** has an ambiguity in its lookup semantics—if **find** returns **#f**, you cannot tell (in general) if it found a **#f** element that satisfied *predicate*, or if it did not find any element at all. In many situations, this ambiguity cannot arise—either the list being searched is known not to contain any **#f** elements, or the list is guaranteed to have an element satisfying *predicate*. However, in cases where this ambiguity can arise, you should use **find-tail** instead of **find**—**find-tail** has no such ambiguity:

```
(cond ((find-tail pred lis)
       => (lambda (pair) ...)) ; Handle (CAR PAIR)
      (else ...)) ; Search failed.
```

The non-standard **find-matching-item** procedure (and its alias **list-search-positive**) works identically except that its argument order is reversed. **list-search-negative** is similar to **list-search-positive** but the sense of the predicate is reversed.

find-tail *predicate list*   [procedure]

    (SRFI 1) Returns the first pair of *list* whose car satisfies *predicate*; returns **#f** if there's no such pair. **find-tail** can be viewed as a general-predicate variant of *memv*.

memq *object list*   [procedure]
memv *object list*   [procedure]
member *object list*   [procedure]

    These procedures return the first pair of *list* whose car is *object*; the returned pair is always one from which *list* is composed. If *object* does not occur in *list*, **#f** (n.b.: not the empty list) is returned. **memq** uses **eq?** to compare *object* with the elements of *list*, while **memv** uses **eqv?** and **member** uses **equal?**.[3]

```
(memq 'a '(a b c))              ⇒ (a b c)
(memq 'b '(a b c))              ⇒ (b c)
(memq 'a '(b c d))              ⇒ #f
(memq (list 'a) '(b (a) c))     ⇒ #f
(member (list 'a) '(b (a) c))   ⇒ ((a) c)
(memq 101 '(100 101 102))       ⇒ unspecified
(memv 101 '(100 101 102))       ⇒ (101 102)
```

member-procedure *predicate*   [procedure]

    Returns a procedure similar to **memq**, except that *predicate*, which must be an equivalence predicate, is used instead of **eq?**. This could be used to define **memv** as follows:

```
(define memv (member-procedure eqv?))
```

---

[3] Although they are often used as predicates, **memq**, **memv**, and **member** do not have question marks in their names because they return useful values rather than just **#t** or **#f**.

7.7 Mapping of Lists

map *procedure list list . . .*   [procedure]
> *Procedure* must be a procedure taking as many arguments as there are *lists*. If more
> than one *list* is given, then they must all be the same length. `map` applies *procedure*
> element-wise to the elements of the *lists* and returns a list of the results, in order from
> left to right. The dynamic order in which *procedure* is applied to the elements of the
> *lists* is unspecified; use `for-each` to sequence side effects.
>
> ```
> (map cadr '((a b) (d e) (g h)))           ⇒ (b e h)
> (map (lambda (n) (expt n n)) '(1 2 3 4))  ⇒ (1 4 27 256)
> (map + '(1 2 3) '(4 5 6))                 ⇒ (5 7 9)
> (let ((count 0))
>   (map (lambda (ignored)
>          (set! count (+ count 1))
>          count)
>        '(a b c)))                         ⇒ unspecified
> ```

map* *initial-value procedure list1 list2 . . .*   [procedure]
> Similar to `map`, except that the resulting list is terminated by *initial-value* rather than
> the empty list. The following are equivalent:
>
> ```
> (map procedure list list ...)
> (map* '() procedure list list ...)
> ```

append-map *procedure list list . . .*   [procedure]
append-map* *initial-value procedure list list . . .*   [procedure]
> Similar to `map` and `map*`, respectively, except that the results of applying *procedure*
> to the elements of *lists* are concatenated together by `append` rather than by `cons`.
> The following are equivalent, except that the former is more efficient:
>
> ```
> (append-map procedure list list ...)
> (apply append (map procedure list list ...))
> ```

append-map! *procedure list list . . .*   [procedure]
append-map*! *initial-value procedure list list . . .*   [procedure]
> Similar to `map` and `map*`, respectively, except that the results of applying *procedure*
> to the elements of *lists* are concatenated together by `append!` rather than by `cons`.
> The following are equivalent, except that the former is more efficient:
>
> ```
> (append-map! procedure list list ...)
> (apply append! (map procedure list list ...))
> ```

for-each *procedure list list . . .*   [procedure]
> The arguments to `for-each` are like the arguments to `map`, but `for-each` calls *procedure* for its side effects rather than for its values. Unlike `map`, `for-each` is guaranteed
> to call *procedure* on the elements of the *lists* in order from the first element to the
> last, and the value returned by `for-each` is unspecified.

```
(let ((v (make-vector 5)))
  (for-each (lambda (i)
              (vector-set! v i (* i i)))
            '(0 1 2 3 4))
  v)                            ⇒ #(0 1 4 9 16)
```

7.8 Reduction of Lists

reduce-left *procedure initial list*   [procedure]
> Combines all the elements of *list* using the binary operation *procedure*. For example, using + one can add up all the elements:

```
(reduce-left + 0 list-of-numbers)
```

> The argument *initial* is used only if *list* is empty; in this case *initial* is the result of the call to reduce-left. If *list* has a single argument, it is returned. Otherwise, the arguments are reduced in a left-associative fashion. For example:

```
(reduce-left + 0 '(1 2 3 4))        ⇒ 10
(reduce-left + 0 '(1 2))            ⇒ 3
(reduce-left + 0 '(1))             ⇒ 1
(reduce-left + 0 '())              ⇒ 0
(reduce-left + 0 '(foo))           ⇒ foo
(reduce-left list '() '(1 2 3 4))   ⇒ (((1 2) 3) 4)
```

reduce-right *procedure initial list*   [procedure]
> Like reduce-left except that it is right-associative.

```
(reduce-right list '() '(1 2 3 4))   ⇒ (1 (2 (3 4)))
```

fold-right *procedure initial list*   [procedure]
> Combines all of the elements of *list* using the binary operation *procedure*. Unlike reduce-left and reduce-right, *initial* is always used:

```
(fold-right + 0 '(1 2 3 4))        ⇒ 10
(fold-right + 0 '(foo))            [error]  Illegal datum
(fold-right list '() '(1 2 3 4))    ⇒ (1 (2 (3 (4 ()))))
```

Fold-right has interesting properties because it establishes a homomorphism between (cons, ()) and (*procedure*, *initial*). It can be thought of as replacing the pairs in the spine of the list with *procedure* and replacing the () at the end with *initial*. Many of the classical list-processing procedures can be expressed in terms of fold-right, at least for the simple versions that take a fixed number of arguments:

```
(define (copy-list list)
  (fold-right cons '() list))

(define (append list1 list2)
  (fold-right cons list2 list1))

(define (map p list)
  (fold-right (lambda (x r) (cons (p x) r)) '() list))

(define (reverse items)
  (fold-right (lambda (x r) (append r (list x))) '() items))
```

fold-left *procedure initial list*   [procedure]

Combines all the elements of *list* using the binary operation *procedure*. Elements are combined starting with *initial* and then the elements of *list* from left to right. Whereas **fold-right** is recursive in nature, capturing the essence of **cdr**-ing down a list and then computing a result, *fold-left* is iterative in nature, combining the elements as the list is traversed.

```
(fold-left list '() '(1 2 3 4))          ⇒ ((((() 1) 2) 3) 4)


(define (length list)
  (fold-left (lambda (sum element) (+ sum 1)) 0 list))

(define (reverse items)
  (fold-left (lambda (x y) (cons y x)) () items))
```

any *predicate list list . . .*   [procedure]

(SRFI 1) Applies *predicate* across the *lists*, returning true if *predicate* returns true on any application.

If there are *n* list arguments *list1 . . . listn*, then *predicate* must be a procedure taking *n* arguments and returning a boolean result.

any applies *predicate* to the first elements of the *list* parameters. If this application returns a true value, **any** immediately returns that value. Otherwise, it iterates, applying *predicate* to the second elements of the *list* parameters, then the third, and so forth. The iteration stops when a true value is produced or one of the lists runs out of values; in the latter case, **any** returns #f. The application of *predicate* to the last element of the *lists* is a tail call.

Note the difference between **find** and **any**—**find** returns the element that satisfied the predicate; **any** returns the true value that the *predicate* produced.

Like **every**, **any**'s name does not end with a question mark—this is to indicate that it does not return a simple boolean (#t or #f), but a general value.

```
(any integer? '(a 3 b 2.7))   => #t
(any integer? '(a 3.1 b 2.7)) => #f
(any < '(3 1 4 1 5)
       '(2 7 1 8 2)) => #t
```

The non-standard procedure **there-exists?** is similar, except that it takes a single list and a predicate argument, in that order.

every *predicate list list . . .*   [procedure]

> (SRFI 1) Applies *predicate* across the *lists*, returning true if *predicate* returns true on every application.
>
> If there are *n* list arguments *list1 . . . listn*, then *predicate* must be a procedure taking *n* arguments and returning a boolean result.
>
> **every** applies *predicate* to the first elements of the *list* parameters. If this application returns false, **every** immediately returns false. Otherwise, it iterates, applying *predicate* to the second elements of the *list* parameters, then the third, and so forth. The iteration stops when a false value is produced or one of the *lists* runs out of values. In the latter case, **every** returns the true value produced by its final application of *predicate*. The application of *predicate* to the last element of the *lists* is a tail call.
>
> If one of the *lists* has no elements, **every** simply returns #t.
>
> Like **any**, **every**'s name does not end with a question mark—this is to indicate that it does not return a simple boolean (#t or #f), but a general value.
>
> The non-standard procedure **for-all?** is similar, except that it takes a single list and a predicate argument, in that order.

7.9 Miscellaneous List Operations

circular-list *object . . .*   [procedure]
make-circular-list *k* [*element*]   [procedure]

> These procedures are like **list** and **make-list**, respectively, except that the returned lists are circular. **circular-list** could have been defined like this:
>
> ```
> (define (circular-list . objects)
>   (append! objects objects))
> ```
>
> **circular-list** is compatible with SRFI 1, but extended so that it can be called with no arguments.

reverse *list*   [procedure]

> Returns a newly allocated list consisting of the top-level elements of *list* in reverse order.
>
> ```
> (reverse '(a b c))            ⇒ (c b a)
> (reverse '(a (b c) d (e (f))))  ⇒ ((e (f)) d (b c) a)
> ```

reverse! *list*   [procedure]

> Returns a list consisting of the top-level elements of *list* in reverse order. **reverse!** is like **reverse**, except that it destructively modifies *list*. Because the result may not be **eqv?** to *list*, it is desirable to do something like (set! x (reverse! x)).

sort *sequence procedure*   [procedure]
merge-sort *sequence procedure*   [procedure]
quick-sort *sequence procedure*   [procedure]

> *Sequence* must be either a list or a vector. *Procedure* must be a procedure of two arguments that defines a *total ordering* on the elements of *sequence*. In other words, if x and y are two distinct elements of *sequence*, then it must be the case that

```
(and (procedure x y)
     (procedure y x))
  ⇒ #f
```

If *sequence* is a list (vector), `sort` returns a newly allocated list (vector) whose elements are those of *sequence*, except that they are rearranged to be sorted in the order defined by *procedure*. So, for example, if the elements of *sequence* are numbers, and *procedure* is <, then the resulting elements are sorted in monotonically nondecreasing order. Likewise, if *procedure* is >, the resulting elements are sorted in monotonically nonincreasing order. To be precise, if x and y are any two adjacent elements in the result, where x precedes y, it is the case that

```
(procedure y x)
     ⇒ #f
```

Two sorting algorithms are implemented: `merge-sort` and `quick-sort`. The procedure `sort` is an alias for `merge-sort`.

See also the definition of `sort!`.

8 Vectors

Vectors are heterogenous structures whose elements are indexed by exact non-negative integers. A vector typically occupies less space than a list of the same length, and the average time required to access a randomly chosen element is typically less for the vector than for the list.

The *length* of a vector is the number of elements that it contains. This number is an exact non-negative integer that is fixed when the vector is created. The *valid indexes* of a vector are the exact non-negative integers less than the length of the vector. The first element in a vector is indexed by zero, and the last element is indexed by one less than the length of the vector.

Vectors are written using the notation #(*object* ...). For example, a vector of length 3 containing the number zero in element 0, the list (2 2 2 2) in element 1, and the string "Anna" in element 2 can be written as

        #(0 (2 2 2 2) "Anna")

Note that this is the external representation of a vector, not an expression evaluating to a vector. Like list constants, vector constants must be quoted:

        '#(0 (2 2 2 2) "Anna")   ⇒ #(0 (2 2 2 2) "Anna")

A number of the vector procedures operate on subvectors. A *subvector* is a segment of a vector that is specified by two exact non-negative integers, *start* and *end*. *Start* is the index of the first element that is included in the subvector, and *end* is one greater than the index of the last element that is included in the subvector. Thus if *start* and *end* are the same, they refer to a null subvector, and if *start* is zero and *end* is the length of the vector, they refer to the entire vector. The *valid indexes* of a subvector are the exact integers between *start* inclusive and *end* exclusive.

8.1 Construction of Vectors

make-vector *k* [*object*]   [procedure]
> Returns a newly allocated vector of *k* elements. If *object* is specified, **make-vector** initializes each element of the vector to *object*. Otherwise the initial elements of the result are unspecified.

vector *object* ...   [procedure]
> Returns a newly allocated vector whose elements are the given arguments. **vector** is analogous to **list**.
>
>   (vector 'a 'b 'c)   ⇒ #(a b c)

vector-copy *vector*   [procedure]
> Returns a newly allocated vector that is a copy of *vector*.

list->vector *list*   [procedure]
> Returns a newly allocated vector initialized to the elements of *list*. The inverse of **list->vector** is **vector->list**.
>
>   (list->vector '(dididit dah))   ⇒ #(dididit dah)

`make-initialized-vector` *k initialization*   [procedure]
> Similar to `make-vector`, except that the elements of the result are determined by calling the procedure *initialization* on the indices. For example:
>
>   (make-initialized-vector 5 (lambda (x) (* x x)))
>   ⇒ #(0 1 4 9 16)

`vector-grow` *vector k*   [procedure]
> *K* must be greater than or equal to the length of *vector*. Returns a newly allocated vector of length *k*. The first (`vector-length` *vector*) elements of the result are initialized from the corresponding elements of *vector*. The remaining elements of the result are unspecified.

`vector-map` *procedure vector*   [procedure]
> *Procedure* must be a procedure of one argument. `vector-map` applies *procedure* element-wise to the elements of *vector* and returns a newly allocated vector of the results, in order from left to right. The dynamic order in which *procedure* is applied to the elements of *vector* is unspecified.
>
>   (vector-map cadr '#((a b) (d e) (g h)))   ⇒ #(b e h)
>   (vector-map (lambda (n) (expt n n)) '#(1 2 3 4))
>   ⇒ #(1 4 27 256)
>   (vector-map + '#(5 7 9))   ⇒ #(5 7 9)

8.2 Selecting Vector Components

`vector?` *object*   [procedure]
> Returns `#t` if *object* is a vector; otherwise returns `#f`.

`vector-length` *vector*   [procedure]
> Returns the number of elements in *vector*.

`vector-ref` *vector k*   [procedure]
> Returns the contents of element *k* of *vector*. *K* must be a valid index of *vector*.
>
>   (vector-ref '#(1 1 2 3 5 8 13 21) 5)   ⇒ 8

`vector-set!` *vector k object*   [procedure]
> Stores *object* in element *k* of *vector* and returns an unspecified value. *K* must be a valid index of *vector*.
>
>   (let ((vec (vector 0 '(2 2 2 2) "Anna")))
>   (vector-set! vec 1 '("Sue" "Sue"))
>   vec)
>   ⇒ #(0 ("Sue" "Sue") "Anna")

`vector-first` *vector*   [procedure]
`vector-second` *vector*   [procedure]
`vector-third` *vector*   [procedure]
`vector-fourth` *vector*   [procedure]
`vector-fifth` *vector*   [procedure]
`vector-sixth` *vector*   [procedure]

vector-seventh *vector*   [procedure]
vector-eighth *vector*   [procedure]

These procedures access the first several elements of *vector* in the obvious way. It is an error if the implicit index of one of these procedurs is not a valid index of *vector*.

vector-binary-search *vector key<? unwrap-key key*   [procedure]

Searches *vector* for an element with a key matching *key*, returning the element if one is found or #f if none. The search operation takes time proportional to the logarithm of the length of *vector*. *Unwrap-key* must be a procedure that maps each element of *vector* to a key. *Key<?* must be a procedure that implements a total ordering on the keys of the elements.

```
(define (translate number)
  (vector-binary-search '#((1 . i)
                           (2 . ii)
                           (3 . iii)
                           (6 . vi))
                        < car number))
(translate 2)  ⇒  (2 . ii)
(translate 4)  ⇒  #F
```

8.3 Cutting Vectors

subvector *vector start end*   [procedure]

Returns a newly allocated vector that contains the elements of *vector* between index *start* (inclusive) and *end* (exclusive).

vector-head *vector end*   [procedure]

Equivalent to

```
(subvector vector 0 end)
```

vector-tail *vector start*   [procedure]

Equivalent to

```
(subvector vector start (vector-length vector))
```

8.4 Modifying Vectors

vector-fill! *vector object*   [procedure]
subvector-fill! *vector start end object*   [procedure]

Stores *object* in every element of the vector (subvector) and returns an unspecified value.

subvector-move-left! *vector1 start1 end1 vector2 start2*   [procedure]
subvector-move-right! *vector1 start1 end1 vector2 start2*   [procedure]

Destructively copies the elements of *vector1*, starting with index *start1* (inclusive) and ending with *end1* (exclusive), into *vector2* starting at index *start2* (inclusive). *Vector1*, *start1*, and *end1* must specify a valid subvector, and *start2* must be a valid index for *vector2*. The length of the source subvector must not exceed the length of *vector2* minus the index *start2*.

The elements are copied as follows (note that this is only important when *vector1* and *vector2* are `eqv?`):

`subvector-move-left!`

> The copy starts at the left end and moves toward the right (from smaller indices to larger). Thus if *vector1* and *vector2* are the same, this procedure moves the elements toward the left inside the vector.

`subvector-move-right!`

> The copy starts at the right end and moves toward the left (from larger indices to smaller). Thus if *vector1* and *vector2* are the same, this procedure moves the elements toward the right inside the vector.

`sort!` *vector procedure*   [procedure]
`merge-sort!` *vector procedure*   [procedure]
`quick-sort!` *vector procedure*   [procedure]

Procedure must be a procedure of two arguments that defines a *total ordering* on the elements of *vector*. The elements of *vector* are rearranged so that they are sorted in the order defined by *procedure*. The elements are rearranged in place, that is, *vector* is destructively modified so that its elements are in the new order.

`sort!` returns *vector* as its value.

Two sorting algorithms are implemented: `merge-sort!` and `quick-sort!`. The procedure `sort!` is an alias for `merge-sort!`.

See also the definition of `sort`.

9 Bit Strings

A *bit string* is a sequence of bits. Bit strings can be used to represent sets or to manipulate binary data. The elements of a bit string are numbered from zero up to the number of bits in the string less one, in *right to left order*, (the rightmost bit is numbered zero). When you convert from a bit string to an integer, the zero-th bit is associated with the zero-th power of two, the first bit is associated with the first power, and so on.

Bit strings are encoded very densely in memory. Each bit occupies exactly one bit of storage, and the overhead for the entire bit string is bounded by a small constant. However, accessing a bit in a bit string is slow compared to accessing an element of a vector or character string. If performance is of overriding concern, it is better to use character strings to store sets of boolean values even though they occupy more space.

The *length* of a bit string is the number of bits that it contains. This number is an exact non-negative integer that is fixed when the bit string is created. The *valid indexes* of a bit string are the exact non-negative integers less than the length of the bit string.

Bit strings may contain zero or more bits. They are not limited by the length of a machine word. In the printed representation of a bit string, the contents of the bit string are preceded by '#*'. The contents are printed starting with the most significant bit (highest index).

Note that the external representation of bit strings uses a bit ordering that is the reverse of the representation for bit strings in Common Lisp. It is likely that MIT/GNU Scheme's representation will be changed in the future, to be compatible with Common Lisp. For the time being this representation should be considered a convenience for viewing bit strings rather than a means of entering them as data.

```
#*11111
#*1010
#*00000000
#*
```

All of the bit-string procedures are MIT/GNU Scheme extensions.

9.1 Construction of Bit Strings

make-bit-string *k initialization*   [procedure]
    Returns a newly allocated bit string of length *k*. If *initialization* is #f, the bit string is filled with 0 bits; otherwise, the bit string is filled with 1 bits.

```
(make-bit-string 7 #f)                    ⇒   #*0000000
```

bit-string-allocate *k*   [procedure]
    Returns a newly allocated bit string of length *k*, but does not initialize it.

bit-string-copy *bit-string*   [procedure]
    Returns a newly allocated copy of *bit-string*.

9.2 Selecting Bit String Components

bit-string? *object*   [procedure]
  Returns #t if *object* is a bit string; otherwise returns #f.

bit-string-length *bit-string*   [procedure]
  Returns the length of *bit-string*.

bit-string-ref *bit-string k*   [procedure]
  Returns #t if the *k*th bit is 1; otherwise returns #f. *K* must be a valid index of
  bit-string.

bit-string-set! *bit-string k*   [procedure]
  Sets the *k*th bit in *bit-string* to 1 and returns an unspecified value. *K* must be a valid
  index of *bit-string*.

bit-string-clear! *bit-string k*   [procedure]
  Sets the *k*th bit in *bit-string* to 0 and returns an unspecified value. *K* must be a valid
  index of *bit-string*.

bit-substring-find-next-set-bit *bit-string start end*   [procedure]
  Returns the index of the first occurrence of a set bit in the substring of *bit-string*
  from *start* (inclusive) to *end* (exclusive). If none of the bits in the substring are set
  #f is returned. The index returned is relative to the whole bit string, not substring.

  The following procedure uses **bit-substring-find-next-set-bit** to find all the set
  bits and display their indexes:

```
(define (scan-bitstring bs)
  (let ((end (bit-string-length bs)))
    (let loop ((start 0))
      (let ((next
             (bit-substring-find-next-set-bit bs start end)))
        (if next
            (begin
              (write-line next)
              (if (< next end)
                  (loop (+ next 1)))))))))
```

9.3 Cutting and Pasting Bit Strings

bit-string-append *bit-string-1 bit-string-2*   [procedure]
  Appends the two bit string arguments, returning a newly allocated bit string as its
  result. In the result, the bits copied from *bit-string-1* are less significant (smaller
  indices) than those copied from *bit-string-2*.

bit-substring *bit-string start end*   [procedure]
  Returns a newly allocated bit string whose bits are copied from *bit-string*, starting
  at index *start* (inclusive) and ending at *end* (exclusive).

9.4 Bitwise Operations on Bit Strings

bit-string-zero? *bit-string*   [procedure]
> Returns #t if *bit-string* contains only 0 bits; otherwise returns #f.

bit-string=? *bit-string-1 bit-string-2*   [procedure]
> Compares the two bit string arguments and returns #t if they are the same length and contain the same bits; otherwise returns #f.

bit-string-not *bit-string*   [procedure]
> Returns a newly allocated bit string that is the bitwise-logical negation of *bit-string*.

bit-string-movec! *target-bit-string bit-string*   [procedure]
> The destructive version of **bit-string-not**. The arguments *target-bit-string* and *bit-string* must be bit strings of the same length. The bitwise-logical negation of *bit-string* is computed and the result placed in *target-bit-string*. The value of this procedure is unspecified.

bit-string-and *bit-string-1 bit-string-2*   [procedure]
> Returns a newly allocated bit string that is the bitwise-logical "and" of the arguments. The arguments must be bit strings of identical length.

bit-string-andc *bit-string-1 bit-string-2*   [procedure]
> Returns a newly allocated bit string that is the bitwise-logical "and" of *bit-string-1* with the bitwise-logical negation of *bit-string-2*. The arguments must be bit strings of identical length.

bit-string-or *bit-string-1 bit-string-2*   [procedure]
> Returns a newly allocated bit string that is the bitwise-logical "inclusive or" of the arguments. The arguments must be bit strings of identical length.

bit-string-xor *bit-string-1 bit-string-2*   [procedure]
> Returns a newly allocated bit string that is the bitwise-logical "exclusive or" of the arguments. The arguments must be bit strings of identical length.

bit-string-and! *target-bit-string bit-string*   [procedure]
bit-string-or! *target-bit-string bit-string*   [procedure]
bit-string-xor! *target-bit-string bit-string*   [procedure]
bit-string-andc! *target-bit-string bit-string*   [procedure]
> These are destructive versions of the above operations. The arguments *target-bit-string* and *bit-string* must be bit strings of the same length. Each of these procedures performs the corresponding bitwise-logical operation on its arguments, places the result into *target-bit-string*, and returns an unspecified result.

9.5 Modification of Bit Strings

bit-string-fill! *bit-string initialization*   [procedure]
> Fills *bit-string* with zeroes if *initialization* is #f; otherwise fills *bit-string* with ones. Returns an unspecified value.

`bit-string-move!` *target-bit-string bit-string*   [procedure]
> Moves the contents of *bit-string* into *target-bit-string*. Both arguments must be bit strings of the same length. The results of the operation are undefined if the arguments are the same bit string.

`bit-substring-move-right!` *bit-string-1 start1 end1 bit-string-2 start2*   [procedure]
> Destructively copies the bits of *bit-string-1*, starting at index *start1* (inclusive) and ending at *end1* (exclusive), into *bit-string-2* starting at index *start2* (inclusive). *Start1* and *end1* must be valid substring indices for *bit-string-1*, and *start2* must be a valid index for *bit-string-2*. The length of the source substring must not exceed the length of *bit-string-2* minus the index *start2*.
>
> The bits are copied starting from the MSB and working towards the LSB; the direction of copying only matters when *bit-string-1* and *bit-string-2* are `eqv?`.

9.6 Integer Conversions of Bit Strings

`unsigned-integer->bit-string` *length integer*   [procedure]
> Both *length* and *integer* must be exact non-negative integers. Converts *integer* into a newly allocated bit string of *length* bits. Signals an error of type `condition-type:bad-range-argument` if *integer* is too large to be represented in *length* bits.

`signed-integer->bit-string` *length integer*   [procedure]
> *Length* must be an exact non-negative integer, and *integer* may be any exact integer. Converts *integer* into a newly allocated bit string of *length* bits, using two's complement encoding for negative numbers. Signals an error of type `condition-type:bad-range-argument` if *integer* is too large to be represented in *length* bits.

`bit-string->unsigned-integer` *bit-string*   [procedure]
`bit-string->signed-integer` *bit-string*   [procedure]
> Converts *bit-string* into an exact integer. `bit-string->signed-integer` regards *bit-string* as a two's complement representation of a signed integer, and produces an integer of like sign and absolute value. `bit-string->unsigned-integer` regards *bit-string* as an unsigned quantity and converts to an integer accordingly.

10 Miscellaneous Datatypes

10.1 Booleans

The *boolean objects* are *true* and *false*. The boolean constant true is written as '#t', and the boolean constant false is written as '#f'.

The primary use for boolean objects is in the conditional expressions if, cond, and, and or; the behavior of these expressions is determined by whether objects are true or false. These expressions count only #f as false. They count everything else, including #t, pairs, symbols, numbers, strings, vectors, and procedures as true (but see Section 1.2.5 [True and False], page 8).

Programmers accustomed to other dialects of Lisp should note that Scheme distinguishes #f and the empty list from the symbol nil. Similarly, #t is distinguished from the symbol t. In fact, the boolean objects (and the empty list) are not symbols at all.

Boolean constants evaluate to themselves, so you don't need to quote them.

```
#t                                    ⇒   #t
#f                                    ⇒   #f
'#f                                   ⇒   #f
t                                     error   Unbound variable
```

false   [variable]
true   [variable]

> These variables are bound to the objects #f and #t respectively. The compiler, given the usual-integrations declaration, replaces references to these variables with their respective values.
>
> Note that the symbol true is not equivalent to #t, and the symbol false is not equivalent to #f.

boolean? *object*   [procedure]

> Returns #t if *object* is either #t or #f; otherwise returns #f.
>
> ```
> (boolean? #f)                         ⇒   #t
> (boolean? 0)                          ⇒   #f
> ```

not *object*   [procedure]
false? *object*   [procedure]

> These procedures return #t if *object* is false; otherwise they return #f. In other words they *invert* boolean values. These two procedures have identical semantics; their names are different to give different connotations to the test.
>
> ```
> (not #t)                              ⇒   #f
> (not 3)                               ⇒   #f
> (not (list 3))                        ⇒   #f
> (not #f)                              ⇒   #t
> ```

boolean=? *obj1 obj2*   [procedure]

> This predicate is true iff *obj1* and *obj2* are either both true or both false.

`boolean/and` *object* ...   [procedure]
> This procedure returns **#t** if none of its arguments are **#f**. Otherwise it returns **#f**.

`boolean/or` *object* ...   [procedure]
> This procedure returns **#f** if all of its arguments are **#f**. Otherwise it returns **#t**.

10.2 Symbols

MIT/GNU Scheme provides two types of symbols: *interned* and *uninterned*. Interned symbols are far more common than uninterned symbols, and there are more ways to create them. Interned symbols have an external representation that is recognized by the procedure **read**; uninterned symbols do not.[1]

Interned symbols have an extremely useful property: any two interned symbols whose names are the same, in the sense of **string=?**, are the same object (i.e. they are **eq?** to one another). The term *interned* refers to the process of *interning* by which this is accomplished. Uninterned symbols do not share this property.

The names of interned symbols are not distinguished by their alphabetic case. Because of this, MIT/GNU Scheme converts all alphabetic characters in the name of an interned symbol to a specific case (lower case) when the symbol is created. When the name of an interned symbol is referenced (using **symbol->string**) or written (using **write**) it appears in this case. It is a bad idea to depend on the name being lower case. In fact, it is preferable to take this one step further: don't depend on the name of a symbol being in a uniform case.

The rules for writing an interned symbol are the same as the rules for writing an identifier (see Section 1.3.3 [Identifiers], page 10). Any interned symbol that has been returned as part of a literal expression, or read using the **read** procedure and subsequently written out using the **write** procedure, will read back in as the identical symbol (in the sense of **eq?**).

Usually it is also true that reading in an interned symbol that was previously written out produces the same symbol. An exception are symbols created by the procedures **string->symbol** and **intern**; they can create symbols for which this write/read invariance may not hold because the symbols' names contain special characters or letters in the non-standard case.[2]

The external representation for uninterned symbols is special, to distinguish them from interned symbols and prevent them from being recognized by the **read** procedure:

---

[1] In older dialects of Lisp, uninterned symbols were fairly important. This was true because symbols were complicated data structures: in addition to having value cells (and sometimes, function cells), these structures contained *property lists*. Because of this, uninterned symbols were often used merely for their property lists — sometimes an uninterned symbol used this way was referred to as a *disembodied property list*. In MIT/GNU Scheme, symbols do not have property lists, or any other components besides their names. There is a different data structure similar to disembodied property lists: one-dimensional tables (see Section 11.2 [1D Tables], page 149). For these reasons, uninterned symbols are not very useful in MIT/GNU Scheme. In fact, their primary purpose is to simplify the generation of unique variable names in programs that generate Scheme code.

[2] MIT/GNU Scheme reserves a specific set of interned symbols for its own use. If you use these reserved symbols it is possible that you could break specific pieces of software that depend on them. The reserved symbols all have names beginning with the characters '#[' and ending with the character ']'; thus none of these symbols can be read by the procedure **read** and hence are not likely to be used by accident. For example, (**intern** "#[unnamed-procedure]") produces a reserved symbol.

```
(string->uninterned-symbol "foo")
    ⇒  #[uninterned-symbol 30 foo]
```

In this section, the procedures that return symbols as values will either always return interned symbols, or always return uninterned symbols. The procedures that accept symbols as arguments will always accept either interned or uninterned symbols, and do not distinguish the two.

symbol? *object*   [procedure]

Returns #t if *object* is a symbol, otherwise returns #f.

```
(symbol? 'foo)                             ⇒   #t
(symbol? (car '(a b)))                     ⇒   #t
(symbol? "bar")                            ⇒   #f
```

symbol->string *symbol*   [procedure]

Returns the name of *symbol* as a string. If *symbol* was returned by `string->symbol`, the value of this procedure will be identical (in the sense of `string=?`) to the string that was passed to `string->symbol`. It is an error to apply mutation procedures such as `string-set!` to strings returned by this procedure.

```
(symbol->string 'flying-fish)          ⇒   "flying-fish"
(symbol->string 'Martin)               ⇒   "martin"
(symbol->string (string->symbol "Malvina"))
                                       ⇒   "Malvina"
```

Note that two distinct uninterned symbols can have the same name.

intern *string*   [procedure]

Returns the interned symbol whose name is *string*. Converts *string* to the standard alphabetic case before generating the symbol. This is the preferred way to create interned symbols, as it guarantees the following independent of which case the implementation uses for symbols' names:

```
(eq? 'bitBlt (intern "bitBlt")) ⇒     #t
```

The user should take care that *string* obeys the rules for identifiers (see Section 1.3.3 [Identifiers], page 10), otherwise the resulting symbol cannot be read as itself.

intern-soft *string*   [procedure]

Returns the interned symbol whose name is *string*. Converts *string* to the standard alphabetic case before generating the symbol. If no such interned symbol exists, returns #f.

This is exactly like `intern`, except that it will not create an interned symbol, but only returns symbols that already exist.

string->symbol *string*   [procedure]

Returns the interned symbol whose name is *string*. Although you can use this procedure to create symbols with names containing special characters or lowercase letters, it's usually a bad idea to create such symbols because they cannot be read as themselves. See `symbol->string`.

```
(eq? 'mISSISSIppi 'mississippi)        ⇒   #t
(string->symbol "mISSISSIppi")
        ⇒   the symbol with the name "mISSISSIppi"
(eq? 'bitBlt (string->symbol "bitBlt")) ⇒   #f
(eq? 'JollyWog
        (string->symbol
          (symbol->string 'JollyWog)))   ⇒   #t
(string=? "K. Harper, M.D."
              (symbol->string
                (string->symbol
                  "K. Harper, M.D.")))   ⇒   #t
```

string->uninterned-symbol *string*   [procedure]

Returns a newly allocated uninterned symbol whose name is *string*. It is unimportant what case or characters are used in *string*.

Note: this is the fastest way to make a symbol.

generate-uninterned-symbol [*object*]   [procedure]

Returns a newly allocated uninterned symbol that is guaranteed to be different from any other object. The symbol's name consists of a prefix string followed by the (exact non-negative integer) value of an internal counter. The counter is initially zero, and is incremented after each call to this procedure.

The optional argument *object* is used to control how the symbol is generated. It may take one of the following values:

- If *object* is omitted or **#f**, the prefix is **"G"**.

- If *object* is an exact non-negative integer, the internal counter is set to that integer prior to generating the result.

- If *object* is a string, it is used as the prefix.

- If *object* is a symbol, its name is used as the prefix.

  ```
  (generate-uninterned-symbol)
      ⇒   #[uninterned-symbol 31 G0]
  (generate-uninterned-symbol)
      ⇒   #[uninterned-symbol 32 G1]
  (generate-uninterned-symbol 'this)
      ⇒   #[uninterned-symbol 33 this2]
  (generate-uninterned-symbol)
      ⇒   #[uninterned-symbol 34 G3]
  (generate-uninterned-symbol 100)
      ⇒   #[uninterned-symbol 35 G100]
  (generate-uninterned-symbol)
      ⇒   #[uninterned-symbol 36 G101]
  ```

symbol-append *symbol* ...   [procedure]

Returns the interned symbol whose name is formed by concatenating the names of the given symbols. This procedure preserves the case of the names of its arguments, so if one or more of the arguments' names has non-standard case, the result will also have non-standard case.

```
(symbol-append 'foo- 'bar)              ⇒  foo-bar
;; the arguments may be uninterned:
(symbol-append 'foo- (string->uninterned-symbol "baz"))
                                        ⇒  foo-baz
;; the result has the same case as the arguments:
(symbol-append 'foo- (string->symbol "BAZ"))   ⇒  foo-BAZ
```

symbol-hash *symbol*   [procedure]

> Returns a hash number for *symbol*, which is computed by calling `string-hash` on *symbol*'s name. The hash number is an exact non-negative integer.

symbol-hash-mod *symbol modulus*   [procedure]

> *Modulus* must be an exact positive integer. Equivalent to

```
(modulo (symbol-hash symbol) modulus)
```

> This procedure is provided for convenience in constructing hash tables. However, it is normally preferable to use `make-strong-eq-hash-table` to build hash tables keyed by symbols, because `eq?` hash tables are much faster.

symbol<? *symbol1 symbol2*   [procedure]

> This procedure computes a total order on symbols. It is equivalent to

```
(string<? (symbol->string symbol1)
          (symbol->string symbol2))
```

10.3 Cells

Cells are data structures similar to pairs except that they have only one element. They are useful for managing state.

cell? *object*   [procedure]

> Returns #t if *object* is a cell; otherwise returns #f.

make-cell *object*   [procedure]

> Returns a newly allocated cell whose contents is *object*.

cell-contents *cell*   [procedure]

> Returns the current contents of *cell*.

set-cell-contents! *cell object*   [procedure]

> Alters the contents of *cell* to be *object*. Returns an unspecified value.

bind-cell-contents! *cell object thunk*   [procedure]

> Alters the contents of *cell* to be *object*, calls *thunk* with no arguments, then restores the original contents of *cell* and returns the value returned by *thunk*. This is completely equivalent to dynamic binding of a variable, including the behavior when continuations are used (see Section 2.3 [Dynamic Binding], page 18).

10.4 Records

MIT/GNU Scheme provides a *record* abstraction, which is a simple and flexible mechanism for building structures with named components. Records can be defined and accessed using the procedures defined in this section. A less flexible but more concise way to manipulate records is to use the **define-structure** special form (see Section 2.10 [Structure Definitions], page 29).

make-record-type *type-name field-names*   [procedure]

> Returns a *record-type descriptor*, a value representing a new data type, disjoint from all others. The *type-name* argument must be a string, but is only used for debugging purposes (such as the printed representation of a record of the new type). The *field-names* argument is a list of symbols naming the *fields* of a record of the new type. It is an error if the list contains any duplicates. It is unspecified how record-type descriptors are represented.

record-constructor *record-type* [*field-names*]   [procedure]

> Returns a procedure for constructing new members of the type represented by *record-type*. The returned procedure accepts exactly as many arguments as there are symbols in the given list, *field-names*; these are used, in order, as the initial values of those fields in a new record, which is returned by the constructor procedure. The values of any fields not named in the list of *field-names* are unspecified. The *field-names* argument defaults to the list of field-names in the call to **make-record-type** that created the type represented by *record-type*; if the *field-names* argument is provided, it is an error if it contains any duplicates or any symbols not in the default list.

record-keyword-constructor *record-type*   [procedure]

> Returns a procedure for constructing new members of the type represented by *record-type*. The returned procedure accepts arguments in a *keyword list*, which is an alternating sequence of names and values. In other words, the number of arguments must be a multiple of two, and every other argument, starting with the first argument, must be a symbol that is one of the field names for *record-type*.

> The returned procedure may be called with a keyword list that contains multiple instances of the same keyword. In this case, the leftmost instance is used and the other instances are ignored. This allows keyword lists to be accumulated using **cons** or **cons***, and new bindings added to the front of the list override old bindings at the end.

record-predicate *record-type*   [procedure]

> Returns a procedure for testing membership in the type represented by *record-type*. The returned procedure accepts exactly one argument and returns **#t** if the argument is a member of the indicated record type; it returns **#f** otherwise.

record-accessor *record-type field-name*   [procedure]

> Returns a procedure for reading the value of a particular field of a member of the type represented by *record-type*. The returned procedure accepts exactly one argument which must be a record of the appropriate type; it returns the current value of the field named by the symbol *field-name* in that record. The symbol *field-name* must be a member of the list of field names in the call to **make-record-type** that created the type represented by *record-type*.

record-modifier *record-type field-name*   [procedure]

> Returns a procedure for writing the value of a particular field of a member of the type represented by *record-type*. The returned procedure accepts exactly two arguments: first, a record of the appropriate type, and second, an arbitrary Scheme value; it modifies the field named by the symbol *field-name* in that record to contain the given value. The returned value of the modifier procedure is unspecified. The symbol *field-name* must be a member of the list of field names in the call to `make-record-type` that created the type represented by *record-type*.

record? *object*   [procedure]

> Returns `#t` if *object* is a record of any type and `#f` otherwise. Note that `record?` may be true of any Scheme value; of course, if it returns `#t` for some particular value, then `record-type-descriptor` is applicable to that value and returns an appropriate descriptor.

record-type-descriptor *record*   [procedure]

> Returns the record-type descriptor representing the type of *record*. That is, for example, if the returned descriptor were passed to `record-predicate`, the resulting predicate would return `#t` when passed *record*. Note that it is not necessarily the case that the returned descriptor is the one that was passed to `record-constructor` in the call that created the constructor procedure that created *record*.

record-type? *object*   [procedure]

> Returns `#t` if *object* is a record-type descriptor; otherwise returns `#f`.

record-type-name *record-type*   [procedure]

> Returns the type name associated with the type represented by *record-type*. The returned value is `eqv?` to the *type-name* argument given in the call to `make-record-type` that created the type represented by *record-type*.

record-type-field-names *record-type*   [procedure]

> Returns a list of the symbols naming the fields in members of the type represented by *record-type*. The returned value is `equal?` to the *field-names* argument given in the call to `make-record-type` that created the type represented by *record-type*.[3]

10.5 Promises

delay *expression*   [special form]

> The `delay` construct is used together with the procedure `force` to implement *lazy evaluation* or *call by need*. (`delay` *expression*) returns an object called a *promise* which at some point in the future may be asked (by the `force` procedure) to evaluate *expression* and deliver the resulting value.

force *promise*   [procedure]

> Forces the value of *promise*. If no value has been computed for the promise, then a value is computed and returned. The value of the promise is cached (or "memoized") so that if it is forced a second time, the previously computed value is returned without any recomputation.

---

[3] In MIT/GNU Scheme, the returned list is always newly allocated.

```
(force (delay (+ 1 2)))                    ⇒  3

(let ((p (delay (+ 1 2))))
  (list (force p) (force p)))              ⇒  (3 3)

(define head car)

(define tail
  (lambda (stream)
    (force (cdr stream))))

(define a-stream
  (letrec ((next
            (lambda (n)
              (cons n (delay (next (+ n 1)))))))
    (next 0)))

(head (tail (tail a-stream)))             ⇒  2
```

promise? *object*   [procedure]
>   Returns #t if *object* is a promise; otherwise returns #f.

promise-forced? *promise*   [procedure]
>   Returns #t if *promise* has been forced and its value cached; otherwise returns #f.

promise-value *promise*   [procedure]
>   If *promise* has been forced and its value cached, this procedure returns the cached value. Otherwise, an error is signalled.

force and delay are mainly intended for programs written in functional style. The following examples should not be considered to illustrate good programming style, but they illustrate the property that the value of a promise is computed at most once.

```
(define count 0)

(define p
  (delay
    (begin
      (set! count (+ count 1))
      (* x 3))))

(define x 5)

count                                  ⇒  0
p                                      ⇒  #[promise 54]
(force p)                              ⇒  15
p                                      ⇒  #[promise 54]
count                                  ⇒  1
(force p)                              ⇒  15
count                                  ⇒  1
```

Here is a possible implementation of `delay` and `force`. We define the expression

```
(delay expression)
```

to have the same meaning as the procedure call

```
(make-promise (lambda () expression))
```

where `make-promise` is defined as follows:

```
(define make-promise
  (lambda (proc)
    (let ((already-run? #f)
          (result #f))
      (lambda ()
        (cond ((not already-run?)
               (set! result (proc))
               (set! already-run? #t)))
        result))))
```

Promises are implemented here as procedures of no arguments, and `force` simply calls its argument.

```
(define force
  (lambda (promise)
    (promise)))
```

Various extensions to this semantics of `delay` and `force` are supported in some implementations (none of these are currently supported in MIT/GNU Scheme):

- Calling `force` on an object that is not a promise may simply return the object.

- It may be the case that there is no means by which a promise can be operationally distinguished from its forced value. That is, expressions like the following may evaluate to either `#t` or `#f`, depending on the implementation:

  ```
  (eqv? (delay 1) 1)            ⇒   unspecified
  (pair? (delay (cons 1 2)))    ⇒   unspecified
  ```

- Some implementations will implement "implicit forcing", where the value of a promise is forced by primitive procedures like `car` and `+`:

  ```
  (+ (delay (* 3 7)) 13)        ⇒   34
  ```

10.6 Streams

In addition to promises, MIT/GNU Scheme supports a higher-level abstraction called *streams*. Streams are similar to lists, except that the tail of a stream is not computed until it is referred to. This allows streams to be used to represent infinitely long lists.

stream *object . . .*   [procedure]
> Returns a newly allocated stream whose elements are the arguments. Note that the expression `(stream)` returns the empty stream, or end-of-stream marker.

list->stream *list*   [procedure]
> Returns a newly allocated stream whose elements are the elements of *list*. Equivalent to `(apply stream list)`.

`stream->list` *stream*   [procedure]

Returns a newly allocated list whose elements are the elements of *stream*. If *stream* has infinite length this procedure will not terminate. This could have been defined by

```
(define (stream->list stream)
  (if (stream-null? stream)
      '()
      (cons (stream-car stream)
            (stream->list (stream-cdr stream)))))
```

`cons-stream` *object expression*   [special form]

Returns a newly allocated stream pair. Equivalent to `(cons object (delay expression))`.

`stream-pair?` *object*   [procedure]

Returns `#t` if *object* is a pair whose cdr contains a promise. Otherwise returns `#f`. This could have been defined by

```
(define (stream-pair? object)
  (and (pair? object)
       (promise? (cdr object))))
```

`stream-car` *stream*   [procedure]
`stream-first` *stream*   [procedure]

Returns the first element in *stream*. `stream-car` is equivalent to `car`. `stream-first` is a synonym for `stream-car`.

`stream-cdr` *stream*   [procedure]
`stream-rest` *stream*   [procedure]

Returns the first tail of *stream*. Equivalent to `(force (cdr stream))`. `stream-rest` is a synonym for `stream-cdr`.

`stream-null?` *stream*   [procedure]

Returns `#t` if *stream* is the end-of-stream marker; otherwise returns `#f`. This is equivalent to `null?`, but should be used whenever testing for the end of a stream.

`stream-length` *stream*   [procedure]

Returns the number of elements in *stream*. If *stream* has an infinite number of elements this procedure will not terminate. Note that this procedure forces all of the promises that comprise *stream*.

`stream-ref` *stream k*   [procedure]

Returns the element of *stream* that is indexed by k; that is, the kth element. K must be an exact non-negative integer strictly less than the length of *stream*.

`stream-head` *stream k*   [procedure]

Returns the first k elements of *stream* as a list. K must be an exact non-negative integer strictly less than the length of *stream*.

stream-tail *stream k*   [procedure]

> Returns the tail of *stream* that is indexed by *k*; that is, the *k*th tail. This is equivalent to performing **stream-cdr** *k* times. *K* must be an exact non-negative integer strictly less than the length of *stream*.

stream-map *procedure stream stream* ...   [procedure]

> Returns a newly allocated stream, each element being the result of invoking *procedure* with the corresponding elements of the *streams* as its arguments.

10.7 Weak References

Weak references are a mechanism for building data structures that point at objects without protecting them from garbage collection. An example of such a data structure might be an entry in a lookup table that should be removed if the rest of the program does not reference its key. Such an entry must still point at its key to carry out comparisons, but should not in itself prevent its key from being garbage collected.

A *weak reference* is a reference that points at an object without preventing it from being garbage collected. The term *strong reference* is used to distinguish normal references from weak ones. If there is no path of strong references to some object, the garbage collector will reclaim that object and mark any weak references to it to indicate that it has been reclaimed.

If there is a path of strong references from an object *A* to an object *B*, *A* is said to hold *B* *strongly*. If there is a path of references from an object *A* to an object *B*, but every such path traverses at least one weak reference, *A* is said to hold *B* *weakly*.

MIT Scheme provides two mechanisms for using weak references. *Weak pairs* are like normal pairs, except that their car slot is a weak reference (but the cdr is still strong). The heavier-weight *ephemerons* additionally arrange that the ephemeron does not count as holding the object in its key field strongly even if the object in its datum field does.

Warning: Working with weak references is subtle and requires careful analysis; most programs should avoid working with them directly. The most common use cases for weak references ought to be served by hash tables (see Section 11.4 [Hash Tables], page 151), which can employ various flavors of weak entry types, 1d tables (see Section 11.2 [1D Tables], page 149), which hold their keys weakly, and the association table (see Section 11.3 [The Association Table], page 150), which also holds its keys weakly.

10.7.1 Weak Pairs

The car of a *weak pair* holds its pointer weakly, while the cdr holds its pointer strongly. If the object in the car of a weak pair is not held strongly by any other data structure, it will be garbage-collected.

Note: weak pairs can be defeated by cross references among their slots. Consider a weak pair *P* holding an object *A* in its car and an object *D* in its cdr. *P* points to *A* weakly and to *D* strongly. If *D* holds *A* strongly, however, then *P* ends up holding *A* strongly after all. If avoiding this is worth a heavier-weight structure, See Section 10.7.2 [Ephemerons], page 144.

Note: weak pairs are *not* pairs; that is, they do not satisfy the predicate **pair?**.

`weak-pair?` *object*   [procedure]
>   Returns #t if *object* is a weak pair; otherwise returns #f.

`weak-cons` *car cdr*   [procedure]
>   Allocates and returns a new weak pair, with components *car* and *cdr*. The *car* component is held weakly.

`weak-pair/car?` *weak-pair*   [procedure]
>   This predicate returns #f if the car of *weak-pair* has been garbage-collected; otherwise returns #t. In other words, it is true if *weak-pair* has a valid car component.

`weak-car` *weak-pair*   [procedure]
>   Returns the car component of *weak-pair*. If the car component has been garbage-collected, this operation returns #f, but it can also return #f if that is the value that was stored in the car.

Normally, `weak-pair/car?` is used to determine if `weak-car` would return a valid value. An obvious way of doing this would be:

```
(if (weak-pair/car? x)
    (weak-car x)
    ...)
```

However, since a garbage collection could occur between the call to `weak-pair/car?` and `weak-car`, this would not always work correctly. Instead, the following should be used, which always works:

```
(or (weak-car x)
    (and (not (weak-pair/car? x))
         ...))
```

The reason that the latter expression works is that `weak-car` returns #f in just two instances: when the car component is #f, and when the car component has been garbage-collected. In the former case, if a garbage collection happens between the two calls, it won't matter, because #f will never be garbage-collected. And in the latter case, it also won't matter, because the car component no longer exists and cannot be affected by the garbage collector.

`weak-set-car!` *weak-pair object*   [procedure]
>   Sets the car component of *weak-pair* to *object* and returns an unspecified result.

`weak-cdr` *weak-pair*   [procedure]
>   Returns the cdr component of *weak-pair*.

`weak-set-cdr!` *weak-pair object*   [procedure]
>   Sets the cdr component of *weak-pair* to *object* and returns an unspecified result.

10.7.2 Ephemerons

An *ephemeron* is an object with two weakly referenced components called its *key* and *datum*. The garbage collector drops an ephemeron's references to both key and datum, rendering the ephemeron *broken*, if and only if the garbage collector can prove that there are no strong references to the key. In other words, an ephemeron is broken when nobody else cares about its key. In particular, the datum holding a reference to the key will not in itself prevent the ephemeron from becoming broken; in contrast, See Section 10.7.1 [Weak Pairs], page 143. Once broken, ephemerons never cease to be broken; setting the key or datum of a broken ephemeron with `set-ephemeron-key!` or `set-ephemeron-datum!` has no effect. Note that an ephemeron's reference to its datum may be dropped even if the datum is still reachable; all that matters is whether the key is reachable.

Ephemerons are considerably heavier-weight than weak pairs, because garbage-collecting ephemerons is more complicated than garbage-collecting weak pairs. Each ephemeron needs five words of storage, rather than the two words needed by a weak pair. However, while the garbage collector spends more time on ephemerons than on other objects, the amount of time it spends on ephemerons scales linearly with the number of live ephemerons, which is how its running time scales with the total number of live objects anyway.

`ephemeron?` *object*   [procedure]
> Returns `#t` if *object* is a ephemeron; otherwise returns `#f`.

`make-ephemeron` *key datum*   [procedure]
> Allocates and returns a new ephemeron, with components *key* and *datum*.

`ephemeron-broken?` *ephemeron*   [procedure]
> Returns `#t` if the garbage collector has dropped *ephemeron*'s references to its key and datum; otherwise returns `#f`.

`ephemeron-key` *ephemeron*   [procedure]
`ephemeron-datum` *ephemeron*   [procedure]
> These return the key or datum component, respectively, of *ephemeron*. If *ephemeron* has been broken, these operations return `#f`, but they can also return `#f` if that is the value that was stored in the key or value component.

`set-ephemeron-key!` *ephemeron object*   [procedure]
`set-ephemeron-datum!` *ephemeron object*   [procedure]
> These set the key or datum component, respectively, of *ephemeron* to *object* and return an unspecified result. If *ephemeron* is broken, neither of these operations has any effect.

Like `weak-pair/car?`, `ephemeron-broken?` must be used with care. If (ephemeron-broken? *ephemeron*) yields false, it guarantees only that prior evaluations of (ephemeron-key *ephemeron*) or (ephemeron-datum *ephemeron*) yielded the key or datum that was stored in the ephemeron, but it makes no guarantees about subsequent calls to `ephemeron-key` or `ephemeron-datum`: the garbage collector may run and break the ephemeron immediately after `ephemeron-broken?` returns. Thus, the correct idiom to fetch an ephemeron's key and datum and use them if the ephemeron is not broken is

```
(let ((key (ephemeron-key ephemeron))
      (datum (ephemeron-datum ephemeron)))
  (if (ephemeron-broken? ephemeron)
      ... broken case ...
      ... code using key and datum ...))
```

11 Associations

MIT/GNU Scheme provides several mechanisms for associating objects with one another. Each of these mechanisms creates a link between one or more objects, called *keys*, and some other object, called a *datum*. Beyond this common idea, however, each of the mechanisms has various different properties that make it appropriate in different situations:

- *Association lists* are one of Lisp's oldest association mechanisms. Because they are made from ordinary pairs, they are easy to build and manipulate, and very flexible in use. However, the average lookup time for an association list is linear in the number of associations.

- *1D tables* have a very simple interface, making them easy to use, and offer the feature that they do not prevent their keys from being reclaimed by the garbage collector. Like association lists, their average lookup time is linear in the number of associations; but 1D tables aren't as flexible.

- *The association table* is MIT/GNU Scheme's equivalent to the *property lists* of Lisp. It has the advantages that the keys may be any type of object and that it does not prevent the keys from being reclaimed by the garbage collector. However, two linear-time lookups must be performed, one for each key, whereas for traditional property lists only one lookup is required for both keys.

- *Hash tables* are a powerful mechanism with constant-time access to large amounts of data. Hash tables are not as flexible as association lists, but because their access times are independent of the number of associations in the table, for most applications they are the mechanism of choice.

- *Balanced binary trees* are another association mechanism that is useful for applications in which the keys are ordered. Binary trees have access times that are proportional to the logarithm of the number of associations in the tree. While they aren't as fast as hash tables, they offer the advantage that the contents of the tree can be converted to a sorted alist in linear time. Additionally, two trees can be compared for equality in worst-case linear time.

- *Red-Black trees* are a kind of balanced binary tree. The implementation supports destructive insertion and deletion operations with a good constant factor.

- *Weight-Balanced trees* are a kind of balanced binary tree. The implementation provides non-destructive operations. There is a comprehensive set of operations, including: a constant-time size operation; many high-level operations such as the set operations union, intersection and difference; and indexing of elements by position.

11.1 Association Lists

An *association list*, or *alist*, is a data structure used very frequently in Scheme. An alist is a list of pairs, each of which is called an *association*. The car of an association is called the *key*.

An advantage of the alist representation is that an alist can be incrementally augmented simply by adding new entries to the front. Moreover, because the searching procedures `assv` et al. search the alist in order, new entries can "shadow" old entries. If an alist is viewed as a mapping from keys to data, then the mapping can be not only augmented but also altered in a non-destructive manner by adding new entries to the front of the alist.[1]

alist? *object*   [procedure]

> Returns #t if *object* is an association list (including the empty list); otherwise returns #f. Any *object* satisfying this predicate also satisfies list?.

assq *object alist*   [procedure]
assv *object alist*   [procedure]
assoc *object alist*   [procedure]

> These procedures find the first pair in *alist* whose car field is *object*, and return that pair; the returned pair is always an *element* of *alist*, *not* one of the pairs from which *alist* is composed. If no pair in *alist* has *object* as its car, #f (n.b.: not the empty list) is returned. assq uses eq? to compare *object* with the car fields of the pairs in *alist*, while assv uses eqv? and assoc uses equal?.[2]
>
> ```
> (define e '((a 1) (b 2) (c 3)))
> (assq 'a e)                          ⇒  (a 1)
> (assq 'b e)                          ⇒  (b 2)
> (assq 'd e)                          ⇒  #f
> (assq (list 'a) '(((a)) ((b)) ((c))))   ⇒  #f
> (assoc (list 'a) '(((a)) ((b)) ((c))))  ⇒  ((a))
> (assq 5 '((2 3) (5 7) (11 13)))      ⇒  unspecified
> (assv 5 '((2 3) (5 7) (11 13)))      ⇒  (5 7)
> ```

association-procedure *predicate selector*   [procedure]

> Returns an association procedure that is similar to assv, except that *selector* (a procedure of one argument) is used to select the key from the association, and *predicate* (an equivalence predicate) is used to compare the key to the given item. This can be used to make association lists whose elements are, say, vectors instead of pairs (also see Section 7.6 [Searching Lists], page 119).
>
> For example, here is how assv could be implemented:
>
> ```
> (define assv (association-procedure eqv? car))
> ```
>
> Another example is a "reverse association" procedure:
>
> ```
> (define rassv (association-procedure eqv? cdr))
> ```

del-assq *object alist*   [procedure]
del-assv *object alist*   [procedure]
del-assoc *object alist*   [procedure]

> These procedures return a newly allocated copy of *alist* in which all associations with keys equal to *object* have been removed. Note that while the returned copy is a newly allocated list, the association pairs that are the elements of the list are shared with *alist*, not copied. del-assq uses eq? to compare *object* with the keys, while del-assv uses eqv? and del-assoc uses equal?.

---

[1] This introduction is taken from *Common Lisp, The Language*, second edition, p. 431.

[2] Although they are often used as predicates, assq, assv, and assoc do not have question marks in their names because they return useful values rather than just #t or #f.

```
(define a
  '((butcher . "231 e22nd St.")
    (baker . "515 w23rd St.")
    (hardware . "988 Lexington Ave.")))

(del-assq 'baker a)
    ⇒
    ((butcher . "231 e22nd St.")
     (hardware . "988 Lexington Ave."))
```

del-assq! *object alist*   [procedure]
del-assv! *object alist*   [procedure]
del-assoc! *object alist*   [procedure]
> These procedures remove from *alist* all associations with keys equal to *object*. They
> return the resulting list. del-assq! uses eq? to compare *object* with the keys,
> while del-assv! uses eqv? and del-assoc! uses equal?. These procedures are like
> del-assq, del-assv, and del-assoc, respectively, except that they destructively
> modify *alist*.

delete-association-procedure *deletor predicate selector*   [procedure]
> This returns a deletion procedure similar to del-assv or del-assq!. The *predicate*
> and *selector* arguments are the same as those for association-procedure, while the
> *deletor* argument should be either the procedure list-deletor (for non-destructive
> deletions), or the procedure list-deletor! (for destructive deletions).
>
> For example, here is a possible implementation of del-assv:

```
(define del-assv
  (delete-association-procedure list-deletor eqv? car))
```

alist-copy *alist*   [procedure]
> Returns a newly allocated copy of *alist*. This is similar to list-copy except that the
> "association" pairs, i.e. the elements of the list *alist*, are also copied. alist-copy
> could have been implemented like this:

```
(define (alist-copy alist)
  (if (null? alist)
      '()
      (cons (cons (car (car alist)) (cdr (car alist)))
            (alist-copy (cdr alist)))))
```

11.2 1D Tables

1D tables ("one-dimensional" tables) are similar to association lists. In a 1D table, unlike
an association list, the keys of the table are held *weakly*: if a key is garbage-collected, its
associated value in the table is removed. 1D tables compare their keys for equality using
eq?.

1D tables can often be used as a higher-performance alternative to the two-dimensional
association table (see Section 11.3 [The Association Table], page 150). If one of the keys
being associated is a compound object such as a vector, a 1D table can be stored in one

of the vector's slots. Under these circumstances, accessing items in a 1D table will be comparable in performance to using a property list in a conventional Lisp.

make-1d-table   [procedure]
    Returns a newly allocated empty 1D table.

1d-table? *object*   [procedure]
    Returns #t if *object* is a 1D table, otherwise returns #f. Any object that satisfies this predicate also satisfies list?.

1d-table/put! *1d-table key datum*   [procedure]
    Creates an association between *key* and *datum* in *1d-table*. Returns an unspecified value.

1d-table/remove! *1d-table key*   [procedure]
    Removes any association for *key* in *1d-table* and returns an unspecified value.

1d-table/get *1d-table key default*   [procedure]
    Returns the *datum* associated with *key* in *1d-table*. If there is no association for *key*, *default* is returned.

1d-table/lookup *1d-table key if-found if-not-found*   [procedure]
    If-found must be a procedure of one argument, and *if-not-found* must be a procedure of no arguments. If *1d-table* contains an association for *key*, *if-found* is invoked on the *datum* of the association. Otherwise, *if-not-found* is invoked with no arguments. In either case, the result of the invoked procedure is returned as the result of 1d-table/lookup.

1d-table/alist *1d-table*   [procedure]
    Returns a newly allocated association list that contains the same information as *1d-table*.

11.3 The Association Table

MIT/GNU Scheme provides a generalization of the property-list mechanism found in most other implementations of Lisp: a global two-dimensional *association table*. This table is indexed by two keys, called *x-key* and *y-key* in the following procedure descriptions. These keys and the datum associated with them can be arbitrary objects. eq? is used to discriminate keys.

Think of the association table as a matrix: a single datum can be accessed using both keys, a column using *x-key* only, and a row using *y-key* only.

2d-put! *x-key y-key datum*   [procedure]
    Makes an entry in the association table that associates *datum* with *x-key* and *y-key*. Returns an unspecified result.

2d-remove! *x-key y-key*   [procedure]
    If the association table has an entry for *x-key* and *y-key*, it is removed. Returns an unspecified result.

`2d-get` *x-key y-key*   [procedure]

>   Returns the *datum* associated with *x-key* and *y-key*. Returns #f if no such association exists.

`2d-get-alist-x` *x-key*   [procedure]

>   Returns an association list of all entries in the association table that are associated with *x-key*. The result is a list of (`y-key` . `datum`) pairs. Returns the empty list if no entries for *x-key* exist.
>
> ```
> (2d-put! 'foo 'bar 5)
> (2d-put! 'foo 'baz 6)
> (2d-get-alist-x 'foo)          ⇒  ((baz . 6) (bar . 5))
> ```

`2d-get-alist-y` *y-key*   [procedure]

>   Returns an association list of all entries in the association table that are associated with *y-key*. The result is a list of (`x-key` . `datum`) pairs. Returns the empty list if no entries for *y-key* exist.
>
> ```
> (2d-put! 'bar 'foo 5)
> (2d-put! 'baz 'foo 6)
> (2d-get-alist-y 'foo)          ⇒  ((baz . 6) (bar . 5))
> ```

11.4 Hash Tables

Hash tables are a fast, powerful mechanism for storing large numbers of associations. MIT/GNU Scheme's hash tables feature automatic resizing, customizable growth parameters, customizable hash procedures, and many options for weak references to keys or data.

The average times for the insertion, deletion, and lookup operations on a hash table are bounded by a constant. The space required by the table is proportional to the number of associations in the table; the constant of proportionality is described below (see Section 11.4.3 [Resizing of Hash Tables], page 157).

In addition to the hash table interface described in the following, MIT Scheme implements SRFI 69: "Basic hash tables". The reason for supporting two interfaces is partly historical—MIT Scheme supported hash tables prior to the existence of SRFI 69—and partly technical—SFRI 69 fails to specify certain optimization-enabling exceptions to its semantics, forcing a correct implementation to pay the non-negligible performance cost of completely safe behavior.[3] The MIT Scheme native hash table interface, in contrast, specifies the minor exceptions it needs, and is therefore implemented more efficiently. We do not describe the SRFI-69-compliant interface here, as that would be redundant with the SRFI document.

(Previously, the hash-table implementation was a run-time-loadable option, but as of release 7.7.0 it is loaded by default. It's no longer necessary to call `load-option` prior to using hash tables.)

---

[3] SRFI 69 does not give hash functions the flexibility to return new hash values after a garbage collection, which prevents a system whose garbage collector may relocate objects from hashing based on the addresses of objects in memory (see Section 11.4.4 [Address Hashing], page 159). SRFI 69 also does not specify circumstances when procedures passed as arguments to hash table operations may not themselves modify the hash table, which requires defensive copying and defensive repetitions of lookups.

11.4.1 Construction of Hash Tables

The next few procedures are hash-table constructors. All hash table constructors are procedures that accept one optional argument, *initial-size*, and return a newly allocated hash table. If *initial-size* is given, it must be an exact non-negative integer or `#f`. The meaning of *initial-size* is discussed below (see Section 11.4.3 [Resizing of Hash Tables], page 157).

Hash tables are normally characterized by two things: the equivalence predicate that is used to compare keys, and how the table allows its keys and data to be reclaimed by the garbage collector. If a table prevents its keys and data from being reclaimed by the garbage collector, it is said to hold its keys and data *strongly*; other arrangements are possible, where a table may hold keys or data *weakly* or *ephemerally* (see Section 10.7 [Weak References], page 143).

`make-strong-eq-hash-table` [*initial-size*]   [procedure]
    Returns a newly allocated hash table that accepts arbitrary objects as keys, and compares those keys with `eq?`. The keys and data are held strongly. These are the fastest of the standard hash tables.

`make-key-weak-eq-hash-table` [*initial-size*]   [procedure]
    Returns a newly allocated hash table that accepts arbitrary objects as keys, and compares those keys with `eq?`. The keys are held weakly, but the data are held strongly. Note that if a datum holds a key strongly, the table will effectively hold that key strongly.

`make-key-ephemeral-eq-hash-table` [*initial-size*]   [procedure]
    Returns a newly allocated hash table that accepts arbitrary objects as keys, and compares those keys with `eq?`. The keys are held weakly, even if some of the data should hold some of the keys strongly.

`make-strong-eqv-hash-table` [*initial-size*]   [procedure]
    Returns a newly allocated hash table that accepts arbitrary objects as keys, and compares those keys with `eqv?`. The keys and data are held strongly. These hash tables are a little slower than those made by `make-strong-eq-hash-table`.

`make-key-weak-eqv-hash-table` [*initial-size*]   [procedure]
    Returns a newly allocated hash table that accepts arbitrary objects as keys, and compares those keys with `eqv?`. The keys are held weakly, except that booleans, characters, numbers, and interned symbols are held strongly. The data are held strongly. Note that if a datum holds a key strongly, the table will effectively hold that key strongly.

`make-key-ephemeral-eqv-hash-table` [*initial-size*]   [procedure]
    Returns a newly allocated hash table that accepts arbitrary objects as keys, and compares those keys with `eqv?`. The keys are held weakly, except that booleans, characters, numbers, and interned symbols are held strongly. The keys are effectively held weakly even if some of the data should hold some of the keys strongly.

`make-equal-hash-table` [*initial-size*]   [procedure]
    Returns a newly allocated hash table that accepts arbitrary objects as keys, and compares those keys with `equal?`. The keys and data are held strongly. These hash tables are quite a bit slower than those made by `make-strong-eq-hash-table`.

make-string-hash-table [*initial-size*]   [procedure]
    Returns a newly allocated hash table that accepts character strings as keys, and compares them with **string=?**. The keys and data are held strongly.

The next procedure is used to create new hash-table constructors. All of the above hash table constructors could have been created by calls to this "constructor-constructor"; see the examples below.

hash-table/constructor *key-hash key=? rehash-after-gc? entry-type*   [procedure]
    This procedure accepts four arguments and returns a hash-table constructor. The *key=?* argument is an equivalence predicate for the keys of the hash table. The *key-hash* argument is a procedure that computes a hash number. Specifically, *key-hash* accepts two arguments, a key and an exact positive integer (the *modulus*), and returns an exact non-negative integer that is less than the modulus.

    The argument *rehash-after-gc?*, if true, says that the values returned by *key-hash* might change after a garbage collection. If so, the hash-table implementation arranges for the table to be rehashed when necessary. (See Section 11.4.4 [Address Hashing], page 159, for information about hash procedures that have this property.) Otherwise, it is assumed that *key-hash* always returns the same value for the same arguments.

    The argument *entry-type* determines the strength with which the hash table will hold its keys and values. It must be one of **hash-table-entry-type:strong**, **hash-table-entry-type:key-weak**, **hash-table-entry-type:datum-weak**, **hash-table-entry-type:key/datum-weak**, **hash-table-entry-type:key-ephemeral**, **hash-table-entry-type:datum-ephemeral**, or **hash-table-entry-type:key&datum-ephemeral**.

hash-table-entry-type:strong   [variable]
    The entry type for hash tables that hold both keys and data strongly.

hash-table-entry-type:key-weak   [variable]
    An entry type for hash tables that hold keys weakly and data strongly. An entry of this type is a weak pair (see Section 10.7.1 [Weak Pairs], page 143) whose weak (car) slot holds the key of the entry and whose strong (cdr) slot holds the datum of the entry. If a key of such a hash table is garbage collected, the corresponding entry will be removed. Note that if some datum holds some key strongly, the table will effectively hold that key strongly.

hash-table-entry-type:datum-weak   [variable]
    An entry type for hash tables that hold keys strongly and data weakly. An entry of this type is a weak pair (see Section 10.7.1 [Weak Pairs], page 143) whose weak (car) slot holds the datum of the entry and whose strong (cdr) slot holds the key of the entry. If a datum of such a hash table is garbage collected, all corresponding entries will be removed. Note that if some key holds some datum strongly, the table will effectively hold that datum strongly.

hash-table-entry-type:key/datum-weak   [variable]
    The entry type for hash tables that hold both keys and data weakly. An entry of this type is a weak list, holding both the key and the datum in the weak (car) slot of weak

pairs (see Section 10.7.1 [Weak Pairs], page 143). If either a key or datum of such a
hash table is garbage collected, all corresponding entries will be removed.

`hash-table-entry-type:key-ephemeral`   [variable]

>An entry type for hash tables that hold data ephemerally, keyed by the keys. An
>entry of this type is an ephemeron (see Section 10.7.2 [Ephemerons], page 144) whose
>key is the key of the entry and whose datum is the datum of the entry. If a key of such
>a hash table is garbage collected, the corresponding entry will be removed. Note that
>the table holds all its keys weakly even if some data should hold some keys strongly.

`hash-table-entry-type:datum-ephemeral`   [variable]

>An entry type for hash tables that hold keys ephemerally, keyed by the data. An
>entry of this type is an ephemeron (see Section 10.7.2 [Ephemerons], page 144) whose
>key is the datum of the entry and whose datum is the key of the entry. If a datum
>of such a hash table is garbage collected, all corresponding entries will be removed.
>Note that the table holds all its data weakly even if some keys should hold some data
>strongly.

`hash-table-entry-type:key&datum-ephemeral`   [variable]

>The entry type for hash tables that hold both keys and data ephemerally keyed on each
>other. An entry of this type is a pair of ephemerons (see Section 10.7.2 [Ephemerons],
>page 144), one holding the datum keyed by the key and the other holding the key
>keyed by the datum. If both the key and the datum of any entry of such a hash table
>are garbage collected, the entry will be removed. The table holds all its keys and data
>weakly itself, but will prevent any key or datum from being garbage collected if there
>are strong references to its datum or key, respectively.

Some examples showing how some standard hash-table constructors could have been
defined:

```
(define make-weak-eq-hash-table
  (hash-table/constructor eq-hash-mod eq? #t
    hash-table-entry-type:key-weak))

(define make-equal-hash-table
  (hash-table/constructor equal-hash-mod equal? #t
    hash-table-entry-type:strong))

(define make-string-hash-table
  (hash-table/constructor string-hash-mod string=? #f
    hash-table-entry-type:strong))
```

The following procedure is sometimes useful in conjunction with weak and ephemeral
hash tables. Normally it is not needed, because such hash tables clean themselves automatically as they are used.

`hash-table/clean!` *hash-table*   [procedure]

>If *hash-table* is a type of hash table that holds its keys or data weakly or ephemerally,
>this procedure recovers any space that was being used to record associations for
>objects that have been reclaimed by the garbage collector. Otherwise, this procedure
>does nothing. In either case, it returns an unspecified result.

The following procedures are provided only for backward compatibility. They should be considered **deprecated** and should not be used in new programs.

make-weak-eq-hash-table [*initial-size*]   [procedure]
make-eq-hash-table [*initial-size*]   [procedure]
>   These are aliases of `make-key-weak-eq-hash-table`.

make-weak-eqv-hash-table [*initial-size*]   [procedure]
make-eqv-hash-table [*initial-size*]   [procedure]
>   These are aliases of `make-key-weak-eqv-hash-table`.

strong-hash-table/constructor *key-hash key=?* [*rehash-after-gc?*]   [procedure]
>   Like `hash-table/constructor` but always uses `hash-table-entry-type:strong`. If *rehash-after-gc?* is omitted, it defaults to `#f`.

weak-hash-table/constructor *key-hash key=?* [*rehash-after-gc?*]   [procedure]
>   Like `hash-table/constructor` but always uses `hash-table-entry-type:key-weak`. If *rehash-after-gc?* is omitted, it defaults to `#f`.

11.4.2 Basic Hash Table Operations

The procedures described in this section are the basic operations on hash tables. They provide the functionality most often needed by programmers. Subsequent sections describe other operations that provide additional functionality needed by some applications.

hash-table? *object*   [procedure]
>   Returns `#t` if *object* is a hash table, otherwise returns `#f`.

hash-table/put! *hash-table key datum*   [procedure]
>   Associates *datum* with *key* in *hash-table* and returns an unspecified result. The average time required by this operation is bounded by a constant.

hash-table/get *hash-table key default*   [procedure]
>   Returns the datum associated with *key* in *hash-table*. If there is no association for *key*, *default* is returned. The average time required by this operation is bounded by a constant.

hash-table/remove! *hash-table key*   [procedure]
>   If *hash-table* has an association for *key*, removes it. Returns an unspecified result. The average time required by this operation is bounded by a constant.

hash-table/clear! *hash-table*   [procedure]
>   Removes all associations in *hash-table* and returns an unspecified result. The average and worst-case times required by this operation are bounded by a constant.

hash-table/count *hash-table*   [procedure]
>   Returns the number of associations in *hash-table* as an exact non-negative integer. If *hash-table* does not hold its keys and data strongly, this is a conservative upper bound that may count some associations whose keys or data have recently been reclaimed by the garbage collector. The average and worst-case times required by this operation are bounded by a constant.

hash-table->alist *hash-table*   [procedure]

Returns the contents of *hash-table* as a newly allocated alist. Each element of the alist is a pair (`key . datum`) where *key* is one of the keys of *hash-table*, and *datum* is its associated datum. The average and worst-case times required by this operation are linear in the number of associations in the table.

hash-table/key-list *hash-table*   [procedure]

Returns a newly allocated list of the keys in *hash-table*. The average and worst-case times required by this operation are linear in the number of associations in the table.

hash-table/datum-list *hash-table*   [procedure]

Returns a newly allocated list of the datums in *hash-table*. Each element of the list corresponds to one of the associations in *hash-table*; if the table contains multiple associations with the same datum, so will this list. The average and worst-case times required by this operation are linear in the number of associations in the table.

hash-table/for-each *hash-table procedure*   [procedure]

Procedure must be a procedure of two arguments. Invokes *procedure* once for each association in *hash-table*, passing the association's *key* and *datum* as arguments, in that order. Returns an unspecified result. *Procedure* must not modify *hash-table*, with one exception: it is permitted to call `hash-table/remove!` to remove the association being processed.

The following procedure is useful when there is no sensible default value for `hash-table/get` and the caller must choose between different actions depending on whether there is a datum associated with the key.

hash-table/lookup *hash-table key if-found if-not-found*   [procedure]

If-found must be a procedure of one argument, and *if-not-found* must be a procedure of no arguments. If *hash-table* contains an association for *key*, *if-found* is invoked on the datum of the association. Otherwise, *if-not-found* is invoked with no arguments. In either case, the result yielded by the invoked procedure is returned as the result of `hash-table/lookup` (`hash-table/lookup` *reduces* into the invoked procedure, i.e. calls it tail-recursively). The average time required by this operation is bounded by a constant.

hash-table/modify! *hash-table key default procedure*   [procedure]

Procedure must be a procedure of one argument. Applies *procedure* to the datum associated with *key* in *hash-table* or to *default* if there is no association for *key*, associates the result with *key*, and returns that same result. *Procedure* must not use *hash-table*. The average time required by this operation is bounded by a constant.

hash-table/intern! *hash-table key get-default*   [procedure]

Get-default must be a procedure of no arguments. Ensures that *hash-table* has an association for *key* and returns the associated datum. If *hash-table* did not have a datum associated with *key*, `hash-table/intern!` applies *get-default* to zero arguments to generate one. As with `hash-table/modify!`, *get-default* must not use *hash-table*. The average time required by this operation is bounded by a constant.

11.4.3 Resizing of Hash Tables

Normally, hash tables automatically resize themselves according to need. Because of this, the programmer need not be concerned with management of the table's size. However, some limited control over the table's size is provided, which will be discussed below. This discussion involves two concepts, *usable size* and *physical size*, which we will now define.

The *usable size* of a hash table is the number of associations that the table can hold at a given time. If the number of associations in the table exceeds the usable size, the table will automatically grow, increasing the usable size to a new value that is sufficient to hold the associations.

The *physical size* is an abstract measure of a hash table that specifies how much space is allocated to hold the associations of the table. The physical size is always greater than or equal to the usable size. The physical size is not interesting in itself; it is interesting only for its effect on the performance of the hash table. While the average performance of a hash-table lookup is bounded by a constant, the worst-case performance is not. For a table containing a given number of associations, increasing the physical size of the table decreases the probability that worse-than-average performance will occur.

The physical size of a hash table is statistically related to the number of associations. However, it is possible to place bounds on the physical size, and from this to estimate the amount of space used by the table:

```
(define (hash-table-space-bounds count rehash-size rehash-threshold)
  (let ((tf (/ 1 rehash-threshold)))
    (values (if (exact-integer? rehash-size)
                (- (* count (+ 4 tf))
                   (* tf (+ rehash-size rehash-size)))
                (* count (+ 4 (/ tf (* rehash-size rehash-size)))))
            (* count (+ 4 tf)))))
```

What this formula shows is that, for a "normal" rehash size (that is, not an exact integer), the amount of space used by the hash table is proportional to the number of associations in the table. The constant of proportionality varies statistically, with the low bound being

```
(+ 4 (/ (/ 1 rehash-threshold) (* rehash-size rehash-size)))
```

and the high bound being

```
(+ 4 (/ 1 rehash-threshold))
```

which, for the default values of these parameters, are `4.25` and `5`, respectively. Reducing the rehash size will tighten these bounds, but increases the amount of time spent resizing, so you can see that the rehash size gives some control over the time-space tradeoff of the table.

The programmer can control the size of a hash table by means of three parameters:

- Each table's *initial-size* may be specified when the table is created.

- Each table has a *rehash size* that specifies how the size of the table is changed when it is necessary to grow or shrink the table.

- Each table has a *rehash threshold* that specifies the relationship of the table's physical size to its usable size.

If the programmer knows that the table will initially contain a specific number of items, *initial-size* can be given when the table is created. If *initial-size* is an exact non-negative integer, it specifies the initial usable size of the hash table; the table will not change size until the number of items in the table exceeds *initial-size*, after which automatic resizing is enabled and *initial-size* no longer has any effect. Otherwise, if *initial-size* is not given or is #f, the table is initialized to an unspecified size and automatic resizing is immediately enabled.

The *rehash size* specifies how much to increase the usable size of the hash table when it becomes full. It is either an exact positive integer, or a real number greater than one. If it is an integer, the new size is the sum of the old size and the rehash size. Otherwise, it is a real number, and the new size is the product of the old size and the rehash size. Increasing the rehash size decreases the average cost of an insertion, but increases the average amount of space used by the table. The rehash size of a table may be altered dynamically by the application in order to optimize the resizing of the table; for example, if the table will grow quickly for a known period and afterwards will not change size, performance might be improved by using a large rehash size during the growth phase and a small one during the static phase. The default rehash size of a newly constructed hash table is 2.0.

Warning: The use of an exact positive integer for a rehash size is almost always undesirable; this option is provided solely for compatibility with the Common Lisp hash-table mechanism. The reason for this has to do with the time penalty for resizing the hash table. The time needed to resize a hash table is proportional to the number of associations in the table. This resizing cost is *amortized* across the insertions required to fill the table to the point where it needs to grow again. If the table grows by an amount proportional to the number of associations, then the cost of resizing and the increase in size are both proportional to the number of associations, so the *amortized cost* of an insertion operation is still bounded by a constant. However, if the table grows by a constant amount, this is not true: the amortized cost of an insertion is not bounded by a constant. Thus, using a constant rehash size means that the average cost of an insertion increases proportionally to the number of associations in the hash table.

The *rehash threshold* is a real number, between zero exclusive and one inclusive, that specifies the ratio between a hash table's usable size and its physical size. Decreasing the rehash threshold decreases the probability of worse-than-average insertion, deletion, and lookup times, but increases the physical size of the table for a given usable size. The default rehash threshold of a newly constructed hash table is 1.

hash-table/size *hash-table*   [procedure]
> Returns the usable size of *hash-table* as an exact positive integer. This is the number of associations that *hash-table* can hold before it will grow.

hash-table/rehash-size *hash-table*   [procedure]
> Returns the rehash size of *hash-table*.

set-hash-table/rehash-size! *hash-table x*   [procedure]
> *X* must be either an exact positive integer, or a real number that is greater than one. Sets the rehash size of *hash-table* to *x* and returns an unspecified result. This operation adjusts the "shrink threshold" of the table; the table might shrink if the number of associations is less than the new threshold.

hash-table/rehash-threshold *hash-table*   [procedure]
> Returns the rehash threshold of *hash-table*.

`set-hash-table/rehash-threshold!` *hash-table x*   [procedure]

> *X* must be a real number between zero exclusive and one inclusive. Sets the rehash threshold of *hash-table* to *x* and returns an unspecified result. This operation does not change the usable size of the table, but it usually changes the physical size of the table, which causes the table to be rehashed.

11.4.4 Address Hashing

The procedures described in this section may be used to make very efficient key-hashing procedures for arbitrary objects. All of these procedures are based on *address hashing*, which uses the address of an object as its hash number. The great advantage of address hashing is that converting an arbitrary object to a hash number is extremely fast and takes the same amount of time for any object.

The disadvantage of address hashing is that the garbage collector changes the addresses of most objects. The hash-table implementation compensates for this disadvantage by automatically rehashing tables that use address hashing when garbage collections occur. Thus, in order to use these procedures for key hashing, it is necessary to tell the hash-table implementation (by means of the *rehash-after-gc?* argument to the "constructor-constructor" procedure) that the hash numbers computed by your key-hashing procedure must be recomputed after a garbage collection.

`eq-hash` *object*   [procedure]
`eqv-hash` *object*   [procedure]
`equal-hash` *object*   [procedure]

> These procedures return a hash number for *object*. The result is always a non-negative integer, and in the case of `eq-hash`, a non-negative fixnum. Two objects that are equivalent according to `eq?`, `eqv?`, or `equal?`, respectively, will produce the same hash number when passed as arguments to these procedures, provided that the garbage collector does not run during or between the two calls.

The following procedures are the key-hashing procedures used by the standard address-hash-based hash tables.

`eq-hash-mod` *object modulus*   [procedure]

> This procedure is the key-hashing procedure used by `make-strong-eq-hash-table`.

`eqv-hash-mod` *object modulus*   [procedure]

> This procedure is the key-hashing procedure used by `make-strong-eqv-hash-table`.

`equal-hash-mod` *object modulus*   [procedure]

> This procedure is the key-hashing procedure used by `make-equal-hash-table`.

11.5 Object Hashing

The MIT/GNU Scheme object-hashing facility provides a mechanism for generating a unique hash number for an arbitrary object. This hash number, unlike an object's address, is unchanged by garbage collection. The object-hashing facility is useful in conjunction with hash tables, but it may be used for other things as well. In particular, it is used in the generation of the written representation for many objects (see Section 14.7 [Custom Output], page 200).

All of these procedures accept an optional argument called *table*; this table contains the object-integer associations. If given, this argument must be an object-hash table as constructed by `hash-table/make` (see below). If not given, a default table is used.

hash *object* [*table*]   [procedure]

> `hash` associates an exact non-negative integer with *object* and returns that integer. If `hash` was previously called with *object* as its argument, the integer returned is the same as was returned by the previous call. `hash` guarantees that distinct objects (in the sense of `eq?`) are associated with distinct integers.

unhash *k* [*table*]   [procedure]

> `unhash` takes an exact non-negative integer *k* and returns the object associated with that integer. If there is no object associated with *k*, or if the object previously associated with *k* has been reclaimed by the garbage collector, an error of type `condition-type:bad-range-argument` is signalled. In other words, if `hash` previously returned *k* for some object, and that object has not been reclaimed, it is the value of the call to `unhash`.

An object that is passed to `hash` as an argument is not protected from being reclaimed by the garbage collector. If all other references to that object are eliminated, the object will be reclaimed. Subsequently calling `unhash` with the hash number of the (now reclaimed) object will signal an error.

```
(define x (cons 0 0))           ⇒   unspecified
(hash x)                        ⇒   77
(eqv? (hash x) (hash x))        ⇒   #t
(define x 0)                    ⇒   unspecified
(gc-flip)                       ;force a garbage collection
(unhash 77)                     error
```

object-hashed? *object* [*table*]   [procedure]

> This predicate is true if *object* has an associated hash number. Otherwise it is false.

valid-hash-number? *k* [*table*]   [procedure]

> This predicate is true if *k* is the hash number associated with some object. Otherwise it is false.

The following two procedures provide a lower-level interface to the object-hashing mechanism.

object-hash *object* [*table* [*insert?*]]   [procedure]

> `object-hash` is like `hash`, except that it accepts an additional optional argument, *insert?*. If *insert?* is supplied and is `#f`, `object-hash` will return an integer for *object* only if there is already an association in the table; otherwise, it will return `#f`. If *insert?* is not supplied, or is not `#f`, `object-hash` always returns an integer, creating an association in the table if necessary.

> `object-hash` additionally treats `#f` differently than does `hash`. Calling `object-hash` with `#f` as its argument will return an integer that, when passed to `unhash`, will signal an error rather than returning `#f`. Likewise, `valid-hash-number?` will return `#f` for this integer.

`object-unhash` *k* [*table*]   [procedure]
>   `object-unhash` is like `unhash`, except that when *k* is not associated with any object
>   or was previously associated with an object that has been reclaimed, `object-unhash`
>   returns `#f`. This means that there is an ambiguity in the value returned by
>   `object-unhash`: if `#f` is returned, there is no way to tell if *k* is associated with `#f`
>   or is not associated with any object at all.

Finally, this procedure makes new object-hash tables:

`hash-table/make`   [procedure]
>   This procedure creates and returns a new, empty object-hash table that is suitable
>   for use as the optional *table* argument to the above procedures. The returned table
>   contains no associations.

11.6 Red-Black Trees

Balanced binary trees are a useful data structure for maintaining large sets of associations
whose keys are ordered. While most applications involving large association sets should use
hash tables, some applications can benefit from the use of binary trees. Binary trees have
two advantages over hash tables:

- The contents of a binary tree can be converted to an alist, sorted by key, in time
  proportional to the number of associations in the tree. A hash table can be converted
  into an unsorted alist in linear time; sorting it requires additional time.

- Two binary trees can be compared for equality in linear time. Hash tables, on the other
  hand, cannot be compared at all; they must be converted to alists before comparison
  can be done, and alist comparison is quadratic unless the alists are sorted.

MIT/GNU Scheme provides an implementation of *red-black* trees. The red-black tree-
balancing algorithm provides generally good performance because it doesn't try to keep the
tree very closely balanced. At any given node in the tree, one side of the node can be twice
as high as the other in the worst case. With typical data the tree will remain fairly well
balanced anyway.

A red-black tree takes space that is proportional to the number of associations in the
tree. For the current implementation, the constant of proportionality is eight words per
association.

Red-black trees hold their keys *strongly*. In other words, if a red-black tree contains an
association for a given key, that key cannot be reclaimed by the garbage collector.

The red-black tree implementation is a run-time-loadable option. To use red-black trees,
execute

```
(load-option 'rb-tree)
```

once before calling any of the procedures defined here.

`make-rb-tree` *key=?* *key<?*   [procedure]
>   This procedure creates and returns a newly allocated red-black tree. The tree con-
>   tains no associations. *Key=?* and *key<?* are predicates that compare two keys and
>   determine whether they are equal to or less than one another, respectively. For any
>   two keys, at most one of these predicates is true.

rb-tree? *object*   [procedure]
  Returns #t if *object* is a red-black tree, otherwise returns #f.

rb-tree/insert! *rb-tree key datum*   [procedure]
  Associates *datum* with *key* in *rb-tree* and returns an unspecified value. If *rb-tree*
  already has an association for *key*, that association is replaced. The average and
  worst-case times required by this operation are proportional to the logarithm of the
  number of assocations in *rb-tree*.

rb-tree/lookup *rb-tree key default*   [procedure]
  Returns the datum associated with *key* in *rb-tree*. If *rb-tree* doesn't contain an
  association for *key*, *default* is returned. The average and worst-case times required
  by this operation are proportional to the logarithm of the number of assocations in
  rb-tree.

rb-tree/delete! *rb-tree key*   [procedure]
  If *rb-tree* contains an association for *key*, removes it. Returns an unspecified value.
  The average and worst-case times required by this operation are proportional to the
  logarithm of the number of assocations in *rb-tree*.

rb-tree->alist *rb-tree*   [procedure]
  Returns the contents of *rb-tree* as a newly allocated alist. Each element of the alist
  is a pair (**key . datum**) where *key* is one of the keys of *rb-tree*, and *datum* is its
  associated datum. The alist is sorted by key according to the *key<?* argument used
  to construct *rb-tree*. The time required by this operation is proportional to the
  number of associations in the tree.

rb-tree/key-list *rb-tree*   [procedure]
  Returns a newly allocated list of the keys in *rb-tree*. The list is sorted by key according
  to the *key<?* argument used to construct *rb-tree*. The time required by this operation
  is proportional to the number of associations in the tree.

rb-tree/datum-list *rb-tree*   [procedure]
  Returns a newly allocated list of the datums in *rb-tree*. Each element of the list
  corresponds to one of the associations in *rb-tree*, so if the tree contains multiple
  associations with the same datum, so will this list. The list is sorted by the keys of
  the associations, even though they do not appear in the result. The time required by
  this operation is proportional to the number of associations in the tree.

  This procedure is equivalent to:

```
(lambda (rb-tree) (map cdr (rb-tree->alist rb-tree)))
```

rb-tree/equal? *rb-tree-1 rb-tree-2 datum=?*   [procedure]
  Compares *rb-tree-1* and *rb-tree-2* for equality, returning #t iff they are equal and
  #f otherwise. The trees must have been constructed with the same equality and
  order predicates (same in the sense of eq?). The keys of the trees are compared
  using the *key=?* predicate used to build the trees, while the datums of the trees are
  compared using the equivalence predicate *datum=?*. The worst-case time required by
  this operation is proportional to the number of associations in the tree.

rb-tree/empty? *rb-tree*   [procedure]

Returns #t iff *rb-tree* contains no associations. Otherwise returns #f.

rb-tree/size *rb-tree*   [procedure]

Returns the number of associations in *rb-tree*, an exact non-negative integer. The average and worst-case times required by this operation are proportional to the number of associations in the tree.

rb-tree/height *rb-tree*   [procedure]

Returns the height of *rb-tree*, an exact non-negative integer. This is the length of the longest path from a leaf of the tree to the root. The average and worst-case times required by this operation are proportional to the number of associations in the tree.

The returned value satisfies the following:

```
(lambda (rb-tree)
  (let ((size (rb-tree/size rb-tree))
        (lg (lambda (x) (/ (log x) (log 2)))))
    (<= (lg size)
        (rb-tree/height rb-tree)
        (* 2 (lg (+ size 1)))))))
```

rb-tree/copy *rb-tree*   [procedure]

Returns a newly allocated copy of *rb-tree*. The copy is identical to *rb-tree* in all respects, except that changes to *rb-tree* do not affect the copy, and vice versa. The time required by this operation is proportional to the number of associations in the tree.

alist->rb-tree *alist key=? key<?*   [procedure]

Returns a newly allocated red-black tree that contains the same associations as *alist*. This procedure is equivalent to:

```
(lambda (alist key=? key<?)
  (let ((tree (make-rb-tree key=? key<?)))
    (for-each (lambda (association)
                (rb-tree/insert! tree
                                 (car association)
                                 (cdr association)))
              alist)
    tree))
```

The following operations provide access to the smallest and largest members in a red/black tree. They are useful for implementing priority queues.

rb-tree/min *rb-tree default*   [procedure]

Returns the smallest key in *rb-tree*, or *default* if the tree is empty.

rb-tree/min-datum *rb-tree default*   [procedure]

Returns the datum associated with the smallest key in *rb-tree*, or *default* if the tree is empty.

rb-tree/min-pair *rb-tree*   [procedure]
> Finds the smallest key in *rb-tree* and returns a pair containing that key and its associated datum. If the tree is empty, returns **#f**.

rb-tree/max *rb-tree default*   [procedure]
> Returns the largest key in *rb-tree*, or *default* if the tree is empty.

rb-tree/max-datum *rb-tree default*   [procedure]
> Returns the datum associated with the largest key in *rb-tree*, or *default* if the tree is empty.

rb-tree/max-pair *rb-tree*   [procedure]
> Finds the largest key in *rb-tree* and returns a pair containing that key and its associated datum. If the tree is empty, returns **#f**.

rb-tree/delete-min! *rb-tree default*   [procedure]
rb-tree/delete-min-datum! *rb-tree default*   [procedure]
rb-tree/delete-min-pair! *rb-tree*   [procedure]
rb-tree/delete-max! *rb-tree default*   [procedure]
rb-tree/delete-max-datum! *rb-tree default*   [procedure]
rb-tree/delete-max-pair! *rb-tree*   [procedure]
> These operations are exactly like the accessors above, in that they return information associated with the smallest or largest key, except that they simultaneously delete that key.

11.7 Weight-Balanced Trees

Balanced binary trees are a useful data structure for maintaining large sets of ordered objects or sets of associations whose keys are ordered. MIT/GNU Scheme has a comprehensive implementation of weight-balanced binary trees which has several advantages over the other data structures for large aggregates:

- In addition to the usual element-level operations like insertion, deletion and lookup, there is a full complement of collection-level operations, like set intersection, set union and subset test, all of which are implemented with good orders of growth in time and space. This makes weight-balanced trees ideal for rapid prototyping of functionally derived specifications.

- An element in a tree may be indexed by its position under the ordering of the keys, and the ordinal position of an element may be determined, both with reasonable efficiency.

- Operations to find and remove minimum element make weight-balanced trees simple to use for priority queues.

- The implementation is *functional* rather than *imperative*. This means that operations like 'inserting' an association in a tree do not destroy the old tree, in much the same way that (+ 1 x) modifies neither the constant 1 nor the value bound to x. The trees are referentially transparent thus the programmer need not worry about copying the trees. Referential transparency allows space efficiency to be achieved by sharing subtrees.

These features make weight-balanced trees suitable for a wide range of applications, especially those that require large numbers of sets or discrete maps. Applications that have a few global databases and/or concentrate on element-level operations like insertion and lookup are probably better off using hash tables or red-black trees.

The *size* of a tree is the number of associations that it contains. Weight-balanced binary trees are balanced to keep the sizes of the subtrees of each node within a constant factor of each other. This ensures logarithmic times for single-path operations (like lookup and insertion). A weight-balanced tree takes space that is proportional to the number of associations in the tree. For the current implementation, the constant of proportionality is six words per association.

Weight-balanced trees can be used as an implementation for either discrete sets or discrete maps (associations). Sets are implemented by ignoring the datum that is associated with the key. Under this scheme if an association exists in the tree this indicates that the key of the association is a member of the set. Typically a value such as (), #t or #f is associated with the key.

Many operations can be viewed as computing a result that, depending on whether the tree arguments are thought of as sets or maps, is known by two different names. An example is `wt-tree/member?`, which, when regarding the tree argument as a set, computes the set membership operation, but, when regarding the tree as a discrete map, `wt-tree/member?` is the predicate testing if the map is defined at an element in its domain. Most names in this package have been chosen based on interpreting the trees as sets, hence the name `wt-tree/member?` rather than `wt-tree/defined-at?`.

The weight-balanced tree implementation is a run-time-loadable option. To use weight-balanced trees, execute

```
(load-option 'wt-tree)
```

once before calling any of the procedures defined here.

11.7.1 Construction of Weight-Balanced Trees

Binary trees require there to be a total order on the keys used to arrange the elements in the tree. Weight-balanced trees are organized by *types*, where the type is an object encapsulating the ordering relation. Creating a tree is a two-stage process. First a tree type must be created from the predicate that gives the ordering. The tree type is then used for making trees, either empty or singleton trees or trees from other aggregate structures like association lists. Once created, a tree 'knows' its type and the type is used to test compatibility between trees in operations taking two trees. Usually a small number of tree types are created at the beginning of a program and used many times throughout the program's execution.

`make-wt-tree-type` *key<?*   [procedure]

  This procedure creates and returns a new tree type based on the ordering predicate *key<?*. *Key<?* must be a total ordering, having the property that for all key values a, b and c:

```
(key<? a a)                          ⇒ #f
(and (key<? a b) (key<? b a))        ⇒ #f
(if (and (key<? a b) (key<? b c))
    (key<? a c)
    #t)                              ⇒ #t
```

Two key values are assumed to be equal if neither is less than the other by *key<?*.

Each call to `make-wt-tree-type` returns a distinct value, and trees are only compatible if their tree types are `eq?`. A consequence is that trees that are intended to be used in binary-tree operations must all be created with a tree type originating from the same call to `make-wt-tree-type`.

`number-wt-type`   [variable]
> A standard tree type for trees with numeric keys. `Number-wt-type` could have been defined by
>
>   (define number-wt-type (make-wt-tree-type <))

`string-wt-type`   [variable]
> A standard tree type for trees with string keys. `String-wt-type` could have been defined by
>
>   (define string-wt-type (make-wt-tree-type string<?))

`make-wt-tree` *wt-tree-type*   [procedure]
> This procedure creates and returns a newly allocated weight-balanced tree. The tree is empty, i.e. it contains no associations. *Wt-tree-type* is a weight-balanced tree type obtained by calling `make-wt-tree-type`; the returned tree has this type.

`singleton-wt-tree` *wt-tree-type key datum*   [procedure]
> This procedure creates and returns a newly allocated weight-balanced tree. The tree contains a single association, that of *datum* with *key*. *Wt-tree-type* is a weight-balanced tree type obtained by calling `make-wt-tree-type`; the returned tree has this type.

`alist->wt-tree` *tree-type alist*   [procedure]
> Returns a newly allocated weight-balanced tree that contains the same associations as *alist*. This procedure is equivalent to:
>
>   (lambda (type alist)
>   (let ((tree (make-wt-tree type)))
>   (for-each (lambda (association)
>   (wt-tree/add! tree
>   (car association)
>   (cdr association)))
>   alist)
>   tree))

11.7.2 Basic Operations on Weight-Balanced Trees

This section describes the basic tree operations on weight-balanced trees. These operations are the usual tree operations for insertion, deletion and lookup, some predicates and a procedure for determining the number of associations in a tree.

`wt-tree?` *object*   [procedure]
> Returns `#t` if *object* is a weight-balanced tree, otherwise returns `#f`.

`wt-tree/empty?` *wt-tree*   [procedure]
> Returns `#t` if *wt-tree* contains no associations, otherwise returns `#f`.

wt-tree/size *wt-tree*   [procedure]

> Returns the number of associations in *wt-tree*, an exact non-negative integer. This operation takes constant time.

wt-tree/add *wt-tree key datum*   [procedure]

> Returns a new tree containing all the associations in *wt-tree* and the association of *datum* with *key*. If *wt-tree* already had an association for *key*, the new association overrides the old. The average and worst-case times required by this operation are proportional to the logarithm of the number of associations in *wt-tree*.

wt-tree/add! *wt-tree key datum*   [procedure]

> Associates *datum* with *key* in *wt-tree* and returns an unspecified value. If *wt-tree* already has an association for *key*, that association is replaced. The average and worst-case times required by this operation are proportional to the logarithm of the number of associations in *wt-tree*.

wt-tree/member? *key wt-tree*   [procedure]

> Returns #t if *wt-tree* contains an association for *key*, otherwise returns #f. The average and worst-case times required by this operation are proportional to the logarithm of the number of associations in *wt-tree*.

wt-tree/lookup *wt-tree key default*   [procedure]

> Returns the datum associated with *key* in *wt-tree*. If *wt-tree* doesn't contain an association for *key*, *default* is returned. The average and worst-case times required by this operation are proportional to the logarithm of the number of associations in *wt-tree*.

wt-tree/delete *wt-tree key*   [procedure]

> Returns a new tree containing all the associations in *wt-tree*, except that if *wt-tree* contains an association for *key*, it is removed from the result. The average and worst-case times required by this operation are proportional to the logarithm of the number of associations in *wt-tree*.

wt-tree/delete! *wt-tree key*   [procedure]

> If *wt-tree* contains an association for *key* the association is removed. Returns an unspecified value. The average and worst-case times required by this operation are proportional to the logarithm of the number of associations in *wt-tree*.

11.7.3 Advanced Operations on Weight-Balanced Trees

In the following the *size* of a tree is the number of associations that the tree contains, and a *smaller* tree contains fewer associations.

wt-tree/split< *wt-tree bound*   [procedure]

> Returns a new tree containing all and only the associations in *wt-tree* that have a key that is less than *bound* in the ordering relation of the tree type of *wt-tree*. The average and worst-case times required by this operation are proportional to the logarithm of the size of *wt-tree*.

wt-tree/split> *wt-tree bound*   [procedure]

Returns a new tree containing all and only the associations in *wt-tree* that have a key that is greater than *bound* in the ordering relation of the tree type of *wt-tree*. The average and worst-case times required by this operation are proportional to the logarithm of the size of *wt-tree*.

wt-tree/union *wt-tree-1 wt-tree-2*   [procedure]

Returns a new tree containing all the associations from both trees. This operation is asymmetric: when both trees have an association for the same key, the returned tree associates the datum from *wt-tree-2* with the key. Thus if the trees are viewed as discrete maps then **wt-tree/union** computes the map override of *wt-tree-1* by *wt-tree-2*. If the trees are viewed as sets the result is the set union of the arguments. The worst-case time required by this operation is proportional to the sum of the sizes of both trees. If the minimum key of one tree is greater than the maximum key of the other tree then the worst-case time required is proportional to the logarithm of the size of the larger tree.

wt-tree/intersection *wt-tree-1 wt-tree-2*   [procedure]

Returns a new tree containing all and only those associations from *wt-tree-1* that have keys appearing as the key of an association in *wt-tree-2*. Thus the associated data in the result are those from *wt-tree-1*. If the trees are being used as sets the result is the set intersection of the arguments. As a discrete map operation, **wt-tree/intersection** computes the domain restriction of *wt-tree-1* to (the domain of) *wt-tree-2*. The worst-case time required by this operation is proportional to the sum of the sizes of the trees.

wt-tree/difference *wt-tree-1 wt-tree-2*   [procedure]

Returns a new tree containing all and only those associations from *wt-tree-1* that have keys that *do not* appear as the key of an association in *wt-tree-2*. If the trees are viewed as sets the result is the asymmetric set difference of the arguments. As a discrete map operation, it computes the domain restriction of *wt-tree-1* to the complement of (the domain of) *wt-tree-2*. The worst-case time required by this operation is proportional to the sum of the sizes of the trees.

wt-tree/subset? *wt-tree-1 wt-tree-2*   [procedure]

Returns **#t** iff the key of each association in *wt-tree-1* is the key of some association in *wt-tree-2*, otherwise returns **#f**. Viewed as a set operation, **wt-tree/subset?** is the improper subset predicate. A proper subset predicate can be constructed:

```
(define (proper-subset? s1 s2)
  (and (wt-tree/subset? s1 s2)
       (< (wt-tree/size s1) (wt-tree/size s2)))))
```

As a discrete map operation, **wt-tree/subset?** is the subset test on the domain(s) of the map(s). In the worst-case the time required by this operation is proportional to the size of *wt-tree-1*.

wt-tree/set-equal? *wt-tree-1 wt-tree-2*   [procedure]

Returns **#t** iff for every association in *wt-tree-1* there is an association in *wt-tree-2* that has the same key, and *vice versa*.

Viewing the arguments as sets, `wt-tree/set-equal?` is the set equality predicate. As a map operation it determines if two maps are defined on the same domain.

This procedure is equivalent to

```
(lambda (wt-tree-1 wt-tree-2)
  (and (wt-tree/subset? wt-tree-1 wt-tree-2
       (wt-tree/subset? wt-tree-2 wt-tree-1)))
```

In the worst case the time required by this operation is proportional to the size of the smaller tree.

`wt-tree/fold` *combiner initial wt-tree*   [procedure]

This procedure reduces *wt-tree* by combining all the associations, using an reverse in-order traversal, so the associations are visited in reverse order. *Combiner* is a procedure of three arguments: a key, a datum and the accumulated result so far. Provided *combiner* takes time bounded by a constant, `wt-tree/fold` takes time proportional to the size of *wt-tree*.

A sorted association list can be derived simply:

```
(wt-tree/fold (lambda (key datum list)
                (cons (cons key datum) list))
              '()
              wt-tree))
```

The data in the associations can be summed like this:

```
(wt-tree/fold (lambda (key datum sum) (+ sum datum))
              0
              wt-tree)
```

`wt-tree/for-each` *action wt-tree*   [procedure]

This procedure traverses *wt-tree* in order, applying *action* to each association. The associations are processed in increasing order of their keys. *Action* is a procedure of two arguments that takes the key and datum respectively of the association. Provided *action* takes time bounded by a constant, `wt-tree/for-each` takes time proportional to the size of *wt-tree*. The example prints the tree:

```
(wt-tree/for-each (lambda (key value)
                    (display (list key value)))
                  wt-tree))
```

`wt-tree/union-merge` *wt-tree-1 wt-tree-2 merge*   [procedure]

Returns a new tree containing all the associations from both trees. If both trees have an association for the same key, the datum associated with that key in the result tree is computed by applying the procedure *merge* to the key, the value from *wt-tree-1* and the value from *wt-tree-2*. *Merge* is of the form

```
(lambda (key datum-1 datum-2) ...)
```

If some key occurs only in one tree, that association will appear in the result tree without being processed by *merge*, so for this operation to make sense, either *merge* must have both a right and left identity that correspond to the association being absent in one of the trees, or some guarantee must be made, for example, all the keys in one tree are known to occur in the other.

These are all reasonable procedures for *merge*

```
(lambda (key val1 val2) (+ val1 val2))
(lambda (key val1 val2) (append val1 val2))
(lambda (key val1 val2) (wt-tree/union val1 val2))
```

However, a procedure like

```
(lambda (key val1 val2) (- val1 val2))
```

would result in a subtraction of the data for all associations with keys occuring in both trees but associations with keys occuring in only the second tree would be copied, not negated, as is presumably be intent. The programmer might ensure that this never happens.

This procedure has the same time behavior as `wt-tree/union` but with a slightly worse constant factor. Indeed, `wt-tree/union` might have been defined like this:

```
(define (wt-tree/union tree1 tree2)
  (wt-tree/union-merge tree1 tree2
                       (lambda (key val1 val2) val2)))
```

The *merge* procedure takes the *key* as a parameter in case the data are not independent of the key.

11.7.4 Indexing Operations on Weight-Balanced Trees

Weight-balanced trees support operations that view the tree as sorted sequence of associations. Elements of the sequence can be accessed by position, and the position of an element in the sequence can be determined, both in logarthmic time.

wt-tree/index *wt-tree index* [procedure]
wt-tree/index-datum *wt-tree index* [procedure]
wt-tree/index-pair *wt-tree index* [procedure]

Returns the 0-based *index*th association of *wt-tree* in the sorted sequence under the tree's ordering relation on the keys. `wt-tree/index` returns the *index*th key, `wt-tree/index-datum` returns the datum associated with the *index*th key and `wt-tree/index-pair` returns a new pair (*key . datum*) which is the `cons` of the *index*th key and its datum. The average and worst-case times required by this operation are proportional to the logarithm of the number of associations in the tree.

These operations signal a condition of type `condition-type:bad-range-argument` if *index*<0 or if *index* is greater than or equal to the number of associations in the tree. If the tree is empty, they signal an anonymous error.

Indexing can be used to find the median and maximum keys in the tree as follows:

```
median:  (wt-tree/index wt-tree
                        (quotient (wt-tree/size wt-tree)
                                  2))

maximum: (wt-tree/index wt-tree
                        (- (wt-tree/size wt-tree)
                           1))
```

wt-tree/rank *wt-tree key* [procedure]

Determines the 0-based position of *key* in the sorted sequence of the keys under the tree's ordering relation, or `#f` if the tree has no association with for *key*. This procedure returns either an exact non-negative integer or #f. The average and worst-case times required by this operation are proportional to the logarithm of the number of associations in the tree.

wt-tree/min *wt-tree*   [procedure]
wt-tree/min-datum *wt-tree*   [procedure]
wt-tree/min-pair *wt-tree*   [procedure]

Returns the association of *wt-tree* that has the least key under the tree's ordering relation. wt-tree/min returns the least key, wt-tree/min-datum returns the datum associated with the least key and wt-tree/min-pair returns a new pair (key . datum) which is the cons of the minimum key and its datum. The average and worst-case times required by this operation are proportional to the logarithm of the number of associations in the tree.

These operations signal an error if the tree is empty. They could have been written

```
(define (wt-tree/min tree)
  (wt-tree/index tree 0))
(define (wt-tree/min-datum tree)
  (wt-tree/index-datum tree 0))
(define (wt-tree/min-pair tree)
  (wt-tree/index-pair tree 0))
```

wt-tree/delete-min *wt-tree*   [procedure]

Returns a new tree containing all of the associations in *wt-tree* except the association with the least key under the *wt-tree*'s ordering relation. An error is signalled if the tree is empty. The average and worst-case times required by this operation are proportional to the logarithm of the number of associations in the tree. This operation is equivalent to

```
(wt-tree/delete wt-tree (wt-tree/min wt-tree))
```

wt-tree/delete-min! *wt-tree*   [procedure]

Removes the association with the least key under the *wt-tree*'s ordering relation. An error is signalled if the tree is empty. The average and worst-case times required by this operation are proportional to the logarithm of the number of associations in the tree. This operation is equivalent to

```
(wt-tree/delete! wt-tree (wt-tree/min wt-tree))
```

12 Procedures

Procedures are created by evaluating `lambda` expressions (see Section 2.1 [Lambda Expressions], page 15); the `lambda` may either be explicit or may be implicit as in a "procedure `define`" (see Section 2.4 [Definitions], page 20). Also there are special built-in procedures, called *primitive procedures*, such as `car`; these procedures are not written in Scheme but in the language used to implement the Scheme system. MIT/GNU Scheme also provides *application hooks*, which support the construction of data structures that act like procedures.

In MIT/GNU Scheme, the written representation of a procedure tells you the type of the procedure (compiled, interpreted, or primitive):

```
pp
      ⇒  #[compiled-procedure 56 ("pp" #x2) #x10 #x307578]
(lambda (x) x)
      ⇒  #[compound-procedure 57]
(define (foo x) x)
foo
      ⇒  #[compound-procedure 58 foo]
car
      ⇒  #[primitive-procedure car]
(call-with-current-continuation (lambda (x) x))
      ⇒  #[continuation 59]
```

Note that interpreted procedures are called "compound" procedures (strictly speaking, compiled procedures are also compound procedures). The written representation makes this distinction for historical reasons, and may eventually change.

12.1 Procedure Operations

`apply` *procedure object object ...*   [procedure]
> Calls *procedure* with the elements of the following list as arguments:
>
> > (`cons*` *object object ...*)
>
> The initial *objects* may be any objects, but the last *object* (there must be at least one *object*) must be a list.
>
> ```
> (apply + (list 3 4 5 6))           ⇒   18
> (apply + 3 4 '(5 6))               ⇒   18
>
> (define compose
>   (lambda (f g)
>     (lambda args
>       (f (apply g args)))))
> ((compose sqrt *) 12 75)           ⇒   30
> ```

`procedure?` *object*   [procedure]
> Returns #t if *object* is a procedure; otherwise returns #f. If #t is returned, exactly one of the following predicates is satisfied by *object*: `compiled-procedure?`, `compound-procedure?`, or `primitive-procedure?`.

`compiled-procedure?` *object*   [procedure]
> Returns #t if *object* is a compiled procedure; otherwise returns #f.

`compound-procedure?` *object*   [procedure]
> Returns #t if *object* is a compound (i.e. interpreted) procedure; otherwise returns #f.

`primitive-procedure?` *object*   [procedure]
> Returns #t if *object* is a primitive procedure; otherwise returns #f.

`procedure-environment` *procedure*   [procedure]
> Returns the closing environment of *procedure*. Signals an error if *procedure* is a primitive procedure, or if *procedure* is a compiled procedure for which the debugging information is unavailable.

12.2 Arity

Each procedure has an *arity*, which is the minimum and (optionally) maximum number of arguments that it will accept. MIT/GNU Scheme provides an abstraction that represents arity, and tests for the apparent arity of a procedure.

Arity objects come in two forms: the simple form, an exact non-negative integer, represents a fixed number of arguments. The general form is a pair whose `car` represents the minimum number of arguments and whose `cdr` is the maximum number of arguments.

`make-procedure-arity` *min* [*max* [*simple-ok?*]]   [procedure]
> Returns an arity object made from *min* and *max*. *Min* must be an exact non-negative integer. *Max* must be an exact non-negative integer at least as large as *min*. Alternatively, *max* may be omitted or given as '#f', which represents an arity with no upper bound.
>
> If *simple-ok?* is true, the returned arity is in the simple form (an exact non-negative integer) when possible, and otherwise is always in the general form. *Simple-ok?* defaults to '#f'.

`procedure-arity?` *object*   [procedure]
> Returns '#t' if *object* is an arity object, and '#f' otherwise.

`guarantee-procedure-arity` *object caller*   [procedure]
> Signals an error if *object* is not an arity object. *Caller* is a symbol that is printed as part of the error message and is intended to be the name of the procedure where the error occurs.

`procedure-arity-min` *arity*   [procedure]
`procedure-arity-max` *arity*   [procedure]
> Return the lower and upper bounds of *arity*, respectively.

The following procedures test for the apparent arity of a procedure. The results of the test may be less restrictive than the effect of calling the procedure. In other words, these procedures may indicate that the procedure will accept a given number of arguments, but if you call the procedure it may signal a `condition-type:wrong-number-of-arguments` error. For example, here is a procedure that appears to accept any number of arguments, but when called will signal an error if the number of arguments is not one:

```
(lambda arguments (apply car arguments))
```

`procedure-arity` *procedure*   [procedure]

Returns the arity that *procedure* accepts. The result may be in either simple or general form.

```
(procedure-arity (lambda () 3))        ⇒  (0 . 0)
(procedure-arity (lambda (x) x))       ⇒  (1 . 1)
(procedure-arity car)                  ⇒  (1 . 1)
(procedure-arity (lambda x x))         ⇒  (0 . #f)
(procedure-arity (lambda (x . y) x))   ⇒  (1 . #f)
(procedure-arity (lambda (x #!optional y) x))
                                       ⇒  (1 . 2)
```

`procedure-arity-valid?` *procedure arity*   [procedure]

Returns '#t' if *procedure* accepts *arity*, and '#f' otherwise.

`procedure-of-arity?` *object arity*   [procedure]

Returns '#t' if *object* is a procedure that accepts *arity*, and '#f' otherwise. Equivalent to:

```
(and (procedure? object)
     (procedure-arity-valid? object arity))
```

`guarantee-procedure-of-arity` *object arity caller*   [procedure]

Signals an error if *object* is not a procedure accepting *arity*. *Caller* is a symbol that is printed as part of the error message and is intended to be the name of the procedure where the error occurs.

`thunk?` *object*   [procedure]

Returns '#t' if *object* is a procedure that accepts zero arguments, and '#f' otherwise. Equivalent to:

```
(procedure-of-arity? object 0)
```

`guarantee-thunk` *object caller*   [procedure]

Signals an error if *object* is not a procedure accepting zero arguments. *Caller* is a symbol that is printed as part of the error message and is intended to be the name of the procedure where the error occurs.

12.3 Primitive Procedures

`make-primitive-procedure` *name* [*arity*]   [procedure]

Name must be a symbol. *Arity* must be an exact non-negative integer, -1, #f, or #t; if not supplied it defaults to #f. Returns the primitive procedure called *name*. May perform further actions depending on *arity*:

#f   If the primitive procedure is not implemented, signals an error.

#t   If the primitive procedure is not implemented, returns #f.

integer If the primitive procedure is implemented, signals an error if its arity is not equal to *arity*. If the primitive procedure is not implemented, returns an unimplemented primitive procedure object that accepts *arity* arguments. An *arity* of -1 means it accepts any number of arguments.

primitive-procedure-name *primitive-procedure*   [procedure]
>   Returns the name of *primitive-procedure*, a symbol.

>   (primitive-procedure-name car)   ⇒   car

implemented-primitive-procedure? *primitive-procedure*   [procedure]
>   Returns #t if *primitive-procedure* is implemented; otherwise returns #f. Useful be-
>   cause the code that implements a particular primitive procedure is not necessarily
>   linked into the executable Scheme program.

12.4 Continuations

call-with-current-continuation *procedure*   [procedure]
>   *Procedure* must be a procedure of one argument. Packages up the current continua-
>   tion (see below) as an *escape procedure* and passes it as an argument to *procedure*.
>   The escape procedure is a Scheme procedure of one argument that, if it is later passed
>   a value, will ignore whatever continuation is in effect at that later time and will give
>   the value instead to the continuation that was in effect when the escape procedure
>   was created. The escape procedure created by call-with-current-continuation
>   has unlimited extent just like any other procedure in Scheme. It may be stored in
>   variables or data structures and may be called as many times as desired.

>   The following examples show only the most common uses of this procedure. If all real
>   programs were as simple as these examples, there would be no need for a procedure
>   with the power of call-with-current-continuation.

```
(call-with-current-continuation
  (lambda (exit)
    (for-each (lambda (x)
                (if (negative? x)
                    (exit x)))
              '(54 0 37 -3 245 19))
    #t))                                      ⇒   -3


(define list-length
  (lambda (obj)
    (call-with-current-continuation
      (lambda (return)
        (letrec ((r
                  (lambda (obj)
                    (cond ((null? obj) 0)
                          ((pair? obj) (+ (r (cdr obj)) 1))
                          (else (return #f))))))
          (r obj))))))
(list-length '(1 2 3 4))                      ⇒   4
(list-length '(a b . c))                      ⇒   #f
```

A common use of call-with-current-continuation is for structured, non-local
exits from loops or procedure bodies, but in fact call-with-current-continuation
is quite useful for implementing a wide variety of advanced control structures.

Whenever a Scheme expression is evaluated a continuation exists that wants the result of the expression. The continuation represents an entire (default) future for the computation. If the expression is evaluated at top level, for example, the continuation will take the result, print it on the screen, prompt for the next input, evaluate it, and so on forever. Most of the time the continuation includes actions specified by user code, as in a continuation that will take the result, multiply it by the value stored in a local variable, add seven, and give the answer to the top-level continuation to be printed. Normally these ubiquitous continuations are hidden behind the scenes and programmers don't think much about them. On the rare occasions that you may need to deal explicitly with continuations, `call-with-current-continuation` lets you do so by creating a procedure that acts just like the current continuation.

`continuation?` *object*   [procedure]
>   Returns `#t` if *object* is a continuation; otherwise returns `#f`.

`within-continuation` *continuation thunk*   [procedure]
>   *Thunk* must be a procedure of no arguments. Conceptually, `within-continuation` invokes *continuation* on the result of invoking *thunk*, but *thunk* is executed in the dynamic context of *continuation*. In other words, the "current" continuation is abandoned before *thunk* is invoked.

`dynamic-wind` *before thunk after*   [procedure]
>   Calls *thunk* without arguments, returning the result(s) of this call. *Before* and *after* are called, also without arguments, as required by the following rules (note that in the absence of calls to continuations captured using `call-with-current-continuation` the three arguments are called once each, in order). *Before* is called whenever execution enters the dynamic extent of the call to *thunk* and *after* is called whenever it exits that dynamic extent. The dynamic extent of a procedure call is the period between when the call is initiated and when it returns. In Scheme, because of `call-with-current-continuation`, the dynamic extent of a call may not be a single, connected time period. It is defined as follows:
>
>   - The dynamic extent is entered when execution of the body of the called procedure begins.
>   - The dynamic extent is also entered when execution is not within the dynamic extent and a continuation is invoked that was captured (using `call-with-current-continuation`) during the dynamic extent.
>   - It is exited when the called procedure returns.
>   - It is also exited when execution is within the dynamic extent and a continuation is invoked that was captured while not within the dynamic extent.

If a second call to `dynamic-wind` occurs within the dynamic extent of the call to *thunk* and then a continuation is invoked in such a way that the *after*s from these two invocations of `dynamic-wind` are both to be called, then the *after* associated with the second (inner) call to `dynamic-wind` is called first.

If a second call to `dynamic-wind` occurs within the dynamic extent of the call to *thunk* and then a continuation is invoked in such a way that the *before*s from these two invocations of `dynamic-wind` are both to be called, then the *before* associated with the first (outer) call to `dynamic-wind` is called first.

If invoking a continuation requires calling the *before* from one call to `dynamic-wind` and the *after* from another, then the *after* is called first.

The effect of using a captured continuation to enter or exit the dynamic extent of a call to *before* or *after* is undefined.

```
(let ((path '())
      (c #f))
  (let ((add (lambda (s)
               (set! path (cons s path)))))
    (dynamic-wind
      (lambda () (add 'connect))
      (lambda ()
        (add (call-with-current-continuation
               (lambda (c0)
                 (set! c c0)
                 'talk1))))
      (lambda () (add 'disconnect)))
    (if (< (length path) 4)
        (c 'talk2)
        (reverse path)))))
```

⇒ (connect talk1 disconnect connect talk2 disconnect)

The following two procedures support multiple values.

call-with-values *thunk procedure*   [procedure]
> *Thunk* must be a procedure of no arguments, and *procedure* must be a procedure. *Thunk* is invoked with a continuation that expects to receive multiple values; specifically, the continuation expects to receive the same number of values that *procedure* accepts as arguments. *Thunk* must return multiple values using the `values` procedure. Then *procedure* is called with the multiple values as its arguments. The result yielded by *procedure* is returned as the result of `call-with-values`.

values *object ...*   [procedure]
> Returns multiple values. The continuation in effect when this procedure is called must be a multiple-value continuation that was created by `call-with-values`. Furthermore it must accept as many values as there are *objects*.

12.5 Application Hooks

Application hooks are objects that can be applied like procedures. Each application hook has two parts: a *procedure* that specifies what to do when the application hook is applied, and an arbitrary object, called *extra*. Often the procedure uses the extra object to determine what to do.

There are two kinds of application hooks, which differ in what arguments are passed to the procedure. When an *apply hook* is applied, the procedure is passed exactly the same arguments that were passed to the apply hook. When an *entity* is applied, the entity itself is passed as the first argument, followed by the other arguments that were passed to the entity.

Both apply hooks and entities satisfy the predicate `procedure?`. Each satisfies either `compiled-procedure?`, `compound-procedure?`, or `primitive-procedure?`, depending on its procedure component. An apply hook is considered to accept the same number of arguments as its procedure, while an entity is considered to accept one less argument than its procedure.

`make-apply-hook` *procedure object*   [procedure]
> Returns a newly allocated apply hook with a procedure component of *procedure* and an extra component of *object*.

`apply-hook?` *object*   [procedure]
> Returns `#t` if *object* is an apply hook; otherwise returns `#f`.

`apply-hook-procedure` *apply-hook*   [procedure]
> Returns the procedure component of *apply-hook*.

`set-apply-hook-procedure!` *apply-hook procedure*   [procedure]
> Changes the procedure component of *apply-hook* to be *procedure*. Returns an unspecified value.

`apply-hook-extra` *apply-hook*   [procedure]
> Returns the extra component of *apply-hook*.

`set-apply-hook-extra!` *apply-hook object*   [procedure]
> Changes the extra component of *apply-hook* to be *object*. Returns an unspecified value.

`make-entity` *procedure object*   [procedure]
> Returns a newly allocated entity with a procedure component of *procedure* and an extra component of *object*.

`entity?` *object*   [procedure]
> Returns `#t` if *object* is an entity; otherwise returns `#f`.

`entity-procedure` *entity*   [procedure]
> Returns the procedure component of *entity*.

`set-entity-procedure!` *entity procedure*   [procedure]
> Changes the procedure component of *entity* to be *procedure*. Returns an unspecified value.

`entity-extra` *entity*   [procedure]
> Returns the extra component of *entity*.

`set-entity-extra!` *entity object*   [procedure]
> Changes the extra component of *entity* to be *object*. Returns an unspecified value.

12.6 Generic Dispatch

MIT/GNU Scheme provides a generic dispatch mechanism that can choose an action to take based on the types of a set of objects. Performance is guaranteed by the use of a hash-based method cache.

This is *not* an object-oriented programming system, although it can provide the basis for such systems. The difference is that the generic dispatch doesn't have any model for the relationship between object types. Instead, there is a flat space of types and methods are selected by procedural examination of the given operand types.

12.6.1 Generic Procedures

The core of the dispatch mechanism is the *generic procedure*. This is a procedure that is called in the usual way, but which dispatches to a particular *method* based on the types of its arguments.

make-generic-procedure *arity* [*name*]   [procedure]

Returns a new generic procedure accepting *arity*. *Arity* must specify a minimum of one argument.

Name is used for debugging: it is a symbol that has no role in the semantics of the generic procedure. *Name* may be **#f** to indicate that the generic procedure is anonymous. If *name* is not specified, it defaults to '**#f**'.

Examples:

```
(define foo-bar (make-generic-procedure 2 'bar))

(define foo-baz (make-generic-procedure '(1 . 2) 'foo-baz))

(define foo-mum (make-generic-procedure '(1 . #f)))
```

generic-procedure? *object*   [procedure]

Returns '**#t**' if *object* is a generic procedure, and '**#f**' otherwise.

guarantee-generic-procedure *object caller*   [procedure]

Signals an error if *object* is not a generic procedure. *Caller* is a symbol that is printed as part of the error message and is intended to be the name of the procedure where the error occurs.

generic-procedure-arity *generic*   [procedure]

Returns the arity of *generic*, as given to **make-generic-procedure**.

generic-procedure-name *generic*   [procedure]

Returns the name of *generic*, as given to **make-generic-procedure**.

generic-procedure-applicable? *generic operands*   [procedure]

Returns '**#t**' if *generic* is applicable to *operands* (which must be a list of objects), and '**#f**' otherwise.

condition-type:no-applicable-methods *operator operands*   [condition type]

This condition type is signalled when a generic procedure is applied and there are no applicable methods for the given operands. The condition's *operator* field contains the generic procedure and the *operands* field contains the given operands.

condition-type:extra-applicable-methods *operator operands*   [condition type]
> This condition type is signalled when a generic procedure is applied and there are more than one applicable methods for the given operands. The condition's *operator* field contains the generic procedure and the *operands* field contains the given operands.

12.6.2 Method Generators

Generic-procedure methods are dynamically chosen by *generators*, which are procedures of two arguments. Each generic procedure has a set of associated generators. Whenever the procedure is applied, each associated generator is applied to two arguments: the generic procedure and a list of the dispatch tags for the operands. The return value from the generator is either a *method* (a procedure accepting that number of arguments) or '**#f**'. In order for the application to succeed, exactly one of the generic procedure's generators must return a method.

Once a method has been chosen, it is cached. A subsequent call to the generic procedure with operands of the same types will reuse that cached method. Consequently, it is important that generators be *functional*: they must always compute the same value from the same arguments.

add-generic-procedure-generator *generic generator*   [procedure]
> Adds *generator* to *generic*'s set of generators and returns an unspecified value.

remove-generic-procedure-generator *generic generator*   [procedure]
> Removes *generator* from *generic*'s set of generators and returns an unspecified value.

remove-generic-procedure-generators *generic tags*   [procedure]
> Calls each of *generic*'s set of generators on *tags* and removes each generator that returns a method. Returns an unspecified value.

generic-procedure-generator-list *generic*   [procedure]
> Returns a list of *generic*'s generators.

As a convenience, each generic procedure can have a *default generator*, which is called only when all of the other generators have returned '**#f**'. When created, a generic procedure has no default generator.

generic-procedure-default-generator *generic*   [procedure]
> Returns *generic*'s default generator.

set-generic-procedure-default-generator! *generic generator*   [procedure]
> Sets *generic*'s default generator to *generator* and returns an unspecified value.

12.6.3 Dispatch Tags

A dispatch tag is an object that represents the "type" of an object, for the purposes of generic dispatch. Every object has an associated dispatch tag. Built-in objects like pairs or booleans have predefined tags, while dynamically typed objects like records have tags that are created as needed.

dispatch-tag *object*   [procedure]
> Returns the dispatch tag for *object*.

```
(dispatch-tag #f)        ⇒ #[dispatch-tag 17 (boolean)]
(dispatch-tag #t)        ⇒ #[dispatch-tag 17 (boolean)]
(dispatch-tag (list))    ⇒ #[dispatch-tag 18 (null)]
(dispatch-tag (list 3))  ⇒ #[dispatch-tag 19 (pair list)]
```

built-in-dispatch-tag *name*   [procedure]

Returns the built-in dispatch tag called *name*. *Name* must be a symbol that is the name of a known built-in dispatch tag.

```
(built-in-dispatch-tag 'boolean) ⇒ #[dispatch-tag 17 (boolean)]
(built-in-dispatch-tag 'null)    ⇒ #[dispatch-tag 18 (null)]
(built-in-dispatch-tag 'pair)    ⇒ #[dispatch-tag 19 (pair list)]
(built-in-dispatch-tag 'list)    ⇒ #[dispatch-tag 19 (pair list)]
```

built-in-dispatch-tags   [procedure]

Returns a list of the built-in dispatch tags.

record-type-dispatch-tag *record-type*   [procedure]

Returns the dispatch tag associate with *record-type*. See See Section 10.4 [Records], page 138, for more information about record types.

dispatch-tag? *object*   [procedure]

Returns '#t' if *object* is a dispatch tag, and '#f' otherwise.

guarantee-dispatch-tag *object caller*   [procedure]

Signals an error if *object* is not a dispatch tag. *Caller* is a symbol that is printed as part of the error message and is intended to be the name of the procedure where the error occurs.

13 Environments

13.1 Environment Operations

Environments are first-class objects in MIT/GNU Scheme. An environment consists of some bindings and possibly a parent environment, from which other bindings are inherited. The operations in this section reveal the frame-like structure of environments by permitting you to examine the bindings of a particular environment separately from those of its parent.

There are several types of bindings that can occur in an environment. The most common is the simple variable binding, which associates a value (any Scheme object) with an identifier (a symbol). A variable binding can also be *unassigned*, which means that it has no value. An unassigned variable is bound, in that is will shadow other bindings of the same name in ancestor environments, but a reference to that variable will signal an error of type `condition-type:unassigned-variable`. An unassigned variable can be *assigned* (using `set!` or `environment-assign!`) to give it a value.

In addition to variable bindings, an environment can also have *keyword bindings*. A keyword binding associates a syntactic keyword (usually a macro transformer) with an identifier. Keyword bindings are special in that they are considered "bound", but ordinary variable references don't work on them. So an attempt to reference or assign a keyword binding results in an error of type `condition-type:macro-binding`. However, keyword bindings can be redefined using `define` or `environment-define`.

environment? *object*   [procedure]
>   Returns #t if *object* is an environment; otherwise returns #f.

environment-has-parent? *environment*   [procedure]
>   Returns #t if *environment* has a parent environment; otherwise returns #f.

environment-parent *environment*   [procedure]
>   Returns the parent environment of *environment*. It is an error if *environment* has no parent.

environment-bound-names *environment*   [procedure]
>   Returns a newly allocated list of the names (symbols) that are bound by *environment*. This does not include the names that are bound by the parent environment of *environment*. It does include names that are unassigned or keywords in *environment*.

environment-macro-names *environment*   [procedure]
>   Returns a newly allocated list of the names (symbols) that are bound to syntactic keywords in *environment*.

environment-bindings *environment*   [procedure]
>   Returns a newly allocated list of the bindings of *environment*; does not include the bindings of the parent environment. Each element of this list takes one of two forms: (*symbol*) indicates that *symbol* is bound but unassigned, while (*symbol object*) indicates that *symbol* is bound, and its value is *object*.

environment-reference-type *environment symbol*   [procedure]

Returns a symbol describing the *reference type* of *symbol* in *environment* or one of its ancestor environments. The result is one of the following:

normal   means *symbol* is a variable binding with a normal value.

unassigned

means *symbol* is a variable binding with no value.

macro   means *symbol* is a keyword binding.

unbound   means *symbol* has no associated binding.

environment-bound? *environment symbol*   [procedure]

Returns #t if *symbol* is bound in *environment* or one of its ancestor environments; otherwise returns #f. This is equivalent to

```
(not (eq? 'unbound
          (environment-reference-type environment symbol)))
```

environment-assigned? *environment symbol*   [procedure]

Returns #t if *symbol* is bound in *environment* or one of its ancestor environments, and has a normal value. Returns #f if it is bound but unassigned. Signals an error if it is unbound or is bound to a keyword.

environment-lookup *environment symbol*   [procedure]

Symbol must be bound to a normal value in *environment* or one of its ancestor environments. Returns the value to which it is bound. Signals an error if unbound, unassigned, or a keyword.

environment-lookup-macro *environment symbol*   [procedure]

If *symbol* is a keyword binding in *environment* or one of its ancestor environments, returns the value of the binding. Otherwise, returns #f. Does not signal any errors other than argument-type errors.

environment-assignable? *environment symbol*   [procedure]

Symbol must be bound in *environment* or one of its ancestor environments. Returns #t if the binding may be modified by side effect.

environment-assign! *environment symbol object*   [procedure]

Symbol must be bound in *environment* or one of its ancestor environments, and must be assignable. Modifies the binding to have *object* as its value, and returns an unspecified result.

environment-definable? *environment symbol*   [procedure]

Returns #t if *symbol* is definable in *environment*, and #f otherwise. At present, this is false for environments generated by application of compiled procedures, and true for all other environments.

environment-define *environment symbol object*   [procedure]

Defines *symbol* to be bound to *object* in *environment*, and returns an unspecified value. Signals an error if *symbol* isn't definable in *environment*.

`environment-define-macro` *environment symbol transformer*   [procedure]

> Defines *symbol* to be a keyword bound to *transformer* in *environment*, and returns an
> unspecified value. Signals an error if *symbol* isn't definable in *environment*. The type
> of *transformer* is defined by the syntax engine and is not checked by this procedure.
> If the type is incorrect this will subsequently signal an error during syntax expansion.

`eval` *expression environment*   [procedure]

> Evaluates *expression*, a list-structure representation (sometimes called s-expression
> representation) of a Scheme expression, in *environment*. You rarely need `eval` in
> ordinary programs; it is useful mostly for evaluating expressions that have been cre-
> ated "on the fly" by a program. `eval` is relatively expensive because it must convert
> *expression* to an internal form before it is executed.
>
> ```
> (define foo (list '+ 1 2))
> (eval foo (the-environment))            ⇒   3
> ```

13.2 Environment Variables

The `user-initial-environment` is where the top-level read-eval-print (REP) loop evaluates
expressions and binds definitions. It is a child of `system-global-environment`, which is
where all of the Scheme system definitions are bound. All of the bindings in `system-global-
environment` are available when the current environment is `user-initial-environment`.
However, any new bindings that you create in the REP loop (with `define` forms or by
loading files containing `define` forms) occur in `user-initial-environment`.

`system-global-environment`   [variable]

> The variable `system-global-environment` is bound to the distinguished
> environment that's the ancestor of most other environments (except for those
> created by `make-root-top-level-environment`). It is the parent environment of
> `user-initial-environment`. Primitives, system procedures, and most syntactic
> keywords are bound (and sometimes closed) in this environment.

`user-initial-environment`   [variable]

> The variable `user-initial-environment` is bound to the default environment in
> which typed expressions are evaluated by the top-level REP loop.
>
> Although all bindings in `system-global-environment` are visible to the REP loop,
> definitions that are typed at, or loaded by, the REP loop occur in the `user-initial-
> environment`. This is partly a safety measure: if you enter a definition that happens
> to have the same name as a critical system procedure, your definition will be visible
> only to the procedures you define in the `user-initial-environment`; the MIT/GNU
> Scheme system procedures, which are defined in `system-global-environment`, will
> continue to see the original definition.

13.3 REPL Environment

`nearest-repl/environment`   [procedure]

> Returns the current REP loop environment (i.e. the current environment of the closest
> enclosing REP loop). When Scheme first starts up, this is the same as `user-initial-
> environment`.

ge *environment*   [procedure]

>   Changes the current REP loop environment to *environment*. *Environment* can be either an environment or a procedure object. If it's a procedure, the environment in which that procedure was closed is the new environment.

13.4 Top-level Environments

The operations in this section manipulate *top-level environments*, as opposed to environments created by the application of procedures. For historical reasons, top-level environments are referred to as *interpreter environments*.

the-environment   [special form]

>   Returns the current environment. This form may only be evaluated in a top-level environment. An error is signalled if it appears elsewhere.

top-level-environment? *object*   [procedure]
interpreter-environment? *object*   [procedure]

>   Returns #t if *object* is an top-level environment; otherwise returns #f.
>
>   **interpreter-environment?** is an alias for **top-level-environment?**.

extend-top-level-environment *environment* [*names* [*values*]]   [procedure]
make-top-level-environment [*names* [*values*]]   [procedure]
make-root-top-level-environment [*names* [*values*]]   [procedure]

>   Returns a newly allocated top-level environment. **extend-top-level-environment** creates an environment that has parent *environment*, **make-top-level-environment** creates an environment that has parent **system-global-environment**, and **make-root-top-level-environment** creates an environment that has no parent.
>
>   The optional arguments *names* and *values* are used to specify initial bindings in the new environment. If specified, *names* must be a list of symbols, and *values* must be a list of objects. If only *names* is specified, each name in *names* will be bound in the environment, but unassigned. If *names* and *values* are both specified, they must be the same length, and each name in *names* will be bound to the corresponding value in *values*. If neither *names* nor *values* is specified, the environment will have no initial bindings.

link-variables *environment1 symbol1 environment2 symbol2*   [procedure]

>   Defines *symbol1* in *environment1* to have the same binding as *symbol2* in *environment2*, and returns an unspecified value. Prior to the call, *symbol2* must be bound in *environment2*, but the type of binding is irrelevant; it may be a normal binding, an unassigned binding, or a keyword binding. Signals an error if *symbol1* isn't definable in *environment1*, or if *symbol2* is unbound in *environment2*.
>
>   By "the same binding", we mean that the value cell is shared between the two environments. If a value is assigned to *symbol1* in *environment1*, a subsequent reference to *symbol2* in *environment2* will see that value, and vice versa.

unbind-variable *environment symbol*   [procedure]

>   If *symbol* is bound in *environment* or one of its ancestor environments, removes the binding, so that subsequent accesses to that symbol behave as if the binding never existed. Returns #t if there was a binding prior to the call, and #f if there wasn't.

14 Input/Output

This chapter describes the procedures that are used for input and output (I/O). The chapter first describes *ports* and how they are manipulated, then describes the I/O operations. Finally, some low-level procedures are described that permit the implementation of custom ports and high-performance I/O.

14.1 Ports

Scheme uses ports for I/O. A *port*, which can be treated like any other Scheme object, serves as a source or sink for data. A port must be open before it can be read from or written to. The standard I/O port, `console-i/o-port`, is opened automatically when you start Scheme. When you use a file for input or output, you need to explicitly open and close a port to the file (with procedures described in this chapter). Additional procedures let you open ports to strings.

Many input procedures, such as `read-char` and `read`, read data from the current input port by default, or from a port that you specify. The current input port is initially `console-i/o-port`, but Scheme provides procedures that let you change the current input port to be a file or string.

Similarly, many output procedures, such as `write-char` and `display`, write data to the current output port by default, or to a port that you specify. The current output port is initially `console-i/o-port`, but Scheme provides procedures that let you change the current output port to be a file or string.

Nearly all ports read or write Unicode characters; the exceptions are those for which non-Unicode character coding has been specified.

Every port is either an input port, an output port, or both. The following predicates distinguish all of the possible cases.

`port?` *object*   [procedure]
> Returns `#t` if *object* is a port, otherwise returns `#f`.

`input-port?` *object*   [procedure]
> Returns `#t` if *object* is an input port, otherwise returns `#f`. Any object satisfying this predicate also satisfies `port?`.

`output-port?` *object*   [procedure]
> Returns `#t` if *object* is an output port, otherwise returns `#f`. Any object satisfying this predicate also satisfies `port?`.

`i/o-port?` *object*   [procedure]
> Returns `#t` if *object* is both an input port and an output port, otherwise returns `#f`. Any object satisfying this predicate also satisfies `port?`, `input-port?`, and `output-port?`.

`guarantee-port` *object*   [procedure]
`guarantee-input-port` *object*   [procedure]
`guarantee-output-port` *object*   [procedure]

guarantee-i/o-port *object*   [procedure]

> These procedures check the type of *object*, signalling an error of type
> `condition-type:wrong-type-argument` if it is not a port, input port, output port,
> or I/O port, respectively. Otherwise they return *object*.

The next five procedures return the runtime system's *standard ports*. All of the standard
ports are dynamically bound by the REP loop; this means that when a new REP loop is
started, for example by an error, each of these ports is dynamically bound to the I/O port
of the REP loop. When the REP loop exits, the ports revert to their original values.

current-input-port   [procedure]

> Returns the current input port. This is the default port used by many input proce-
> dures. Initially, `current-input-port` returns the value of `console-i/o-port`.

current-output-port   [procedure]

> Returns the current output port. This is the default port used by many output
> procedures. Initially, `current-output-port` returns the value of `console-i/o-port`.

notification-output-port   [procedure]

> Returns an output port suitable for generating "notifications", that is, messages to
> the user that supply interesting information about the execution of a program. For
> example, the `load` procedure writes messages to this port informing the user that
> a file is being loaded. Initially, `notification-output-port` returns the value of
> `console-i/o-port`.

trace-output-port   [procedure]

> Returns an output port suitable for generating "tracing" information about a pro-
> gram's execution. The output generated by the `trace` procedure is sent to this port.
> Initially, `trace-output-port` returns the value of `console-i/o-port`.

interaction-i/o-port   [procedure]

> Returns an I/O port suitable for querying or prompting the user. The standard
> prompting procedures use this port by default (see Section 14.8 [Prompting],
> page 202). Initially, `interaction-i/o-port` returns the value of `console-i/o-port`.

with-input-from-port *input-port thunk*   [procedure]
with-output-to-port *output-port thunk*   [procedure]
with-notification-output-port *output-port thunk*   [procedure]
with-trace-output-port *output-port thunk*   [procedure]
with-interaction-i/o-port *i/o-port thunk*   [procedure]

> *Thunk* must be a procedure of no arguments. Each of these procedures binds one
> of the standard ports to its first argument, calls *thunk* with no arguments, restores
> the port to its original value, and returns the result that was yielded by *thunk*. This
> temporary binding is performed the same way as dynamic binding of a variable,
> including the behavior in the presence of continuations (see Section 2.3 [Dynamic
> Binding], page 18).
>
> `with-input-from-port` binds the current input port, `with-output-to-port` binds
> the current output port, `with-notification-output-port` binds the "notification"
> output port, `with-trace-output-port` binds the "trace" output port, and
> `with-interaction-i/o-port` binds the "interaction" I/O port.

```
set-current-input-port! input-port                              [procedure]
set-current-output-port! output-port                            [procedure]
set-notification-output-port! output-port                       [procedure]
set-trace-output-port! output-port                              [procedure]
set-interaction-i/o-port! i/o-port                              [procedure]
```
> Each of these procedures alters the binding of one of the standard ports and returns an unspecified value. The binding that is modified corresponds to the name of the procedure.

```
console-i/o-port                                                  [variable]
```
> `console-i/o-port` is an I/O port that communicates with the "console". Under unix, the console is the controlling terminal of the Scheme process. Under Windows, the console is the window that is created when Scheme starts up.
>
> This variable is rarely used; instead programs should use one of the standard ports defined above. This variable should not be modified.

```
close-port port                                                 [procedure]
```
> Closes *port* and returns an unspecified value. If *port* is a file port, the file is closed.

```
close-input-port port                                           [procedure]
```
> Closes *port* and returns an unspecified value. *Port* must be an input port or an I/O port; if it is an I/O port, then only the input side of the port is closed.

```
close-output-port port                                          [procedure]
```
> Closes *port* and returns an unspecified value. *Port* must be an output port or an I/O port; if it is an I/O port, then only the output side of the port is closed.

14.2 File Ports

Before Scheme can access a file for reading or writing, it is necessary to open a port to the file. This section describes procedures used to open ports to files. Such ports are closed (like any other port) by **close-port**. File ports are automatically closed if and when they are reclaimed by the garbage collector.

Before opening a file for input or output, by whatever method, the *filename* argument is converted to canonical form by calling the procedure **merge-pathnames** with *filename* as its sole argument. Thus, *filename* can be either a string or a pathname, and it is merged with the current pathname defaults to produce the pathname that is then opened.

Any file can be opened in one of two modes, *normal* or *binary*. Normal mode is for accessing text files, and binary mode is for accessing other files. Unix does not distinguish these modes, but Windows do: in normal mode, their file ports perform *newline translation*, mapping between the carriage-return/linefeed sequence that terminates text lines in files, and the **#\newline** that terminates lines in Scheme. In binary mode, such ports do not perform newline translation. Unless otherwise mentioned, the procedures in this section open files in normal mode.

```
open-input-file filename                                        [procedure]
```
> Takes a filename referring to an existing file and returns an input port capable of delivering characters from the file. If the file cannot be opened, an error of type **condition-type:file-operation-error** is signalled.

open-output-file *filename* [*append?*]   [procedure]

Takes a filename referring to an output file to be created and returns an output port capable of writing characters to a new file by that name. If the file cannot be opened, an error of type `condition-type:file-operation-error` is signalled.

The optional argument *append?* is an MIT/GNU Scheme extension. If *append?* is given and not `#f`, the file is opened in *append* mode. In this mode, the contents of the file are not overwritten; instead any characters written to the file are appended to the end of the existing contents. If the file does not exist, append mode creates the file and writes to it in the normal way.

open-i/o-file *filename*   [procedure]

Takes a filename referring to an existing file and returns an I/O port capable of both reading and writing the file. If the file cannot be opened, an error of type `condition-type:file-operation-error` is signalled.

This procedure is often used to open special files. For example, under unix this procedure can be used to open terminal device files, PTY device files, and named pipes.

open-binary-input-file *filename*   [procedure]
open-binary-output-file *filename* [*append?*]   [procedure]
open-binary-i/o-file *filename*   [procedure]

These procedures open files in binary mode. In all other respects they are identical to `open-input-file`, `open-output-file`, and `open-i/o-file`, respectively.

close-all-open-files   [procedure]

This procedure closes all file ports that are open at the time that it is called, and returns an unspecified value.

call-with-input-file *filename procedure*   [procedure]
call-with-output-file *filename procedure*   [procedure]

These procedures call *procedure* with one argument: the port obtained by opening the named file for input or output, respectively. If the file cannot be opened, an error of type `condition-type:file-operation-error` is signalled. If *procedure* returns, then the port is closed automatically and the value yielded by *procedure* is returned. If *procedure* does not return, then the port will not be closed automatically unless it is reclaimed by the garbage collector.[1]

call-with-binary-input-file *filename procedure*   [procedure]
call-with-binary-output-file *filename procedure*   [procedure]

These procedures open files in binary mode. In all other respects they are identical to `call-with-input-file` and `call-with-output-file`, respectively.

with-input-from-file *filename thunk*   [procedure]
with-output-to-file *filename thunk*   [procedure]

Thunk must be a procedure of no arguments. The file is opened for input or output, an input or output port connected to it is made the default value returned

---

[1] Because Scheme's escape procedures have unlimited extent, it is possible to escape from the current continuation but later to escape back in. If implementations were permitted to close the port on any escape from the current continuation, then it would be impossible to write portable code using both `call-with-current-continuation` and `call-with-input-file` or `call-with-output-file`.

by `current-input-port` or `current-output-port`, and the *thunk* is called with no arguments. When the *thunk* returns, the port is closed and the previous default is restored. `with-input-from-file` and `with-output-to-file` return the value yielded by *thunk*. If an escape procedure is used to escape from the continuation of these procedures, their behavior is implementation-dependent; in that situation MIT/GNU Scheme leaves the files open.

`with-input-from-binary-file` *filename thunk*   [procedure]
`with-output-to-binary-file` *filename thunk*   [procedure]
> These procedures open files in binary mode. In all other respects they are identical to `with-input-from-file` and `with-output-to-file`, respectively.

14.3 String Ports

This section describes the simplest kinds of ports: input ports that read their input from given strings, and output ports that accumulate their output and return it as a string. It also describes "truncating" output ports, which can limit the length of the resulting string to a given value.

`open-input-string` *string* [*start* [*end*]]   [procedure]
> Returns a new string port that delivers characters from *string*. The optional arguments *start* and *end* may be used to specify that the string port delivers characters from a substring of *string*; if not given, *start* defaults to 0 and *end* defaults to (`string-length` *string*).

`with-input-from-string` *string thunk*   [procedure]
> *Thunk* must be a procedure of no arguments. `with-input-from-string` creates a new input port that reads from *string*, makes that port the current input port, and calls *thunk*. When *thunk* returns, `with-input-from-string` restores the previous current input port and returns the result yielded by *thunk*.
>
>   (with-input-from-string "(a b c) (d e f)" read) ⇒ (a b c)
>
> Note: this procedure is equivalent to:
>
>   (with-input-from-port (open-input-string string) thunk)

`open-output-string`   [procedure]
`get-output-string`   [procedure]
> `open-output-string` returns a new output port that accumulates in a buffer everything that is written to it. The accumulated output can subsequently be obtained by calling `get-output-string` on the port.

`call-with-output-string` *procedure*   [procedure]
> *Procedure* is called with one argument, an output port. The value yielded by *procedure* is ignored. When *procedure* returns, `call-with-output-string` returns the port's accumulated output as a newly allocated string. This is equivalent to:
>
>   (define (call-with-output-string procedure)
>   (let ((port (open-output-string)))
>   (procedure port)
>   (get-output-string port)))

`with-output-to-string` *thunk*   [procedure]

> *Thunk* must be a procedure of no arguments. `with-output-to-string` creates a new output port that accumulates output, makes that port the default value returned by `current-output-port`, and calls *thunk* with no arguments. When *thunk* returns, `with-output-to-string` restores the previous default and returns the accumulated output as a newly allocated string.

```
(with-output-to-string
  (lambda ()
    (write 'abc)))                        ⇒   "abc"
```

> Note: this procedure is equivalent to:

```
(call-with-output-string
  (lambda (port)
    (with-output-to-port port thunk)))
```

`with-output-to-truncated-string` *k thunk*   [procedure]

> Similar to `with-output-to-string`, except that the output is limited to *k* characters. If *thunk* attempts to write more than *k* characters, it will be aborted by invoking an escape procedure that returns from `with-output-to-truncated-string`.

> The value of this procedure is a pair; the car of the pair is `#t` if *thunk* attempted to write more than *k* characters, and `#f` otherwise. The cdr of the pair is a newly allocated string containing the accumulated output.

> This procedure is helpful for displaying circular lists, as shown in this example:

```
(define inf (list 'inf))
(with-output-to-truncated-string 40
  (lambda ()
    (write inf)))                         ⇒   (#f . "(inf)")
(set-cdr! inf inf)
(with-output-to-truncated-string 40
  (lambda ()
    (write inf)))
       ⇒   (#t . "(inf inf inf inf inf inf inf inf inf inf")
```

`write-to-string` *object* [*k*]   [procedure]

> Writes *object* to a string output port, and returns the resulting newly allocated string. If *k* is supplied and not `#f`, this procedure is equivalent to

```
(with-output-to-truncated-string k
  (lambda ()
    (write object)))
```

> otherwise it is equivalent to

```
(with-output-to-string
  (lambda ()
    (write object)))
```

14.4 Input Procedures

This section describes the procedures that read input. Input procedures can read either from the current input port or from a given port. Remember that to read from a file, you must first open a port to the file.

Input ports can be divided into two types, called *interactive* and *non-interactive*. Interactive input ports are ports that read input from a source that is time-dependent; for example, a port that reads input from a terminal or from another program. Non-interactive input ports read input from a time-independent source, such as an ordinary file or a character string.

All optional arguments called *input-port*, if not supplied, default to the current input port.

read-char [*input-port*]   [procedure]

>   Returns the next character available from *input-port*, updating *input-port* to point to the following character. If no more characters are available, an end-of-file object is returned.

>   In MIT/GNU Scheme, if *input-port* is an interactive input port and no characters are immediately available, **read-char** will hang waiting for input, even if the port is in non-blocking mode.

peek-char [*input-port*]   [procedure]

>   Returns the next character available from *input-port*, *without* updating *input-port* to point to the following character. If no more characters are available, an end-of-file object is returned.[2]

>   In MIT/GNU Scheme, if *input-port* is an interactive input port and no characters are immediately available, **peek-char** will hang waiting for input, even if the port is in non-blocking mode.

char-ready? [*input-port*]   [procedure]

>   Returns **#t** if a character is ready on *input-port* and returns **#f** otherwise. If **char-ready?** returns **#t** then the next **read-char** operation on *input-port* is guaranteed not to hang. If *input-port* is a file port at end of file then **char-ready?** returns **#t**.[3]

read [*input-port* [*environment*]]   [procedure]

>   Converts external representations of Scheme objects into the objects themselves. **read** returns the next object parsable from *input-port*, updating *input-port* to point to the first character past the end of the written representation of the object. If an end

---

[2] The value returned by a call to **peek-char** is the same as the value that would have been returned by a call to **read-char** on the same port. The only difference is that the very next call to **read-char** or **peek-char** on that *input-port* will return the value returned by the preceding call to **peek-char**. In particular, a call to **peek-char** on an interactive port will hang waiting for input whenever a call to **read-char** would have hung.

[3] **char-ready?** exists to make it possible for a program to accept characters from interactive ports without getting stuck waiting for input. Any input editors associated with such ports must make sure that characters whose existence has been asserted by **char-ready?** cannot be rubbed out. If **char-ready?** were to return **#f** at end of file, a port at end of file would be indistinguishable from an interactive port that has no ready characters.

of file is encountered in the input before any characters are found that can begin an object, read returns an end-of-file object. The *input-port* remains open, and further attempts to read will also return an end-of-file object. If an end of file is encountered after the beginning of an object's written representation, but the written representation is incomplete and therefore not parsable, an error is signalled.

Environment is used to look up the values of control variables such as '*parser-radix*'. If not supplied, it defaults to the REP environment.

eof-object? *object*   [procedure]
> Returns #t if *object* is an end-of-file object; otherwise returns #f.

read-char-no-hang [*input-port*]   [procedure]
> If *input-port* can deliver a character without blocking, this procedure acts exactly like read-char, immediately returning that character. Otherwise, #f is returned, unless *input-port* is a file port at end of file, in which case an end-of-file object is returned. In no case will this procedure block waiting for input.

read-string *char-set* [*input-port*]   [procedure]
> Reads characters from *input-port* until it finds a terminating character that is a member of *char-set* (see Section 5.6 [Character Sets], page 84) or encounters end of file. The port is updated to point to the terminating character, or to end of file if no terminating character was found. read-string returns the characters, up to but excluding the terminating character, as a newly allocated string.
>
> This procedure ignores the blocking mode of the port, blocking unconditionally until it sees either a delimiter or end of file. If end of file is encountered before any characters are read, an end-of-file object is returned.
>
> On many input ports, this operation is significantly faster than the following equivalent code using peek-char and read-char:
>
> ```
> (define (read-string char-set input-port)
>   (let ((char (peek-char input-port)))
>     (if (eof-object? char)
>         char
>         (list->string
>          (let loop ((char char))
>            (if (or (eof-object? char)
>                    (char-set-member? char-set char))
>                '()
>                (begin
>                  (read-char input-port)
>                  (cons char
>                        (loop (peek-char input-port)))))))))))
> ```

read-line [*input-port*]   [procedure]
> read-line reads a single line of text from *input-port*, and returns that line as a newly allocated string. The #\newline terminating the line, if any, is discarded and does not appear in the returned string.

This procedure ignores the blocking mode of the port, blocking unconditionally until it has read an entire line. If end of file is encountered before any characters are read, an end-of-file object is returned.

read-string! *string* [*input-port*]   [procedure]
read-substring! *string start end* [*input-port*]   [procedure]
> **read-string!** and **read-substring!** fill the specified region of *string* with characters read from *input-port* until the region is full or else there are no more characters available from the port. For **read-string!**, the region is all of *string*, and for **read-substring!**, the region is that part of *string* specified by *start* and *end*.

> The returned value is the number of characters filled into the region. However, there are several interesting cases to consider:

> - If **read-string!** (**read-substring!**) is called when *input-port* is at "end-of-file", then the returned value is 0. Note that "end-of-file" can mean a file port that is at the file's end, a string port that is at the string's end, or any other port that will never produce more characters.

> - If *input-port* is an interactive port (e.g. a terminal), and one or more characters are immediately available, the region is filled using the available characters. The procedure then returns immediately, without waiting for further characters, even if the number of available characters is less than the size of the region. The returned value is the number of characters actually filled in.

> - If *input-port* is an interactive port and no characters are immediately available, the result of the operation depends on the blocking mode of the port. If the port is in non-blocking mode, **read-string!** (**read-substring!**) immediately returns the value **#f**. Otherwise, the operation blocks until a character is available. As soon as at least one character is available, the region is filled using the available characters. The procedure then returns immediately, without waiting for further characters, even if the number of available characters is less than the size of the region. The returned value is the number of characters actually filled in.

> The importance of **read-string!** and **read-substring!** are that they are both flexible and extremely fast, especially for large amounts of data.

The following variables may be bound or assigned to change the behavior of the **read** procedure. They are looked up in the environment that is passed to **read**, and so may have different values in different environments. It is recommended that the global bindings of these variables be left unchanged; make local changes by shadowing the global bindings in nested environments.

parser-radix   [variable]
> This variable defines the radix used by the reader when it parses numbers. This is similar to passing a radix argument to **string->number**. The value of this variable must be one of 2, 8, 10, or 16; any other value is ignored, and the reader uses radix 10.

> Note that much of the number syntax is invalid for radixes other than 10. The reader detects cases where such invalid syntax is used and signals an error. However, problems can still occur when ***parser-radix*** is set to 16, because syntax that

normally denotes symbols can now denote numbers (e.g. abc). Because of this, it is usually undesirable to set this variable to anything other than the default.

The default value of this variable is 10.

parser-canonicalize-symbols?   [variable]

> This variable controls how the parser handles case-sensitivity of symbols. If it is bound to its default value of #t, symbols read by the parser are converted to lower case before being interned. Otherwise, symbols are interned without case conversion.
>
> In general, it is a bad idea to use this feature, as it doesn't really make Scheme case-sensitive, and therefore can break features of the Scheme runtime that depend on case-insensitive symbols.

14.5 Output Procedures

Output ports may or may not support *buffering* of output, in which output characters are collected together in a buffer and then sent to the output device all at once. (Most of the output ports implemented by the runtime system support buffering.) Sending all of the characters in the buffer to the output device is called *flushing* the buffer. In general, output procedures do not flush the buffer of an output port unless the buffer is full.

However, the standard output procedures described in this section perform what is called *discretionary* flushing of the buffer. Discretionary output flushing works as follows. After a procedure performs its output (writing characters to the output buffer), it checks to see if the port implements an operation called `discretionary-flush-output`. If so, then that operation is invoked to flush the buffer. At present, only the console port defines `discretionary-flush-output`; this is used to guarantee that output to the console appears immediately after it is written, without requiring calls to `flush-output`.

All optional arguments called *output-port*, if not supplied, default to the current output port.

write-char *char* [*output-port*]   [procedure]

> Writes *char* (the character itself, not a written representation of the character) to *output-port*, performs discretionary output flushing, and returns an unspecified value.

write-string *string* [*output-port*]   [procedure]

> Writes *string* to *output-port*, performs discretionary output flushing, and returns an unspecified value. This is equivalent to writing the contents of *string*, one character at a time using **write-char**, except that it is usually much faster.

write-substring *string start end* [*output-port*]   [procedure]

> Writes the substring defined by *string*, *start*, and *end* to *output-port*, performs discretionary output flushing, and returns an unspecified value. This is equivalent to writing the contents of the substring, one character at a time using **write-char**, except that it is usually much faster.

write *object* [*output-port*]   [procedure]

> Writes a written representation of *object* to *output-port*, and returns an unspecified value. If *object* has a standard external representation, then the written representation generated by **write** shall be parsable by **read** into an equivalent object. Thus

strings that appear in the written representation are enclosed in doublequotes, and within those strings backslash and doublequote are escaped by backslashes. `write` performs discretionary output flushing and returns an unspecified value.

`display` *object* [*output-port*]   [procedure]

Writes a representation of *object* to *output-port*. Strings appear in the written representation as if written by `write-string` instead of by `write`. Character objects appear in the representation as if written by `write-char` instead of by `write`. `display` performs discretionary output flushing and returns an unspecified value.[4]

`newline` [*output-port*]   [procedure]

Writes an end-of-line to *output-port*, performs discretionary output flushing, and returns an unspecified value. Equivalent to (`write-char #\newline` *output-port*).

`fresh-line` [*output-port*]   [procedure]

Most output ports are able to tell whether or not they are at the beginning of a line of output. If *output-port* is such a port, this procedure writes an end-of-line to the port only if the port is not already at the beginning of a line. If *output-port* is not such a port, this procedure is identical to `newline`. In either case, `fresh-line` performs discretionary output flushing and returns an unspecified value.

`write-line` *object* [*output-port*]   [procedure]

Like `write`, except that it writes an end-of-line to *output-port* after writing *object*'s representation. This procedure performs discretionary output flushing and returns an unspecified value.

`flush-output` [*output-port*]   [procedure]

If *output-port* is buffered, this causes the contents of its buffer to be written to the output device. Otherwise it has no effect. Returns an unspecified value.

`beep` [*output-port*]   [procedure]

Performs a "beep" operation on *output-port*, performs discretionary output flushing, and returns an unspecified value. On the console port, this usually causes the console bell to beep, but more sophisticated interactive ports may take other actions, such as flashing the screen. On most output ports, e.g. file and string output ports, this does nothing.

`clear` [*output-port*]   [procedure]

"Clears the screen" of *output-port*, performs discretionary output flushing, and returns an unspecified value. On a terminal or window, this has a well-defined effect. On other output ports, e.g. file and string output ports, this does nothing.

`pp` *object* [*output-port* [*as-code?*]]   [procedure]

`pp` prints *object* in a visually appealing and structurally revealing manner on *output-port*. If object is a procedure, `pp` attempts to print the source text. If the optional argument *as-code?* is true, `pp` prints lists as Scheme code, providing appropriate indentation; by default this argument is false. `pp` performs discretionary output flushing and returns an unspecified value.

---

[4] `write` is intended for producing machine-readable output and `display` is for producing human-readable output.

The following variables may be dynamically bound to change the behavior of the `write`
and `display` procedures.

unparser-radix   [variable]

This variable specifies the default radix used to print numbers. Its value must be one
of the exact integers 2, 8, 10, or 16; the default is 10. If *unparser-radix* is not
10, numbers are prefixed to indicate their radix.

unparser-list-breadth-limit   [variable]

This variable specifies a limit on the length of the printed representation of a list or
vector; for example, if the limit is 4, only the first four elements of any list are printed,
followed by ellipses to indicate any additional elements. The value of this variable
must be an exact non-negative integer, or `#f` meaning no limit; the default is `#f`.

```
(fluid-let ((*unparser-list-breadth-limit* 4))
  (write-to-string '(a b c d)))
                               ⇒ "(a b c d)"
(fluid-let ((*unparser-list-breadth-limit* 4))
  (write-to-string '(a b c d e)))
                               ⇒ "(a b c d ...)"
```

unparser-list-depth-limit   [variable]

This variable specifies a limit on the nesting of lists and vectors in the printed representation. If lists (or vectors) are more deeply nested than the limit, the part of the
representation that exceeds the limit is replaced by ellipses. The value of this variable
must be an exact non-negative integer, or `#f` meaning no limit; the default is `#f`.

```
(fluid-let ((*unparser-list-depth-limit* 4))
  (write-to-string '((((a))) b c d)))
                               ⇒ "((((a))) b c d)"
(fluid-let ((*unparser-list-depth-limit* 4))
  (write-to-string '(((((a)))) b c d)))
                               ⇒ "((((...))) b c d)"
```

unparser-string-length-limit   [variable]

This variable specifies a limit on the length of the printed representation of strings.
If a string's length exceeds this limit, the part of the printed representation for the
characters exceeding the limit is replaced by ellipses. The value of this variable must
be an exact non-negative integer, or `#f` meaning no limit; the default is `#f`.

```
(fluid-let ((*unparser-string-length-limit* 4))
  (write-to-string "abcd"))
                               ⇒ "\"abcd\""
(fluid-let ((*unparser-string-length-limit* 4))
  (write-to-string "abcde"))
                               ⇒ "\"abcd...\""
```

unparse-with-maximum-readability?   [variable]

This variable, which takes a boolean value, tells the printer to use a special printed
representation for objects that normally print in a form that cannot be recognized by
`read`. These objects are printed using the representation #@*n*, where *n* is the result

of calling **hash** on the object to be printed. The reader recognizes this syntax, calling **unhash** on n to get back the original object. Note that this printed representation can only be recognized by the Scheme program in which it was generated, because these hash numbers are different for each invocation of Scheme.

14.6 Format

The procedure **format** is very useful for producing nicely formatted text, producing good-looking messages, and so on. MIT/GNU Scheme's implementation of **format** is similar to that of Common Lisp, except that Common Lisp defines many more directives.[5]

format is a run-time-loadable option. To use it, execute

```
(load-option 'format)
```

once before calling it.

format *destination control-string argument ...*   [procedure]

> Writes the characters of *control-string* to *destination*, except that a tilde (~) introduces a *format directive*. The character after the tilde, possibly preceded by prefix parameters and modifiers, specifies what kind of formatting is desired. Most directives use one or more *argument*s to create their output; the typical directive puts the next *argument* into the output, formatted in some special way. It is an error if no argument remains for a directive requiring an argument, but it is not an error if one or more arguments remain unprocessed by a directive.
>
> The output is sent to *destination*. If *destination* is #f, a string is created that contains the output; this string is returned as the value of the call to **format**. In all other cases **format** returns an unspecified value. If *destination* is #t, the output is sent to the current output port. Otherwise, *destination* must be an output port, and the output is sent there.
>
> This procedure performs discretionary output flushing (see Section 14.5 [Output Procedures], page 196).
>
> A **format** directive consists of a tilde (~), optional prefix parameters separated by commas, optional colon (:) and at-sign (@) modifiers, and a single character indicating what kind of directive this is. The alphabetic case of the directive character is ignored. The prefix parameters are generally integers, notated as optionally signed decimal numbers. If both the colon and at-sign modifiers are given, they may appear in either order.
>
> In place of a prefix parameter to a directive, you can put the letter 'V' (or 'v'), which takes an *argument* for use as a parameter to the directive. Normally this should be an exact integer. This feature allows variable-width fields and the like. You can also use the character '#' in place of a parameter; it represents the number of arguments remaining to be processed.
>
> It is an error to give a format directive more parameters than it is described here as accepting. It is also an error to give colon or at-sign modifiers to a directive in a combination not specifically described here as being meaningful.

---

[5] This description of **format** is adapted from *Common Lisp, The Language*, second edition, section 22.3.3.

~A   The next *argument*, which may be any object, is printed as if by `display`.
          *~mincol*A inserts spaces on the right, if necessary, to make the width at
          least *mincol* columns. The @ modifier causes the spaces to be inserted on
          the left rather than the right.

~S   The next *argument*, which may be any object, is printed as if by `write`.
          *~mincol*S inserts spaces on the right, if necessary, to make the width at
          least *mincol* columns. The @ modifier causes the spaces to be inserted on
          the left rather than the right.

~%   This outputs a `#\newline` character. *~n*% outputs *n* newlines. No *ar-
          gument* is used. Simply putting a newline in *control-string* would work,
          but ~% is often used because it makes the control string look nicer in the
          middle of a program.

~~   This outputs a tilde. *~n~* outputs *n* tildes.

~newline Tilde immediately followed by a newline ignores the newline and any
          following non-newline whitespace characters. With an @, the newline is
          left in place, but any following whitespace is ignored. This directive is
          typically used when *control-string* is too long to fit nicely into one line of
          the program:

```
(define (type-clash-error procedure arg spec actual)
  (format
   #t
   "~%Procedure ~S~%requires its %A argument ~
    to be of type ~S,~%but it was called with ~
    an argument of type ~S.~%"
   procedure arg spec actual))

(type-clash-error 'vector-ref
                  "first"
                  'integer
                  'vector)
```

          prints

```
Procedure vector-ref
requires its first argument to be of type integer,
but it was called with an argument of type vector.
```

          Note that in this example newlines appear in the output only as specified
          by the ~% directives; the actual newline characters in the control string
          are suppressed because each is preceded by a tilde.

14.7 Custom Output

MIT/GNU Scheme provides hooks for specifying that certain kinds of objects have special
written representations. There are no restrictions on the written representations, but only
a few kinds of objects may have custom representation specified for them, specifically:

records (see Section 10.4 [Records], page 138), vectors that have special tags in their zero-th elements (see Chapter 8 [Vectors], page 125), and pairs that have special tags in their car fields (see Chapter 7 [Lists], page 109). There is a different procedure for specifying the written representation of each of these types.

set-record-type-unparser-method! *record-type unparser-method*   [procedure]
> Changes the unparser method of the type represented by *record-type* to be *unparser-method*, and returns an unspecified value. Subsequently, when the unparser encounters a record of this type, it will invoke *unparser-method* to generate the written representation.

unparser/set-tagged-vector-method! *tag unparser-method*   [procedure]
> Changes the unparser method of the vector type represented by *tag* to be *unparser-method*, and returns an unspecified value. Subsequently, when the unparser encounters a vector with *tag* as its zero-th element, it will invoke *unparser-method* to generate the written representation.

unparser/set-tagged-pair-method! *tag unparser-method*   [procedure]
> Changes the unparser method of the pair type represented by *tag* to be *unparser-method*, and returns an unspecified value. Subsequently, when the unparser encounters a pair with *tag* in its car field, it will invoke *unparser-method* to generate the written representation.

An *unparser method* is a procedure that is invoked with two arguments: an unparser state and an object. An unparser method generates a written representation for the object, writing it to the output port specified by the unparser state. The value yielded by an unparser method is ignored. Note that an unparser state is not an output port, rather it is an object that contains an output port as one of its components. Application programs generally do not construct or examine unparser state objects, but just pass them along.

There are two ways to create an unparser method (which is then registered by one of the above procedures). The first, and easiest, is to use **standard-unparser-method**. The second is to define your own method using the procedure **with-current-unparser-state**. We encourage the use of the first method, as it results in a more uniform appearance for objects. Many predefined datatypes, for example procedures and environments, already have this appearance.

standard-unparser-method *name procedure*   [procedure]
> Returns a standard unparser method. *Name* may be any object, and is used as the name of the type with which the unparser method is associated; *name* is usually a symbol. *Procedure* must be **#f** or a procedure of two arguments.
>
> If *procedure* is **#f**, the returned method generates an external representation of this form:
>
> > `#[name hash]`
>
> Here *name* is the external representation of the argument *name*, as generated by **write**,[6] and *hash* is the external representation of an exact non-negative integer unique to the object being printed (specifically, it is the result of calling **hash** on the object). Subsequently, the expression

---

[6] Except that if the argument *name* is a string, its external representation is generated by **write-string**.

> `#@hash`

is notation for an expression evaluating to the object.

If *procedure* is supplied, the returned method generates a slightly different external representation:

> `#[name hash output]`

Here *name* and *hash* are as above, and *output* is the output generated by *procedure*. The representation is constructed in three stages:

1. The first part of the format (up to *output*) is written to the output port specified by the unparser state. This is `"#["`, *name*, `" "`, and *hash*.

2. *Procedure* is invoked on two arguments: the object and an output port.

3. The closing bracket is written to the output port.

The following procedure is useful for writing more general kinds of unparser methods.

`with-current-unparser-state` *unparser-state procedure*   [procedure]

    This procedure calls *procedure* with one argument, the output port from *unparser-state*. Additionally, it arranges for the remaining components of *unparser-state* to be given to the printer when they are needed. The *procedure* generates some output by writing to the output port using the usual output operations, and the value yielded by *procedure* is returned from `with-current-unparser-state`.

    The port passed to *procedure* should only be used within the dynamic extent of *procedure*.

14.8 Prompting

This section describes procedures that prompt the user for input. Why should the programmer use these procedures when it is possible to do prompting using ordinary input and output procedures? One reason is that the prompting procedures are more succinct. However, a second and better reason is that the prompting procedures can be separately customized for each user interface, providing more natural interaction. The interfaces for Edwin and for GNU Emacs have already been customized in this fashion; because Edwin and Emacs are very similar editors, their customizations provide very similar behavior.

Each of these procedure accepts an optional argument called *port*, which if given must be an I/O port. If not given, this port defaults to the value of (`interaction-i/o-port`); this is initially the console I/O port.

`prompt-for-command-expression` *prompt* [*port* [*environment*]]   [procedure]

    Prompts the user for an expression that is to be executed as a command. This is the procedure called by the REP loop to read the user's expressions.

    If *prompt* is a string, it is used verbatim as the prompt string. Otherwise, it must be a pair whose car is the symbol '`standard`' and whose cdr is a string; in this case the prompt string is formed by prepending to the string the current REP loop "level number" and a space. Also, a space is appended to the string, unless it already ends in a space or is an empty string.

    If *environment* is given, it is passed as the second argument to `read`.

The default behavior of this procedure is to print a fresh line, a newline, and the prompt string; flush the output buffer; then read an object and return it.

Under Edwin and Emacs, before the object is read, the interaction buffer is put into a mode that allows expressions to be edited and submitted for input using specific editor commands. The first expression that is submitted is returned as the value of this procedure.

prompt-for-command-char *prompt* [*port*]   [procedure]
Prompts the user for a single character that is to be executed as a command; the returned character is guaranteed to satisfy **char-graphic?**. If at all possible, the character is read from the user interface using a mode that reads the character as a single keystroke; in other words, it should not be necessary for the user to follow the character with a carriage return or something similar.

This is the procedure called by **debug** and **where** to read the user's commands.

If *prompt* is a string, it is used verbatim as the prompt string. Otherwise, it must be a pair whose car is **standard** and whose cdr is a string; in this case the prompt string is formed by prepending to the string the current REP loop "level number" and a space. Also, a space is appended to the string, unless it already ends in a space or is an empty string.

The default behavior of this procedure is to print a fresh line, a newline, and the prompt string; flush the output buffer; read a character in raw mode, echo that character, and return it.

Under Edwin and Emacs, instead of reading a character, the interaction buffer is put into a mode in which graphic characters submit themselves as input. After this mode change, the first such character submitted is returned as the value of this procedure.

prompt-for-expression *prompt* [*port* [*environment*]]   [procedure]
Prompts the user for an expression.

The prompt string is formed by appending a colon and a space to *prompt*, unless *prompt* already ends in a space or is the null string.

If *environment* is given, it is passed as the second argument to **read**.

The default behavior of this procedure is to print a fresh line, a newline, and the prompt string; flush the output buffer; then read an object and return it.

Under Edwin and Emacs, the expression is read in the minibuffer.

prompt-for-evaluated-expression *prompt* [*environment* [*port*]]   [procedure]
Prompts the user for an evaluated expression. Calls **prompt-for-expression** to read an expression, then evaluates the expression using *environment*; if *environment* is not given, the REP loop environment is used.

prompt-for-confirmation *prompt* [*port*]   [procedure]
Prompts the user for confirmation. The result yielded by this procedure is a boolean.

The prompt string is formed by appending the string " (y or n)? " to *prompt*, unless *prompt* already ends in a space or is the null string.

The default behavior of this procedure is to print a fresh line, a newline, and the prompt string; flush the output buffer; then read a character in raw mode. If the character is #\y, #\Y, or #\space, the procedure returns #t; If the character is #\n, #\N, or #\rubout, the procedure returns #f. Otherwise the prompt is repeated.

Under Edwin or Emacs, the confirmation is read in the minibuffer.

14.9 Port Primitives

This section describes the low-level operations that can be used to build and manipulate I/O ports.

The purpose of these operations is twofold: to allow programmers to construct new kinds of I/O ports, and to provide faster I/O operations than those supplied by the standard high level procedures. The latter is useful because the standard I/O operations provide defaulting and error checking, and sometimes other features, which are often unnecessary. This interface provides the means to bypass such features, thus improving performance.

The abstract model of an I/O port, as implemented here, is a combination of a set of named operations and a state. The state is an arbitrary object, the meaning of which is determined by the operations. The operations are defined by a mapping from names to procedures.

The set of named operations is represented by an object called a *port type*. A port type is constructed from a set of named operations, and is subsequently used to construct a port. The port type completely specifies the behavior of the port. Port types also support a simple form of inheritance, allowing you to create new ports that are similar to existing ports.

The port operations are divided into two classes:

Standard operations

> There is a specific set of standard operations for input ports, and a different set for output ports. Applications can assume that the standard input operations are implemented for all input ports, and likewise the standard output operations are implemented for all output ports.

Custom operations

> Some ports support additional operations. For example, ports that implement output to terminals (or windows) may define an operation named y-size that returns the height of the terminal in characters. Because only some ports will implement these operations, programs that use custom operations must test each port for their existence, and be prepared to deal with ports that do not implement them.

14.9.1 Port Types

The procedures in this section provide means for constructing port types with standard and custom operations, and accessing their operations.

make-port-type *operations port-type*   [procedure]
> Creates and returns a new port type. *Operations* must be a list; each element is a list of two elements, the name of the operation (a symbol) and the procedure that implements it. *Port-type* is either #f or a port type; if it is a port type, any operations implemented by *port-type* but not specified in *operations* will be implemented by the resulting port type.

Operations need not contain definitions for all of the standard operations; the procedure will provide defaults for any standard operations that are not defined. At a minimum, the following operations must be defined: for input ports, `read-char` and `peek-char`; for output ports, either `write-char` or `write-substring`. I/O ports must supply the minimum operations for both input and output.

If an operation in *operations* is defined to be `#f`, then the corresponding operation in *port-type* is *not* inherited.

If `read-char` is defined in *operations*, then any standard input operations defined in *port-type* are ignored. Likewise, if `write-char` or `write-substring` is defined in *operations*, then any standard output operations defined in *port-type* are ignored. This feature allows overriding the standard operations without having to enumerate them.

`port-type?` *object*	[procedure]
`input-port-type?` *object*	[procedure]
`output-port-type?` *object*	[procedure]
`i/o-port-type?` *object*	[procedure]

These predicates return `#t` if *object* is a port type, input-port type, output-port type, or I/O-port type, respectively. Otherwise, they return `#f`.

`port-type/operations` *port-type*   [procedure]

Returns a newly allocated list containing all of the operations implemented by *port-type*. Each element of the list is a list of two elements — the name and its associated operation.

`port-type/operation-names` *port-type*   [procedure]

Returns a newly allocated list whose elements are the names of the operations implemented by *port-type*.

`port-type/operation` *port-type symbol*   [procedure]

Returns the operation named *symbol* in *port-type*. If *port-type* has no such operation, returns `#f`.

14.9.2 Constructors and Accessors for Ports

The procedures in this section provide means for constructing ports, accessing the type of a port, and manipulating the state of a port.

`make-port` *port-type state*   [procedure]

Returns a new port with type *port-type* and the given *state*. The port will be an input, output, or I/O port according to *port-type*.

`port/type` *port*   [procedure]

Returns the port type of *port*.

`port/state` *port*   [procedure]

Returns the state component of *port*.

`set-port/state!` *port object*   [procedure]

Changes the state component of *port* to be *object*. Returns an unspecified value.

port/operation *port symbol*   [procedure]
    Equivalent to

        `(port-type/operation (port/type port) symbol)`

port/operation-names *port*   [procedure]
    Equivalent to

        `(port-type/operation-names (port/type port))`

make-eof-object *input-port*   [procedure]
    Returns an object that satisfies the predicate `eof-object?`. This is sometimes useful
    when building input ports.

14.9.3 Input Port Operations

This section describes the standard operations on input ports. Following that, some useful
custom operations are described.

read-char *input-port*   [operation on **input port**]
    Removes the next character available from *input-port* and returns it. If *input-port*
    has no more characters and will never have any (e.g. at the end of an input file), this
    operation returns an end-of-file object. If *input-port* has no more characters but will
    eventually have some more (e.g. a terminal where nothing has been typed recently),
    and it is in non-blocking mode, `#f` is returned; otherwise the operation hangs until
    input is available.

peek-char *input-port*   [operation on **input port**]
    Reads the next character available from *input-port* and returns it. The character is
    not removed from *input-port*, and a subsequent attempt to read from the port will
    get that character again. In other respects this operation behaves like `read-char`.

char-ready? *input-port k*   [operation on **input port**]
    `char-ready?` returns `#t` if at least one character is available to be read from *input-
    port*. If no characters are available, the operation waits up to *k* milliseconds before
    returning `#f`, returning immediately if any characters become available while it is
    waiting.

read-string *input-port char-set*   [operation on **input port**]
discard-chars *input-port char-set*   [operation on **input port**]
    These operations are like `read-char`, except that they read or discard multiple char-
    acters at once. All characters up to, but excluding, the first character in *char-set*
    (or end of file) are read from *input-port*. `read-string` returns these characters as a
    newly allocated string, while `discard-chars` discards them and returns an unspeci-
    fied value. These operations hang until sufficient input is available, even if *input-port*
    is in non-blocking mode. If end of file is encountered before any input characters,
    `read-string` returns an end-of-file object.

read-substring *input-port string start end*   [operation on **input port**]
    Reads characters from *input-port* into the substring defined by *string*, *start*, and *end*
    until either the substring has been filled or there are no more characters available.
    Returns the number of characters written to the substring.

If *input-port* is an interactive port, and at least one character is immediately available, the available characters are written to the substring and this operation returns immediately. If no characters are available, and *input-port* is in blocking mode, the operation blocks until at least one character is available. Otherwise, the operation returns #f immediately.

This is an extremely fast way to read characters from a port.

`input-port/read-char` *input-port*	[procedure]
`input-port/peek-char` *input-port*	[procedure]
`input-port/char-ready?` *input-port k*	[procedure]
`input-port/read-string` *input-port char-set*	[procedure]
`input-port/discard-chars` *input-port char-set*	[procedure]
`input-port/read-substring` *input-port string start end*	[procedure]

Each of these procedures invokes the respective operation on *input-port*. For example, the following are equivalent:

```
(input-port/read-char input-port)

((port/operation input-port 'read-char) input-port)
```

The following custom operations are implemented for input ports to files, and will also work with some other kinds of input ports:

`eof?` *input-port*   [operation on `input port`]

> Returns #t if *input-port* is known to be at end of file, otherwise it returns #f.

`chars-remaining` *input-port*   [operation on `input port`]

> Returns an estimate of the number of characters remaining to be read from *input-port*. This is useful only when *input-port* is a file port in binary mode; in other cases, it returns #f.

`buffered-input-chars` *input-port*   [operation on `input port`]

> Returns the number of unread characters that are stored in *input-port*'s buffer. This will always be less than or equal to the buffer's size.

`input-buffer-size` *input-port*   [operation on `input port`]

> Returns the maximum number of characters that *input-port*'s buffer can hold.

`set-input-buffer-size` *input-port size*   [operation on `input port`]

> Resizes *input-port*'s buffer so that it can hold at most *size* characters. Characters in the buffer are discarded. *Size* must be an exact non-negative integer.

14.9.4 Output Port Operations

This section describes the standard operations on output ports. Following that, some useful custom operations are described.

`write-char` *output-port char*   [operation on `output port`]

> Writes *char* to *output-port* and returns an unspecified value.

`write-substring` *output-port string start end*   [operation on `output port`]

> Writes the substring specified by *string*, *start*, and *end* to *output-port* and returns an unspecified value. Equivalent to writing the characters of the substring, one by one, to *output-port*, but is implemented very efficiently.

fresh-line *output-port*   [operation on `output` port]
> Most output ports are able to tell whether or not they are at the beginning of a line
> of output. If *output-port* is such a port, end-of-line is written to the port only if the
> port is not already at the beginning of a line. If *output-port* is not such a port, an
> end-of-line is unconditionally written to the port. Returns an unspecified value.

flush-output *output-port*   [operation on `output` port]
> If *output-port* is buffered, this causes its buffer to be written out. Otherwise it has
> no effect. Returns an unspecified value.

discretionary-flush-output *output-port*   [operation on `output` port]
> Normally, this operation does nothing. However, ports that support discretionary
> output flushing implement this operation identically to `flush-output`.

output-port/write-char *output-port char*   [procedure]
output-port/write-substring *output-port string start end*   [procedure]
output-port/fresh-line *output-port*   [procedure]
output-port/flush-output *output-port*   [procedure]
output-port/discretionary-flush-output *output-port*   [procedure]
> Each of these procedures invokes the respective operation on *output-port*. For exam-
> ple, the following are equivalent:

```
(output-port/write-char output-port char)
((port/operation output-port 'write-char)
 output-port char)
```

output-port/write-string *output-port string*   [procedure]
> Writes *string* to *output-port*. Equivalent to

```
(output-port/write-substring output-port
                             string
                             0
                             (string-length string))
```

The following custom operations are generally useful.

buffered-output-chars *output-port*   [operation on `output` port]
> Returns the number of unwritten characters that are stored in *output-port*'s buffer.
> This will always be less than or equal to the buffer's size.

output-buffer-size *output-port*   [operation on `output` port]
> Returns the maximum number of characters that *output-port*'s buffer can hold.

set-output-buffer-size *output-port size*   [operation on `output` port]
> Resizes *output-port*'s buffer so that it can hold at most *size* characters. Characters
> in the buffer are discarded. *Size* must be an exact non-negative integer.

x-size *output-port*   [operation on `output` port]
> Returns an exact positive integer that is the width of *output-port* in characters. If
> *output-port* has no natural width, e.g. if it is a file port, `#f` is returned.

y-size *output-port*   [operation on `output port`]

   Returns an exact positive integer that is the height of *output-port* in characters. If
   output-port has no natural height, e.g. if it is a file port, `#f` is returned.

output-port/x-size *output-port*   [procedure]

   This procedure invokes the custom operation whose name is the symbol `x-size`, if it
   exists. If the `x-size` operation is both defined and returns a value other than `#f`, that
   value is returned as the result of this procedure. Otherwise, `output-port/x-size`
   returns a default value (currently 80).

   `output-port/x-size` is useful for programs that tailor their output to the width
   of the display (a fairly common practice). If the output device is not a display,
   such programs normally want some reasonable default width to work with, and this
   procedure provides exactly that.

output-port/y-size *output-port*   [procedure]

   This procedure invokes the custom operation whose name is the symbol `y-size`, if
   it exists. If the `y-size` operation is defined, the value it returns is returned as the
   result of this procedure; otherwise, `#f` is returned.

14.9.5 Blocking Mode

An interactive port is always in one of two modes: *blocking* or *non-blocking*. This mode
is independent of the terminal mode: each can be changed independent of the other. Furthermore, if it is an interactive I/O port, there are separate blocking modes for input and
for output.

If an input port is in blocking mode, attempting to read from it when no input is available
will cause Scheme to "block", i.e. suspend itself, until input is available. If an input port is
in non-blocking mode, attempting to read from it when no input is available will cause the
reading procedure to return immediately, indicating the lack of input in some way (exactly
how this situation is indicated is separately specified for each procedure or operation).

An output port in blocking mode will block if the output device is not ready to accept
output. In non-blocking mode it will return immediately after performing as much output
as the device will allow (again, each procedure or operation reports this situation in its own
way).

Interactive ports are initially in blocking mode; this can be changed at any time with
the procedures defined in this section.

These procedures represent blocking mode by the symbol `blocking`, and non-blocking
mode by the symbol `nonblocking`. An argument called *mode* must be one of these symbols.
A *port* argument to any of these procedures may be any port, even if that port does not
support blocking mode; in that case, the port is not modified in any way.

port/input-blocking-mode *port*   [procedure]

   Returns the input blocking mode of *port*.

port/set-input-blocking-mode *port mode*   [procedure]

   Changes the input blocking mode of *port* to be *mode*. Returns an unspecified value.

port/with-input-blocking-mode *port mode thunk*   [procedure]

> *Thunk* must be a procedure of no arguments. `port/with-input-blocking-mode`
> binds the input blocking mode of *port* to be *mode*, executes *thunk*, restores the input
> blocking mode of *port* to what it was when `port/with-input-blocking-mode` was
> called, and returns the value that was yielded by *thunk*. This binding is performed by
> `dynamic-wind`, which guarantees that the input blocking mode is restored if *thunk*
> escapes from its continuation.

port/output-blocking-mode *port*   [procedure]

> Returns the output blocking mode of *port*.

port/set-output-blocking-mode *port mode*   [procedure]

> Changes the output blocking mode of *port* to be *mode*. Returns an unspecified value.

port/with-output-blocking-mode *port mode thunk*   [procedure]

> *Thunk* must be a procedure of no arguments. `port/with-output-blocking-mode`
> binds the output blocking mode of *port* to be *mode*, executes *thunk*, restores the
> output blocking mode of *port* to what it was when `port/with-output-blocking-`
> `mode` was called, and returns the value that was yielded by *thunk*. This binding
> is performed by `dynamic-wind`, which guarantees that the output blocking mode is
> restored if *thunk* escapes from its continuation.

14.9.6 Terminal Mode

A port that reads from or writes to a terminal has a *terminal mode*; this is either *cooked*
or *raw*. This mode is independent of the blocking mode: each can be changed independent
of the other. Furthermore, a terminal I/O port has independent terminal modes both for
input and for output.

A terminal port in cooked mode provides some standard processing to make the terminal
easy to communicate with. For example, under unix, cooked mode on input reads from the
terminal a line at a time and provides rubout processing within the line, while cooked
mode on output might translate linefeeds to carriage-return/linefeed pairs. In general, the
precise meaning of cooked mode is operating-system dependent, and furthermore might
be customizable by means of operating system utilities. The basic idea is that cooked
mode does whatever is necessary to make the terminal handle all of the usual user-interface
conventions for the operating system, while keeping the program's interaction with the port
as normal as possible.

A terminal port in raw mode disables all of that processing. In raw mode, characters are
directly read from and written to the device without any translation or interpretation by
the operating system. On input, characters are available as soon as they are typed, and are
not echoed on the terminal by the operating system. In general, programs that put ports
in raw mode have to know the details of interacting with the terminal. In particular, raw
mode is used for writing programs such as text editors.

Terminal ports are initially in cooked mode; this can be changed at any time with the
procedures defined in this section.

These procedures represent cooked mode by the symbol `cooked`, and raw mode by the
symbol `raw`. Additionally, the value `#f` represents "no mode"; it is the terminal mode of a
port that is not a terminal. An argument called *mode* must be one of these three values.

A *port* argument to any of these procedures may be any port, even if that port does not support terminal mode; in that case, the port is not modified in any way.

port/input-terminal-mode *port*   [procedure]
>   Returns the input terminal mode of *port*.

port/set-input-terminal-mode *port mode*   [procedure]
>   Changes the input terminal mode of *port* to be *mode*. Returns an unspecified value.

port/with-input-terminal-mode *port mode thunk*   [procedure]
>   *Thunk* must be a procedure of no arguments. `port/with-input-terminal-mode` binds the input terminal mode of *port* to be *mode*, executes *thunk*, restores the input terminal mode of *port* to what it was when `port/with-input-terminal-mode` was called, and returns the value that was yielded by *thunk*. This binding is performed by `dynamic-wind`, which guarantees that the input terminal mode is restored if *thunk* escapes from its continuation.

port/output-terminal-mode *port*   [procedure]
>   Returns the output terminal mode of *port*.

port/set-output-terminal-mode *port mode*   [procedure]
>   Changes the output terminal mode of *port* to be *mode*. Returns an unspecified value.

port/with-output-terminal-mode *port mode thunk*   [procedure]
>   *Thunk* must be a procedure of no arguments. `port/with-output-terminal-mode` binds the output terminal mode of *port* to be *mode*, executes *thunk*, restores the output terminal mode of *port* to what it was when `port/with-output-terminal-mode` was called, and returns the value that was yielded by *thunk*. This binding is performed by `dynamic-wind`, which guarantees that the output terminal mode is restored if *thunk* escapes from its continuation.

14.10 Parser Buffers

The *parser buffer* mechanism facilitates construction of parsers for complex grammars. It does this by providing an input stream with unbounded buffering and backtracking. The amount of buffering is under program control. The stream can backtrack to any position in the buffer.

The mechanism defines two data types: the *parser buffer* and the *parser-buffer pointer*. A parser buffer is like an input port with buffering and backtracking. A parser-buffer pointer is a pointer into the stream of characters provided by a parser buffer.

Note that all of the procedures defined here consider a parser buffer to contain a stream of Unicode characters.

There are several constructors for parser buffers:

input-port->parser-buffer *port*   [procedure]
>   Returns a parser buffer that buffers characters read from *port*.

substring->parser-buffer *string start end*   [procedure]
>   Returns a parser buffer that buffers the characters in the argument substring. This is equivalent to creating a string input port and calling `input-port->parser-buffer`, but it runs faster and uses less memory.

string->parser-buffer *string*   [procedure]
Like `substring->parser-buffer` but buffers the entire string.

source->parser-buffer *source*   [procedure]
Returns a parser buffer that buffers the characters returned by calling *source*. *Source* is a procedure of three arguments: a string, a start index, and an end index (in other words, a substring specifier). Each time *source* is called, it writes some characters in the substring, and returns the number of characters written. When there are no more characters available, it returns zero. It must not return zero in any other circumstance.

Parser buffers and parser-buffer pointers may be distinguished from other objects:

parser-buffer? *object*   [procedure]
Returns `#t` if *object* is a parser buffer, otherwise returns `#f`.

parser-buffer-pointer? *object*   [procedure]
Returns `#t` if *object* is a parser-buffer pointer, otherwise returns `#f`.

Characters can be read from a parser buffer much as they can be read from an input port. The parser buffer maintains an internal pointer indicating its current position in the input stream. Additionally, the buffer remembers all characters that were previously read, and can look at characters arbitrarily far ahead in the stream. It is this buffering capability that facilitates complex matching and backtracking.

read-parser-buffer-char *buffer*   [procedure]
Returns the next character in *buffer*, advancing the internal pointer past that character. If there are no more characters available, returns `#f` and leaves the internal pointer unchanged.

peek-parser-buffer-char *buffer*   [procedure]
Returns the next character in *buffer*, or `#f` if no characters are available. Leaves the internal pointer unchanged.

parser-buffer-ref *buffer index*   [procedure]
Returns a character in *buffer*. *Index* is a non-negative integer specifying the character to be returned. If *index* is zero, returns the next available character; if it is one, returns the character after that, and so on. If *index* specifies a position after the last character in *buffer*, returns `#f`. Leaves the internal pointer unchanged.

The internal pointer of a parser buffer can be read or written:

get-parser-buffer-pointer *buffer*   [procedure]
Returns a parser-buffer pointer object corresponding to the internal pointer of *buffer*.

set-parser-buffer-pointer! *buffer pointer*   [procedure]
Sets the internal pointer of *buffer* to the position specified by *pointer*. *Pointer* must have been returned from a previous call of `get-parser-buffer-pointer` on *buffer*. Additionally, if some of *buffer*'s characters have been discarded by `discard-parser-buffer-head!`, *pointer* must be outside the range that was discarded.

`get-parser-buffer-tail` *buffer pointer*   [procedure]

> Returns a newly-allocated string consisting of all of the characters in *buffer* that fall between *pointer* and *buffer*'s internal pointer. *Pointer* must have been returned from a previous call of `get-parser-buffer-pointer` on *buffer*. Additionally, if some of *buffer*'s characters have been discarded by `discard-parser-buffer-head!`, *pointer* must be outside the range that was discarded.

`discard-parser-buffer-head!` *buffer*   [procedure]

> Discards all characters in *buffer* that have already been read; in other words, all characters prior to the internal pointer. After this operation has completed, it is no longer possible to move the internal pointer backwards past the current position by calling `set-parser-buffer-pointer!`.

The next rather large set of procedures does conditional matching against the contents of a parser buffer. All matching is performed relative to the buffer's internal pointer, so the first character to be matched against is the next character that would be returned by `peek-parser-buffer-char`. The returned value is always `#t` for a successful match, and `#f` otherwise. For procedures whose names do not end in '`-no-advance`', a successful match also moves the internal pointer of the buffer forward to the end of the matched text; otherwise the internal pointer is unchanged.

`match-parser-buffer-char` *buffer char*   [procedure]
`match-parser-buffer-char-ci` *buffer char*   [procedure]
`match-parser-buffer-not-char` *buffer char*   [procedure]
`match-parser-buffer-not-char-ci` *buffer char*   [procedure]
`match-parser-buffer-char-no-advance` *buffer char*   [procedure]
`match-parser-buffer-char-ci-no-advance` *buffer char*   [procedure]
`match-parser-buffer-not-char-no-advance` *buffer char*   [procedure]
`match-parser-buffer-not-char-ci-no-advance` *buffer char*   [procedure]

> Each of these procedures compares a single character in *buffer* to *char*. The basic comparison `match-parser-buffer-char` compares the character to *char* using `char=?`. The procedures whose names contain the '`-ci`' modifier do case-insensitive comparison (i.e. they use `char-ci=?`). The procedures whose names contain the '`not-`' modifier are successful if the character *doesn't* match *char*.

`match-parser-buffer-char-in-set` *buffer char-set*   [procedure]
`match-parser-buffer-char-in-set-no-advance` *buffer char-set*   [procedure]

> These procedures compare the next character in *buffer* against *char-set* using `char-set-member?`.

`match-parser-buffer-string` *buffer string*   [procedure]
`match-parser-buffer-string-ci` *buffer string*   [procedure]
`match-parser-buffer-string-no-advance` *buffer string*   [procedure]
`match-parser-buffer-string-ci-no-advance` *buffer string*   [procedure]

> These procedures match *string* against *buffer*'s contents. The '`-ci`' procedures do case-insensitive matching.

`match-parser-buffer-substring` *buffer string start end*   [procedure]
`match-parser-buffer-substring-ci` *buffer string start end*   [procedure]

`match-parser-buffer-substring-no-advance` *buffer string start end*   [procedure]
`match-parser-buffer-substring-ci-no-advance` *buffer string start*   [procedure]
      end
> These procedures match the specified substring against *buffer*'s contents. The '`-ci`' procedures do case-insensitive matching.

The remaining procedures provide information that can be used to identify locations in a parser buffer's stream.

`parser-buffer-position-string` *pointer*   [procedure]
> Returns a string describing the location of *pointer* in terms of its character and line indexes. This resulting string is meant to be presented to an end user in order to direct their attention to a feature in the input stream. In this string, the indexes are presented as one-based numbers.
>
> *Pointer* may alternatively be a parser buffer, in which case it is equivalent to having specified the buffer's internal pointer.

`parser-buffer-pointer-index` *pointer*   [procedure]
`parser-buffer-pointer-line` *pointer*   [procedure]
> Returns the character or line index, respectively, of *pointer*. Both indexes are zero-based.

14.11 Parser Language

Although it is possible to write parsers using the parser-buffer abstraction (see Section 14.10 [Parser Buffers], page 211), it is tedious. The problem is that the abstraction isn't closely matched to the way that people think about syntactic structures. In this section, we introduce a higher-level mechanism that greatly simplifies the implementation of a parser.

The *parser language* described here allows the programmer to write BNF-like specifications that are translated into efficient Scheme code at compile time. The language is declarative, but it can be freely mixed with Scheme code; this allows the parsing of grammars that aren't conveniently described in the language.

The language also provides backtracking. For example, this expression matches any sequence of alphanumeric characters followed by a single alphabetic character:

```
(*matcher
 (seq (* (char-set char-set:alphanumeric))
      (char-set char-set:alphabetic)))
```

The way that this works is that the matcher matches alphanumeric characters in the input stream until it finds a non-alphanumeric character. It then tries to match an alphabetic character, which of course fails. At this point, if it matched at least one alphanumeric character, it *backtracks*: the last matched alphanumeric is "unmatched", and it again attempts to match an alphabetic character. The backtracking can be arbitrarily deep; the matcher will continue to back up until it finds a way to match the remainder of the expression.

So far, this sounds a lot like regular-expression matching (see Section 6.8 [Regular Expressions], page 100). However, there are some important differences.

- The parser language uses a Scheme-like syntax that is easier to read and write than regular-expression notation.

- The language provides macros so that common syntactic constructs can be abstracted.

- The language mixes easily with Scheme code, allowing the full power of Scheme to be applied to program around limitations in the parser language.

- The language provides expressive facilities for converting syntax into parsed structure. It also makes it easy to convert parsed strings into meaningful objects (e.g. numbers).

- The language is compiled into machine language; regular expressions are usually interpreted.

Here is an example that shows off several of the features of the parser language. The example is a parser for XML start tags:

```
(*parser
 (with-pointer p
   (seq "<"
        parse-name
        parse-attribute-list
        (alt (match ">")
             (match "/>")
             (sexp
              (lambda (b)
                (error
                 (string-append
                  "Unterminated start tag at "
                  (parser-buffer-position-string p)))))))))
```

This shows that the basic description of a start tag is very similar to its BNF. Non-terminal symbols `parse-name` and `parse-attribute-list` do most of the work, and the noise strings `"<"` and `">"` are the syntactic markers delimiting the form. There are two alternate endings for start tags, and if the parser doesn't find either of the endings, the Scheme code (wrapped in `sexp`) is run to signal an error. The error procedure `perror` takes a pointer p, which it uses to indicate the position in the input stream at which the error occurred. In this case, that is the beginning of the start tag, i.e. the position of the leading `"<"` marker.

This example still looks pretty complicated, mostly due to the error-signalling code. In practice, this is abstracted into a macro, after which the expression is quite succinct:

```
(*parser
 (bracket "start tag"
     (seq (noise (string "<")) parse-name)
     (match (alt (string ">") (string "/>")))
   parse-attribute-list))
```

The `bracket` macro captures the pattern of a bracketed item, and hides much of the detail.

The parser language actually consists of two languages: one for defining matchers, and one for defining parsers. The languages are intentionally very similar, and are meant to be used together. Each sub-language is described below in its own section.

The parser language is a run-time-loadable option; to use it, execute

```
(load-option '*parser)
```

once before compiling any code that uses the language.

14.11.1 *Matcher

The *matcher language* is a declarative language for specifying a *matcher procedure*. A matcher procedure is a procedure that accepts a single parser-buffer argument and returns a boolean value indicating whether the match it performs was successful. If the match succeeds, the internal pointer of the parser buffer is moved forward over the matched text. If the match fails, the internal pointer is unchanged.

For example, here is a matcher procedure that matches the character 'a':

```
(lambda (b) (match-parser-buffer-char b #\a))
```

Here is another example that matches two given characters, *c1* and *c2*, in sequence:

```
(lambda (b)
  (let ((p (get-parser-buffer-pointer b)))
    (if (match-parser-buffer-char b c1)
        (if (match-parser-buffer-char b c2)
            #t
            (begin
              (set-parser-buffer-pointer! b p)
              #f))
        #f)))
```

This is code is clear, but has lots of details that get in the way of understanding what it is doing. Here is the same example in the matcher language:

```
(*matcher (seq (char c1) (char c2)))
```

This is much simpler and more intuitive. And it generates virtually the same code:

```
(pp (*matcher (seq (char c1) (char c2))))
⊣ (lambda (#[b1])
⊣    (let ((#[p1] (get-parser-buffer-pointer #[b1])))
⊣      (and (match-parser-buffer-char #[b1] c1)
⊣           (if (match-parser-buffer-char #[b1] c2)
⊣               #t
⊣               (begin
⊣                 (set-parser-buffer-pointer! #[b1] #[p1])
⊣                 #f)))))
```

Now that we have seen an example of the language, it's time to look at the detail. The *matcher special form is the interface between the matcher language and Scheme.

*matcher *mexp*   [special form]

    The operand *mexp* is an expression in the matcher language. The *matcher expression expands into Scheme code that implements a matcher procedure.

Here are the predefined matcher expressions. New matcher expressions can be defined using the macro facility (see Section 14.11.3 [Parser-language Macros], page 222). We will start with the primitive expressions.

char *expression*   [matcher expression]
char-ci *expression*   [matcher expression]
not-char *expression*   [matcher expression]

`not-char-ci` *expression*   [matcher expression]

These expressions match a given character. In each case, the *expression* operand is a Scheme expression that must evaluate to a character at run time. The '`-ci`' expressions do case-insensitive matching. The '`not-`' expressions match any character other than the given one.

`string` *expression*   [matcher expression]
`string-ci` *expression*   [matcher expression]

These expressions match a given string. The *expression* operand is a Scheme expression that must evaluate to a string at run time. The `string-ci` expression does case-insensitive matching.

`char-set` *expression*   [matcher expression]

These expressions match a single character that is a member of a given character set. The *expression* operand is a Scheme expression that must evaluate to a character set at run time.

`end-of-input`   [matcher expression]

The `end-of-input` expression is successful only when there are no more characters available to be matched.

`discard-matched`   [matcher expression]

The `discard-matched` expression always successfully matches the null string. However, it isn't meant to be used as a matching expression; it is used for its effect. `discard-matched` causes all of the buffered text prior to this point to be discarded (i.e. it calls `discard-parser-buffer-head!` on the parser buffer).

Note that `discard-matched` may not be used in certain places in a matcher expression. The reason for this is that it deliberately discards information needed for backtracking, so it may not be used in a place where subsequent backtracking will need to back over it. As a rule of thumb, use `discard-matched` only in the last operand of a `seq` or `alt` expression (including any `seq` or `alt` expressions in which it is indirectly contained).

In addition to the above primitive expressions, there are two convenient abbreviations. A character literal (e.g. '`#\A`') is a legal primitive expression, and is equivalent to a `char` expression with that literal as its operand (e.g. '`(char #\A)`'). Likewise, a string literal is equivalent to a `string` expression (e.g. '`(string "abc")`').

Next there are several combinator expressions. These closely correspond to similar combinators in regular expressions. Parameters named *mexp* are arbitrary expressions in the matcher language.

`seq` *mexp* ...   [matcher expression]

This matches each *mexp* operand in sequence. For example,

```
(seq (char-set char-set:alphabetic)
     (char-set char-set:numeric))
```

matches an alphabetic character followed by a numeric character, such as '`H4`'.

Note that if there are no *mexp* operands, the `seq` expression successfully matches the null string.

`alt` *mexp* ...   [matcher expression]

This attempts to match each *mexp* operand in order from left to right. The first one that successfully matches becomes the match for the entire `alt` expression.

The `alt` expression participates in backtracking. If one of the *mexp* operands matches, but the overall match in which this expression is embedded fails, the backtracking mechanism will cause the `alt` expression to try the remaining *mexp* operands. For example, if the expression

```
(seq (alt "ab" "a") "b")
```

is matched against the text 'abc', the `alt` expression will initially match its first operand. But it will then fail to match the second operand of the `seq` expression. This will cause the `alt` to be restarted, at which time it will match 'a', and the overall match will succeed.

Note that if there are no *mexp* operands, the `alt` match will always fail.

`*` *mexp*   [matcher expression]

This matches zero or more occurrences of the *mexp* operand. (Consequently this match always succeeds.)

The * expression participates in backtracking; if it matches N occurrences of *mexp*, but the overall match fails, it will backtrack to *N-1* occurrences and continue. If the overall match continues to fail, the * expression will continue to backtrack until there are no occurrences left.

`+` *mexp*   [matcher expression]

This matches one or more occurrences of the *mexp* operand. It is equivalent to

```
(seq mexp (* mexp))
```

`?` *mexp*   [matcher expression]

This matches zero or one occurrences of the *mexp* operand. It is equivalent to

```
(alt mexp (seq))
```

`sexp` *expression*   [matcher expression]

The `sexp` expression allows arbitrary Scheme code to be embedded inside a matcher. The *expression* operand must evaluate to a matcher procedure at run time; the procedure is called to match the parser buffer. For example,

```
(*matcher
 (seq "a"
      (sexp parse-foo)
      "b"))
```

expands to

```
(lambda (#[b1])
  (let ((#[p1] (get-parser-buffer-pointer #[b1])))
    (and (match-parser-buffer-char #[b1] #\a)
         (if (parse-foo #[b1])
             (if (match-parser-buffer-char #[b1] #\b)
                 #t
                 (begin
                   (set-parser-buffer-pointer! #[b1] #[p1])
                   #f))
             (begin
               (set-parser-buffer-pointer! #[b1] #[p1])
               #f)))))
```

The case in which *expression* is a symbol is so common that it has an abbreviation:
'(sexp *symbol*)' may be abbreviated as just *symbol*.

with-pointer *identifier mexp*   [matcher expression]
    The **with-pointer** expression fetches the parser buffer's internal pointer (using
    get-parser-buffer-pointer), binds it to *identifier*, and then matches the pattern
    specified by *mexp*. *Identifier* must be a symbol.

    This is meant to be used on conjunction with **sexp**, as a way to capture a pointer to
    a part of the input stream that is outside the **sexp** expression. An example of the
    use of **with-pointer** appears above (see [with-pointer example], page 215).

14.11.2 *Parser

The *parser language* is a declarative language for specifying a *parser procedure*. A parser
procedure is a procedure that accepts a single parser-buffer argument and parses some of
the input from the buffer. If the parse is successful, the procedure returns a vector of objects
that are the result of the parse, and the internal pointer of the parser buffer is advanced
past the input that was parsed. If the parse fails, the procedure returns **#f** and the internal
pointer is unchanged. This interface is much like that of a matcher procedure, except that
on success the parser procedure returns a vector of values rather than **#t**.

The ***parser** special form is the interface between the parser language and Scheme.

*parser *pexp*   [special form]
    The operand *pexp* is an expression in the parser language. The ***parser** expression
    expands into Scheme code that implements a parser procedure.

There are several primitive expressions in the parser language. The first two provide a
bridge to the matcher language (see Section 14.11.1 [*Matcher], page 216):

match *mexp*   [parser expression]
    The **match** expression performs a match on the parser buffer. The match to be
    performed is specified by *mexp*, which is an expression in the matcher language. If
    the match is successful, the result of the **match** expression is a vector of one element:
    a string containing that text.

noise *mexp*   [parser expression]
    The **noise** expression performs a match on the parser buffer. The match to be
    performed is specified by *mexp*, which is an expression in the matcher language. If

the match is successful, the result of the `noise` expression is a vector of zero elements. (In other words, the text is matched and then thrown away.)

The *mexp* operand is often a known character or string, so in the case that *mexp* is a character or string literal, the `noise` expression can be abbreviated as the literal. In other words, '(noise "foo")' can be abbreviated just '"foo"'.

`values` *expression* ...   [parser expression]

Sometimes it is useful to be able to insert arbitrary values into the parser result. The `values` expression supports this. The *expression* arguments are arbitrary Scheme expressions that are evaluated at run time and returned in a vector. The `values` expression always succeeds and never modifies the internal pointer of the parser buffer.

`discard-matched`   [parser expression]

The `discard-matched` expression always succeeds, returning a vector of zero elements. In all other respects it is identical to the `discard-matched` expression in the matcher language.

Next there are several combinator expressions. Parameters named *pexp* are arbitrary expressions in the parser language. The first few combinators are direct equivalents of those in the matcher language.

`seq` *pexp* ...   [parser expression]

The `seq` expression parses each of the *pexp* operands in order. If all of the *pexp* operands successfully match, the result is the concatenation of their values (by `vector-append`).

`alt` *pexp* ...   [parser expression]

The `alt` expression attempts to parse each *pexp* operand in order from left to right. The first one that successfully parses produces the result for the entire `alt` expression.

Like the `alt` expression in the matcher language, this expression participates in backtracking.

`*` *pexp*   [parser expression]

The `*` expression parses zero or more occurrences of *pexp*. The results of the parsed occurrences are concatenated together (by `vector-append`) to produce the expression's result.

Like the `*` expression in the matcher language, this expression participates in backtracking.

`+` *pexp*   [parser expression]

The `*` expression parses one or more occurrences of *pexp*. It is equivalent to

```
(seq pexp (* pexp))
```

`?` *pexp*   [parser expression]

The `*` expression parses zero or one occurrences of *pexp*. It is equivalent to

```
(alt pexp (seq))
```

The next three expressions do not have equivalents in the matcher language. Each accepts a single *pexp* argument, which is parsed in the usual way. These expressions perform transformations on the returned values of a successful match.

transform *expression pexp*   [parser expression]

The `transform` expression performs an arbitrary transformation of the values returned by parsing *pexp*. *Expression* is a Scheme expression that must evaluate to a procedure at run time. If *pexp* is successfully parsed, the procedure is called with the vector of values as its argument, and must return a vector or `#f`. If it returns a vector, the parse is successful, and those are the resulting values. If it returns `#f`, the parse fails and the internal pointer of the parser buffer is returned to what it was before *pexp* was parsed.

For example:

```
(transform (lambda (v) (if (= 0 (vector-length v)) #f v)) ...)
```

encapsulate *expression pexp*   [parser expression]

The `encapsulate` expression transforms the values returned by parsing *pexp* into a single value. *Expression* is a Scheme expression that must evaluate to a procedure at run time. If *pexp* is successfully parsed, the procedure is called with the vector of values as its argument, and may return any Scheme object. The result of the `encapsulate` expression is a vector of length one containing that object. (And consequently `encapsulate` doesn't change the success or failure of *pexp*, only its value.)

For example:

```
(encapsulate vector->list ...)
```

map *expression pexp*   [parser expression]

The `map` expression performs a per-element transform on the values returned by parsing *pexp*. *Expression* is a Scheme expression that must evaluate to a procedure at run time. If *pexp* is successfully parsed, the procedure is mapped (by `vector-map`) over the values returned from the parse. The mapped values are returned as the result of the `map` expression. (And consequently `map` doesn't change the success or failure of *pexp*, nor the number of values returned.)

For example:

```
(map string->symbol ...)
```

Finally, as in the matcher language, we have `sexp` and `with-pointer` to support embedding Scheme code in the parser.

sexp *expression*   [parser expression]

The `sexp` expression allows arbitrary Scheme code to be embedded inside a parser. The *expression* operand must evaluate to a parser procedure at run time; the procedure is called to parse the parser buffer. This is the parser-language equivalent of the `sexp` expression in the matcher language.

The case in which *expression* is a symbol is so common that it has an abbreviation: '(sexp *symbol*)' may be abbreviated as just *symbol*.

with-pointer *identifier pexp*   [parser expression]

The `with-pointer` expression fetches the parser buffer's internal pointer (using `get-parser-buffer-pointer`), binds it to *identifier*, and then parses the pattern specified by *pexp*. *Identifier* must be a symbol. This is the parser-language equivalent of the `with-pointer` expression in the matcher language.

14.11.3 Parser-language Macros

The parser and matcher languages provide a macro facility so that common patterns can be abstracted. The macro facility allows new expression types to be independently defined in the two languages. The macros are defined in hierarchically organized tables, so that different applications can have private macro bindings.

define-*matcher-macro *formals expression*   [special form]
define-*parser-macro *formals expression*   [special form]

> These special forms are used to define macros in the matcher and parser language, respectively. *Formals* is like the *formals* list of a `define` special form, and *expression* is a Scheme expression.
>
> If *formals* is a list (or improper list) of symbols, the first symbol in the list is the name of the macro, and the remaining symbols are interpreted as the *formals* of a lambda expression. A lambda expression is formed by combining the latter *formals* with the *expression*, and this lambda expression, when evaluated, becomes the *expander*. The defined macro accepts the same number of operands as the expander. A macro instance is expanded by applying the expander to the list of operands; the result of the application is interpreted as a replacement expression for the macro instance.
>
> If *formals* is a symbol, it is the name of the macro. In this case, the expander is a procedure of no arguments whose body is *expression*. When the *formals* symbol appears by itself as an expression in the language, the expander is called with no arguments, and the result is interpreted as a replacement expression for the symbol.

define-*matcher-expander *identifier expander*   [procedure]
define-*parser-expander *identifier expander*   [procedure]

> These procedures provide a procedural interface to the macro-definition mechanism. *Identifier* must be a symbol, and *expander* must be an expander procedure, as defined above. Instances of the `define-*matcher-macro` and `define-*parser-macro` special forms expand into calls to these procedures.

The remaining procedures define the interface to the parser-macros table abstraction. Each parser-macro table has a separate binding space for macros in the matcher and parser languages. However, the table inherits bindings from one specified table; it's not possible to inherit matcher-language bindings from one table and parser-language bindings from another.

make-parser-macros *parent-table*   [procedure]

> Create and return a new parser-macro table that inherits from *parent-table*. *Parent-table* must be either a parser-macro table, or `#f`; usually it is specified as the value of `global-parser-macros`.

parser-macros? *object*   [procedure]

> This is a predicate for parser-macro tables.

global-parser-macros   [procedure]

> Return the global parser-macro table. This table is predefined and contains all of the bindings documented here.

There is a "current" table at all times, and macro definitions are always placed in this table. By default, the current table is the global macro table, but the following procedures allow this to be changed.

current-parser-macros   [procedure]
  Return the current parser-macro table.

set-current-parser-macros! *table*   [procedure]
  Change the current parser-macro table to *table*, which must satisfy **parser-macros?**.

with-current-parser-macros *table thunk*   [procedure]
  Bind the current parser-macro table to *table*, call *thunk* with no arguments, then restore the original table binding. The value returned by *thunk* is the returned as the value of this procedure. *Table* must satisfy **parser-macros?**, and *thunk* must be a procedure of no arguments.

14.12 XML Support

MIT/GNU Scheme provides a simple non-validating XML parser. This parser is believed to be conformant with XML 1.0. It passes all of the tests in the "xmltest" directory of the XML conformance tests (dated 2001-03-15). The parser supports XML namespaces; it doesn't support external document type declarations (DTDs), and it doesn't yet support XML 1.1. The output of the parser is a record tree that closely reflects the structure of the XML document.

MIT/GNU Scheme also provides support for writing an XML record tree to an output port. There is no guarantee that parsing an XML document and writing it back out will make a verbatim copy of the document. The output will be semantically identical but may have small syntactic differences. For example, entities are substituted during the parsing process.

The purpose of the XML support is to provide a mechanism for reading and writing simple XML documents. In the future this support may be further developed to support a standard interface such as DOM or SAX.

The XML support is a run-time-loadable option; to use it, execute

```
(load-option 'xml)
```

once before running any code that uses it.

14.12.1 XML Input

The primary entry point for the XML parser is **read-xml**, which reads characters from a port and returns an XML document record. The character coding of the input is determined by reading some of the input stream and looking for a byte order mark and/or an encoding in the XML declaration. We support all ISO 8859 codings, as well as UTF-8, UTF-16, and UTF-32.

When an XHTML document is read, the parser provides entity definitions for all of the named XHTML characters; for example, it defines '** **' and '**©**'. In order for a document to be recognized as XHTML, it must contain an XHTML DTD, such as this:

```
<!DOCTYPE html
        PUBLIC "-//W3C//DTD XHTML 1.0 Strict//EN"
        "http://www.w3.org/TR/xhtml1/DTD/xhtml1-strict.dtd">
```

At present the parser recognizes XHTML Strict 1.0 and XHTML 1.1 documents.

read-xml *port* [*pi-handlers*]   [procedure]

> Read an XML document from *port* and return the corresponding XML document record.
>
> *Pi-handlers*, if specified, must be an association list. Each element of *pi-handlers* must be a list of two elements: a symbol and a procedure. When the parser encounters processing instructions with a name that appears in *pi-handlers*, the procedure is called with one argument, which is the text of the processing instructions. The procedure must return a list of XML structure records that are legal for the context of the processing instructions.

read-xml-file *pathname* [*pi-handlers*]   [procedure]

> This convenience procedure simplifies reading XML from a file. It is roughly equivalent to

```
(define (read-xml-file pathname #!optional pi-handlers)
  (call-with-input-file pathname
    (lambda (port)
      (read-xml port pi-handlers))))
```

string->xml *string* [*start* [*end* [*pi-handlers*]]]   [procedure]

> This convenience procedure simplifies reading XML from a string. The *string* argument may be a string or a wide string. It is roughly equivalent to

```
(define (string->xml string #!optional start end pi-handlers)
  (read-xml (open-input-string string start end)
            pi-handlers))
```

14.12.2 XML Output

The following procedures serialize XML document records into character sequences. All are virtually identical except for the way that the character sequence is represented.

Each procedure will accept either an **xml-document** record or any of the other XML record types. This makes it possible to write fragments of XML documents, although you should keep in mind that such fragments aren't documents and won't generally be accepted by any XML parser.

If the *xml* being written is an **xml-document** record, the procedures **write-xml** and **write-xml-file** will look for a contained **xml-declaration** record and its **encoding** attribute. If the **encoding** is a supported value, the output will be encoded as specified; otherwise it will be encoded as UTF-8.

When an XHTML document record is written, named XHTML characters are translated into their corresponding entities. For example, the character '#\U+00A0' is written as ' '. In order for an XML document record to be recognized as XHTML, it must have a DTD record that satisfies the predicate **html-dtd?**.

write-xml *xml port*   [procedure]

Write *xml* to *port*. Note that character encoding will only be done if *port* supports it.

write-xml-file *xml pathname*   [procedure]

Write *xml* to the file specified by *pathname*. Roughly equivalent to

```
(define (write-xml-file xml pathname)
  (call-with-output-file pathname
    (lambda (port)
      (write-xml xml port))))
```

xml->wide-string *xml*   [procedure]

Convert *xml* to a wide string. No character encoding is used, since wide strings can represent all characters without encoding. Roughly equivalent to

```
(define (xml->wide-string xml)
  (call-with-wide-output-string
   (lambda (port)
     (write-xml xml port))))
```

xml->string *xml*   [procedure]

Convert *xml* to a character string encoded as UTF-8. Roughly equivalent to

```
(define (xml->string xml)
  (wide-string->utf8-string (xml->wide-string xml)))
```

14.12.3 XML Names

MIT/GNU Scheme implements XML names in a slightly complex way. Unfortunately, this complexity is a direct consequence of the definition of XML names rather than a mis-feature of this implementation.

The reason that XML names are complex is that XML namespace support, which was added after XML was standardized, is not very well integrated with the core XML definition. The most obvious problem is that names can't have associated namespaces when they appear in the DTD of a document, even if the body of the document uses them. Consequently, it must be possible to compare non-associated names with associated names.

An XML name consists of two parts: the *qname*, which is a symbol, possibly including a namespace prefix; and the *Uniform Resource Identifier* (URI), which identifies an optional namespace.

make-xml-name *qname uri*   [procedure]

Creates and returns an XML name. *Qname* must be a symbol whose name satisfies **string-is-xml-name?**. *Uri* must satisfy either **absolute-uri?** or **null-xml-namespace-uri?**. The returned value is an XML name that satisfies **xml-name?**.

If *uri* is the *null* namespace (satisfies **null-xml-namespace-uri?**), the returned value is a symbol equivalent to *qname*. This means that an ordinary symbol can be used as an XML name when there is no namespace associated with the name.

For convenience, *qname* may be a string, in which case it is converted to a symbol using **make-xml-qname**.

For convenience, *uri* may be any object that `->uri` is able to convert to a URI record, provided the resulting URI meets the above restrictions.

`xml-name?` *object*   [procedure]
    Returns `#t` if *object* is an XML name, and `#f` otherwise.

`xml-name->symbol` *xml-name*   [procedure]
    Returns the symbol part of *xml-name*.

`xml-name-uri` *xml-name*   [procedure]
    Returns the *URI* of *xml-name*. The result always satisfies `absolute-uri?` or
    `null-xml-namespace-uri?`.

`xml-name-string` *xml-name*   [procedure]
    Returns the *qname* of *xml-name* as a string. Equivalent to

```
(symbol-name (xml-name->symbol xml-name))
```

The next two procedures get the *prefix* and *local part* of an XML name, respectively. The prefix of an XML name is the part of the qname to the left of the colon, while the local part is the part of the qname to the right of the colon. If there is no colon in the qname, the local part is the entire qname, and the prefix is the null symbol (i.e. '||').

`xml-name-prefix` *xml-name*   [procedure]
    Returns the *prefix* of *xml-name* as a symbol.

`xml-name-local` *xml-name*   [procedure]
    Returns the *local part* of *xml-name* as a symbol.

The next procedure compares two XML names for equality. The rules for equality are slightly complex, in order to permit comparing names in the DTD with names in the document body. So, if both of the names have non-null namespace URIs, then the names are equal if and only if their local parts are equal and their URIs are equal. (The prefixes of the names are not considered in this case.) Otherwise, the names are equal if and only if their qnames are equal.

`xml-name=?` *xml-name-1 xml-name-2*   [procedure]
    Returns `#t` if *xml-name-1* and *xml-name-2* are the same name, and `#f` otherwise.

These next procedures define the data abstraction for qnames. While qnames are represented as symbols, only symbols whose names satisfy `string-is-xml-name?` are qnames.

`make-xml-qname` *string*   [procedure]
    String must satisfy `string-is-xml-name?`. Returns the qname corresponding to
    string (the symbol whose name is *string*).

`xml-qname?` *object*   [procedure]
    Returns `#t` if *object* is a qname, otherwise returns `#f`.

`xml-qname-prefix` *qname*   [procedure]
    Returns the prefix of *qname* as a symbol.

xml-qname-local *qname*   [procedure]
> Returns the local part of *qname* as a symbol.

The prefix of a qname or XML name may be absent if there is no colon in the name. The absent, or null, prefix is abstracted by the next two procedures. Note that the null prefix is a symbol, just like non-null prefixes.

null-xml-name-prefix   [procedure]
> Returns the null prefix.

null-xml-name-prefix? *object*   [procedure]
> Returns #t if *object* is the null prefix, otherwise returns #f.

The namespace URI of an XML name may be null, meaning that there is no namespace associated with the name. This namespace is represented by a relative URI record whose string representation is the null string.

null-xml-namespace-uri   [procedure]
> Returns the null namespace URI record.

null-xml-namespace-uri? *object*   [procedure]
> Returns #t if *object* is the null namespace URI record, otherwise returns #f.

The following values are two distinguished URI records.

xml-uri   [variable]
> **xml-uri** is the URI reserved for use by the XML recommendation. This URI must be used with the 'xml' prefix.

xmlns-uri   [variable]
> **xmlns-uri** is the URI reserved for use by the XML namespace recommendation. This URI must be used with the 'xmlns' prefix.

make-xml-nmtoken *string*   [procedure]

xml-nmtoken? *object*   [procedure]

string-is-xml-name? *string*   [procedure]

string-is-xml-nmtoken? *string*   [procedure]

14.12.4 XML Structure

The output from the XML parser and the input to the XML output procedure is a complex data structure composed of a hierarchy of typed components. Each component is a record whose fields correspond to parts of the XML structure that the record represents. There are no special operations on these records; each is a tuple with named subparts. The root record type is **xml-document**, which represents a complete XML document.

Each record type *type* has the following associated bindings:

<type>   is a variable bound to the record-type descriptor for *type*. The record-type descriptor may be used as a specializer in SOS method definitions, which greatly simplifies code to dispatch on these types.

type?   is a predicate for records of type *type*. It accepts one argument, which can be any object, and returns #t if the object is a record of this type, or #f otherwise.

make-*type*

is a constructor for records of type *type*. It accepts one argument for each field of *type*, in the same order that they are written in the type description, and returns a newly-allocated record of that type.

type-field

is an accessor procedure for the field *field* in records of type *type*. It accepts one argument, which must be a record of that type, and returns the contents of the corresponding field in the record.

set-*type*-field!

is a modifier procedure for the field *field* in records of type *type*. It accepts two arguments: the first must be a record of that type, and the second is a new value for the corresponding field. The record's field is modified to have the new value.

xml-document *declaration misc-1 dtd misc-2 root misc-3*   [record type]
The xml-document record is the top-level record representing a complete XML document. *Declaration* is either an xml-declaration object or #f. *Dtd* is either an xml-dtd object or #f. *Root* is an xml-element object. *Misc-1*, *misc-2*, and *misc-3* are lists of miscellaneous items; a miscellaneous item is either an xml-comment object, an xml-processing-instructions object, or a string of whitespace.

xml-declaration *version encoding standalone*   [record type]
The xml-declaration record represents the '<?xml ... ?>' declaration that optionally appears at the beginning of an XML document. *Version* is a version string, typically "1.0". *Encoding* is either an encoding string or #f. *Standalone* is either "yes", "no", or #f.

xml-element *name attributes contents*   [record type]
The xml-element record represents general XML elements; the bulk of a typical XML document consists of these elements. *Name* is the element name (an XML name). *Attributes* is a list of XML attribute objects. *Contents* is a list of the contents of the element. Each element of this list is either a string, an xml-element record or an xml-processing-instructions record.

xml-processing-instructions *name text*   [record type]
The xml-processing-instructions record represents processing instructions, which have the form '<?*name* ... ?>'. These instructions are intended to contain non-XML data that will be processed by another interpreter; for example they might contain PHP programs. The *name* field is the processor name (a symbol), and the *text* field is the body of the instructions (a string).

xml-dtd *root external internal*   [record type]
The xml-dtd record represents a document type declaration. The *root* field is an XML name for the root element of the document. *External* is either an xml-external-id record or #f. *Internal* is a list of DTD element records (e.g. xml-!element, xml-!attlist, etc.).

The remaining record types are valid only within a DTD.

xml-!element *name content-type*   [record type]

The `xml-!element` record represents an element-type declaration. *Name* is the XML name of the type being declared (a symbol). *Content-type* describes the type and can have several different values, as follows:

- The XML names 'EMPTY' and 'ANY' correspond to the XML keywords of the same name.

- A list '(MIX *type* ...)' corresponds to the '(#PCDATA | *type* | ...)' syntax.

xml-!attlist *name definitions*   [record type]

The `xml-!attlist` record represents an attribute-list declaration. *Name* is the XML name of the type for which attributes are being declared (a symbol). *Definitions* is a list of attribute definitions, each of which is a list of three elements (`name type default`). *Name* is an XML name for the name of the attribute (a symbol). *Type* describes the attribute type, and can have one of the following values:

- The XML names 'CDATA', 'IDREFS', 'IDREF', 'ID', 'ENTITY', 'ENTITIES', 'NMTOKENS', and 'NMTOKEN' correspond to the XML keywords of the same names.

- A list '(NOTATION *name1 name2* ...)' corresponds to the 'NOTATION (*name1* | *name2* ...)' syntax.

- A list '(ENUMERATED *name1 name2* ...)' corresponds to the '(*name1* | *name2* ...)' syntax.

Default describes the default value for the attribute, and can have one of the following values:

- The XML names '#REQUIRED' and '#IMPLIED' correspond to the XML keywords of the same names.

- A list '(#FIXED *value*)' corresponds to the '#FIXED "*value*"' syntax. *Value* is represented as a string.

- A list '(DEFAULT *value*)' corresponds to the '"*value*"' syntax. *Value* is represented as a string.

xml-!entity *name value*   [record type]

The `xml-!entity` record represents a general entity declaration. *Name* is an XML name for the entity. *Value* is the entity's value, either a string or an `xml-external-id` record.

xml-parameter-!entity *name value*   [record type]

The `xml-parameter-!entity` record represents a parameter entity declaration. *Name* is an XML name for the entity. *Value* is the entity's value, either a string or an `xml-external-id` record.

xml-unparsed-!entity *name id notation*   [record type]

The `xml-unparsed-!entity` record represents an unparsed entity declaration. `Name` is an XML name for the entity. *Id* is an `xml-external-id` record. *Notation* is an XML name for the notation.

xml-!notation *name id*   [record type]

The `xml-!notation` record represents a notation declaration. `Name` is an XML name for the notation. *Id* is an `xml-external-id` record.

xml-external-id *id uri*   [record type]

The `xml-external-id` record is a reference to an external DTD. This reference consists of two parts: *id* is a public ID literal, corresponding to the 'PUBLIC' keyword, while *uri* is a system literal, corresponding to the 'SYSTEM' keyword. Either or both may be present, depending on the context. *Id* is represented as a string, while *uri* is represented as a URI record.

15 Operating-System Interface

The Scheme standard provides a simple mechanism for reading and writing files: file ports. MIT/GNU Scheme provides additional tools for dealing with other aspects of the operating system:

- *Pathnames* are a reasonably operating-system independent tool for manipulating the component parts of file names. This can be useful for implementing defaulting of file name components.

- Control over the *current working directory*: the place in the file system from which relative file names are interpreted.

- Procedures that rename, copy, delete, and test for the existence of files. Also, procedures that return detailed information about a particular file, such as its type (directory, link, etc.) or length.

- Procedures for reading the contents of a directory.

- Procedures for obtaining times in various formats, converting between the formats, and generating human-readable time strings.

- Procedures to run other programs as subprocesses of Scheme, to read their output, and write input to them.

- A means to determine the operating system Scheme is running under.

15.1 Pathnames

MIT/GNU Scheme programs need to use names to designate files. The main difficulty in dealing with names of files is that different file systems have different naming formats for files. For example, here is a table of several file systems (actually, operating systems that provide file systems) and what equivalent file names might look like for each one:

```
System          File Name
------          ---------
TOPS-20         <LISPIO>FORMAT.FASL.13
TOPS-10         FORMAT.FAS[1,4]
ITS             LISPIO;FORMAT FASL
MULTICS         >udd>LispIO>format.fasl
TENEX           <LISPIO>FORMAT.FASL;13
VAX/VMS         [LISPIO]FORMAT.FAS;13
UNIX            /usr/lispio/format.fasl
DOS             C:\USR\LISPIO\FORMAT.FAS
```

It would be impossible for each program that deals with file names to know about each different file name format that exists; a new operating system to which Scheme was ported might use a format different from any of its predecessors. Therefore, MIT/GNU Scheme provides *two* ways to represent file names: *filenames* (also called *namestrings*), which are strings in the implementation-dependent form customary for the file system, and *pathnames*, which are special abstract data objects that represent file names in an implementation-independent way. Procedures are provided to convert between these two representations, and all manipulations of files can be expressed in machine-independent terms by using pathnames.

In order to allow MIT/GNU Scheme programs to operate in a network environment that may have more than one kind of file system, the pathname facility allows a file name to specify which file system is to be used. In this context, each file system is called a *host*, in keeping with the usual networking terminology.[1]

Note that the examples given in this section are specific to unix pathnames. Pathnames for other operating systems have different external representations.

15.1.1 Filenames and Pathnames

Pathname objects are usually created by parsing filenames (character strings) into component parts. MIT/GNU Scheme provides operations that convert filenames into pathnames and vice versa.

->pathname *object*   [procedure]
> Returns a pathname that is the equivalent of *object*. *Object* must be a pathname or a string. If *object* is a pathname, it is returned. If *object* is a string, this procedure returns the pathname that corresponds to the string; in this case it is equivalent to (parse-namestring *object* #f #f).
>
> > (->pathname "foo")   ⇒ #[pathname 65 "foo"]
> > (->pathname "/usr/morris") ⇒ #[pathname 66 "/usr/morris"]

parse-namestring *thing* [*host* [*defaults*]]   [procedure]
> This turns *thing* into a pathname. *Thing* must be a pathname or a string. If *thing* is a pathname, it is returned. If *thing* is a string, this procedure returns the pathname that corresponds to the string, parsed according to the syntax of the file system specified by *host*.
>
> This procedure *does not* do defaulting of pathname components.
>
> The optional arguments are used to determine what syntax should be used for parsing the string. In general this is only really useful if your implementation of MIT/GNU Scheme supports more than one file system, otherwise you would use **->pathname**. If given, *host* must be a host object or **#f**, and *defaults* must be a pathname. *Host* specifies the syntax used to parse the string. If *host* is not given or **#f**, the host component from *defaults* is used instead; if *defaults* is not given, the host component from *default-pathname-defaults* is used.

->namestring *pathname*   [procedure]
> **->namestring** returns a newly allocated string that is the filename corresponding to *pathname*.
>
> > (->namestring (->pathname "/usr/morris/minor.van"))
> >   ⇒ "/usr/morris/minor.van"

pathname-simplify *pathname*   [procedure]
> Returns a pathname that locates the same file or directory as *pathname*, but is in some sense simpler. Note that **pathname-simplify** might not always be able to simplify the pathname, e.g. on unix with symbolic links the directory /usr/morris/../ need not be the same as /usr/. In cases of uncertainty the behavior is conservative, returning the original or a partly simplified pathname.

---

[1] This introduction is adapted from *Common Lisp, The Language*, second edition, section 23.1.

```
(pathname-simplify "/usr/morris/../morris/dance")
     ⇒  #[pathname "/usr/morris/dance"]
```

15.1.2 Components of Pathnames

A pathname object always has six components, described below. These components are the common interface that allows programs to work the same way with different file systems; the mapping of the pathname components into the concepts peculiar to each file system is taken care of by the Scheme implementation.

host	The name of the file system on which the file resides. In the current implementation, this component is always a host object that is filled in automatically by the runtime system. When specifying the host component, use either **#f** or the value of the variable `local-host`.
device	Corresponds to the "device" or "file structure" concept in many host file systems: the name of a (logical or physical) device containing files. This component is the drive letter for PC file systems, and is unused for unix file systems.
directory	Corresponds to the "directory" concept in many host file systems: the name of a group of related files (typically those belonging to a single user or project). This component is always used for all file systems.
name	The name of a group of files that can be thought of as conceptually the "same" file. This component is always used for all file systems.
type	Corresponds to the "filetype" or "extension" concept in many host file systems. This says what kind of file this is. Files with the same name but different type are usually related in some specific way, such as one being a source file, another the compiled form of that source, and a third the listing of error messages from the compiler. This component is currently used for all file systems, and is formed by taking the characters that follow the last dot in the namestring.
version	Corresponds to the "version number" concept in many host file systems. Typically this is a number that is incremented every time the file is modified. This component is currently unused for all file systems.

Note that a pathname is not necessarily the name of a specific file. Rather, it is a specification (possibly only a partial specification) of how to access a file. A pathname need not correspond to any file that actually exists, and more than one pathname can refer to the same file. For example, the pathname with a version of **newest** may refer to the same file as a pathname with the same components except a certain number as the version. Indeed, a pathname with version **newest** may refer to different files as time passes, because the meaning of such a pathname depends on the state of the file system. In file systems with such facilities as "links", multiple file names, logical devices, and so on, two pathnames that look quite different may turn out to address the same file. To access a file given a pathname, one must do a file-system operation such as **open-input-file**.

Two important operations involving pathnames are *parsing* and *merging*. Parsing is the conversion of a filename (which might be something supplied interactively by the users when asked to supply the name of a file) into a pathname object. This operation is implementation-dependent, because the format of filenames is implementation-dependent.

Merging takes a pathname with missing components and supplies values for those components from a source of default values.

Not all of the components of a pathname need to be specified. If a component of a pathname is missing, its value is #f. Before the file system interface can do anything interesting with a file, such as opening the file, all the missing components of a pathname must be filled in. Pathnames with missing components are used internally for various purposes; in particular, parsing a namestring that does not specify certain components will result in a pathname with missing components.

Any component of a pathname may be the symbol unspecific, meaning that the component simply does not exist, for file systems in which such a value makes no sense. For example, unix and Windows file systems usually do not support version numbers, so the version component for such a host might be unspecific.[2]

In addition to #f and unspecific, the components of a pathname may take on the following meaningful values:

host   An implementation-defined type which may be tested for using the host? predicate.

device   On systems that support this component (Windows), it may be specified as a string containing a single alphabetic character, for which the alphabetic case is ignored.

directory A non-empty list, which represents a *directory path*: a sequence of directories, each of which has a name in the previous directory, the last of which is the directory specified by the entire path. Each element in such a path specifies the name of the directory relative to the directory specified by the elements to its left. The first element of the list is either the symbol absolute or the symbol relative. If the first element in the list is the symbol absolute, then the directory component (and subsequently the pathname) is *absolute*; the first component in the sequence is to be found at the "root" of the file system. If the directory is *relative* then the first component is to be found in some as yet unspecified directory; typically this is later specified to be the *current working directory*.

           Aside from absolute and relative, which may only appear as the first element of the list, each subsequent element in the list is either: a string, which is a literal component; the symbol wild, meaningful only when used in conjunction with the directory reader; or the symbol up, meaning the next directory is the "parent" of the previous one. up corresponds to the file .. in unix and PC file systems.

           (The following note does not refer to any file system currently supported by MIT/GNU Scheme, but is included for completeness.) In file systems that do not have "hierarchical" structure, a specified directory component will always be a list whose first element is absolute. If the system does not support directories other than a single global directory, the list will have no other elements. If the system supports "flat" directories, i.e. a global set of directories with no subdirectories, then the list will contain a second element, which is either a

---

[2] This description is adapted from *Common Lisp, The Language*, second edition, section 23.1.1.

string or `wild`. In other words, a non-hierarchical file system is treated as if it were hierarchical, but the hierarchical features are unused. This representation is somewhat inconvenient for such file systems, but it discourages programmers from making code depend on the lack of a file hierarchy.

name A string, which is a literal component; or the symbol `wild`, meaningful only when used in conjunction with the directory reader.

type A string, which is a literal component; or the symbol `wild`, meaningful only when used in conjunction with the directory reader.

version An exact positive integer, which is a literal component; the symbol `newest`, which means to choose the largest available version number for that file; the symbol `oldest`, which means to choose the smallest version number; or the symbol `wild`, meaningful only when used in conjunction with the directory reader. In the future some other possible values may be added, e.g. `installed`. Note that currently no file systems support version numbers; thus this component is not used and should be specified as `#f`.

`make-pathname` *host device directory name type version*   [procedure]
Returns a pathname object whose components are the respective arguments. Each argument must satisfy the restrictions for the corresponding component, which were outlined above.

```
(make-pathname #f
               #f
               '(absolute "usr" "morris")
               "foo"
               "scm"
               #f)
    ⇒  #[pathname 67 "/usr/morris/foo.scm"]
```

`pathname-host` *pathname*   [procedure]
`pathname-device` *pathname*   [procedure]
`pathname-directory` *pathname*   [procedure]
`pathname-name` *pathname*   [procedure]
`pathname-type` *pathname*   [procedure]
`pathname-version` *pathname*   [procedure]
Returns a particular component of *pathname*.

```
(define x (->pathname "/usr/morris/foo.scm"))
(pathname-host x)        ⇒  #[host 1]
(pathname-device x)      ⇒  unspecific
(pathname-directory x)   ⇒  (absolute "usr" "morris")
(pathname-name x)        ⇒  "foo"
(pathname-type x)        ⇒  "scm"
(pathname-version x)     ⇒  unspecific
```

`pathname-new-device` *pathname device*   [procedure]
`pathname-new-directory` *pathname directory*   [procedure]
`pathname-new-name` *pathname name*   [procedure]

`pathname-new-type` *pathname type*   [procedure]

`pathname-new-version` *pathname version*   [procedure]

> Returns a new copy of *pathname* with the respective component replaced by the second argument. *Pathname* is unchanged. Portable programs should not explicitly replace a component with `unspecific` because this might not be permitted in some situations.

```
(define p (->pathname "/usr/blisp/rel15"))
p
    ⇒  #[pathname 71 "/usr/blisp/rel15"]
(pathname-new-name p "rel100")
    ⇒  #[pathname 72 "/usr/blisp/rel100"]
(pathname-new-directory p '(relative "test" "morris"))
    ⇒  #[pathname 73 "test/morris/rel15"]
p
    ⇒  #[pathname 71 "/usr/blisp/rel15"]
```

`pathname-default-device` *pathname device*   [procedure]

`pathname-default-directory` *pathname directory*   [procedure]

`pathname-default-name` *pathname name*   [procedure]

`pathname-default-type` *pathname type*   [procedure]

`pathname-default-version` *pathname version*   [procedure]

> These operations are similar to the `pathname-new-`*component* operations, except that they only change the specified *component* if it has the value `#f` in *pathname*.

15.1.3 Operations on Pathnames

`pathname?` *object*   [procedure]

> Returns `#t` if *object* is a pathname; otherwise returns `#f`.

`pathname=?` *pathname1 pathname2*   [procedure]

> Returns `#t` if *pathname1* is equivalent to *pathname2*; otherwise returns `#f`. Pathnames are equivalent if all of their components are equivalent, hence two pathnames that are equivalent must identify the same file or equivalent partial pathnames. However, the converse is not true: non-equivalent pathnames may specify the same file (e.g. via absolute and relative directory components), and pathnames that specify no file at all (e.g. name and directory components unspecified) may be equivalent.

`pathname-absolute?` *pathname*   [procedure]

> Returns `#t` if *pathname* is an absolute rather than relative pathname object; otherwise returns `#f`. Specifically, this procedure returns `#t` when the directory component of *pathname* is a list starting with the symbol `absolute`, and returns `#f` in all other cases. All pathnames are either absolute or relative, so if this procedure returns `#f`, the argument is a relative pathname.

`directory-pathname?` *pathname*   [procedure]

> Returns `#t` if *pathname* has only directory components and no file components. This is roughly equivalent to

```
(define (directory-pathname? pathname)
  (string-null? (file-namestring pathname)))
```

except that it is faster.

pathname-wild? *pathname*   [procedure]
  Returns **#t** if *pathname* contains any wildcard components; otherwise returns **#f**.

merge-pathnames *pathname* [*defaults* [*default-version*]]   [procedure]
  Returns a pathname whose components are obtained by combining those of *pathname*
  and *defaults*. *Defaults* defaults to the value of ***default-pathname-defaults*** and
  default-version defaults to **newest**.

  The pathnames are combined by components: if *pathname* has a non-missing component, that is the resulting component, otherwise the component from *defaults* is
  used. The default version can be **#f** to preserve the information that the component
  was missing from *pathname*. The directory component is handled specially: if both
  pathnames have directory components that are lists, and the directory component
  from *pathname* is relative (i.e. starts with **relative**), then the resulting directory
  component is formed by appending *pathname*'s component to *defaults*'s component.
  For example:

```
(define path1 (->pathname "scheme/foo.scm"))
(define path2 (->pathname "/usr/morris"))
path1
      ⇒  #[pathname 74 "scheme/foo.scm"]
path2
      ⇒  #[pathname 75 "/usr/morris"]
(merge-pathnames path1 path2)
      ⇒  #[pathname 76 "/usr/scheme/foo.scm"]
(merge-pathnames path2 path1)
      ⇒  #[pathname 77 "/usr/morris.scm"]
```

  The merging rules for the version are more complex and depend on whether *pathname*
  specifies a name. If *pathname* does not specify a name, then the version, if not
  provided, will come from *defaults*. However, if *pathname* does specify a name then
  the version is not affected by *defaults*. The reason is that the version "belongs to"
  some other file name and is unlikely to have anything to do with the new one. Finally,
  if this process leaves the version missing, then *default-version* is used.

  The net effect is that if the user supplies just a name, then the host, device, directory
  and type will come from *defaults*, but the version will come from *default-version*. If
  the user supplies nothing, or just a directory, the name, type and version will come
  over from *defaults* together.

default-pathname-defaults   [variable]
  This is the default pathname-defaults pathname; if any pathname primitive that
  needs a set of defaults is not given one, it uses this one. **set-working-directory-**
  pathname! sets this variable to a new value, computed by merging the new working
  directory with the variable's old value.

pathname-default *pathname device directory name type version*   [procedure]
  This procedure defaults all of the components of *pathname* simultaneously. It could
  have been defined by:

```
(define (pathname-default pathname
                          device directory name type version)
  (make-pathname (pathname-host pathname)
                 (or (pathname-device pathname) device)
                 (or (pathname-directory pathname) directory)
                 (or (pathname-name pathname) name)
                 (or (pathname-type pathname) type)
                 (or (pathname-version pathname) version)))
```

file-namestring *pathname*   [procedure]
directory-namestring *pathname*   [procedure]
host-namestring *pathname*   [procedure]
enough-namestring *pathname* [*defaults*]   [procedure]

These procedures return a string corresponding to a subset of the *pathname* information. `file-namestring` returns a string representing just the *name*, *type* and *version* components of *pathname*; the result of `directory-namestring` represents just the *host*, *device*, and *directory* components; and `host-namestring` returns a string for just the *host* portion.

`enough-namestring` takes another argument, *defaults*. It returns an abbreviated namestring that is just sufficient to identify the file named by *pathname* when considered relative to the *defaults* (which defaults to `*default-pathname-defaults*`).

```
(file-namestring "/usr/morris/minor.van")
    ⇒  "minor.van"
(directory-namestring "/usr/morris/minor.van")
    ⇒  "/usr/morris/"
(enough-namestring "/usr/morris/men")
    ⇒  "men"          ;perhaps
```

file-pathname *pathname*   [procedure]
directory-pathname *pathname*   [procedure]
enough-pathname *pathname* [*defaults*]   [procedure]

These procedures return a pathname corresponding to a subset of the *pathname* information. `file-pathname` returns a pathname with just the *name*, *type* and *version* components of *pathname*. The result of `directory-pathname` is a pathname containing the *host*, *device* and *directory* components of *pathname*.

`enough-pathname` takes another argument, *defaults*. It returns an abbreviated pathname that is just sufficient to identify the file named by *pathname* when considered relative to the *defaults* (which defaults to `*default-pathname-defaults*`).

These procedures are similar to `file-namestring`, `directory-namestring` and `enough-namestring`, but they return pathnames instead of strings.

directory-pathname-as-file *pathname*   [procedure]

Returns a pathname that is equivalent to *pathname*, but in which the directory component is represented as a file. The last directory is removed from the directory component and converted into name and type components. This is the inverse operation to `pathname-as-directory`.

```
(directory-pathname-as-file (->pathname "/usr/blisp/"))
    ⇒  #[pathname "/usr/blisp"]
```

pathname-as-directory *pathname*   [procedure]

Returns a pathname that is equivalent to *pathname*, but in which any file components have been converted to a directory component. If *pathname* does not have name, type, or version components, it is returned without modification. Otherwise, these file components are converted into a string, and the string is added to the end of the list of directory components. This is the inverse operation to `directory-pathname-as-file`.

```
(pathname-as-directory (->pathname "/usr/blisp/rel5"))
    ⇒  #[pathname "/usr/blisp/rel5/"]
```

15.1.4 Miscellaneous Pathname Procedures

This section gives some standard operations on host objects, and some procedures that return some useful pathnames.

local-host   [variable]

This variable has as its value the host object that describes the local host's file system.

host? *object*   [procedure]

Returns #t if *object* is a pathname host; otherwise returns #f.

host=? *host1 host2*   [procedure]

Returns #t if *host1* and *host2* denote the same pathname host; otherwise returns #f.

init-file-pathname [*host*]   [procedure]

Returns a pathname for the user's initialization file on *host*. The *host* argument defaults to the value of `local-host`. If the initialization file does not exist this procedure returns #f.

Under unix, the init file is called `.scheme.init`; under Windows, the init file is called `scheme.ini`. In either case, it is located in the user's home directory, which is computed by `user-homedir-pathname`.

user-homedir-pathname [*host*]   [procedure]

Returns a pathname for the user's "home directory" on *host*. The *host* argument defaults to the value of `local-host`. The concept of a "home directory" is itself somewhat implementation-dependent, but it should be the place where the user keeps personal files, such as initialization files and mail.

Under unix, the user's home directory is specified by the HOME environment variable. If this variable is undefined, the user name is computed using the `getlogin` system call, or if that fails, the `getuid` system call. The resulting user name is passed to the `getpwnam` system call to obtain the home directory.

Under Windows, several heuristics are tried to find the user's home directory. The user's home directory is computed by examining several environment variables, in the following order:

- HOMEDRIVE and HOMEPATH are both defined and %HOMEDRIVE%%HOMEPATH% is an existing directory. (These variables are automatically defined by Windows NT.)

- `HOME` is defined and `%HOME%` is an existing directory.
- `USERDIR` and `USERNAME` are defined and `%USERDIR%\%USERNAME%` is an existing directory.
- `USERDIR` and `USER` are defined and `%USERDIR%\%USER%` is an existing directory.
- `USERNAME` is defined and `%USERNAME%` is an existing directory on the Windows system drive.
- `USER` is defined and `%USER%` is an existing directory on the Windows system drive.
- Finally, if all else fails, the Windows system drive is used as the home directory.

`system-library-pathname` *pathname*   [procedure]

> Locates *pathname* in MIT/GNU Scheme's system library directory. An error of type `condition-type:file-operation-error` is signalled if *pathname* cannot be located on the library search path.
>
>   (system-library-pathname "compiler.com")
>   ⇒ #[pathname 45 "/usr/local/lib/mit-scheme/compiler.com"]

`system-library-directory-pathname` *pathname*   [procedure]

> Locates the pathname of an MIT/GNU Scheme system library directory. An error of type `condition-type:file-operation-error` is signalled if *pathname* cannot be located on the library search path.
>
>   (system-library-directory-pathname "options")
>   ⇒ #[pathname 44 "/usr/local/lib/mit-scheme/options/"]

15.2 Working Directory

When MIT/GNU Scheme is started, the *current working directory* (or simply, *working directory*) is initialized in an operating-system dependent manner; usually, it is the directory in which Scheme was invoked. The working directory can be determined from within Scheme by calling the `pwd` procedure, and changed by calling the `cd` procedure. Each REP loop has its own working directory, and inferior REP loops initialize their working directory from the value in effect in their superior at the time they are created.

`working-directory-pathname`   [procedure]
`pwd`   [procedure]

> Returns the current working directory as a pathname that has no name, type, or version components, just host, device, and directory components. `pwd` is an alias for `working-directory-pathname`; the long name is intended for programs and the short name for interactive use.

`set-working-directory-pathname!` *filename*   [procedure]
`cd` *filename*   [procedure]

> Makes *filename* the current working directory and returns the new current working directory as a pathname. *Filename* is coerced to a pathname using `pathname-as-directory`. `cd` is an alias for `set-working-directory-pathname!`; the long name is intended for programs and the short name for interactive use.
>
> Additionally, `set-working-directory-pathname!` modifies the value of `*default-pathname-defaults*` by merging the new working directory into it.

When this procedure is executed in the top-level REP loop, it changes the working directory of the running Scheme executable.

```
(set-working-directory-pathname! "/usr/morris/blisp")
    ⇒ #[pathname "/usr/morris/blisp/"]
(set-working-directory-pathname! "~")
    ⇒ #[pathname "/usr/morris/"]
```

This procedure signals an error if *filename* does not refer to an existing directory.

If *filename* describes a relative rather than absolute pathname, this procedure interprets it as relative to the current working directory, before changing the working directory.

```
(working-directory-pathname)
    ⇒ #[pathname "/usr/morris/"]
(set-working-directory-pathname! "foo")
    ⇒ #[pathname "/usr/morris/foo/"]
```

with-working-directory-pathname *filename thunk*   [procedure]
This procedure temporarily rebinds the current working directory to *filename*, invokes *thunk* (a procedure of no arguments), then restores the previous working directory and returns the value yielded by *thunk*. *Filename* is coerced to a pathname using **pathname-as-directory**. In addition to binding the working directory, **with-working-directory-pathname** also binds the variable ***default-pathname-defaults***, merging the old value of that variable with the new working directory pathname. Both bindings are performed in exactly the same way as dynamic binding of a variable (see Section 2.3 [Dynamic Binding], page 18).

15.3 File Manipulation

This section describes procedures that manipulate files and directories. Any of these procedures can signal a number of errors for many reasons. The specifics of these errors are much too operating-system dependent to document here. However, if such an error is signalled by one of these procedures, it will be of type **condition-type:file-operation-error**.

file-exists? *filename*   [procedure]
file-exists-direct? *filename*   [procedure]
file-exists-indirect? *filename*   [procedure]
These procedures return **#t** if *filename* is an existing file or directory; otherwise they return **#f**. In operating systems that support symbolic links, if the file is a symbolic link, **file-exists-direct?** tests for the existence of the link, while **file-exists-indirect?** and **file-exists?** test for the existence of the file pointed to by the link.

copy-file *source-filename target-filename*   [procedure]
Makes a copy of the file named by *source-filename*. The copy is performed by creating a new file called *target-filename*, and filling it with the same data as *source-filename*.

rename-file *source-filename target-filename*   [procedure]
Changes the name of *source-filename* to be *target-filename*. In the unix implementation, this will not rename across file systems.

delete-file *filename* [procedure]

Deletes the file named *filename*.

delete-file-no-errors *filename* [procedure]

Like `delete-file`, but returns a boolean value indicating whether an error occurred during the deletion. If no errors occurred, `#t` is returned. If an error of type `condition-type:file-error` or `condition-type:port-error` is signalled, `#f` is returned.

hard-link-file *source-filename target-filename* [procedure]

Makes a hard link from *source-filename* to *target-filename*. This operation gives the file specified by *source-filename* a new name, in addition to the old name.

This currently works only on unix systems. It is further restricted to work only when *source-filename* and *target-filename* refer to names in the same file system.

soft-link-file *source-filename target-filename* [procedure]

Creates a new soft link called *target-filename* that points at the file *source-filename*. (Soft links are also sometimes called *symbolic* links.) Note that *source-filename* will be interpreted as a string (although you may specify it as a pathname object, if you wish). The contents of this string will be stored in the file system as the soft link. When a file operation attempts to open the link, the contents of the link are interpreted relative to the link's location at that time.

This currently works only on unix systems.

make-directory *filename* [procedure]

Creates a new directory named *filename*. Signals an error if *filename* already exists, or if the directory cannot be created.

delete-directory *filename* [procedure]

Deletes the directory named *filename*. Signals an error if the directory does not exist, is not a directory, or contains any files or subdirectories.

->truename *filename* [procedure]

This procedure attempts to discover and return the "true name" of the file associated with *filename* within the file system. An error of type `condition-type:file-operation-error` is signalled if the appropriate file cannot be located within the file system.

call-with-temporary-file-pathname *procedure* [procedure]

Calls `temporary-file-pathname` to create a temporary file, then calls *procedure* with one argument, the pathname referring to that file. When *procedure* returns, if the temporary file still exists, it is deleted; then, the value yielded by *procedure* is returned. If *procedure* escapes from its continuation, and the file still exists, it is deleted.

temporary-file-pathname [*directory*] [procedure]

Creates a new empty temporary file and returns a pathname referring to it. The temporary file is created with Scheme's default permissions, so barring unusual circumstances it can be opened for input and/or output without error. The temporary

file will remain in existence until explicitly deleted. If the file still exists when the
Scheme process terminates, it will be deleted.

If *directory* is specified, the temporary file will be stored there. If it is not specified, or if it is #f, the temporary file will be stored in the directory returned by
`temporary-directory-pathname`.

`temporary-directory-pathname`   [procedure]
    Returns the pathname of an existing directory that can be used to store temporary
    files. These directory names are tried, in order, until a writeable directory is found:

- The directories specified by the environment variables `TMPDIR`, `TEMP`, or `TMP`.

- Under unix, the directories `/var/tmp`, `/usr/tmp`, or `/tmp`.

- Under Windows, the following directories on the system drive: `\temp`, `\tmp`, or
  `\`.

- Under Windows, the current directory, as specified by `*default-pathname-`
  `defaults*`.

`file-directory?` *filename*   [procedure]
    Returns #t if the file named *filename* exists and is a directory. Otherwise returns #f.
    In operating systems that support symbolic links, if *filename* names a symbolic link,
    this examines the file linked to, not the link itself.

    This is equivalent to

```
(eq? 'directory (file-type-indirect filename))
```

`file-regular?` *filename*   [procedure]
    Returns #t if the file named *filename* exists and is a regular file (i.e. not a directory,
    symbolic link, device file, etc.). Otherwise returns #f. In operating systems that
    support symbolic links, if *filename* names a symbolic link, this examines the file
    linked to, not the link itself.

    This is equivalent to

```
(eq? 'regular (file-type-indirect filename))
```

`file-symbolic-link?` *filename*   [procedure]
    In operating systems that support symbolic links, if the file named *filename* exists and
    is a symbolic link, this procedure returns the contents of the symbolic link as a newly
    allocated string. The returned value is the name of the file that the symbolic link
    points to and must be interpreted relative to the directory of *filename*. If *filename*
    either does not exist or is not a symbolic link, or if the operating system does not
    support symbolic links, this procedure returns #f.

`file-type-direct` *filename*   [procedure]
`file-type-indirect` *filename*   [procedure]
    If the file named *filename* exists, `file-type-direct` returns a symbol specifying what
    type of file it is. For example, if *filename* refers to a directory, the symbol `directory`
    is returned. If *filename* doesn't refer to an existing file, #f is returned.

    If *filename* refers to a symbolic link, `file-type-direct` returns the type of the link
    itself, while `file-type-indirect` returns the type of the file linked to.

At this time, the symbols that can be returned are the following. The names are intended to be self-explanatory. Most of these names can only be returned on particular operating systems, and so the operating-system name is prefixed to the name.

```
regular
directory
unix-symbolic-link
unix-character-device
unix-block-device
unix-named-pipe
unix-socket
win32-named-pipe
```

file-readable? *filename*   [procedure]

> Returns **#t** if *filename* names a file that can be opened for input; i.e. a *readable* file. Otherwise returns **#f**.

file-writeable? *filename*   [procedure]

> Returns **#t** if *filename* names a file that can be opened for output; i.e. a *writeable* file. Otherwise returns **#f**.

file-executable? *filename*   [procedure]

> Returns **#t** if *filename* names a file that can be executed. Otherwise returns **#f**. Under unix, an executable file is identified by its mode bits. Under Windows, an executable file has one of the file extensions **.exe**, **.com**, or **.bat**.

file-access *filename mode*   [procedure]

> *Mode* must be an exact integer between 0 and 7 inclusive; it is a bitwise-encoded predicate selector with 1 meaning "executable", 2 meaning "writeable", and 4 meaning "readable". **file-access** returns **#t** if *filename* exists and satisfies the predicates selected by *mode*. For example, if *mode* is 5, then *filename* must be both readable and executable. If *filename* doesn't exist, or if it does not satisfy the selected predicates, **#f** is returned.

file-eq? *filename1 filename2*   [procedure]

> Determines whether *filename1* and *filename2* refer to the same file. Under unix, this is done by comparing the inodes and devices of the two files. Under Windows, this is done by comparing the filename strings.

file-modes *filename*   [procedure]

> If *filename* names an existing file, **file-modes** returns an exact non-negative integer encoding the file's permissions. The encoding of this integer is operating-system dependent. Under unix, it is the least-significant 12 bits of the **st_mode** element of the **struct stat** structure. Under Windows, it is the file attribute bits, which are described below. If *filename* does not name an existing file, **#f** is returned.

set-file-modes! *filename modes*   [procedure]

> *Filename* must name an existing file. *Modes* must be an exact non-negative integer that could have been returned by a call to **file-modes**. **set-file-modes!** modifies the file's permissions to be those encoded by *modes*.

`nt-file-mode/read-only`	[variable]
`nt-file-mode/hidden`	[variable]
`nt-file-mode/system`	[variable]
`nt-file-mode/directory`	[variable]
`nt-file-mode/archive`	[variable]
`nt-file-mode/normal`	[variable]
`nt-file-mode/temporary`	[variable]
`nt-file-mode/compressed`	[variable]

The values of these variables are the "mode bits" that comprise the value returned by `file-modes` under Windows. These bits are small integers that are combined by adding to form a complete set of modes. The integer zero represents a set of modes in which none of these bits are set.

`file-modification-time` *filename*   [procedure]

Returns the modification time of *filename* as an exact non-negative integer. The result may be compared to other file times using ordinary integer arithmetic. If *filename* names a file that does not exist, `file-modification-time` returns `#f`.

In operating systems that support symbolic links, if *filename* names a symbolic link, `file-modification-time` returns the modification time of the file linked to. An alternate procedure, `file-modification-time-direct`, returns the modification time of the link itself; in all other respects it is identical to `file-modification-time`. For symmetry, `file-modification-time-indirect` is a synonym of `file-modification-time`.

`file-access-time` *filename*   [procedure]

Returns the access time of *filename* as an exact non-negative integer. The result may be compared to other file times using ordinary integer arithmetic. If *filename* names a file that does not exist, `file-access-time` returns `#f`.

In operating systems that support symbolic links, if *filename* names a symbolic link, `file-access-time` returns the access time of the file linked to. An alternate procedure, `file-access-time-direct`, returns the access time of the link itself; in all other respects it is identical to `file-access-time`. For symmetry, `file-access-time-indirect` is a synonym of `file-access-time`.

`set-file-times!` *filename access-time modification-time*   [procedure]

Filename must name an existing file, while *access-time* and *modification-time* must be valid file times that might have been returned by `file-access-time` and `file-modification-time`, respectively. `set-file-times!` alters the access and modification times of the file specified by *filename* to the values given by *access-time* and *modification-time*, respectively. For convenience, either of the time arguments may be specified as `#f`; in this case the corresponding time is not changed. `set-file-times!` returns an unspecified value.

`current-file-time`   [procedure]

Returns the current time as an exact non-negative integer, in the same format used by the above file-time procedures. This number can be compared to other file times using ordinary arithmetic operations.

`file-touch` *filename*   [procedure]
> *Touches* the file named *filename*. If the file already exists, its modification time is set to the current file time and `#f` is returned. Otherwise, the file is created and `#t` is returned. This is an atomic test-and-set operation, so it is useful as a synchronization mechanism.

`file-length` *filename*   [procedure]
> Returns the length, in bytes, of the file named *filename* as an exact non-negative integer.

`file-attributes` *filename*   [procedure]
> This procedure determines if the file named *filename* exists, and returns information about it if so; if the file does not exist, it returns `#f`.
>
> In operating systems that support symbolic links, if *filename* names a symbolic link, `file-attributes` returns the attributes of the link itself. An alternate procedure, `file-attributes-indirect`, returns the attributes of the file linked to; in all other respects it is identical to `file-attributes`. For symmetry, `file-attributes-direct` is a synonym of `file-attributes`.

The information returned by `file-attributes` is decoded by accessor procedures. The following accessors are defined in all operating systems:

`file-attributes/type` *attributes*   [procedure]
> The file type: `#t` if the file is a directory, a character string (the name linked to) if a symbolic link, or `#f` for all other types of file.

`file-attributes/access-time` *attributes*   [procedure]
> The last access time of the file, an exact non-negative integer.

`file-attributes/modification-time` *attributes*   [procedure]
> The last modification time of the file, an exact non-negative integer.

`file-attributes/change-time` *attributes*   [procedure]
> The last change time of the file, an exact non-negative integer.

`file-attributes/length` *attributes*   [procedure]
> The length of the file in bytes.

`file-attributes/mode-string` *attributes*   [procedure]
> The mode string of the file, a newly allocated string showing the file's mode bits. Under unix, this string is in unix format. Under Windows, this string shows the standard "DOS" attributes in their usual format.

`file-attributes/n-links` *attributes*   [procedure]
> The number of links to the file, an exact positive integer. Under Windows, this is always 1.

The following additional accessors are defined under unix:

`file-attributes/uid` *attributes*   [procedure]
> The user id of the file's owner, an exact non-negative integer.

`file-attributes/gid` *attributes*   [procedure]
> The group id of the file's group, an exact non-negative integer.

`file-attributes/inode-number` *attributes*   [procedure]
> The inode number of the file, an exact non-negative integer.

The following additional accessor is defined under Windows:

`file-attributes/modes` *attributes*   [procedure]
> The attribute bits of the file. This is an exact non-negative integer containing the
> file's attribute bits, exactly as specified by the operating system's API.

15.4 Directory Reader

`directory-read` *directory* [*sort?*]   [procedure]
> *Directory* must be an object that can be converted into a pathname by
> `->pathname`. The directory specified by *directory* is read, and the contents of the
> directory is returned as a newly allocated list of absolute pathnames. The result
> is sorted according to the usual sorting conventions for directories, unless *sort?* is
> specified as `#f`. If *directory* has name, type, or version components, the returned
> list contains only those pathnames whose name, type, and version components match
> those of *directory*; `wild` or `#f` as one of these components means "match anything".
>
> The Windows implementation supports "globbing", in which the characters `*` and `?`
> are interpreted to mean "match anything" and "match any character", respectively.
> This "globbing" is supported only in the file part of *directory*.

15.5 Date and Time

MIT/GNU Scheme provides a simple set of procedures for manipulating date and time
information. There are four time representations, each of which serves a different purpose.
Each representation may be converted to any of the others.

The primary time representation, *universal time*, is an exact non-negative integer count-
ing the number of seconds that have elapsed since midnight January 1, 1900 UTC. (UTC
stands for *Coordinated Universal Time*, and is the modern name for Greenwich Mean Time.)
This format is produced by `get-universal-time` and `decoded-time->universal-time`.

The second representation, *decoded time*, is a record structure in which the time is
broken down into components, such as month, minute, etc. Decoded time is always relative
to a particular time zone, which is a component of the structure. This format is produced
by `global-decoded-time` and `local-decoded-time`.

The third representation, *file time*, is an exact non-negative integer that is larger
for increasing time. Unlike universal time, this representation is operating-system
dependent. This format is produced by all of the file-attribute procedures, for example
`file-modification-time` and `file-attributes`.

The fourth representation, the *time string*, is an external representation for time. This
format is defined by RFC-822, *Standard for the format of ARPA Internet text messages*,
with the modification that years are represented as four-digit numbers rather than two-
digit numbers. This format is the standard format for Internet email and numerous other
network protocols.

Within this section, argument variables named *universal-time*, *decoded-time*, *file-time*, and *time-string* are respectively required to be of the corresponding format.

15.5.1 Universal Time

get-universal-time   [procedure]
>   Return the current time in universal format.
>
>   (get-universal-time) ⇒ 3131453078

epoch   [variable]
>   epoch is the representation of midnight January 1, 1970 UTC in universal-time format.
>
>   epoch ⇒ 2208988800

15.5.2 Decoded Time

Objects representing standard time components, such as seconds and minutes, are required to be exact non-negative integers. Seconds and minutes must be inclusively between 0 and 59; hours between 0 and 23; days between 1 and 31; months between 1 and 12; years are represented in "four-digit" form, in which 1999 is represented as 1999 — *not* 99.

local-decoded-time   [procedure]
>   Return the current time in decoded format. The decoded time is represented in the local time zone.
>
>   (pp (local-decoded-time))
>   ⊣ #[decoded-time 76]
>   ⊣ (second 2)
>   ⊣ (minute 12)
>   ⊣ (hour 11)
>   ⊣ (day 27)
>   ⊣ (month 4)
>   ⊣ (year 1999)
>   ⊣ (day-of-week 1)
>   ⊣ (daylight-savings-time 1)
>   ⊣ (zone 5)

global-decoded-time   [procedure]
>   Return the current time in decoded format. The decoded time is represented in UTC.
>
>   (pp (global-decoded-time))
>   ⊣ #[decoded-time 77]
>   ⊣ (second 8)
>   ⊣ (minute 12)
>   ⊣ (hour 15)
>   ⊣ (day 27)
>   ⊣ (month 4)
>   ⊣ (year 1999)
>   ⊣ (day-of-week 1)
>   ⊣ (daylight-savings-time 0)
>   ⊣ (zone 0)

`make-decoded-time` *second minute hour day month year* [*zone*]   [procedure]
> Return a new decoded-time object representing the given time. The arguments must be valid components according to the above rules, and must form a valid date.

> If *zone* is not supplied or is `#f`, the resulting decoded time will be represented in the local time zone. Otherwise, *zone* must be a valid time zone, and the result will be represented in that zone.

> **Warning**: because this procedure depends on the operating system's runtime library, it is not capable of representing all dates. In particular, on most unix systems, it is not possible to encode dates that occur prior to midnight, January 1, 1970 UTC. Attempting to do this will signal an error.

> ```
> (pp (make-decoded-time 0 9 11 26 3 1999))
> ⊣ #[decoded-time 19]
> ⊣ (second 0)
> ⊣ (minute 9)
> ⊣ (hour 11)
> ⊣ (day 26)
> ⊣ (month 3)
> ⊣ (year 1999)
> ⊣ (day-of-week 4)
> ⊣ (daylight-savings-time 0)
> ⊣ (zone 5)
>
> (pp (make-decoded-time 0 9 11 26 3 1999 3))
> ⊣ #[decoded-time 80]
> ⊣ (second 0)
> ⊣ (minute 9)
> ⊣ (hour 11)
> ⊣ (day 26)
> ⊣ (month 3)
> ⊣ (year 1999)
> ⊣ (day-of-week 4)
> ⊣ (daylight-savings-time 0)
> ⊣ (zone 3)
> ```

`decoded-time/second` *decoded-time*   [procedure]
`decoded-time/minute` *decoded-time*   [procedure]
`decoded-time/hour` *decoded-time*   [procedure]
`decoded-time/day` *decoded-time*   [procedure]
`decoded-time/month` *decoded-time*   [procedure]
`decoded-time/year` *decoded-time*   [procedure]
> Return the corresponding component of *decoded-time*.

> ```
> (decoded-time/second (local-decoded-time)) ⇒ 17
> (decoded-time/year (local-decoded-time)) ⇒ 1999
> (decoded-time/day (local-decoded-time)) ⇒ 26
> ```

`decoded-time/day-of-week` *decoded-time*   [procedure]
> Return the day of the week on which *decoded-time* falls, encoded as an exact integer between 0 (Monday) and 6 (Sunday), inclusive.
>
>   (decoded-time/day-of-week (local-decoded-time)) ⇒ 4

`decoded-time/daylight-savings-time?` *decoded-time*   [procedure]
> Return #t if *decoded-time* is represented using daylight savings time. Otherwise return #f.
>
>   (decoded-time/daylight-savings-time? (local-decoded-time))
>   ⇒ #f

`decoded-time/zone` *decoded-time*   [procedure]
> Return the time zone in which *decoded-time* is represented. This is an exact rational number between -24 and +24 inclusive, that when multiplied by 3600 is an integer. The value is the number of hours west of UTC.
>
>   (decoded-time/zone (local-decoded-time)) ⇒ 5

`time-zone?` *object*   [procedure]
> Returns #t if *object* is an exact number between -24 and +24 inclusive, that when multiplied by 3600 is an integer.
>
>   (time-zone? -5)   ⇒ #t
>   (time-zone? 11/2) ⇒ #t
>   (time-zone? 11/7) ⇒ #f

`month/max-days` *month*   [procedure]
> Returns the maximum number of days possible in *month*. *Month* must be an exact integer between 1 and 12 inclusive.
>
>   (month/max-days 2) ⇒ 29
>   (month/max-days 3) ⇒ 31
>   (month/max-days 4) ⇒ 30

15.5.3 File Time

As stated above, file time is operating-system dependent. As of this writing, two formats are used. For unix and Windows systems, file time is the number of seconds since midnight January 1, 1970 UTC (the standard unix time convention).

The following procedures generate their results in file-time format:

```
file-access-time
file-access-time-direct
file-access-time-indirect
file-modification-time
file-modification-time-direct
file-modification-time-indirect
file-attributes/access-time
file-attributes/modification-time
file-attributes/change-time
```

Additionally, `set-file-times!` accepts its time arguments in file-time format.

15.5.4 Time-Format Conversion

The procedures described in this section convert times from one format to another.

universal-time->local-decoded-time *universal-time*   [procedure]
universal-time->global-decoded-time *universal-time*   [procedure]
>   Converts an argument in universal-time format to decoded-time format. The result
>   is in the local time zone or UTC, respectively.

```
(pp (universal-time->local-decoded-time (get-universal-time)))
⊣ #[decoded-time 21]
⊣ (second 23)
⊣ (minute 57)
⊣ (hour 17)
⊣ (day 29)
⊣ (month 4)
⊣ (year 1999)
⊣ (day-of-week 3)
⊣ (daylight-savings-time 1)
⊣ (zone 5)


(pp (universal-time->global-decoded-time
     (get-universal-time)))
⊣ #[decoded-time 22]
⊣ (second 27)
⊣ (minute 57)
⊣ (hour 21)
⊣ (day 29)
⊣ (month 4)
⊣ (year 1999)
⊣ (day-of-week 3)
⊣ (daylight-savings-time 0)
⊣ (zone 0)
```

universal-time->file-time *universal-time*   [procedure]
>   Converts an argument in universal-time format to file-time format.

```
(universal-time->file-time (get-universal-time))
    ⇒ 925422988
```

universal-time->local-time-string *universal-time*   [procedure]
universal-time->global-time-string *universal-time*   [procedure]
>   Converts an argument in universal-time format to a time string. The result is in the
>   local time zone or UTC, respectively.

```
(universal-time->local-time-string (get-universal-time))
    ⇒ "Thu, 29 Apr 1999 17:55:31 -0400"
(universal-time->global-time-string (get-universal-time))
    ⇒ "Thu, 29 Apr 1999 21:55:51 +0000"
```

decoded-time->universal-time *decoded-time*   [procedure]
>   Converts an argument in decoded-time format to universal-time format.

```
(decoded-time->universal-time (local-decoded-time))
    ⇒ 3134411942
(decoded-time->universal-time (global-decoded-time))
    ⇒ 3134411947
```

decoded-time->file-time *decoded-time*   [procedure]
    Converts an argument in decoded-time format to file-time format.

```
(decoded-time->file-time (local-decoded-time))
    ⇒ 925423191
(decoded-time->file-time (global-decoded-time))
    ⇒ 925423195
```

decoded-time->string *decoded-time*   [procedure]
    Convert an argument in decoded-time format to a time string.

```
(decoded-time->string (local-decoded-time))
    ⇒ "Thu, 29 Apr 1999 18:00:43 -0400"
(decoded-time->string (global-decoded-time))
    ⇒ "Thu, 29 Apr 1999 22:00:46 +0000"
```

file-time->universal-time *file-time*   [procedure]
    Converts an argument in universal-time format to file-time format.

```
(file-time->universal-time (file-modification-time "/"))
    ⇒ 3133891907
```

file-time->local-decoded-time *file-time*   [procedure]
file-time->global-decoded-time *file-time*   [procedure]
    Converts an argument in file-time format to decoded-time format. The result is in
    the local time zone or UTC, respectively.

```
(pp (file-time->local-decoded-time
     (file-modification-time "/")))
⊣ #[decoded-time 26]
⊣ (second 47)
⊣ (minute 31)
⊣ (hour 17)
⊣ (day 23)
⊣ (month 4)
⊣ (year 1999)
⊣ (day-of-week 4)
⊣ (daylight-savings-time 1)
⊣ (zone 5)
```

```
(pp (file-time->global-decoded-time
     (file-modification-time "/")))
⊣ #[decoded-time 27]
⊣ (second 47)
⊣ (minute 31)
⊣ (hour 21)
⊣ (day 23)
⊣ (month 4)
⊣ (year 1999)
⊣ (day-of-week 4)
⊣ (daylight-savings-time 0)
⊣ (zone 0)
```

file-time->local-time-string *file-time*   [procedure]
file-time->global-time-string *file-time*   [procedure]
    Converts an argument in file-time format to a time string. The result is in the local time zone or UTC, respectively.

```
(file-time->local-time-string (file-modification-time "/"))
    ⇒ "Fri, 23 Apr 1999 17:31:47 -0400"
(file-time->global-time-string (file-modification-time "/"))
    ⇒ "Fri, 23 Apr 1999 21:31:47 +0000"
```

string->universal-time *time-string*   [procedure]
    Converts a time-string argument to universal-time format.

```
(string->universal-time "Fri, 23 Apr 1999 21:31:47 +0000")
    ⇒ 3133888307
(string->universal-time "Fri, 23 Apr 1999 17:31:47 -0400")
    ⇒ 3133888307
```

string->decoded-time *time-string*   [procedure]
    Converts a time-string argument to decoded-time format.

```
(pp (string->decoded-time "Fri, 23 Apr 1999 17:31:47 -0400"))
⊣ #[decoded-time 30]
⊣ (second 47)
⊣ (minute 31)
⊣ (hour 17)
⊣ (day 23)
⊣ (month 4)
⊣ (year 1999)
⊣ (day-of-week 4)
⊣ (daylight-savings-time 0)
⊣ (zone 4)
```

string->file-time *time-string*   [procedure]
    Converts a time-string argument to file-time format.

```
(string->file-time "Fri, 23 Apr 1999 17:31:47 -0400")
    ⇒ 924899507
```

15.5.5 External Representation of Time

The normal external representation for time is the time string, as described above. The procedures in this section generate alternate external representations of time which are more verbose and may be more suitable for presentation to human readers.

decoded-time/date-string *decoded-time*   [procedure]
decoded-time/time-string *decoded-time*   [procedure]
These procedures return strings containing external representations of the date and time, respectively, represented by *decoded-time*. The results are implicitly in local time.

```
(decoded-time/date-string (local-decoded-time))
    ⇒ "Tuesday March 30, 1999"
(decoded-time/time-string (local-decoded-time))
    ⇒ "11:22:38 AM"
```

day-of-week/long-string *day-of-week*   [procedure]
day-of-week/short-string *day-of-week*   [procedure]
Returns a string representing the given *day-of-week*. The argument must be an exact non-negative integer between 0 and 6 inclusive. day-of-week/long-string returns a long string that fully spells out the name of the day. day-of-week/short-string returns a shortened string that abbreviates the day to three letters.

```
(day-of-week/long-string 0)  ⇒ "Monday"
(day-of-week/short-string 0) ⇒ "Mon"
(day-of-week/short-string 3) ⇒ "Thu"
```

month/long-string *month*   [procedure]
month/short-string *month*   [procedure]
Returns a string representing the given *month*. The argument must be an exact non-negative integer between 1 and 12 inclusive. month/long-string returns a long string that fully spells out the name of the month. month/short-string returns a shortened string that abbreviates the month to three letters.

```
(month/long-string 1)   ⇒ "January"
(month/short-string 1)  ⇒ "Jan"
(month/short-string 10) ⇒ "Oct"
```

time-zone->string   [procedure]
Returns a string corresponding to the given time zone. This string is the same string that is used to generate RFC-822 time strings.

```
(time-zone->string 5)    ⇒ "-0500"
(time-zone->string -4)   ⇒ "+0400"
(time-zone->string 11/2) ⇒ "-0530"
```

15.6 Machine Time

The previous section dealt with procedures that manipulate clock time. This section describes procedures that deal with computer time: elapsed CPU time, elapsed real time, and so forth. These procedures are useful for measuring the amount of time it takes to execute code.

Some of the procedures in this section manipulate a time representation called *ticks*. A tick is a unit of time that is unspecified here but can be converted to and from seconds by supplied procedures. A count in ticks is represented as an exact integer. At present each tick is one millisecond, but this may change in the future.

`process-time-clock`   [procedure]

> Returns the amount of process time, in ticks, that has elapsed since Scheme was started. Process time is measured by the operating system and is time during which the Scheme process is computing. It does not include time in system calls, but depending on the operating system it may include time used by subprocesses.
>
> `(process-time-clock)` ⇒ `21290`

`real-time-clock`   [procedure]

> Returns the amount of real time, in ticks, that has elapsed since Scheme was started. Real time is the time measured by an ordinary clock.
>
> `(real-time-clock)` ⇒ `33474836`

`internal-time/ticks->seconds` *ticks*   [procedure]

> Returns the number of seconds corresponding to *ticks*. The result is always a real number.
>
> `(internal-time/ticks->seconds 21290)` ⇒ `21.29`
> `(internal-time/ticks->seconds 33474836)` ⇒ `33474.836`

`internal-time/seconds->ticks` *seconds*   [procedure]

> Returns the number of ticks corresponding to *seconds*. *Seconds* must be a real number.
>
> `(internal-time/seconds->ticks 20.88)` ⇒ `20880`
> `(internal-time/seconds->ticks 20.83)` ⇒ `20830`

`system-clock`   [procedure]

> Returns the amount of process time, in seconds, that has elapsed since Scheme was started. Roughly equivalent to:
>
> `(internal-time/ticks->seconds (process-time-clock))`
>
> Example:
>
> `(system-clock)` ⇒ `20.88`

`runtime`   [procedure]

> Returns the amount of process time, in seconds, that has elapsed since Scheme was started. However, it does not include time spent in garbage collection.
>
> `(runtime)` ⇒ `20.83`

`with-timings` *thunk receiver*   [procedure]

> Calls *thunk* with no arguments. After *thunk* returns, *receiver* is called with three arguments describing the time spent while computing *thunk*: the elapsed run time, the amount of time spent in the garbage collector, and the elapsed real time. All three times are in ticks.
>
> This procedure is most useful for doing performance measurements, and is designed to have relatively low overhead.

```
(with-timings
 (lambda () ... hairy computation ...)
 (lambda (run-time gc-time real-time)
   (write (internal-time/ticks->seconds run-time))
   (write-char #\space)
   (write (internal-time/ticks->seconds gc-time))
   (write-char #\space)
   (write (internal-time/ticks->seconds real-time))
   (newline)))
```

measure-interval *runtime? procedure*   [procedure]

Calls *procedure*, passing it the current process time, in seconds, as an argument. The result of this call must be another procedure. When *procedure* returns, the resulting procedure is tail-recursively called with the ending time, in seconds, as an argument.

If *runtime?* is #f, the elapsed time is deducted from the elapsed system time returned by runtime.

While this procedure can be used for time measurement, its interface is somewhat clumsy for that purpose. We recommend that you use with-timings instead, because it is more convenient and has lower overhead.

```
(measure-interval #t
                  (lambda (start-time)
                    (let ((v ... hairy computation ...))
                      (lambda (end-time)
                        (write (- end-time start-time))
                        (newline)
                        v))))
```

15.7 Subprocesses

MIT/GNU Scheme provides the ability to run and control subprocesses. This support is divided into two parts: a low-level set of primitives that maps onto the underlying operating system's process-control primitives, and a high-level set of procedures for starting a subprocess and running it to completion in a single call. Subprocesses that are run in the latter fashion are referred to as *synchronous*, because they are started and stopped in synchrony with a Scheme procedure call.

This chapter documents Scheme's high-level synchronous-subprocess support. The low-level support is not documented but is available for those who are willing to read the source code.

Synchronous-subprocess support is a run-time-loadable option. To use it, execute

```
(load-option 'synchronous-subprocess)
```

once before calling it.

15.7.1 Subprocess Procedures

There are two commands for running synchronous subprocesses under Scheme. run-shell-command is very simple to use, provides access to all shell features, and is to be preferred in most situations. run-synchronous-subprocess allows direct execution of a program and precise control of the command-line arguments passed to the program, but does not provide file globbing, I/O redirection, or other shell features.

run-shell-command *command option* ...   [procedure]

> Runs *command*, which must be a string. *Command* is passed to a command shell for interpretation; how the shell is chosen is detailed below.
>
> The *options* are a sequence of keyword/value pairs that specify optional behavior. See below for more information about options.
>
> **run-shell-command** waits until the subprocess completes its execution and returns the exit code from the subprocess. If the subprocess is killed or stopped, an error is signalled and the procedure does not return.

run-synchronous-subprocess *program arguments option* ...   [procedure]

> Runs *program*, passing it the given command-line *arguments*. *Program* must be either the name of a program on the path, or else a pathname to a specific program. *Arguments* must be a list of strings; each string is a single command-line argument to the program.
>
> The *options* are a sequence of keyword/value pairs that specify optional behavior. See below for more information about options.
>
> **run-synchronous-subprocess** waits until the subprocess completes its execution and returns the exit code from the subprocess. If the subprocess is killed or stopped, an error is signalled and the procedure does not return.

15.7.2 Subprocess Conditions

If a subprocess spawned by one of the above procedures is killed or suspended, then one of the following errors will be signalled.

condition-type:subprocess-signalled *subprocess reason*   [condition type]

> This condition type is a subtype of **condition-type:subprocess-abnormal-termination**. It is signalled when the subprocess is killed.
>
> *Subprocess* is an object that represents the subprocess involved. The internals of this object can be accessed but the interface is not documented at this time; see the source code for details.
>
> *Reason* is interesting only on unix systems, where it is the signal that killed the process. On other systems it has a fixed value that conveys no useful information.

condition-type:subprocess-stopped *subprocess reason*   [condition type]

> This condition type is a subtype of **condition-type:subprocess-abnormal-termination**. It is signalled when the subprocess is stopped or suspended.
>
> *Subprocess* is an object that represents the subprocess involved. The internals of this object can be accessed but the interface is not documented at this time; see the source code for details.
>
> *Reason* is interesting only on unix systems, where it is the signal that stopped the process. On other systems it has a fixed value that conveys no useful information.

`condition-type:subprocess-abnormal-termination`   [condition type]
    subprocess reason
    This condition type is a subtype of `condition-type:error`. This is an abstract type
    that is never signalled. It is provided so that condition handlers can be bound to it.

15.7.3 Subprocess Options

The following subprocess options may be passed to `run-shell-command` or
`run-synchronous-subprocess`. These options are passed as alternating keyword/value
pairs, for example:

```
(run-shell-command "ls /"
                   'output my-output-port
                   'output-buffer-size 8192)
```

The example shows a shell command being run with two options specified: `output` and
`output-buffer-size`.

`input` *port*   [subprocess option]
    Specifies the standard input of the subprocess. *Port* may be an input port, in which
    case characters are read from *port* and fed to the subprocess until *port* reaches end-
    of-file. Alternatively, *port* may be `#f`, indicating that the subprocess has no standard
    input.

    The default value of this option is `#f`.

```
(call-with-input-file "foo.in"
  (lambda (port)
    (run-shell-command "cat > /dev/null" 'input port)))
```

`input-line-translation` *line-ending*   [subprocess option]
    Specifies how line-endings should be translated when writing characters to the subpro-
    cess. Ignored if the `input` option is `#f`. *Line-ending* must be either a string specifying
    the line ending, or the symbol `default`, meaning to use the operating system's stan-
    dard line ending. In either case, newline characters to be written to the `input` port
    are translated to the specified line ending before being written.

    The default value of this option is `default`.

```
(call-with-input-file "foo.in"
  (lambda (port)
    (run-shell-command "cat > /dev/null"
                       'input port
                       'input-line-translation "\r\n")))
```

`input-buffer-size` *n*   [subprocess option]
    Specifies the size of the input buffer for the standard input of the subprocess. (This
    is the buffer on the Scheme side, and has nothing to do with any buffering done on
    the subprocess side.) Ignored if the `input` option is `#f`. *N* must be an exact positive
    integer specifying the number of characters the buffer can hold.

    The default value of this option is `512`.

```
(call-with-input-file "foo.in"
  (lambda (port)
    (run-shell-command "cat > /dev/null"
                       'input port
                       'input-buffer-size 4096)))
```

output *port*   [subprocess option]

Specifies the standard output and standard error of the subprocess. *Port* may be an output port, in which case characters are read from the subprocess and fed to *port* until the subprocess finishes. Alternatively, *port* may be #f, indicating that the subprocess has no standard output or standard error.

The default value of this option is the value of (current-output-port).

```
(call-with-output-file "foo.out"
  (lambda (port)
    (run-shell-command "ls -la /etc" 'output port)))
```

output-line-translation *line-ending*   [subprocess option]

Specifies how line-endings should be translated when reading characters from the standard output of the subprocess. Ignored if the output option is #f. *Line-ending* must be either a string specifying the line ending, or the symbol default, meaning to use the operating system's standard line ending. In either case, newline characters read from the subprocess port are translated to the specified line ending.

The default value of this option is default.

```
(call-with-output-file "foo.out"
  (lambda (port)
    (run-shell-command "ls -la /etc"
                       'output port
                       'output-line-translation "\r\n")))
```

output-buffer-size *n*   [subprocess option]

Specifies the size of the output buffer for the standard output of the subprocess. (This is the buffer on the Scheme side, and has nothing to do with any buffering done on the subprocess side.) Ignored if the output option is #f. *N* must be an exact positive integer specifying the number of characters the buffer can hold.

The default value of this option is 512.

```
(call-with-output-file "foo.out"
  (lambda (port)
    (run-shell-command "ls -la /etc"
                       'output port
                       'output-buffer-size 4096)))
```

redisplay-hook *thunk*   [subprocess option]

Specifies that *thunk* is to be run periodically when output from the subprocess is available. *Thunk* must be a procedure of no arguments, or #f indicating that no hook is supplied. This option is mostly useful for interactive systems. For example, the Edwin text editor uses this to update output buffers when running some subprocesses.

The default value of this option is #f.

```
(run-shell-command "ls -la /etc"
                   'redisplay-hook
                   (lambda ()
                     (update-buffer-contents buffer)))
```

environment *environment*   [subprocess option]

Specifies the environment variables that are to be used for the subprocess. *Environment* must be either a vector of strings or **#f** indicating the default environment. If it is a vector of strings, each string must be a name/value pair where the name and value are separated by an equal sign, for example, `"foo=bar"`. To define a variable with no value, just omit the value, as in `"foo="`.

Note that the variable **scheme-subprocess-environment** is bound to the default subprocess environment.

The default value of this option is **#f**.

```
(run-shell-command "ls -la /etc"
                   'environment
                   (let* ((v scheme-subprocess-environment)
                          (n (vector-length v))
                          (v (vector-grow v (+ n 1))))
                     (vector-set! v n "TERM=none")
                     v))
```

working-directory *pathname*   [subprocess option]

Specifies the working directory in which the subprocess will run.

The default value of this option is (**working-directory-pathname**).

```
(run-shell-command "ls -la" 'working-directory "/etc/")
```

use-pty? *boolean*   [subprocess option]

This option is meaningful only on unix systems; on other systems it is ignored. Specifies whether to communicate with the subprocess using PTY devices; if true, PTYs will be used, otherwise pipes will be used.

The default value of this option is **#f**.

```
(run-shell-command "ls -la /etc" 'use-pty? #t)
```

shell-file-name *pathname*   [subprocess option]

Specifies the shell program to use for **run-shell-command**.

The default value of this option is (**os/shell-file-name**). This is the value of the environment variable **SHELL**, or if **SHELL** is not set, the value is operating-system dependent as follows:

- On unix systems, **/bin/sh** is used.

- On Windows systems, the value of the environment variable **COMSPEC** is used. If that is not set, **cmd.exe** is used for Windows NT, or **command.com** is used for Windows 9x; in each case the shell is found by searching the path.

```
(run-shell-command "ls -la /etc"
                   'shell-file-name "/usr/local/bin/bash")
```

15.8 TCP Sockets

MIT/GNU Scheme provides access to *sockets*, which are a mechanism for inter-process communication. TCP stream sockets are supported, which communicate between computers over a TCP/IP network. TCP sockets are supported on all operating systems.

TCP sockets have two distinct interfaces: one interface to implement a *client* and another to implement a *server*. The basic protocol is that servers set up a listening port and wait for connections from clients. Implementation of clients is simpler and will be treated first.

The socket procedures accept two special arguments, called *host-name* and *service*. *Host-name* is a string which must be the name of an internet host. It is looked up using the ordinary lookup rules for your computer. For example, if your host is `foo.mit.edu` and *host-name* is `"bar"`, then it specifies `bar.mit.edu`.

Service specifies the service to which you will connect. A networked computer normally provides several different services, such as telnet or FTP. Each service is associated with a unique *port number*; for example, the `"www"` service is associated with port 80. The *service* argument specifies the port number, either as a string, or directly as an exact non-negative integer. Port strings are decoded by the operating system using a table; for example, on unix the table is in `/etc/services`. Usually you will use a port string rather than a number.

`open-tcp-stream-socket` *host-name service*   [procedure]
> `open-tcp-stream-socket` opens a connection to the host specified by *host-name*. *Host-name* is looked up using the ordinary lookup rules for your computer. The connection is established to the service specified by *service*. The returned value is an I/O port, to which you can read and write characters using ordinary Scheme I/O procedures such as `read-char` and `write-char`.
>
> When you wish to close the connection, just use `close-port`.
>
> As an example, here is how you can open a connection to a web server:
>
> > `(open-tcp-stream-socket "web.mit.edu" "www")`

Next we will treat setting up a TCP server, which is slightly more complicated. Creating a server is a two-part process. First, you must open a *server socket*, which causes the operating system to listen to the network on a port that you specify. Once the server socket is opened, the operating system will allow clients to connect to your computer on that port.

In the second step of the process, you *accept* the connection, which completes the connection initiated by the client, and allows you to communicate with the client. Accepting a connection does not affect the server socket; it continues to listen for additional client connections. You can have multiple client connections to the same server socket open simultaneously.

`open-tcp-server-socket` *service* [*address*]   [procedure]
> This procedure opens a server socket that listens for connections to *service*; the socket will continue to listen until you close it. The returned value is a server socket object.
>
> An error is signalled if another process is already listening on the service. Additionally, ports whose number is less than 1024 are privileged on many operating systems, and cannot be used by non-privileged processes; if *service* specifies such a port and you do not have administrative privileges, an error may be signalled.

The optional argument *address* specifies the IP address on which the socket will listen. If this argument is not supplied or is given as `#f`, then the socket listens on all IP addresses for this machine. (This is equivalent to passing the result of calling `host-address-any`.)

`tcp-server-connection-accept` *server-socket block? peer-address*   [procedure]
      [*line-translation*]
    Checks to see if a client has connected to *server-socket*. If so, an I/O port is returned. The returned port can be read and written using ordinary Scheme I/O procedures such as `read-char` and `write-char`.

    The argument *block?* says what to do if no client has connected at the time of the call. If `#f`, it says to return immediately with two values of `#f`. Otherwise, the call waits until a client connects.

    The argument *peer-address* is either `#f` or an IP address as allocated by `allocate-host-address`. If it is an IP address, the address is modified to be the address of the client making the connection.

    The optional argument *line-translation* specifies how end-of-line characters will be translated when reading or writing to the returned socket. If this is unspecified or `#f`, then lines will be terminated by CR-LF, which is the standard for most internet protocols. Otherwise, it must be a string, which specifies the line-ending character sequence to use.

    Note that closing the port returned by this procedure does not affect *server-socket*; it just closes the particular client connection that was opened by the call. To close *server-socket*, use `close-tcp-server-socket`.

`close-tcp-server-socket` *server-socket*   [procedure]
    Closes the server socket *server-socket*. The operating system will cease listening for network connections to that service. Client connections to *server-socket* that have already been accepted will not be affected.

15.9 Miscellaneous OS Facilities

This section contains assorted operating-system facilities that don't fit into other categories.

`microcode-id/operating-system`   [variable]
`microcode-id/operating-system-name`   [variable]
    `microcode-id/operating-system` is bound to a symbol that specifies the type of operating system that Scheme is running under. There are two possible values: `unix` or `nt`.

    `microcode-id/operating-system-name` is a string containing the same name as `microcode-id/operating-system`; the latter is created by interning the former as a symbol.

`microcode-id/operating-system-variant`   [variable]
    This variable is a string that identifies the particular variant of the operating system that Scheme is running under. Here are some of the possible values:

```
"GNU/Linux"
"MacOSX"
"Microsoft Windows NT 4.0 (Build 1381; Service Pack 3)"
```

For Windows systems, it is recommended that you match on the prefix of this string and ignore the "Build" suffix. This is because the suffix may contain information about service packs or fixes, while the prefix will be constant for a particular version of Windows.

The next few procedures provide access to the *domain name service* (DNS), which maintains associations between internet host names such as "www.swiss.ai.mit.edu" and IP addresses, such as 18.23.0.16. In MIT/GNU Scheme, we represent an internet host name as a string, and an IP address as a byte vector of length 4 (byte vectors are just character strings that are accessed using vector-8b-ref rather than string-ref). The bytes in an IP address read in the same order as they do when written out:

```
(get-host-by-name "www.swiss") ⇒ #("\022\027\000\020")
```

get-host-by-name *host-name*   [procedure]

> Looks up the internet host name *host-name* using the DNS, returning a vector of IP addresses for the corresponding host, or #f if there is no such host. Usually the returned vector has only one element, but if a host has more than one network interface, the vector might have more than one element.
>
> ```
> (get-host-by-name "www.swiss") ⇒ #("\022\027\000\020")
> ```

get-host-by-address *ip-address*   [procedure]

> Does a reverse DNS lookup on *ip-address*, returning the internet host name corresponding to that address, or #f if there is no such host.
>
> ```
> (get-host-by-address "\022\027\000\020") ⇒ "swissnet.ai.mit.edu"
> ```

canonical-host-name *host-name*   [procedure]

> Finds the "canonical" internet host name for *host-name*. For example:
>
> ```
> (canonical-host-name "zurich")    ⇒ "zurich.ai.mit.edu"
> (canonical-host-name "www.swiss") ⇒ "swissnet.ai.mit.edu"
> ```
>
> In both examples, the default internet domain 'ai.mit.edu' is added to *host-name*. In the second example, "www.swiss" is an alias for another computer named "swissnet".

get-host-name   [procedure]

> Returns the string that identifies the computer that MIT/GNU Scheme is running on. Usually this is an unqualified internet host name, i.e. the host name without the domain suffix:
>
> ```
> (get-host-name) ⇒ "aarau"
> ```

os/hostname   [procedure]

> Returns the canonical internet host name of the computer that MIT/GNU Scheme is running on. So, in contrast to the example for get-host-name:
>
> ```
> (os/hostname) ⇒ "aarau.ai.mit.edu"
> ```

allocate-host-address   [procedure]
>   Allocates and returns an IP address object. This is just a string of a fixed length
>   (current 4 bytes) into which an IP address may be stored. This procedure is used to
>   generate an appropriate argument to be passed to `tcp-server-connection-accept`.

>   `(allocate-host-address)` $\Rightarrow$ `"Xe\034\241"`

host-address-any   [procedure]
>   Return an IP address object that specifies "any host". This object is useful only when
>   passed as the *address* argument to `open-tcp-server-socket`.

>   `(host-address-any)` $\Rightarrow$ `"\000\000\000\000"`

host-address-loopback   [procedure]
>   Return an IP address object that specifies the local *loopback* network interface. The
>   loopback interface is a software network interface that can be used only for commu-
>   nicating between processes on the same computer. This address object is useful only
>   when passed as the *address* argument to `open-tcp-server-socket`.

>   `(host-address-loopback)` $\Rightarrow$ `"\177\000\000\001"`

16 Error System

The MIT/GNU Scheme error system provides a uniform mechanism for the signalling of errors and other exceptional conditions. The simplest and most generally useful procedures in the error system are:

error
: is used to signal simple errors, specifying a message and some irritant objects (see Section 16.1 [Condition Signalling], page 266). Errors are usually handled by stopping the computation and putting the user in an error REPL.

warn
: is used to signal warnings (see Section 16.1 [Condition Signalling], page 266). Warnings are usually handled by printing a message on the console and continuing the computation normally.

ignore-errors
: is used to suppress the normal handling of errors within a given dynamic extent (see Section 16.3 [Condition Handling], page 269). Any error that occurs within the extent is trapped, returning immediately to the caller of ignore-errors.

More demanding applications require more powerful facilities. To give a concrete example, suppose you want floating-point division to return a very large number whenever the denominator is zero. This behavior can be implemented using the error system.

The Scheme arithmetic system can signal many different kinds of errors, including floating-point divide by zero. In our example, we would like to handle this particular condition specially, allowing the system to handle other arithmetic errors in its usual way.

The error system supports this kind of application by providing mechanisms for distinguishing different types of error conditions and for specifying where control should be transferred should a given condition arise. In this example, there is a specific object that represents the "floating-point divide by zero" condition type, and it is possible to dynamically specify an arbitrary Scheme procedure to be executed when a condition of that type is signalled. This procedure then finds the stack frame containing the call to the division operator, and returns the appropriate value from that frame.

Another useful kind of behavior is the ability to specify uniform handling for related classes of conditions. For example, it might be desirable, when opening a file for input, to gracefully handle a variety of different conditions associated with the file system. One such condition might be that the file does not exist, in which case the program will try some other action, perhaps opening a different file instead. Another related condition is that the file exists, but is read protected, so it cannot be opened for input. If these or any other related conditions occur, the program would like to skip this operation and move on to something else.

At the same time, errors unrelated to the file system should be treated in their usual way. For example, calling car on the argument 3 should signal an error. Or perhaps the name given for the file is syntactically incorrect, a condition that probably wants to be handled differently from the case of the file not existing.

To facilitate the handling of classes of conditions, the error system taxonomically organizes all condition types. The types are related to one another by *taxonomical links*, which specify that one type is a "kind of" another type. If two types are linked this way, one is considered to be a *specialization* of the other; or vice-versa, the second is a *generalization* of the first. In our example, all of the errors associated with opening an input file would be specializations of the condition type "cannot open input file".

The taxonomy of condition types permits any condition type to have no more than one immediate generalization. Thus, the condition types form a forest (set of trees). While users can create new trees, the standard taxonomy (see Section 16.7 [Taxonomy], page 280) is rooted at `condition-type:serious-condition`, `condition-type:warning`, `condition-type:simple-condition`, and `condition-type:breakpoint`; users are encouraged to add new subtypes to these condition types rather than create new trees in the forest.

To summarize, the error system provides facilities for the following tasks. The sections that follow will describe these facilities in more detail.

Signalling a condition

> A condition may be signalled in a number of different ways. Simple errors may be signalled, without explicitly defining a condition type, using `error`. The `signal-condition` procedure provides the most general signalling mechanism.

Handling a condition

> The programmer can dynamically specify handlers for particular condition types or for classes of condition types, by means of the `bind-condition-handler` procedure. Individual handlers have complete control over the handling of a condition, and additionally may decide not to handle a particular condition, passing it on to previously bound handlers.

Restarting from a handler

> The `with-restart` procedure provides a means for condition-signalling code to communicate to condition-handling code what must be done to proceed past the condition. Handlers can examine the restarts in effect when a condition was signalled, allowing a structured way to continue an interrupted computation.

Packaging condition state

> Each condition is represented by an explicit object. Condition objects contain information about the nature of the condition, information that describes the state of the computation from which the condition arose, and information about the ways the computation can be restarted.

Classification of conditions

> Each condition has a type, represented by a condition type object. Each condition type may be a specialization of some other condition types. A group of types that share a common generalization can be handled uniformly by specifying a handler for the generalization.

16.1 Condition Signalling

Once a condition instance has been created using `make-condition` (or any condition constructor), it can be *signalled*. The act of signalling a condition is separated from the act of creating the condition to allow more flexibility in how conditions are handled. For example, a condition instance could be returned as the value of a procedure, indicating that something unusual has happened, to allow the caller to clean up some state. The caller could then signal the condition once it is ready.

A more important reason for having a separate condition-signalling mechanism is that it allows *resignalling*. When a signalled condition has been caught by a particular handler, and the handler decides that it doesn't want to process that particular condition, it can signal the condition again. This is one way to allow other handlers to get a chance to see the condition.

error *reason argument . . .* [procedure]

This is the simplest and most common way to signal a condition that requires intervention before a computation can proceed (when intervention is not required, **warn** is more appropriate). **error** signals a condition (using **signal-condition**), and if no handler for that condition alters the flow of control (by invoking a restart, for example) it calls the procedure **standard-error-handler**, which normally prints an error message and stops the computation, entering an error REPL. Under normal circumstances **error** will not return a value (although an interactive debugger can be used to force this to occur).

Precisely what condition is signalled depends on the first argument to **error**. If *reason* is a condition, then that condition is signalled and the *argument*s are ignored. If *reason* is a condition type, then a new instance of this type is generated and signalled; the *argument*s are used to generate the values of the fields for this condition type (they are passed as the *field-plist* argument to **make-condition**). In the most common case, however, *reason* is neither a condition nor a condition type, but rather a string or symbol. In this case a condition of type **condition-type:simple-error** is created with the *message* field containing the *reason* and the *irritants* field containing the *argument*s.

warn *reason argument . . .* [procedure]

When a condition is not severe enough to warrant intervention, it is appropriate to signal the condition with **warn** rather than **error**. As with **error**, **warn** first calls **signal-condition**; the condition that is signalled is chosen exactly as in **error** except that a condition of type **condition-type:simple-warning** is signalled if *reason* is neither a condition nor a condition type. If the condition is not handled, **warn** calls the procedure **standard-warning-handler**, which normally prints a warning message and continues the computation by returning from **warn**.

warn establishes a restart named **muffle-warning** before calling **signal-condition**. This allows a signal handler to prevent the generation of the warning message by calling **muffle-warning**. The value of a call to **warn** is unspecified.

signal-condition *condition* [procedure]

This is the fundamental operation for signalling a condition. The precise operation of **signal-condition** depends on the condition type of which *condition* is an instance, the condition types set by **break-on-signals**, and the handlers established by **bind-condition-handler** and **bind-default-condition-handler**.

If the *condition* is an instance of a type that is a specialization of any of the types specified by **break-on-signals**, then a breakpoint REPL is initiated. Otherwise (or when that REPL returns), the handlers established by **bind-condition-handler** are checked, most recent first. Each applicable handler is invoked, and the search for a handler continues if the handler returns normally. If all applicable handlers return, then the applicable handlers established by `bind-default-condition-handler` are checked, again most recent first. Finally, if no handlers apply (or all return in a normal manner), `signal-condition` returns an unspecified value.

Note: unlike many other systems, the MIT/GNU Scheme runtime library does *not* establish handlers of any kind. (However, the Edwin text editor uses condition handlers extensively.) Thus, calls to `signal-condition` will return to the caller unless there are user supplied condition handlers, as the following example shows:

```
(signal-condition
 (make-condition
  condition-type:error
  (call-with-current-continuation (lambda (x) x))
  '()    ; no restarts
  '()))  ; no fields
⇒  unspecified
```

16.2 Error Messages

By convention, error messages (and in general, the reports generated by `write-condition-report`) should consist of one or more complete sentences. The usual rules for sentences should be followed: the first word of the sentence should be capitalized, and the sentence should be terminated by a period. The message should not contain extraneous whitespace such as line breaks or indentation.

The error system provides a simple formatting language that allows the programmer to have some control over the printing of error messages. This formatting language will probably be redesigned in a future release.

Error messages typically consist of a string describing the error, followed by some irritant objects. The string is printed using `display`, and the irritants are printed using `write`, typically with a space between each irritant. To allow simple formatting, we introduce a *noise* object, printed using `display`. The irritant list may contain ordinary objects interspersed with noise objects. Each noise object is printed using `display`, with no extra whitespace, while each normal object is printed using `write`, prefixed by a single space character.

Here is an example:

```
(define (error-within-procedure message irritant procedure)
  (error message
         irritant
         (error-irritant/noise "within procedure")
         procedure
         (error-irritant/noise ".")))
```

This would format as follows:

```
(error-within-procedure "Bad widget" 'widget-32 'invert-widget)  error
```

```
Bad widget widget-32 within procedure invert-widget.
```

Here are the operations supporting error messages:

format-error-message *message irritants port*   [procedure]
> *Message* is typically a string (although this is not required), *irritants* a list of irritant objects, and *port* an output port. Formats *message* and *irritants* to *port* in the standard way. Note that, during the formatting process, the depth and breadth to which lists are printed are each limited to small numbers, to guarantee that the output from each irritant is not arbitrarily large.

error-irritant/noise *value*   [procedure]
> Creates and returns a noise object whose value is *value*.

16.3 Condition Handling

The occurrence of a condition is signalled using `signal-condition`. `signal-condition` attempts to locate and invoke a *condition handler* that is prepared to deal with the type of condition that has occurred. A condition handler is a procedure of one parameter, the condition that is being signalled. A procedure is installed as a condition handler by calling `bind-condition-handler` (to establish a handler that is in effect only while a particular thunk is executing) or `bind-default-condition-handler` (to establish a handler that is in effect permanently). As implied by the name, handlers created by `bind-default-condition-handler` are invoked only after all other applicable handlers have been invoked.

A *handler* may process a signal in any way it deems appropriate, but the common patterns are:

Ignore the condition.
> By returning from the handler in the usual manner.

Handle the condition.
> By doing some processing and then invoking a restart (or, less preferably, a continuation) that was established at some point prior to the call to `signal-condition`.

Resignal a condition.
> By doing some processing and calling `signal-condition` with either the same condition or a newly created one. In order to support this, `signal-condition` runs *handler* in such a way that a subsequent call to `signal-condition` sees only the handlers that were established prior to this one.

As an aid to debugging condition handlers, Scheme maintains a set of condition types that will cause an interactive breakpoint to occur prior to normal condition signalling. That is, `signal-condition` creates a new REPL prior to its normal operation when its argument is a condition that is a specialization of any of these types. The procedure `break-on-signals` establishes this set of condition types.

ignore-errors *thunk*   [procedure]
> Executes *thunk* with a condition handler that intercepts the signalling of any specialization of `condition-type:error` (including those produced by calls to `error`) and immediately terminates the execution of *thunk* and returns from the call to `ignore-errors` with the signalled condition as its value. If *thunk* returns normally, its value is returned from `ignore-errors`.

Notice that `ignore-errors` does not "turn off signalling" or condition handling. Condition handling takes place in the normal manner but conditions specialized from `condition-type:error` are trapped rather than propogated as they would be by default.

`bind-condition-handler` *condition-types handler thunk* [procedure]

Invokes *thunk* after adding *handler* as a condition handler for the conditions specified by *condition-types*. *Condition-types* must be a list of condition types; signalling a condition whose type is a specialization of any of these types will cause the *handler* to be invoked. See `signal-condition` for a description of the mechanism used to invoke handlers.

By special extension, if *condition-types* is the empty list then the *handler* is called for all conditions.

`bind-default-condition-handler` *condition-types handler* [procedure]

Installs *handler* as a (permanent) condition handler for the conditions specified by *condition-types*. *Condition-types* must be a list of condition types; signalling a condition whose type is a specialization of any of these types will cause the *handler* to be invoked. See `signal-condition` for a description of the mechanism used to invoke handlers.

By special extension, if *condition-types* is the empty list then the *handler* is called for all conditions.

`break-on-signals` *condition-types* [procedure]

Arranges for `signal-condition` to create an interactive REPL before it signals a condition that is a specialization of any of the types in the list of *condition-types*. This can be extremely helpful when trying to debug code that uses custom condition handlers. In order to create a REPL when *any* condition type is signalled it is best to actually put a breakpoint on entry to `signal-condition`.

`standard-error-handler` *condition* [procedure]

Called internally by `error` after it calls `signal-condition`. Normally creates a new REPL with the prompt `"error>"` (but see `standard-error-hook`). In order to simulate the effect of calling `error`, code may call `signal-condition` directly and then call `standard-error-handler` if `signal-condition` returns.

`standard-error-hook` [variable]

This variable controls the behavior of the procedure `standard-error-handler`, and hence `error`. It is intended to be bound with `fluid-let` and is normally `#f`. It may be changed to a procedure of one argument and will then be invoked (with `standard-error-hook` rebound to `#f`) by `standard-error-handler` just prior to starting the error REPL. It is passed one argument, the condition being signalled.

`standard-warning-handler` *condition* [procedure]

This is the procedure called internally by `warn` after it calls `signal-condition`. The normal behavior of `standard-warning-handler` is to print a message (but see `standard-warning-hook`). More precisely, the message is printed to the port returned by `notification-output-port`. The message is formed by first printing the string

"Warning: " to this port, and then calling `write-condition-report` on *condition* and the port.

In order to simulate the effect of calling `warn`, code may call `signal-condition` directly and then call `standard-warning-handler` if `signal-condition` returns. (This is not sufficient to implement the `muffle-warning` protocol, however. For that purpose an explicit restart must be provided.)

`standard-warning-hook`   [variable]

> This variable controls the behavior of the procedure `standard-warning-handler`, and hence `warn`. It is intended to be bound with `fluid-let` and is normally `#f`. It may be changed to a procedure of one argument and will then be invoked (with `standard-warning-hook` rebound to `#f`) by `standard-warning-handler` in lieu of writing the warning message. It is passed one argument, the condition being signalled.

16.4 Restarts

The Scheme error system provides a mechanism, known as *restarts*, that helps coordinate condition-signalling code with condition-handling code. A module of code that detects and signals conditions can provide procedures (using `with-simple-restart` or `with-restart`) to be invoked by handlers that wish to continue, abort, or restart the computation. These procedures, called *restart effectors*, are encapsulated in restart objects.

When a condition object is created, it contains a set of restart objects, each of which contains a restart effector. Condition handlers can inspect the condition they are handling (using `find-restart` to find restarts by name, or `condition/restarts` to see the entire set), and they can invoke the associated effectors (using `invoke-restart` or `invoke-restart-interactively`). Effectors can take arguments, and these may be computed directly by the condition-handling code or by gathering them interactively from the user.

The names of restarts can be chosen arbitrarily, but the choice of name is significant. These names are used to coordinate between the signalling code (which supplies names for restarts) and the handling code (which typically chooses a restart effector by the name of its restart). Thus, the names specify the *restart protocol* implemented by the signalling code and invoked by the handling code. The protocol indicates the number of arguments required by the effector code as well as the semantics of the arguments.

Scheme provides a conventional set of names (hence, protocols) for common use. By choosing the names of restarts from this set, signalling code can indicate that it is able to perform a small set of fairly common actions (`abort`, `continue`, `muffle-warning`, `retry`, `store-value`, `use-value`). In turn, simple condition-handling code can look for the kind of action it wishes to perform and simply invoke it by name. All of Scheme's conventional names are symbols, although in general restart names are not restricted to any particular data type. In addition, the object `#f` is reserved to indicate the "not for automated use" protocol: these restarts should be activated only under human control.

Restarts themselves are first-class objects. They encapsulate their name, a procedure (known as the *effector*) to be executed if they are invoked, and a thunk (known as the *reporter*) that can be invoked to display a description of the restart (used, for example, by the interactive debugger). Invoking a restart is an indication that a handler has chosen to accept control for a condition; as a consequence, the *effector* of the restart should not return, since this would indicate that the handler declined to handle the condition. Thus, the *effector* should call a continuation captured before the condition-signalling process began. The most common pattern of usage by signalling code is encapsulated in `with-simple-restart`.

Within this chapter, a parameter named *restarts* will accept any of the following values:

- A list of restart objects.

- A condition. The procedure `condition/restarts` is called on the condition, and the resulting list of restarts is used in place of the condition.

- The symbol `bound-restarts`. The procedure `bound-restarts` is called (with no arguments), and the resulting list of restarts is used in place of the symbol.

- If the *restarts* parameter is optional and is not supplied, it is equivalent to having specified the symbol `bound-restarts`.

16.4.1 Establishing Restart Code

`with-simple-restart` *name reporter thunk*   [procedure]

Invokes *thunk* in a dynamic environment created by adding a restart named *name* to the existing named restarts. *Reporter* may be used during the execution of *thunk* to produce a description of the newly created restart; it must either be a procedure of one argument (a port) or a string. By convention, the description generated by *reporter* should be a short complete sentence, with first word capitalized and terminated by a period. The sentence should fit on one line with a little room to spare (see the examples below); usually this means that the sentence should be 70 characters or less in length.

If the restart created by `with-simple-restart` is invoked it simply aborts the computation in progress by returning an unspecified value from the call to `with-simple-restart`. Otherwise `with-simple-restart` returns the value computed by *thunk*.

```
(with-simple-restart 'george "This restart is named george."
  (lambda () 3)) ⇒ 3

(with-simple-restart 'george "This restart is named george."
  (lambda ()
    (invoke-restart (find-restart 'george)))) ⇒ unspecific

(with-simple-restart 'george "This restart is named george."
  (lambda () (car 3)))
;The object 3, passed as the first argument to car,
; is not the correct type.
;To continue, call RESTART with an option number:
; (RESTART 3) => Specify an argument to use in its place.
; (RESTART 2) => This restart is named george.
; (RESTART 1) => Return to read-eval-print level 1.
```

`with-restart` *name reporter effector interactor thunk*   [procedure]

Invokes *thunk* in a dynamic environment created by adding a restart named *name* to the existing named restarts. *Reporter* may be used during the execution of *thunk* to produce a description of the newly created restart; it must either be a procedure of one argument (a port) or a string. *Effector* is a procedure which will be called when the restart is invoked by `invoke-restart`. *Interactor* specifies the arguments that are to be passed to *effector* when it is invoked interactively; it may be either a procedure of no arguments, or `#f`. If *interactor* is `#f`, this restart is not meant to be invoked interactively.

The value returned by `with-restart` is the value returned by *thunk*. Should the restart be invoked by a condition handler, however, the *effector* will not return back to the handler that invoked it. Instead, the *effector* should call a continuation created before the condition-signalling process began, and `with-restart` will therefore not return in the normal manner.

```
(define (by-george! thunk)
  ; This code handles conditions that arise while executing thunk
  ; by invoking the GEORGE restart, passing 1 and 2 to the restart's
  ; effector code.
  (bind-condition-handler '() ; All conditions
   (lambda (condition)
     (invoke-restart (find-restart 'george) 1 2))
   thunk))

(define (can-george! thunk)
  ; This code provides a way of handling errors: the GEORGE restart.
  ; In order to GEORGE you must supply two values.
  (lambda ()
    (call-with-current-continuation
     (lambda (kappa)
       (with-restart
        'george                        ; Name
        "This restart is named george." ; Reporter
        (lambda (a b)                  ; Effector
          (kappa (list 'george a b)))
        values                         ; Interactor
        thunk)))))                     ; Thunk

(by-george! (can-george! (lambda () -3))        ⇒ -3
(by-george! (can-george! (lambda () (car 'x)))) ⇒ (george 1 2)
```

16.4.2 Invoking Standard Restart Code

Scheme supports six standard protocols for restarting from a condition, each encapsulated using a named restart (for use by condition-signalling code) and a simple procedure (for use by condition-handling code). Unless otherwise specified, if one of these procedures is unable to find its corresponding restart, it returns immediately with an unspecified value.

Each of these procedures accepts an optional argument *restarts*, which is described above in Section 16.4 [Restarts], page 271.

abort [*restarts*]   [procedure]

> Abort the computation, using the restart named **abort**. The corresponding effector takes no arguments and abandons the current line of computation. This is the restart provided by Scheme's REPL.
>
> If there is no restart named **abort**, this procedure signals an error of type `condition-type:no-such-restart`.

continue [*restarts*]   [procedure]

> Continue the current computation, using the restart named **continue**. The corresponding effector takes no arguments and continues the computation beyond the point at which the condition was signalled.

muffle-warning [*restarts*]   [procedure]

> Continue the current computation, using the restart named **muffle-warning**. The corresponding effector takes no arguments and continues the computation beyond the point at which any warning message resulting from the condition would be presented to the user. The procedure **warn** establishes a **muffle-warning** restart for this purpose.
>
> If there is no restart named **muffle-warning**, this procedure signals an error of type `condition-type:no-such-restart`.

retry [*restarts*]   [procedure]

> Retry the current computation, using the restart named **retry**. The corresponding effector takes no arguments and simply retries the same computation that triggered the condition. The condition may reoccur, of course, if the root cause has not been eliminated. The code that signals a "file does not exist" error can be expected to supply a **retry** restart. The restart would be invoked after first creating the missing file, since the computation is then likely to succeed if it is simply retried.

store-value *new-value* [*restarts*]   [procedure]

> Retry the current computation, using the restart named **store-value**, after first storing *new-value*. The corresponding effector takes one argument, *new-value*, and stores it away in a restart-dependent location, then retries the same computation that triggered the condition. The condition may reoccur, of course, if the root cause has not been eliminated. The code that signals an "unassigned variable" error can be expected to supply a **store-value** restart; this would store the value in the variable and continue the computation.

use-value *new-value* [*restarts*]   [procedure]

> Retry the current computation, using the restart named **use-value**, but substituting *new-value* for a value that previously caused a failure. The corresponding effector takes one argument, *new-value*, and retries the same computation that triggered the condition with the new value substituted for the failing value. The condition may reoccur, of course, if the new value also induces the condition.
>
> The code that signals an "unassigned variable" error can be expected to supply a **use-value** restart; this would simply continue the computation with *new-value* instead of the value of the variable. Contrast this with the **retry** and **store-value** restarts. If the **retry** restart is used it will fail because the variable still has no value.

The `store-value` restart could be used, but it would alter the value of the variable, so that future references to the variable would not be detected.

16.4.3 Finding and Invoking General Restart Code

Restarts are a general mechanism for establishing a protocol between condition-signalling and condition-handling code. The Scheme error system provides "packaging" for a number of common protocols. It also provides lower-level hooks that are intended for implementing customized protocols. The mechanism used by signalling code (`with-restart` and `with-simple-restart`) is used for both purposes.

Four additional operations are provided for the use of condition-handling code. Two operations (`bound-restarts` and `find-restart`) allow condition-handling code to locate active restarts. The other two operations (`invoke-restart` and `invoke-restart-interactively`) allow restart effectors to be invoked once the restart object has been located.

In addition, there is a data abstraction that provides access to the information encapsulated in restart objects.

bound-restarts   [procedure]

    Returns a list of all currently active restart objects, most recently installed first. `bound-restarts` should be used with caution by condition-handling code, since it reveals all restarts that are active at the time it is called, rather than at the time the condition was signalled. It is useful, however, for collecting the list of restarts for inclusion in newly generated condition objects or for inspecting the current state of the system.

find-restart *name* [*restarts*]   [procedure]

    Returns the first restart object named *name* in the list of *restarts* (permissible values for *restarts* are described above in Section 16.4 [Restarts], page 271). When used in a condition handler, `find-restart` is usually passed the name of a particular restart *and* the condition object that has been signalled. In this way the handler finds only restarts that were available when the condition was created (usually the same as when it was signalled). If *restarts* is omitted, the currently active restarts would be used, and these often include restarts added after the condition ocurred.

invoke-restart *restart argument* ...   [procedure]

    Calls the restart effector encapsulated in *restart*, passing the specified *argument*s to it. `invoke-restart` is intended for use by condition-handling code that understands the protocol implemented by *restart*, and can therefore calculate and pass an appropriate set of arguments.

    If a condition handler needs to interact with a user to gather the arguments for an effector (e.g. if it does not understand the protocol implemented by *restart*) `invoke-restart-interactively` should be used instead of `invoke-restart`.

invoke-restart-interactively *restart*   [procedure]

    First calls the interactor encapsulated in *restart* to interactively gather the arguments needed for *restart*'s effector. It then calls the effector, passing these arguments to it.

`invoke-restart-interactively` is intended for calling interactive restarts (those for which `restart/interactor` is not `#f`). For convenience, `invoke-restart-interactively` will call the restart's effector with no arguments if the restart has no interactor; this behavior may change in the future.

16.4.4 The Named Restart Abstraction

A restart object is very simple, since it encapsulates only a name, effector, interactor, and description.

`restart?` *object*   [procedure]
>   Returns `#f` if and only if *object* is not a restart.

`restart/name` *restart*   [procedure]
>   Returns the name of *restart*. While the Scheme error system uses only symbols and the object `#f` for its predefined names, programs may use arbitrary objects (name equivalence is tested using `eq?`).

`restart/effector` *restart*   [procedure]
>   Returns the effector encapsulated in *restart*. Normally this procedure is not used since `invoke-restart` and `invoke-restart-interactively` capture the most common invocation patterns.

`restart/interactor` *restart*   [procedure]
>   Returns the interactor encapsulated in *restart*. This is either a procedure of no arguments or the object `#f`. Normally this procedure is not used since `invoke-restart-interactively` captures the most common usage. Thus `restart/interactor` is most useful as a predicate to determine if *restart* is intended to be invoked interactively.

`write-restart-report` *restart port*   [procedure]
>   Writes a description of *restart* to *port*. This works by either displaying (if it is a string) or calling (if it is a procedure) the *reporter* that was supplied when the restart was created.

16.5 Condition Instances

A *condition*, in addition to the information associated with its type, usually contains other information that is not shared with other conditions of the same type. For example, the condition type associated with "unbound variable" errors does not specify the name of the variable that was unbound. The additional information is captured in a *condition* object, also called a *condition instance*.

In addition to information that is specific to a given type of condition (such as the variable name for "unbound variable" conditions), every condition instance also contains a continuation that encapsulates the state of the computation in which the condition occurred. This continuation is used for analyzing the computation to learn more about the context in which the condition occurred. It is *not* intended to provide a mechanism for continuing the computation; that mechanism is provided by restarts.

16.5.1 Generating Operations on Conditions

Scheme provides four procedures that take a condition type as input and produce operations on the corresponding condition object. These are reminiscent of the operations on record types that produce record operators (see Section 10.4 [Records], page 138). Given a condition type it is possible to generate: a constructor for instances of the type (using `condition-constructor`); an accessor to extract the contents of a field in instances of the type (using `condition-accessor`); a predicate to test for instances of the type (using `condition-predicate`); and a procedure to create and signal an instance of the type (using `condition-signaller`).

Notice that the creation of a condition object is distinct from signalling an occurrence of the condition. Condition objects are first-class; they may be created and never signalled, or they may be signalled more than once. Further notice that there are no procedures for modifying conditions; once created, a condition cannot be altered.

condition-constructor *condition-type field-names*   [procedure]
> Returns a constructor procedure that takes as arguments values for the fields specified in *field-names* and creates a condition of type *condition-type*. *Field-names* must be a list of symbols that is a subset of the *field-names* in *condition-type*. The constructor procedure returned by `condition-constructor` has signature
>
> > `(lambda (continuation restarts . field-values) ...)`
>
> where the *field-names* correspond to the *field-values*. The constructor argument *restarts* is described in Section 16.4 [Restarts], page 271. Conditions created by the constructor procedure have `#f` for the values of all fields other than those specified by *field-names*.
>
> For example, the following procedure `make-simple-warning` constructs a condition of type `condition-type:simple-warning` given a continuation (where the condition occurred), a description of the restarts to be made available, a warning message, and a list of irritants that caused the warning:
>
> > ```
> > (define make-simple-warning
> >   (condition-constructor condition-type:simple-warning
> >                          '(message irritants)))
> > ```

condition-accessor *condition-type field-name*   [procedure]
> Returns a procedure that takes as input a condition object of type *condition-type* and extracts the contents of the specified *field-name*. `condition-accessor` signals `error:bad-range-argument` if the *field-name* isn't one of the named fields of *condition-type*; the returned procedure will signal `error:wrong-type-argument` if passed an object other than a condition of type *condition-type* or one of its specializations.
>
> If it is known in advance that a particular field of a condition will be accessed repeatedly it is worth constructing an accessor for the field using `condition-accessor` rather than using the (possibly more convenient, but slower) `access-condition` procedure.

condition-predicate *condition-type*   [procedure]
> Returns a predicate procedure for testing whether an object is a condition of type *condition-type* or one of its specializations (there is no predefined way to test for a condition of a given type but *not* a specialization of that type).

condition-signaller *condition-type field-names default-handler*   [procedure]
> Returns a signalling procedure with parameters *field-names*. When the signalling procedure is called it creates and signals a condition of type *condition-type*. If the condition isn't handled (i.e. if no handler is invoked that causes an escape from the current continuation) the signalling procedure reduces to a call to *default-handler* with the condition as its argument.

> There are several standard procedures that are conventionally used for *default-handler*. If *condition-type* is a specialization of `condition-type:error`, *default-handler* should be the procedure `standard-error-handler`. If *condition-type* is a specialization of `condition-type:warning`, *default-handler* should be the procedure `standard-warning-handler`. If *condition-type* is a specialization of `condition-type:breakpoint`, *default-handler* should be the procedure `standard-breakpoint-handler`.

16.5.2 Condition Abstraction

The condition data type is abstracted through a predicate `condition?` and a set of accessor procedures.

condition? *object*   [procedure]
> Returns #f if and only if *object* is not a condition.

condition/type *condition*   [procedure]
> Returns the condition type of which *condition* is an instance.

condition/error? *condition*   [procedure]
> Returns #t if the *condition* is an instance of condition type `condition-type:error` or a specialization of it, #f otherwise.

condition/restarts *condition*   [procedure]
> Returns the list of restarts specified when *condition* was created.

condition/continuation *condition*   [procedure]
> Returns the continuation specified when *condition* was created. This is provided for inspecting the state of the system when the condition occurred, *not* for continuing or restarting the computation.

write-condition-report *condition port*   [procedure]
> Writes a description of *condition* to *port*, using the reporter function from the condition type associated with *condition*. See also `condition/report-string`.

16.5.3 Simple Operations on Condition Instances

The simple procedures described in this section are built on top of the more detailed abstraction of condition objects described above. While these procedures are sometimes easier to use, they are often less efficient.

make-condition *condition-type continuation restarts field-plist*   [procedure]

> Create a new condition object as an instance of *condition-type*, associated with *continuation*. The *continuation* is provided for inspection purposes only, *not* for restarting the computation. The *restarts* argument is described in Section 16.4 [Restarts], page 271. The *field-plist* is an alternating list of field names and values for those fields, where the field names are those that would be returned by (condition-type/field-names *condition-type*). It is used to provide values for fields in the condition object; fields with no value specified are set to #f. Once a condition object has been created there is no way to alter the values of these fields.

access-condition *condition field-name*   [procedure]

> Returns the value stored in the field *field-name* within *condition*. *Field-name* must be one of the names returned by (condition-type/field-names (condition/type *condition*)). access-condition looks up the *field-name* at runtime, so it is more efficient to use condition-accessor to create an access function if the same field is to be extracted from several instances of the same condition type.

condition/report-string *condition*   [procedure]

> Returns a string containing a report of the *condition*. This is generated by calling write-condition-report on *condition* and a string output port, and returning the output collected by the port as a string.

16.6 Condition Types

Each condition has a *condition type* object associated with it. These objects are used as a means of focusing on related classes of conditions, first by concentrating all of the information about a specific class of condition in a single place, and second by specifying an inheritance relationship between types. This inheritance relationship forms the taxonomic structure of the condition hierarchy (see Section 16.7 [Taxonomy], page 280).

The following procedures consititute the abstraction for condition types.

make-condition-type *name generalization field-names reporter*   [procedure]

> Creates and returns a (new) condition type that is a specialization of *generalization* (if it is a condition type) or is the root of a new tree of condition types (if *generalization* is #f). For debugging purposes, the condition type has a *name*, and instances of this type contain storage for the fields specified by *field-names* (a list of symbols) in addition to the fields common to all conditions (*type*, *continuation* and *restarts*).

> *Reporter* is used to produce a description of a particular condition of this type. It may be a string describing the condition, a procedure of arity two (the first argument will be a condition of this type and the second a port) that will write the message to the given port, or #f to specify that the reporter should be taken from the condition type *generalization* (or produce an "undocumented condition of type . . ." message if *generalization* is #f). The conventions used to form descriptions are spelled out in Section 16.2 [Error Messages], page 268.

condition-type/error? *condition-type*   [procedure]
    Returns #t if the *condition-type* is condition-type:error or a specialization of it,
    #f otherwise.

condition-type/field-names *condition-type*   [procedure]
    Returns a list of all of the field names for a condition of type *condition-type*. This
    is the set union of the fields specified when this *condition-type* was created with the
    condition-type/field-names of the generalization of this *condition-type*.

condition-type/generalizations *condition-type*   [procedure]
    Returns a list of all of the generalizations of *condition-type*. Notice that every condi-
    tion type is considered a generalization of itself.

condition-type? *object*   [procedure]
    Returns #f if and only if *object* is not a condition type.

16.7 Condition-Type Taxonomy

The MIT/GNU Scheme error system provides a rich set of predefined condition types.
These are organized into a forest through taxonomic links providing the relationships for
"specializes" and "generalizes". The chart appearing below shows these relationships by
indenting all the specializations of a given type relative to the type. Note that the variables
that are bound to these condition types are prefixed by 'condition-type:'; for example, the type appearing in the following table as 'simple-error' is stored in the variable
condition-type:simple-error. Users are encouraged to add new condition types by creating specializations of existing ones.

Following the chart are detailed descriptions of the predefined condition types. Some
of these types are marked as *abstract* types. Abstract types are not intended to be used
directly as the type of a condition; they are to be used as generalizations of other types,
and for binding condition handlers. Types that are not marked as abstract are *concrete*;
they are intended to be explicitly used as a condition's type.

```
serious-condition
    error
        simple-error
        illegal-datum
            wrong-type-datum
                wrong-type-argument
                wrong-number-of-arguments
            datum-out-of-range
                bad-range-argument
            inapplicable-object
        file-error
            file-operation-error
            derived-file-error
        port-error
            derived-port-error
        variable-error
            unbound-variable
            unassigned-variable
        arithmetic-error
            divide-by-zero
            floating-point-overflow
            floating-point-underflow
        control-error
            no-such-restart
        not-loading
        primitive-procedure-error
            system-call-error
    warning
        simple-warning
    simple-condition
    breakpoint
```

condition-type:serious-condition   [condition type]

> This is an abstract type. All serious conditions that require some form of intervention should inherit from this type. In particular, all errors inherit from this type.

condition-type:error   [condition type]

> This is an abstract type. All errors should inherit from this type.

condition-type:simple-error *message irritants*   [condition type]

> This is the condition generated by the **error** procedure when its first argument is not a condition or condition type. The fields *message* and *irritants* are taken directly from the arguments to **error**; *message* contains an object (usually a string) and *irritants* contains a list of objects. The reporter for this type uses **format-error-message** to generate its output from *message* and *irritants*.

condition-type:illegal-datum *datum*   [condition type]

> This is an abstract type. This type indicates the class of errors in which a program discovers an object that lacks specific required properties. Most commonly, the object

is of the wrong type or is outside a specific range. The *datum* field contains the offending object.

condition-type:wrong-type-datum *datum type*   [condition type]

    This type indicates the class of errors in which a program discovers an object that is of the wrong type. The *type* field contains a string describing the type that was expected, and the *datum* field contains the object that is of the wrong type.

```
(error:wrong-type-datum 3.4 "integer")    error
;The object 3.4 is not an integer.
;To continue, call RESTART with an option number:
; (RESTART 1) => Return to read-eval-print level 1.
```

error:wrong-type-datum *datum type*   [procedure]

    This procedure signals a condition of type `condition-type:wrong-type-datum`. The *datum* and *type* fields of the condition are filled in from the corresponding arguments to the procedure.

condition-type:wrong-type-argument *datum type operator*   [condition type]
      operand

    This type indicates that a procedure was passed an argument of the wrong type. The *operator* field contains the procedure (or a symbol naming the procedure), the *operand* field indicates the argument position that was involved (this field contains either a symbol, a non-negative integer, or #f), the *type* field contains a string describing the type that was expected, and the *datum* field contains the offending argument.

```
(+ 'a 3)                                    error
;The object a, passed as the first argument to integer-add,
; is not the correct type.
;To continue, call RESTART with an option number:
; (RESTART 2) => Specify an argument to use in its place.
; (RESTART 1) => Return to read-eval-print level 1.
```

```
(list-copy 3)
;The object 3, passed as an argument to list-copy, is not a list.
;To continue, call RESTART with an option number:
; (RESTART 1) => Return to read-eval-print level 1.
```

error:wrong-type-argument *datum type operator*   [procedure]

    This procedure signals a condition of type `condition-type:wrong-type-argument`. The *datum*, *type* and *operator* fields of the condition are filled in from the corresponding arguments to the procedure; the *operand* field of the condition is set to #f.

condition-type:wrong-number-of-arguments *datum type*   [condition type]
      operands

    This type indicates that a procedure was called with the wrong number of arguments. The *datum* field contains the procedure being called, the *type* field contains the number of arguments that the procedure accepts, and the *operands* field contains a list of the arguments that were passed to the procedure.

```
(car 3 4)                                    [error]
;The procedure car has been called with 2 arguments;
; it requires exactly 1 argument.
;To continue, call RESTART with an option number:
; (RESTART 1) => Return to read-eval-print level 1.
```

error:wrong-number-of-arguments *datum type operands*   [procedure]

This procedure signals a condition of type `condition-type:wrong-number-of-arguments`. The *datum, type* and *operands* fields of the condition are filled in from the corresponding arguments to the procedure.

condition-type:datum-out-of-range *datum*   [condition type]

This type indicates the class of errors in which a program discovers an object that is of the correct type but is otherwise out of range. Most often, this type indicates that an index to some data structure is outside of the range of indices for that structure. The *datum* field contains the offending object.

```
(error:datum-out-of-range 3)                 [error]
;The object 3 is not in the correct range.
;To continue, call RESTART with an option number:
; (RESTART 1) => Return to read-eval-print level 1.
```

error:datum-out-of-range *datum*   [procedure]

This procedure signals a condition of type `condition-type:datum-out-of-range`. The *datum* field of the condition is filled in from the corresponding argument to the procedure.

condition-type:bad-range-argument *datum operator operand*   [condition type]

This type indicates that a procedure was passed an argument that is of the correct type but is otherwise out of range. Most often, this type indicates that an index to some data structure is outside of the range of indices for that structure. The *operator* field contains the procedure (or a symbol naming the procedure), the *operand* field indicates the argument position that was involved (this field contains either a symbol, a non-negative integer, or `#f`), and the *datum* field is the offending argument.

```
(string-ref "abc" 3)                         [error]
;The object 3, passed as the second argument to string-ref,
; is not in the correct range.
;To continue, call RESTART with an option number:
; (RESTART 2) => Specify an argument to use in its place.
; (RESTART 1) => Return to read-eval-print level 1.
```

error:bad-range-argument *datum operator*   [procedure]

This procedure signals a condition of type `condition-type:bad-range-argument`. The *datum* and *operator* fields of the condition are filled in from the corresponding arguments to the procedure; the *operand* field of the condition is set to `#f`.

condition-type:inapplicable-object *datum operands*   [condition type]

This type indicates an error in which a program attempted to apply an object that is not a procedure. The object being applied is saved in the *datum* field, and the arguments being passed to the object are saved as a list in the *operands* field.

```
(3 4)                                                      error
;The object 3 is not applicable.
;To continue, call RESTART with an option number:
; (RESTART 2) => Specify a procedure to use in its place.
; (RESTART 1) => Return to read-eval-print level 1.
```

condition-type:file-error *filename*   [condition type]

    This is an abstract type. It indicates that an error associated with a file has occurred. For example, attempting to delete a nonexistent file will signal an error. The *filename* field contains a filename or pathname associated with the operation that failed.

condition-type:file-operation-error *filename verb noun*   [condition type]
        reason operator operands

    This is the most common condition type for file system errors. The *filename* field contains the filename or pathname that was being operated on. The *verb* field contains a string which is the verb or verb phrase describing the operation being performed, and the *noun* field contains a string which is a noun or noun phrase describing the object being operated on. The *reason* field contains a string describing the error that occurred. The *operator* field contains the procedure performing the operation (or a symbol naming that procedure), and the *operands* field contains a list of the arguments that were passed to that procedure. For example, an attempt to delete a nonexistent file would have the following field values:

```
filename        "/zu/cph/tmp/no-such-file"
verb            "delete"
noun            "file"
reason          "no such file or directory"
operator        file-remove
operands        ("/zu/cph/tmp/no-such-file")
```

and would generate a message like this:

```
(delete-file "/zu/cph/tmp/no-such-file")   error
;Unable to delete file "/zu/cph/tmp/no-such-file" because:
; No such file or directory.
;To continue, call RESTART with an option number:
; (RESTART 3) => Try to delete the same file again.
; (RESTART 2) => Try to delete a different file.
; (RESTART 1) => Return to read-eval-print level 1.
```

error:file-operation-error *filename verb noun reason operator*   [procedure]
        operands

    This procedure signals a condition of type `condition-type:file-operation-error`. The fields of the condition are filled in from the corresponding arguments to the procedure.

condition-type:derived-file-error *filename condition*   [condition type]

    This is another kind of file error, which is generated by obscure file-system errors that do not fit into the standard categories. The *filename* field contains the filename or pathname that was being operated on, and the *condition* field contains a condition describing the error in more detail. Usually the *condition* field contains a condition of type `condition-type:system-call-error`.

`error:derived-file` *filename condition*   [procedure]

   This procedure signals a condition of type `condition-type:derived-file-error`. The *filename* and *condition* fields of the condition are filled in from the corresponding arguments to the procedure.

`condition-type:port-error` *port*   [condition type]

   This is an abstract type. It indicates that an error associated with a I/O port has occurred. For example, writing output to a file port can signal an error if the disk containing the file is full; that error would be signalled as a port error. The *port* field contains the associated port.

`condition-type:derived-port-error` *port condition*   [condition type]

   This is a concrete type that is signalled when port errors occur. The *port* field contains the port associated with the error, and the *condition* field contains a condition object that describes the error in more detail. Usually the *condition* field contains a condition of type `condition-type:system-call-error`.

`error:derived-port` *port condition*   [procedure]

   This procedure signals a condition of type `condition-type:derived-port-error`. The *port* and *condition* fields of the condition are filled in from the corresponding arguments to the procedure.

`condition-type:variable-error` *location environment*   [condition type]

   This is an abstract type. It indicates that an error associated with a variable has occurred. The *location* field contains the name of the variable, and the *environment* field contains the environment in which the variable was referenced.

`condition-type:unbound-variable` *location environment*   [condition type]

   This type is generated when a program attempts to access or modify a variable that is not bound. The *location* field contains the name of the variable, and the *environment* field contains the environment in which the reference occurred.

```
foo                                         error
;Unbound variable: foo
;To continue, call RESTART with an option number:
; (RESTART 3) => Specify a value to use instead of foo.
; (RESTART 2) => Define foo to a given value.
; (RESTART 1) => Return to read-eval-print level 1.
```

`condition-type:unassigned-variable` *location environment* [condition type]

   This type is generated when a program attempts to access a variable that is not assigned. The *location* field contains the name of the variable, and the *environment* field contains the environment in which the reference occurred.

```
foo                                                    error
;Unassigned variable: foo
;To continue, call RESTART with an option number:
; (RESTART 3) => Specify a value to use instead of foo.
; (RESTART 2) => Set foo to a given value.
; (RESTART 1) => Return to read-eval-print level 1.
```

condition-type:arithmetic-error *operator operands*   [condition type]

> This is an abstract type. It indicates that a numerical operation was unable to complete because of an arithmetic error. (For example, division by zero.) The *operator* field contains the procedure that implements the operation (or a symbol naming the procedure), and the *operands* field contains a list of the arguments that were passed to the procedure.

condition-type:divide-by-zero *operator operands*   [condition type]

> This type is generated when a program attempts to divide by zero. The *operator* field contains the procedure that implements the failing operation (or a symbol naming the procedure), and the *operands* field contains a list of the arguments that were passed to the procedure.

```
(/ 1 0)
;Division by zero signalled by /.
;To continue, call RESTART with an option number:
; (RESTART 1) => Return to read-eval-print level 1.
```

error:divide-by-zero *operator operands*   [procedure]

> This procedure signals a condition of type condition-type:divide-by-zero. The *operator* and *operands* fields of the condition are filled in from the corresponding arguments to the procedure.

condition-type:floating-point-overflow *operator operands*   [condition type]

> This type is generated when a program performs an arithmetic operation that results in a floating-point overflow. The *operator* field contains the procedure that implements the operation (or a symbol naming the procedure), and the *operands* field contains a list of the arguments that were passed to the procedure.

condition-type:floating-point-underflow *operator operands*   [condition type]

> This type is generated when a program performs an arithmetic operation that results in a floating-point underflow. The *operator* field contains the procedure that implements the operation (or a symbol naming the procedure), and the *operands* field contains a list of the arguments that were passed to the procedure.

condition-type:primitive-procedure-error *operator*   [condition type]
        operands

> This is an abstract type. It indicates that an error was generated by a primitive procedure call. Primitive procedures are distinguished from ordinary procedures in that they are not written in Scheme but instead in the underlying language of the Scheme implementation. The *operator* field contains the procedure that implements the operation (or a symbol naming the procedure), and the *operands* field contains a list of the arguments that were passed to the procedure.

`condition-type:system-call-error` *operator operands*   [condition type]
      system-call error-type

This is the most common condition type generated by primitive procedures. A condition of this type indicates that the primitive made a system call to the operating system, and that the system call signalled an error. The system-call error is reflected back to Scheme as a condition of this type, except that many common system-call errors are automatically translated by the Scheme implementation into more useful forms; for example, a system-call error that occurs while trying to delete a file will be translated into a condition of type `condition-type:file-operation-error`. The *operator* field contains the procedure that implements the operation (or a symbol naming the procedure), and the *operands* field contains a list of the arguments that were passed to the procedure. The *system-call* and *error-type* fields contain symbols that describe the specific system call that was being made and the error that occurred, respectively; these symbols are completely operating-system dependent.

`condition-type:control-error`   [condition type]

This is an abstract type. It describes a class of errors relating to program control flow.

`condition-type:no-such-restart` *name*   [condition type]

This type indicates that a named restart was not active when it was expected to be. Conditions of this type are signalled by several procedures that look for particular named restarts, for example `muffle-warning`. The *name* field contains the name that was being searched for.

```
(muffle-warning)                        error
;The restart named muffle-warning is not bound.
;To continue, call RESTART with an option number:
; (RESTART 1) => Return to read-eval-print level 1.
```

`error:no-such-restart` *name*   [procedure]

This procedure signals a condition of type `condition-type:no-such-restart`. The *name* field of the condition is filled in from the corresponding argument to the procedure.

`condition-type:not-loading`   [condition type]

A condition of this type is generated when the procedure `current-load-pathname` is called from somewhere other than inside a file being loaded.

```
(current-load-pathname)                 error
;No file being loaded.
;To continue, call RESTART with an option number:
; (RESTART 1) => Return to read-eval-print level 1.
```

`condition-type:warning`   [condition type]

This is an abstract type. All warnings should inherit from this type. Warnings are a class of conditions that are usually handled by informing the user of the condition and proceeding the computation normally.

condition-type:simple-warning *message irritants*   [condition type]
> This is the condition generated by the **warn** procedure. The fields *message* and *irritants* are taken directly from the arguments to **warn**; *message* contains an object (usually a string) and *irritants* contains a list of objects. The reporter for this type uses **format-error-message** to generate its output from *message* and *irritants*.

condition-type:simple-condition *message irritants*   [condition type]
> This is an unspecialized condition that does not fall into any of the standard condition classes. The *message* field contains an object (usually a string) and *irritants* contains a list of objects. The reporter for this type uses **format-error-message** to generate its output from *message* and *irritants*.

condition-type:breakpoint *environment message prompt*   [condition type]
> A condition of this type is generated by the breakpoint mechanism. The contents of its fields are beyond the scope of this document.

17 Graphics

MIT/GNU Scheme has a simple two-dimensional line-graphics interface that is suitable for many graphics applications. In particular it is often used for plotting data points from experiments. The interface is generic in that it can support different types of graphics devices in a uniform manner. At the present time only one type of graphics device is implemented on each operating system.

Procedures are available for drawing points, lines, and text; defining the coordinate system; clipping graphics output; controlling some of the drawing characteristics; and controlling the output buffer (for devices that perform buffering). Additionally, devices may support custom operations, such as control of colors.

There are some constraints on the arguments to the procedures described in this chapter. Any argument named *graphics-device* must be a graphics device object that was returned from a call to `make-graphics-device`. Any argument that is a coordinate must be either an exact integer or an inexact real.

17.1 Opening and Closing of Graphics Devices

`graphics-type-available?` *graphics-device-type*   [procedure]
> This predicate returns `#t` if the graphics system named by the symbol *graphics-device-type* is implemented by the Scheme system. Otherwise it returns `#f`, in which case it is an error to attempt to make a graphics device using *graphics-device-type*.

`enumerate-graphics-types`   [procedure]
> This procedure returns a list of symbols which are the names of all the graphics device types that are supported by the Scheme system. The result is useful in deciding what additional arguments to supply to `make-graphics-device`, as each device type typically has a unique way of specifying the initial size, shape and other attributes.

`make-graphics-device` *graphics-device-type object . . .*   [procedure]
> This operation creates and returns a graphics device object. *Graphics-device-type* is a symbol naming a graphics device type, and both the number and the meaning of the remaining arguments is determined by that type (see the description of each device type for details); *graphics-device-type* must satisfy `graphics-type-available?`. *Graphics-device-type* may also be `#f`, in which case the graphics device type is chosen by the system from what is available. This allows completely portable graphics programs to be written provided no custom graphics operations are used. When *graphics-device-type* is `#f` no further arguments may be given; each graphics device type will use some "sensible" defaults. If more control is required then the program should use one of the two procedures above to dispatch on the available types.
>
> This procedure opens and initializes the device, which remains valid until explicitly closed by the procedure `graphics-close`. Depending on the implementation of the graphics device, if this object is reclaimed by the garbage collector, the graphics device may remain open or it may be automatically closed. While a graphics device remains open the resources associated with it are not released.

`graphics-close` *graphics-device*   [procedure]
> Closes *graphics-device*, releasing its resources. Subsequently it is an error to use *graphics-device*.

17.2 Coordinates for Graphics

Each graphics device has two different coordinate systems associated with it: *device coordinates* and *virtual coordinates*. Device coordinates are generally defined by low-level characteristics of the device itself, and often cannot be changed. Most device coordinate systems are defined in terms of pixels, and usually the upper-left-hand corner is the origin of the coordinate system, with x coordinates increasing to the right and y coordinates increasing downwards.

In contrast, virtual coordinates are more flexible in the units employed, the position of the origin, and even the direction in which the coordinates increase. A virtual coordinate system is defined by assigning coordinates to the edges of a device. Because these edge coordinates are arbitrary real numbers, any Cartesian coordinate system can be defined.

All graphics procedures that use coordinates are defined on virtual coordinates. For example, to draw a line at a particular place on a device, the virtual coordinates for the endpoints of that line are given.

When a graphics device is initialized, its virtual coordinate system is reset so that the left edge corresponds to an x-coordinate of `-1`, the right edge to x-coordinate `1`, the bottom edge to y-coordinate `-1`, and the top edge to y-coordinate `1`.

`graphics-device-coordinate-limits` *graphics-device*   [procedure]
> Returns (as multiple values) the device coordinate limits for *graphics-device*. The values, which are exact non-negative integers, are: *x-left*, *y-bottom*, *x-right*, and *y-top*.

`graphics-coordinate-limits` *graphics-device*   [procedure]
> Returns (as multiple values) the virtual coordinate limits for *graphics-device*. The values, which are real numbers, are: *x-left*, *y-bottom*, *x-right*, and *y-top*.

`graphics-set-coordinate-limits` *graphics-device x-left y-bottom*   [procedure]
>   *x-right y-top*
>
> Changes the virtual coordinate limits of *graphics-device* to the given arguments. *X-left*, *y-bottom*, *x-right*, and *y-top* must be real numbers. Subsequent calls to `graphics-coordinate-limits` will return the new limits. This operation has no effect on the device's displayed contents.
>
> Note: This operation usually resets the clip rectangle, although it is not guaranteed to do so. If a clip rectangle is in effect when this procedure is called, it is necessary to redefine the clip rectangle afterwards.

17.3 Drawing Graphics

The procedures in this section provide the basic drawing capabilities of Scheme's graphics system.

`graphics-clear` *graphics-device*   [procedure]
> Clears the display of *graphics-device*. Unaffected by the current drawing mode.

`graphics-draw-point` *graphics-device x y*   [procedure]
> Draws a single point on *graphics-device* at the virtual coordinates given by *x* and *y*, using the current drawing mode.

`graphics-erase-point` *graphics-device x y*   [procedure]
> Erases a single point on *graphics-device* at the virtual coordinates given by *x* and *y*. This procedure is unaffected by the current drawing mode.

This is equivalent to

```
(lambda (device x y)
  (graphics-bind-drawing-mode device 0
    (lambda ()
      (graphics-draw-point device x y))))
```

`graphics-draw-line` *graphics-device x-start y-start x-end y-end*   [procedure]
> *X-start, y-start, x-end,* and *y-end* must be real numbers. Draws a line on *graphics-device* that connects the points (*x-start, y-start*) and (*x-end, y-end*). The line is drawn using the current drawing mode and line style.

`graphics-draw-text` *graphics-device x y string*   [procedure]
> Draws the characters of *string* at the point (*x, y*) on *graphics-device*, using the current drawing mode. The characteristics of the characters drawn are device-dependent, but all devices are initialized so that the characters are drawn upright, from left to right, with the leftmost edge of the leftmost character at *x*, and the baseline of the characters at *y*.

The following two procedures provide an alternate mechanism for drawing lines, which is more akin to using a plotter. They maintain a *cursor*, which can be positioned to a particular point and then dragged to another point, producing a line. Sequences of connected line segments can be drawn by dragging the cursor from point to point.

Many graphics operations have an unspecified effect on the cursor. The following exceptions are guaranteed to leave the cursor unaffected:

```
graphics-device-coordinate-limits
graphics-coordinate-limits
graphics-enable-buffering
graphics-disable-buffering
graphics-flush
graphics-bind-drawing-mode
graphics-set-drawing-mode
graphics-bind-line-style
graphics-set-line-style
```

The initial state of the cursor is unspecified.

`graphics-move-cursor` *graphics-device x y*   [procedure]
> Moves the cursor for *graphics-device* to the point (*x, y*). The contents of the device's display are unchanged.

`graphics-drag-cursor` *graphics-device x y*   [procedure]
> Draws a line from *graphics-device*'s cursor to the point (*x, y*), simultaneously moving the cursor to that point. The line is drawn using the current drawing mode and line style.

17.4 Characteristics of Graphics Output

Two characteristics of graphics output are so useful that they are supported uniformly by all graphics devices: *drawing mode* and *line style*. A third characteristic, *color*, is equally useful (if not more so), but implementation restrictions prohibit a uniform interface.

The *drawing mode*, an exact integer in the range 0 to 15 inclusive, determines how the figure being drawn is combined with the background over which it is drawn to generate the final result. Initially the drawing mode is set to "source", so that the new output overwrites whatever appears in that place. Useful alternative drawing modes can, for example, erase what was already there, or invert it.

Altogether 16 boolean operations are available for combining the source (what is being drawn) and the destination (what is being drawn over). The source and destination are combined by the device on a pixel-by-pixel basis as follows:

```
Mode    Meaning
----    -------
0       ZERO [erase; use background color]
1       source AND destination
2       source AND (NOT destination)
3       source
4       (NOT source) AND destination
5       destination
6       source XOR destination
7       source OR destination
8       NOT (source OR destination)
9       NOT (source XOR destination)
10      NOT destination
11      source OR (NOT destination)
12      NOT source
13      (NOT source) OR destination
14      (NOT source) OR (NOT destination)
15      ONE [use foreground color]
```

The *line style*, an exact integer in the range 0 to 7 inclusive, determines which parts of a line are drawn in the foreground color, and which in the background color. The default line style, "solid", draws the entire line in the foreground color. Alternatively, the "dash" style alternates between foreground and background colors to generate a dashed line. This capability is useful for plotting several things on the same graph.

Here is a table showing the name and approximate pattern of the different styles. A '1' in the pattern represents a foreground pixel, while a '-' represents a background pixel. Note that the precise output for each style will vary from device to device. The only style that is guaranteed to be the same for every device is "solid".

```
Style   Name                Pattern
-----   -------             -------
0       solid               1111111111111111
1       dash                11111111--------
2       dot                 1-1-1-1-1-1-1-1-
3       dash dot            1111111111111-1-
4       dash dot dot        11111111111-1-1-
5       long dash           11111111111-----
6       center dash         111111111111-11-
7       center dash dash    111111111-11-11-
```

graphics-bind-drawing-mode *graphics-device drawing-mode thunk*   [procedure]
graphics-bind-line-style *graphics-device line-style thunk*   [procedure]
>   These procedures bind the drawing mode or line style, respectively, of *graphics-device*,
>   invoke the procedure *thunk* with no arguments, then undo the binding when *thunk*
>   returns. The value of each procedure is the value returned by *thunk*. Graphics
>   operations performed during *thunk*'s dynamic extent will see the newly bound mode
>   or style as current.

graphics-set-drawing-mode *graphics-device drawing-mode*   [procedure]
graphics-set-line-style *graphics-device line-style*   [procedure]
>   These procedures change the drawing mode or line style, respectively, of *graphics-
>   device*. The mode or style will remain in effect until subsequent changes or bindings.

17.5 Buffering of Graphics Output

To improve performance of graphics output, most graphics devices provide some form of
buffering. By default, Scheme's graphics procedures flush this buffer after every drawing
operation. The procedures in this section allow the user to control the flushing of the output
buffer.

graphics-enable-buffering *graphics-device*   [procedure]
>   Enables buffering for *graphics-device*. In other words, after this procedure is called,
>   graphics operations are permitted to buffer their drawing requests. This usually
>   means that the drawing is delayed until the buffer is flushed explicitly by the user, or
>   until it fills up and is flushed by the system.

graphics-disable-buffering *graphics-device*   [procedure]
>   Disables buffering for *graphics-device*. By default, all graphics devices are initialized
>   with buffering disabled. After this procedure is called, all drawing operations perform
>   their output immediately, before returning.
>
>   Note: **graphics-disable-buffering** flushes the output buffer if necessary.

graphics-flush *graphics-device*   [procedure]
>   Flushes the graphics output buffer for *graphics-device*. This operation has no effect
>   for devices that do not support buffering, or if buffering is disabled for the device.

17.6 Clipping of Graphics Output

Scheme provides a rudimentary mechanism for restricting graphics output to a given rectangular subsection of a graphics device. By default, graphics output that is drawn anywhere within the device's virtual coordinate limits will appear on the device. When a *clip rectangle* is specified, however, output that would have appeared outside the clip rectangle is not drawn.

Note that changing the virtual coordinate limits for a device will usually reset the clip rectangle for that device, as will any operation that affects the size of the device (such as a window resizing operation). However, programs should not depend on this.

graphics-set-clip-rectangle *graphics-device x-left y-bottom x-right*   [procedure]
      y-top
      Specifies the clip rectangle for *graphics-device* in virtual coordinates. *X-left*, *y-bottom*, *x-right*, and *y-top* must be real numbers. Subsequent graphics output is clipped to the intersection of this rectangle and the device's virtual coordinate limits.

graphics-reset-clip-rectangle *graphics-device*   [procedure]
      Eliminates the clip rectangle for *graphics-device*. Subsequent graphics output is clipped to the virtual coordinate limits of the device.

17.7 Custom Graphics Operations

In addition to the standard operations, a graphics device may support *custom operations*. For example, most devices have custom operations to control color. **graphics-operation** is used to invoke custom operations.

graphics-operation *graphics-device name object* ...   [procedure]
      Invokes the graphics operation on *graphics-device* whose name is the symbol *name*, passing it the remaining arguments. This procedure can be used to invoke the standard operations, as well as custom operations that are specific to a particular graphics device type. The names of the standard graphics operations are formed by removing the **graphics-** prefix from the corresponding procedure. For example, the following are equivalent:

```
(graphics-draw-point device x y)
(graphics-operation device 'draw-point x y)
```

For information on the custom operations for a particular device, see the documentation for its type.

17.8 Images

Some graphics device types support images, which are rectangular pieces of picture that may be drawn into a graphics device. Images are often called something else in the host graphics system, such as bitmaps or pixmaps. The operations supported vary between devices, so look under the different device types to see what operations are available. All devices that support images support the following operations.

create-image *width height*   [operation on **graphics-device**]
      Images are created using the **create-image** graphics operation, specifying the *width* and *height* of the image in device coordinates (pixels).

```
(graphics-operation device 'create-image 200 100)
```

The initial contents of an image are unspecified.

`create-image` is a graphics operation rather than a procedure because the kind of image returned depends on the kind of graphics device used and the options specified in its creation. The image may be used freely with other graphics devices created with the same attributes, but the effects of using an image with a graphics device with different attributes (for example, different colors) is undefined. Under X, the image is display dependent.

`draw-image` *x y image*   [operation on `graphics-device`]
> The image is copied into the graphics device at the specified position.

`draw-subimage` *x y image im-x im-y w h*   [operation on `graphics-device`]
> Part of the image is copied into the graphics device at the specified (*x*, *y*) position. The part of the image that is copied is the rectangular region at *im-x* and *im-y* and of width *w* and height *h*. These four numbers are given in device coordinates (pixels).

`image?` *object*   [procedure]
> Returns `#t` if *object* is an image, otherwise returns `#f`.

`image/destroy` *image*   [procedure]
> This procedure destroys *image*, returning storage to the system. Programs should destroy images after they have been used because even modest images may use large amounts of memory. Images are reclaimed by the garbage collector, but they may be implemented using memory outside of Scheme's heap. If an image is reclaimed before being destroyed, the implementation might not deallocate that non-heap memory, which can cause a subsequent call to `create-image` to fail because it is unable to allocate enough memory.

`image/height` *image*   [procedure]
> Returns the height of the image in device coordinates.

`image/width` *image*   [procedure]
> Returns the width of the image in device coordinates.

`image/fill-from-byte-vector` *image bytes*   [procedure]
> The contents of *image* are set in a device-dependent way, using one byte per pixel from *bytes* (a string). Pixels are filled row by row from the top of the image to the bottom, with each row being filled from left to right. There must be at least (`*` (`image/height` *image*) (`image/width` *image*)) bytes in *bytes*.

17.9 X Graphics

MIT/GNU Scheme supports graphics in the X window system (version 11). Arbitrary numbers of displays may be opened, and arbitrary numbers of graphics windows may be created for each display. A variety of operations is available to manipulate various aspects of the windows, to control their size, position, colors, and mapping. The X graphics device type supports images, which are implemented as Xlib `XImage` objects. X display, window, and image objects are automatically closed if they are reclaimed by the garbage collector.

17.9.1 X Graphics Type

A graphics device for X windows is created by passing the symbol x as the graphics device
type name to `make-graphics-device`:

    (make-graphics-device 'x #!optional *display geometry suppress-map?*)

where *display* is either a display object, #f, or a string; *geometry* is either #f or a string;
and *suppress-map?* is a boolean or a vector (see below). A new window is created on the
appropriate display, and a graphics device representing that window is returned.

Display specifies which X display the window is to be opened on; if it is #f or a string,
it is passed as an argument to `x-open-display`, and the value returned by that procedure
is used in place of the original argument. *Geometry* is an X geometry string, or #f which
means to use the default geometry (which is specified as a resource).

Suppress-map?, if given, may take two forms. First, it may be a boolean: if #f (the
default), the window is automatically mapped after it is created; otherwise, #t means to
suppress this automatic mapping. The second form is a vector of three elements. The
first element is a boolean with the same meaning as the boolean form of *suppress-map?*.
The second element is a string, which specifies an alternative resource name to be used for
looking up the window's resources. The third element is also a string, which specifies a class
name for looking up the window's resources. The default value for *suppress-map?* is #f.

The default resource and class names are `"schemeGraphics"` and `"SchemeGraphics"`
respectively.

The window is initialized using the resource and class names specified by *suppress-map?*,
and is sensitive to the following resource properties:

```
Property         Class           Default
--------         -----           -------
geometry         Geometry        512x384+0+0
font             Font            fixed
borderWidth      BorderWidth     2
internalBorder   BorderWidth     [border width]
background       Background      white
foreground       Foreground      black
borderColor      BorderColor     [foreground color]
cursorColor      Foreground      [foreground color]
pointerColor     Foreground      [foreground color]
```

The window is created with a `backing_store` attribute of `Always`. The window's name
and icon name are initialized to `"scheme-graphics"`.

17.9.2 Utilities for X Graphics

`x-graphics/open-display` *display-name*   [procedure]
  Opens a connection to the display whose name is *display-name*, returning a display
  object. If unable to open a connection, #f is returned. *Display-name* is normally a
  string, which is an X display name in the usual form; however, #f is also allowed,
  meaning to use the value of the unix environment variable `DISPLAY`.

`x-graphics/close-display` *display*   [procedure]
> Closes *display*; after calling this procedure, it is an error to use *display* for any purpose. Any windows that were previously opened on *display* are destroyed and their resources returned to the operating system.

`x-close-all-displays`   [procedure]
> Closes all open connections to X displays. Equivalent to calling `x-close-display` on all open displays.

`x-geometry-string` *x y width height*   [procedure]
> This procedure creates and returns a standard X geometry string from the given arguments. *X* and *y* must be either exact integers or `#f`, while *width* and *height* must be either exact non-negative integers or `#f`. Usually either *x* and *y* are both specified or both `#f`; similarly for *width* and *height*. If only one of the elements of such a pair is specified, it is ignored.
>
> Examples:
>
> > ```
> > (x-geometry-string #f #f 100 200) ⇒ "100x200"
> > (x-geometry-string 2 -3 100 200) ⇒ "100x200+2-3"
> > (x-geometry-string 2 -3 #f #f) ⇒ "+2-3"
> > ```
>
> Note that the *x* and *y* arguments cannot distinguish between +0 and -0, even though these have different meanings in X. If either of those arguments is 0, it means +0 in X terminology. If you need to distinguish these two cases you must create your own geometry string using Scheme's string and number primitives.

17.9.3 Custom Operations on X Graphics Devices

Custom operations are invoked using the procedure `graphics-operation`. For example,

> ```
> (graphics-operation device 'set-foreground-color "blue")
> ```

`set-background-color` *color-name*	[operation on `x-graphics-device`]
`set-foreground-color` *color-name*	[operation on `x-graphics-device`]
`set-border-color` *color-name*	[operation on `x-graphics-device`]
`set-mouse-color` *color-name*	[operation on `x-graphics-device`]

> These operations change the colors associated with a window. *Color-name* must be a string, which is the X server's name for the desired color. `set-border-color` and `set-mouse-color` immediately change the border and mouse-cursor colors. `set-background-color` and `set-foreground-color` change the colors to be used when drawing, but have no effect on anything drawn prior to their invocation. Because changing the background color affects the entire window, we recommend calling `graphics-clear` on the window's device afterwards. Color names include both mnemonic names, like `"red"`, and intensity names specified in the `"#rrggbb"` notation.

`draw-arc` *x y radius-x radius-y angle-start*   [operation on `x-graphics-device`]
      angle-sweep fill?
> Operation `draw-arc` draws or fills an arc. An arc is a segment of a circle, which may have been stretched along the x- or y- axis to form an ellipse.

The parameters *x*, *y*, *radius-x* and *radius-y* describe the circle and *angle-start* and *angle-sweep* choose which part of the circle is drawn. The arc is drawn on the graphics device with the center of the circle at the virtual coordinates given by *x* and *y*. *radius-x* and *radius-y* determine the size of the circle in virtual coordinate units.

The parameter *angle-start* determines where the arc starts. It is measured in degrees in an anti-clockwise direction, starting at 3 o'clock. *angle-sweep* determines how much of the circle is drawn. It too is measured anti-clockwise in degrees. A negative value means the measurement is in a clockwise direction.

Note that the angles are determined on a unit circle before it is stretched into an ellipse, so the actual angles that you will see on the computer screen depends on all of: *radius-x* and *radius-y*, the window size, and the virtual coordinates.

If *fill?* is #f then just the segment of the circle is drawn, otherwise the arc is filled in a pie-slice fashion.

This draws a quarter circle pie slice, standing on its point, with point at virtual coordinates (3,5):

```
(graphics-opereration g 'draw-arc 3 5 .5 .5 45 90 #t)
```

draw-circle *x y radius*   [operation on **x-graphics-device**]
fill-circle *x y radius*   [operation on **x-graphics-device**]
These operations draw a circle (outline) or a filled circle (solid) at on the graphics device at the virtual coordinates given by *x* and *y*. These operations could be implemented trivially interms of the **draw-arc** operation.

set-border-width *width*   [operation on **x-graphics-device**]
set-internal-border-width *width*   [operation on **x-graphics-device**]
These operations change the external and internal border widths of a window. *Width* must be an exact non-negative integer, specified in pixels. The change takes place immediately. Note that changing the internal border width can cause displayed graphics to be garbled; we recommend calling **graphics-clear** on the window's device after doing so.

set-font *font-name*   [operation on **x-graphics-device**]
Changes the font used when drawing text in a window. *Font-name* must be a string that is a font name known to the X server. This operation does not affect text drawn prior to its invocation.

set-mouse-shape *shape-number*   [operation on **x-graphics-device**]
Changes the shape of the mouse cursor. *Shape-number* is an exact non-negative integer that is used as an index into the mouse-shape font; when multiplied by 2 this number corresponds to an index in the file
/usr/include/X11/cursorfont.h.

map-window   [operation on **x-graphics-device**]
withdraw-window   [operation on **x-graphics-device**]
These operations control the mapping of windows. They correspond directly to Xlib's **XMapWindow** and **XWithdrawWindow**.

`resize-window` *width height*   [operation on `x-graphics-device`]

> Changes the size of a window. *Width* and *height* must be exact non-negative integers.
> The operation corresponds directly to Xlib's `XResizeWindow`.
>
> This operation resets the virtual coordinate system and the clip rectangle.

`move-window` *x y*   [operation on `x-graphics-device`]

> Changes the position of a window on the display. *X* and *y* must be exact integers.
> The operation corresponds directly to Xlib's `XMoveWindow`. Note that the coordinates
> *x* and *y* do not take the external border into account, and therefore will not position
> the window as you might like. The only reliable way to position a window is to ask
> a window manager to do it for you.

`get-default` *resource property*   [operation on `x-graphics-device`]

> This operation corresponds directly to Xlib's `XGetDefault`. *Resource* and *property*
> must be strings. The operation returns the character string corresponding to the
> association of *resource* and *property*; if no such association exists, `#f` is returned.

`copy-area` *source-x-left source-y-top width height*   [operation on `x-graphics-device`]
          destination-x-left destination-y-top

> This operation copies the contents of the rectangle specified by *source-x-left*, *source-
> y-top*, *width*, and *height* to the rectangle of the same dimensions at *destination-x-left*
> and *destination-y-top*.

`font-structure` *font-name*   [operation on `x-graphics-device`]

> Returns a Scheme equivalent of the X font structure for the font named *font-name*. If
> the string *font-name* does not name a font known to the X server, or names a 16-bit
> font, `#f` is returned.

`x-font-structure/name` *font-structure*   [procedure]
`x-font-structure/direction` *font-structure*   [procedure]
`x-font-structure/all-chars-exist` *font-structure*   [procedure]
`x-font-structure/default-char` *font-structure*   [procedure]
`x-font-structure/min-bounds` *font-structure*   [procedure]
`x-font-structure/max-bounds` *font-structure*   [procedure]
`x-font-structure/start-index` *font-structure*   [procedure]
`x-font-structure/character-bounds` *font-structure*   [procedure]
`x-font-structure/max-ascent` *font-structure*   [procedure]
`x-font-structure/max-descent` *font-structure*   [procedure]

> These procedures extract the components of the font description structure returned by
> the X graphics operation `font-structure`. A more complete description of these com-
> ponents appears in documentation of the `XLoadQueryFont` Xlib call. `start-index` is
> the index of the first character available in the font. The `min-bounds` and `max-bounds`
> components are structures of type `x-character-bounds`, and the `character-bounds`
> component is a vector of the same type.

`x-character-bounds/lbearing` *character-bounds*   [procedure]
`x-character-bounds/rbearing` *character-bounds*   [procedure]
`x-character-bounds/width` *character-bounds*   [procedure]
`x-character-bounds/ascent` *character-bounds*   [procedure]

x-character-bounds/descent *character-bounds*   [procedure]
   These procedures extract components of objects of type `x-character-bounds`. A
   more complete description of them appears in documentation of the
   `XLoadQueryFont` Xlib call.

17.10 Win32 Graphics

MIT/GNU Scheme supports graphics on Microsoft Windows 95, Windows 98, and Windows
NT. In addition to the usual operations, there are operations to control the size, position
and colors of a graphics window. Win32 devices support images, which are implemented as
device independent bitmaps (DIBs).

   The Win32 graphics device type is implemented as a top level window.
`graphics-enable-buffering` is implemented and gives a 2x to 4x speedup on many
graphics operations. As a convenience, when buffering is enabled clicking on the graphics
window's title bar effects a `graphics-flush` operation. The user has the benefit of the
increased performance and the ability to view the progress in drawing at the click of a
mouse button.

17.10.1 Win32 Graphics Type

Win32 graphics devices are created by specifying the symbol `win32` as the *graphics-device-
type* argument to `make-graphics-device`. The Win32 graphics device type is implemented
as a top-level window and supports color drawing in addition to the standard Scheme
graphics operations.

   Graphics devices are opened as follows:

   `(make-graphics-device 'win32 #!optional width height palette)`

where *width* and *height* specify the size, in pixels, of the drawing area in the graphics
window (i.e. excluding the frame). *Palette* determines the colors available for drawing in
the window.

   When a color is specified for drawing, the nearest color available in the palette is used.
Permitted values for *palette* are

`'grayscale`
   The window allocates colors from a grayscale palette of approximately 236
   shades of gray.

`'grayscale-128`
   The window allocates colors from a grayscale palette of 128 shades of gray.

`'standard`
   The standard palette has good selection of colors and grays.

`#f` or `'system`
   The colors available are those in the system palette. There are usually 16
   to 20 colors in the system palette and these are usually sufficent for simple
   applications like line drawings and x-vs-y graphs of mathematical functions.
   Drawing with the system palette can be more efficient.

If *palette* is not specified then the `standard` palette is used.

17.10.2 Custom Operations for Win32 Graphics

Custom operations are invoked using the procedure `graphics-operation`. For example,

    `(graphics-operation device 'set-foreground-color "blue")`

`set-background-color` *color-name*   [operation on `win32-graphics-device`]
`set-foreground-color` *color-name*   [operation on `win32-graphics-device`]

> These operations change the colors associated with a window. *Color-name* must be of one of the valid color specification forms listed below. `set-background-color` and `set-foreground-color` change the colors to be used when drawing, but have no effect on anything drawn prior to their invocation. Because changing the background color affects the entire window, we recommend calling `graphics-clear` on the window's device afterwards.
>
> The foreground color affects the drawing of text, points, lines, ellipses and filled polygons.
>
> Colors are specified in one of three ways:
>
> An integer   This is the Win32 internal RGB value.
>
> By name   A limited number of names are understood by the system. Names are strings, e.g. `"red"`, `"blue"`, `"black"`. More names can be registered with the `define-color` operation.
>
> RGB (Red-Green-Blue) triples
> > A triple is either a vector or list of three integers in the range 0–255 inclusive which specify the intensity of the red, green and blue components of the color. Thus `#(0 0 0)` is black, `(0 0 128)` is dark blue and `#(255 255 255)` is white.
>
> If the color is not available in the graphics device then the nearest available color is used instead.

`define-color` *name spec*   [operation on `win32-graphics-device`]

> Define the string *name* to be the color specified by *spec*. *Spec* may be any acceptable color specification. Note that the color names defined this way are available to any Win32 graphics device, and the names do *not* have to be defined for each device.
>
> Color names defined by this interface may also be used when setting the colors of the Scheme console window, or the colors of Edwin editor windows.

`find-color` *name*   [operation on `win32-graphics-device`]

> Looks up a color previously defined by `define-color`. This returns the color in its most efficient form for operations `set-foreground-color` or `set-background-color`.

`draw-ellipse` *left top right bottom*   [operation on `win32-graphics-device`]

> Draw an ellipse. *Left*, *top*, *right* and *bottom* indicate the coordinates of the bounding rectangle of the ellipse. Circles are merely ellipses with equal width and height. Note that the bounding rectangle has horizontal and vertical sides. Ellipses with rotated axes cannot be drawn. The rectangle applies to the center of the line used to draw the ellipse; if the line width has been set to greater than 1 then the ellipse will spill outside the bounding rectange by half of the line width.

fill-polygon *points*   [operation on `win32-graphics-device`]
Draws a filled polygon using the current foreground color. *Points* is a vector of real numbers. The numbers are in the order x1 y1 x2 y2 ... xn yn. For example,

    (graphics-operation device 'fill-polygon #(0 0 0 1 1 0))

draws a solid triangular region between the points (0, 0), (0, 1) and (1, 0).

load-bitmap *pathname*   [operation on `win32-graphics-device`]
The graphics device contents and size are initialized from the windows bitmap file specified by *pathname*. If no file type is supplied then a "`.BMP`" extension is added. If a clip rectangle is in effect when this procedure is called, it is necessary to redefine the clip rectangle afterwards.

save-bitmap *pathname*   [operation on `win32-graphics-device`]
The graphics device contents are saved as a bitmap to the file specified by *pathname*. If no file type is supplied then a "`.BMP`" extension is added. The saved bitmap may be incorporated into documents or printed.

move-window *x y*   [operation on `win32-graphics-device`]
The graphics device window is moved to the screen position specified by *x* and *y*.

resize-window *width height*   [operation on `win32-graphics-device`]
The graphics device window is resized to the specified *width* and *height* in device coordinates (pixels). If a clip rectangle is in effect when this procedure is called, it is necessary to redefine the clip rectangle afterwards.

set-line-width *width*   [operation on `win32-graphics-device`]
This operation sets the line width for future drawing of lines, points and ellipses. It does not affect existing lines and has no effect on filled polygons. The line width is specified in device units. The default and initial value of this parameter is 1 pixel.

set-window-name *name*   [operation on `win32-graphics-device`]
This sets the window title to the string *name*. The window is given the name "`Scheme Graphics`" at creation.

set-font *handle*   [operation on `win32-graphics-device`]
Sets the font for drawing text. Currently not well supported. If you can get a Win32 font handle it can be used here.

copy-area *source-x-left source-y-top width*   [operation on `win32-graphics-device`]
         height destination-x-left destination-y-top
This operation copies the contents of the rectangle specified by *source-x-left*, *source-y-top*, *width*, and *height* to the rectangle of the same dimensions at *destination-x-left* and *destination-y-top*.

18 Win32 Package Reference

18.1 Overview

The Win32 implementation is still in a state of development. It is expected that changes will be necessary when MIT/GNU Scheme is ported to Windows NT on the DEC Alpha architecture. In particular, the current system is not arranged in a way that adequately distinguishes between issues that are a consequence of the NT operating system and those which are a consequence of the Intel x86 architecture.

Thus this documentation is not definitive, it merely outlines how the current system works. Parts of the system will change and any project implemented using the win32 system must plan for a re-implementation stage.

The Win32 implementation has several components:

- Special microcode primitives.
- A foreign function interface (FFI) for calling procedures in dynamically linked libraries (DLLs).
- An interface for Edwin.
- The Win32 package provides support for using the features of the Windows 3.1 and Windows NT 3.1 environments.
- Device Independent Bitmap utilities. These are used by the win32 Scheme Graphics implementation. (The Scheme Graphics implementation is described in the Reference Manual).

Note that all the names in the Win32 support are part of the `win32` package. The names are bound in the `(win32)` environment, and do not appear as bindings in the user or root environments. An effect of this is that it is far easier to develop Win32 software in the `(win32)` package environment or a child environment.

18.2 Foreign Function Interface

The Win32 foreign function interface (FFI) is a primitive and fairly simple system for calling procedures written in C in a dynamically linked library (DLL). Both user's procedures from a custom DLL and system procedures (e.g. MessageBox) are called using the same mechanism.

Warning: The FFI as it stands has several flaws which make it difficult to use reliably. It is expected that both the interface to and the mechanisms used by the FFI will be changed in the future. We provide it, and this documentation, only to give people an early start in accessing some of the features of Win32 from Scheme. Should you use it in an experiment we welcome any feedback.

The FFI is designed for calling C procedures that use C data types rather than Scheme data objects. Thus it is not possible to write and call a C procedure that returns, for example, a Scheme list. The object returned will always be an integer (which may represent the address of a C data structure).

Warning: It is extremely dangerous to try to pass Scheme callback procedures to C procedures. It is only possible by passing integer 'handles' rather than the actual procedures, and even so, if a garbage collection occurs during the execution of the callback procedure objects in Scheme's heap will have moved. Thus in a foreign procedure that has a callback and a string, after calling the callback the string value may no longer be valid. Playing this game requires a profound knowledge of the implementation.

The interface to the FFI has two main components: a language for declaring the types of values passed to and returned from the foreign procedures and a form for declaring foreign procedures.

18.2.1 Windows Types

Foreign types are designed to represent a correspondence between a Scheme data type that is used to represent an object within the Scheme world and a C data type that represents the data object in the C world. Thus we cannot manipulate true C objects in Scheme, nor can we manipulate Scheme objects in C.

Each foreign type has four aspects that together ensure that the correspondence between the Scheme and C objects is maintained. These aspects are all encoded as procedures that either check for validity or convert between representations. Thus a foreign type is not a declarative type so much as a procedural description of how to pass the type. The underlying foreign procedure call mechanism can pass integers and vector-like Scheme objects, and returns integer values. All other objects must be translated into integers or some other basic type, and must be recovered from integers.

The aspects are:

check   A predicate that returns `#t` if the argument is of an acceptable Scheme type, otherwise returns `#f`. The *check* procedure is used for type-checking.

convert   A procedure of one argument which returns a Scheme object of one of the basic types. It is used to convert an object into a 'simpler' object that will eventually be converted into a C object. The legal simpler objects are integers and strings.

return-convert

       A procedure of one argument that, given an integer, returns a Scheme object of a type satisfying *check*. Its purpose is to convert the result returned by the foreign procedure into a Scheme value.

revert   Some C procedures modify one or more of their arguments. These arguments are passed by reference, i.e. as a pointer to their address. Since a Scheme object might have a different memory layout and storage conventions, it must be passed by copy-in and copy-out rather than by reference. *Revert* is a procedure of two parameters, the original object passed and the result of *convert* on that object. *Revert* may then inspect the converted object and copy back the changes to the original.

define-windows-type *name check convert return revert*   [special form]
define-similar-windows-type *name model* [*check* [*convert* [*return*   [special form]
      [*revert*]]]]
       Both forms define a windows type. The first form defines a type in terms of its aspects as described above. The second defines the type as being like another type, except for certain aspects, which are redefined. *Name* is the name of the type. *Model* is the name of a type. *Check*, *convert*, *return* and *revert* are procedures or the value `#f`. A

#f means use the default value, which in the second form means use the definition provided for *model*. The defaults are

check   (lambda (x) #t), i.e. unchecked.

convert   (lambda (x) x), i.e. no translation performed.

return   (lambda (x) x), i.e. no translation performed.

revert   (lambda (x y) unspecific), i.e. no update performed

The `unchecked` windows type (see below) is defined as:

```
(define-windows-type unchecked #f #f #f #f)
```

Windows types are *not* first class values, so they cannot be stored in variables or defined using `define`:

```
(define my-type unchecked)                      [error]    Unbound variable
(define-similar-windows-type my-type unchecked)
                                                  ;; the correct way
```

Scheme characters must be converted to integers. This is accomplished as follows:

```
(define-windows-type char
    char?               ; check
    char->integer   ; convert
    integer->char   ; convert return value
    #f                  ; cannot be passed by reference
)
```

unchecked   [windows type]
The type which is not checked and undergoes only the basic conversion from a Scheme integer to a C integer or from a Scheme string to a C pointer to the first byte of the string. Returned `unchecked` values are returned as integers.

bool   [windows type]
Scheme booleans are analogous to C integers 0 and 1. Windows type `bool` have been defined as:

```
(define-windows-type bool
    boolean?
    (lambda (x) (if x 1 0))
    (lambda (x) (if (eq? x 0) #f #t))
    #f)
```

char   [windows type]
Scheme characters are converted into C objects of type `char`, which are indistinguishable from small integers.

int   [windows type]
uint   [windows type]
long   [windows type]
ulong   [windows type]
short   [windows type]
ushort   [windows type]

word   [windows type]
byte   [windows type]
    Various integer types that are passed without conversion.

string   [windows type]
    A string that is passed as a C pointer of type `char*` to the first character in the string.

char*   [windows type]
    A string or `#f`. The string is passed as a pointer to characters. The string is correctly
null-terminated. `#f` is passed as the null pointer. This is an example where there is
a more complex mapping between C objects and Scheme objects. C's `char*` type is
represented as one of two Scheme types depending on its value. This allows us us
to distinguish between the C string (pointer) that points to the empty sequence of
characters and the null pointer (which doesnt point anywhere).

handle   [windows type]
hbitmap   [windows type]
hbrush   [windows type]
hcursor   [windows type]
hdc   [windows type]
hicon   [windows type]
hinstance   [windows type]
hmenu   [windows type]
hpalette   [windows type]
hpen   [windows type]
hrgn   [windows type]
hwnd   [windows type]
    Various kinds of Win32 handle. These names correspond to the same, but all up-
percase, names in the Windows C language header files. Win32 API calls are the
source of values of this type and the values are meaningless except as arguments to
other Win32 API calls. Currently these values are represented as integers but we
expect that Win32 handles will in future be represented by allocated Scheme objects
(e.g. records) that will allow predicates (e.g. `hmenu?`) and sensible interlocking with
the garbage collector to free the programmer of the current tedious allocation and
deallocation of handles.

resource-id   [windows type]
    A Windows resource identifier is either a small integer or a string. In C, this distinc-
tion is possible because pointers look like larger integers, so a machine word representing a small integer can be distinguished from a machine word that is a pointer to
the text of the name of the resource.

18.2.2 Windows Foreign Procedures

Foreign procedures are declared as callable entry-points in a module, usually a dynamically
linked library (DLL).

find-module *name*   [procedure]
    Returns a module suitable for use in creating procedures with `windows-procedure`.
Name is a string which is the name of a DLL file. Internally, `find-module` uses the

LoadLibrary Win32 API, so *name* should conform to the specifications for this call. *Name* should be either a full path name of a DLL, or the name of a DLL that resides in the same directory as the Scheme binary SCHEME.EXE or in the system directory.

The module returned is a description for the DLL, and the DLL need not necessarily be linked at or immediately after this call. DLL modules are linked on need and unlinked before Scheme exits and when there are no remaining references to entry points after a garbage-collection. This behavior ensures that the Scheme system can run when a DLL is absent, provided the DLL is not actually used (i.e. no attempt is made to call a procedure in the DLL).

gdi32.dll   [variable]

This variable is bound to the module describing the GDI32.DLL library, which contains the Win32 API graphics calls, e.g. LineTo.

kernel32.dll   [variable]

This variable is bound to the module describing the KERNEL32.DLL library.

user32.dll   [variable]

This variable is bound to the module describing the USER32.DLL library. This module contains many useful Win32 API procedures, like MessageBox and SetWindowText.

windows-procedure (*name* (*parameter type*) ...) *return-type module*   [special form]
      entry-name [*options*]

This form creates a procedure, and could be thought of as "foreign-named-lambda". The form creates a Scheme procedure that calls the C procedure identified by the exported entry point *entry-name* in the module identified by the value of *module*. Both *entry-name* and *module* are evaluated at procedure creation time, so either may be expression. *Entry-name* must evaluate to a string and *module* must evaluate to a module as returned by find-module. These are the only parts of the form that are evaluated at procedure creation time.

Name is the name of the procedure and is for documentation purposes only. This form *does not* define a procedure called *name*. It is more like lambda. The name might be used for debugging and pretty-printing.

A windows procedure has a fixed number of parameters (i.e. no 'rest' parameters or 'varargs'), each of which is named and associated with a windows type *type*. Both the name *parameter* and the windows type *type* must be symbols and are not evaluated. The procedure returns a value of the windows type *return-type*.

The following example creates a procedure that takes a window handle (hwnd) and a string and returns a boolean (bool) result. The procedure does this by calling the SetWindowText entry in the module that is the value of the variable user32.dll. The variable set-window-title is defined to have this procedure as it's value.

```
(define set-window-title
  (windows-procedure
   (set-window-text (window hwnd) (text string))
   bool user32.dll "SetWindowText"))

(set-window-title my-win "Hi")
                              ⇒  #t
                              ;; Changes window's title/text
```

```
set-window-title          ⇒  #[compiled-procedure  ...]
set-window-text         [error]  Unbound variable
```

When there are no *options* the created procedure will (a) check its arguments against the types, (b) convert the arguments, (c) call the C procedure and (d) convert the returned value. No reversion is performed, even if one of the *types* has a reversion defined. (Reverted types are rare [I have never used one], so paying a cost for this unless it is used seems silly).

The following options are allowed:

with-reversions
> The reversions are included in the type conversions.

expand   A synonym for **with-reversions**.

Scheme code
> The *Scheme code* is placed between steps (a) and (b) in the default process. The Scheme code can enforce constraints on the arguments, including constraints between arguments such as checking that an index refers to a valid position in a string.

If both options (i.e. **with-reversions** and Scheme code) are used, **with-reversions** must appear first. There can be arbitrarily many Scheme expression.

18.2.3 Win32 API names and procedures

This section is a moving target.

The **#define** values from **wingdi.h** and **winuser.h** are available as bindings in the **(win32)** package environment. The **#define** symbols are all uppercase; these have been translated to all lowercase Scheme identifiers, thus **WM_LBUTTONUP** is the scheme variable **wm_lbuttonup**. As Scheme is case insensitive, the upper-case version may be used and probably should to make the code look more like conventional Windows code. The Scheme bindings have been produced automagically. Most of the **#define**-symbols contain an underscore so there are not many name clashes. There is one very notable name clash, however: **ERROR** is **#defined** to 0, which shadows the scheme procedure **error** in the root package environment. To signal an error, use **access** to get **error** from the system global environment:

```
(declare (usual-integrations))
...
((access error system-global-environment) "Complain" ...)
```

The set of procedures is incomplete because procedures have been added on a by-need basis for the implementation of other parts of the system, e.g. Scheme Graphics. Look in the implementation for further details.

Win32 API procedure names have been uniformly converted into Scheme identifiers as follows:

- A leading uppercase letter is translated into a lowercase letter.
- Subsequent sequences of uppercase letters are translated into lowercase letters preceeded by a hyphen (minus symbol), i.e. hyphens are inserted at a lowercase to uppercase transition.
- Predicates beginning with `Is` finally have a question-mark appended.

Example: applying these rules to `IsWindow` yields `is-window?`, and `GetDC` is translated into `get-dc`.

18.3 Device Independent Bitmap Utilities

The Device Independent Bitmap (DIB) utilities library `DIBUTILS.DLL` and the associated procedures in `dib.scm` in the Win32 system source is an example of how to use the foreign function interface to access and manipulate non-Scheme objects.

`dib`   [windows type]

In the C world a DIB is a *handle* to a piece of memory containing the bits that represent information about the image and the pixels of the image. The handle is a machine-word sized piece of data which may be thought of as a 32 bit integer. The handle may be null (i.e. zero), indicating that there is no block of memory describing the DIB. The null value is usually returned by C functions that are supposed to create a DIB but failed, for some reason like the memory could not be allocated or a file could not be opened.

In the Scheme world a DIB is a structure containing information about the bitmap (specifically the integer that represents the handle). We also include `#f` in the `dib` windows type to mirror the null handle error value.

```
(define dib-result
  (lambda (handle)
    (if (= handle 0)
        #f
        (make-dib handle))))

(define dib-arg
  (lambda (dib)
    (if dib
        (cell-contents (dib-handle dib))
        0)))

(define-windows-type dib
  (lambda (thing) (or (dib? thing) (eq? thing #f)))
  dib-arg
  dib-result)
```

18.3.1 DIB procedures

The following procedures have typed parameters, using the same convention as `windows-procedure`.

open-dib (*filename string*)   [procedure]
    Return type: *dib*. Calls the `OpenDIB` entry of `DIBUTILS.DLL`. If the return value is
    not `#f` then the file *filename* was found, successfully opened, and the contents were
    suitable for loading into memory as a device independent bitmap.

write-dib (*filename string*) (*dib dib*)   [procedure]
    Return type: *bool*. Calls the `WriteDIB` entry of `DIBUTILS.DLL`. Returns `#t` if the
    file *filename* could be opened and written to. After this operation the file contains
    the bitmap data in a standard format that is understood by `open-dib` and various
    system utilities like the bitmap editor. Any problems resulting in failure are signalled
    by a `#f` return value.

bitmap-from-dib (*dib dib*) (*palette hpalette*)   [procedure]
    Return type: *hbitmap*. Calls the `BitmapFromDib` entry of `DIBUTILS.DLL`. The re-
    turned value is a device dependent bitmap. The colours from the DIB are matched
    against colors in *palette*.

dib-from-bitmap (*bitmap hbitmap*) (*style dword*) (*bits word*) (*palette*   [procedure]
        hpalette)
    Return type: *dib*. Returns a DIB containing the same image as the device dependent
    bitmap *bitmap*. *Style* determines the kind of DIB, e.g. compression style. Calls the
    `DibFromBitmap` entry of `DIBUTILS.DLL`.

dib-blt (*dest hdc*) (*x int*) (*y int*) (*w int*) (*h int*) (*src dib*) (*src-x int*)   [procedure]
        (*src-y int*) (*raster-op long*)
    Return type: *bool*. Calls the `DibBlt` entry of `DIBUTILS.DLL`. Similar to the Win32
    API `BitBlt` call, but draws a DIB rather than a piece of another device context.
    Draws the *dib* on device context *hdc* at position (*x,y*). A rectangle of width *w* and
    height *h* is copied from position (*src-x,src-y*) of *dib*. *Raster-op* is supposed to allow
    the source and destination to be combined but I don't think I got this right so stick
    to `SRCCOPY`.

delete-dib (*dib dib*)   [procedure]
    Return type: *bool*. This procedure reclaims the storage occupied by a DIB. After
    being deleted, the DIB should not be used. This procedure allows the programmer
    to reclaim external heap storage rather than risking it running out before the next
    garbage collection.

dib-height (*dib dib*)   [procedure]
    Return type: *int*. Calls the `DibHeight` expand entry of `DIBUTILS.DLL`, which returns
    the height of the bitmap in pixels.

dib-width (*dib dib*)   [procedure]
    Return type: *int*. Calls the `DibWidth` entry of `DIBUTILS.DLL`, which returns the
    width of the bitmap in pixels.

copy-bitmap (*bm hbitmap*)   [procedure]
    Return type: *hbitmap*. Calls the `CopyBitmap` of `DIBUTILS.DLL`, which creates a new
    bitmap with the same size and contents as the original.

create-dib (*width int*) (*height int*) (*style int*) (*depth int*) (*palette*   [procedure]
        hpalette)
>   Return type: *dib*. Calls the `CreateDIB` entry of `DIBUTILS.DLL`. Creates a DIB of
>   *width* by *height* pixels and *depth* bits of colour information. The *style* parameter
>   determines how the bitmap is stored. I have only ever used `BI_RGB`. If *depth*<=8
>   then the *palette* determines the DIB's colour table.

crop-bitmap (*bm hbitmap*) (*left int*) (*top int*) (*right int*) (*bottom int*)   [procedure]
>   Return type: *hbitmap*. Calls the `CropBitmap` entry of `DIBUTILS.DLL`. Returns a new
>   bitmap containing the image from a region of the original.

dib-set-pixels-unaligned *dib* (*pixels string*)   [procedure]
>   Return type: *bool*. Calls the `DIBSetPixelsUnaligned` entry of
>   `DIBUTILS.DLL`. Stuffs bytes from *pixels* into the bitmap. There are no alignment
>   constraints on *pixels* (the usual way of doing this is to use the `SetDIBits` function
>   which requires that every scan line of the bitmap is 32-bit word aligned, even if the
>   scan lines are not a multiple of 4 bytes long). doing this

18.3.2 Other parts of the DIB Utilities implementation

The `DIBUTILS.DLL` library is an ordinary DLL. See the standard Microsoft Windows documentation on how to create DLLs. Look at the code in the `WIN32/DIBUTILS` directory of
the Scheme source.

Please note:

- For the foreign function interface to find the procedures they must be declared as
  exports in the `.DEF` definition file.

- To load the `.DLL` file use the `find-module` Scheme function. Look at `WIN32/DIB.SCM`
  to see how this is done.

- The current system works with C procedures with the `__stdcall` and `__cdecl` calling
  conventions but *not* the `__fastcall` calling convention.

Appendix A GNU Free Documentation License

Version 1.2, November 2002

Copyright © 2000,2001,2002 Free Software Foundation, Inc.
51 Franklin St, Fifth Floor, Boston, MA 02110-1301, USA

0. PREAMBLE

The purpose of this License is to make a manual, textbook, or other functional and useful document *free* in the sense of freedom: to assure everyone the effective freedom to copy and redistribute it, with or without modifying it, either commercially or non-commercially. Secondarily, this License preserves for the author and publisher a way to get credit for their work, while not being considered responsible for modifications made by others.

This License is a kind of "copyleft", which means that derivative works of the document must themselves be free in the same sense. It complements the GNU General Public License, which is a copyleft license designed for free software.

We have designed this License in order to use it for manuals for free software, because free software needs free documentation: a free program should come with manuals providing the same freedoms that the software does. But this License is not limited to software manuals; it can be used for any textual work, regardless of subject matter or whether it is published as a printed book. We recommend this License principally for works whose purpose is instruction or reference.

1. APPLICABILITY AND DEFINITIONS

This License applies to any manual or other work, in any medium, that contains a notice placed by the copyright holder saying it can be distributed under the terms of this License. Such a notice grants a world-wide, royalty-free license, unlimited in duration, to use that work under the conditions stated herein. The "Document", below, refers to any such manual or work. Any member of the public is a licensee, and is addressed as "you". You accept the license if you copy, modify or distribute the work in a way requiring permission under copyright law.

A "Modified Version" of the Document means any work containing the Document or a portion of it, either copied verbatim, or with modifications and/or translated into another language.

A "Secondary Section" is a named appendix or a front-matter section of the Document that deals exclusively with the relationship of the publishers or authors of the Document to the Document's overall subject (or to related matters) and contains nothing that could fall directly within that overall subject. (Thus, if the Document is in part a textbook of mathematics, a Secondary Section may not explain any mathematics.) The relationship could be a matter of historical connection with the subject or with related matters, or of legal, commercial, philosophical, ethical or political position regarding them.

The "Invariant Sections" are certain Secondary Sections whose titles are designated, as being those of Invariant Sections, in the notice that says that the Document is released

under this License. If a section does not fit the above definition of Secondary then it is
not allowed to be designated as Invariant. The Document may contain zero Invariant
Sections. If the Document does not identify any Invariant Sections then there are none.

The "Cover Texts" are certain short passages of text that are listed, as Front-Cover
Texts or Back-Cover Texts, in the notice that says that the Document is released under
this License. A Front-Cover Text may be at most 5 words, and a Back-Cover Text may
be at most 25 words.

A "Transparent" copy of the Document means a machine-readable copy, represented
in a format whose specification is available to the general public, that is suitable for
revising the document straightforwardly with generic text editors or (for images composed of pixels) generic paint programs or (for drawings) some widely available drawing
editor, and that is suitable for input to text formatters or for automatic translation to
a variety of formats suitable for input to text formatters. A copy made in an otherwise
Transparent file format whose markup, or absence of markup, has been arranged to
thwart or discourage subsequent modification by readers is not Transparent. An image
format is not Transparent if used for any substantial amount of text. A copy that is
not "Transparent" is called "Opaque".

Examples of suitable formats for Transparent copies include plain ASCII without
markup, Texinfo input format, LaTeX input format, SGML or XML using a publicly
available DTD, and standard-conforming simple HTML, PostScript or PDF designed
for human modification. Examples of transparent image formats include PNG, XCF
and JPG. Opaque formats include proprietary formats that can be read and edited
only by proprietary word processors, SGML or XML for which the DTD and/or
processing tools are not generally available, and the machine-generated HTML,
PostScript or PDF produced by some word processors for output purposes only.

The "Title Page" means, for a printed book, the title page itself, plus such following
pages as are needed to hold, legibly, the material this License requires to appear in the
title page. For works in formats which do not have any title page as such, "Title Page"
means the text near the most prominent appearance of the work's title, preceding the
beginning of the body of the text.

A section "Entitled XYZ" means a named subunit of the Document whose title either
is precisely XYZ or contains XYZ in parentheses following text that translates XYZ in
another language. (Here XYZ stands for a specific section name mentioned below, such
as "Acknowledgements", "Dedications", "Endorsements", or "History".) To "Preserve
the Title" of such a section when you modify the Document means that it remains a
section "Entitled XYZ" according to this definition.

The Document may include Warranty Disclaimers next to the notice which states that
this License applies to the Document. These Warranty Disclaimers are considered to
be included by reference in this License, but only as regards disclaiming warranties:
any other implication that these Warranty Disclaimers may have is void and has no
effect on the meaning of this License.

2. VERBATIM COPYING

You may copy and distribute the Document in any medium, either commercially or
noncommercially, provided that this License, the copyright notices, and the license
notice saying this License applies to the Document are reproduced in all copies, and

that you add no other conditions whatsoever to those of this License. You may not use technical measures to obstruct or control the reading or further copying of the copies you make or distribute. However, you may accept compensation in exchange for copies. If you distribute a large enough number of copies you must also follow the conditions in section 3.

You may also lend copies, under the same conditions stated above, and you may publicly display copies.

3. COPYING IN QUANTITY

If you publish printed copies (or copies in media that commonly have printed covers) of the Document, numbering more than 100, and the Document's license notice requires Cover Texts, you must enclose the copies in covers that carry, clearly and legibly, all these Cover Texts: Front-Cover Texts on the front cover, and Back-Cover Texts on the back cover. Both covers must also clearly and legibly identify you as the publisher of these copies. The front cover must present the full title with all words of the title equally prominent and visible. You may add other material on the covers in addition. Copying with changes limited to the covers, as long as they preserve the title of the Document and satisfy these conditions, can be treated as verbatim copying in other respects.

If the required texts for either cover are too voluminous to fit legibly, you should put the first ones listed (as many as fit reasonably) on the actual cover, and continue the rest onto adjacent pages.

If you publish or distribute Opaque copies of the Document numbering more than 100, you must either include a machine-readable Transparent copy along with each Opaque copy, or state in or with each Opaque copy a computer-network location from which the general network-using public has access to download using public-standard network protocols a complete Transparent copy of the Document, free of added material. If you use the latter option, you must take reasonably prudent steps, when you begin distribution of Opaque copies in quantity, to ensure that this Transparent copy will remain thus accessible at the stated location until at least one year after the last time you distribute an Opaque copy (directly or through your agents or retailers) of that edition to the public.

It is requested, but not required, that you contact the authors of the Document well before redistributing any large number of copies, to give them a chance to provide you with an updated version of the Document.

4. MODIFICATIONS

You may copy and distribute a Modified Version of the Document under the conditions of sections 2 and 3 above, provided that you release the Modified Version under precisely this License, with the Modified Version filling the role of the Document, thus licensing distribution and modification of the Modified Version to whoever possesses a copy of it. In addition, you must do these things in the Modified Version:

A. Use in the Title Page (and on the covers, if any) a title distinct from that of the Document, and from those of previous versions (which should, if there were any, be listed in the History section of the Document). You may use the same title as a previous version if the original publisher of that version gives permission.

B. List on the Title Page, as authors, one or more persons or entities responsible for authorship of the modifications in the Modified Version, together with at least five of the principal authors of the Document (all of its principal authors, if it has fewer than five), unless they release you from this requirement.

C. State on the Title page the name of the publisher of the Modified Version, as the publisher.

D. Preserve all the copyright notices of the Document.

E. Add an appropriate copyright notice for your modifications adjacent to the other copyright notices.

F. Include, immediately after the copyright notices, a license notice giving the public permission to use the Modified Version under the terms of this License, in the form shown in the Addendum below.

G. Preserve in that license notice the full lists of Invariant Sections and required Cover Texts given in the Document's license notice.

H. Include an unaltered copy of this License.

I. Preserve the section Entitled "History", Preserve its Title, and add to it an item stating at least the title, year, new authors, and publisher of the Modified Version as given on the Title Page. If there is no section Entitled "History" in the Document, create one stating the title, year, authors, and publisher of the Document as given on its Title Page, then add an item describing the Modified Version as stated in the previous sentence.

J. Preserve the network location, if any, given in the Document for public access to a Transparent copy of the Document, and likewise the network locations given in the Document for previous versions it was based on. These may be placed in the "History" section. You may omit a network location for a work that was published at least four years before the Document itself, or if the original publisher of the version it refers to gives permission.

K. For any section Entitled "Acknowledgements" or "Dedications", Preserve the Title of the section, and preserve in the section all the substance and tone of each of the contributor acknowledgements and/or dedications given therein.

L. Preserve all the Invariant Sections of the Document, unaltered in their text and in their titles. Section numbers or the equivalent are not considered part of the section titles.

M. Delete any section Entitled "Endorsements". Such a section may not be included in the Modified Version.

N. Do not retitle any existing section to be Entitled "Endorsements" or to conflict in title with any Invariant Section.

O. Preserve any Warranty Disclaimers.

If the Modified Version includes new front-matter sections or appendices that qualify as Secondary Sections and contain no material copied from the Document, you may at your option designate some or all of these sections as invariant. To do this, add their titles to the list of Invariant Sections in the Modified Version's license notice. These titles must be distinct from any other section titles.

You may add a section Entitled "Endorsements", provided it contains nothing but endorsements of your Modified Version by various parties—for example, statements of peer review or that the text has been approved by an organization as the authoritative definition of a standard.

You may add a passage of up to five words as a Front-Cover Text, and a passage of up to 25 words as a Back-Cover Text, to the end of the list of Cover Texts in the Modified Version. Only one passage of Front-Cover Text and one of Back-Cover Text may be added by (or through arrangements made by) any one entity. If the Document already includes a cover text for the same cover, previously added by you or by arrangement made by the same entity you are acting on behalf of, you may not add another; but you may replace the old one, on explicit permission from the previous publisher that added the old one.

The author(s) and publisher(s) of the Document do not by this License give permission to use their names for publicity for or to assert or imply endorsement of any Modified Version.

5. COMBINING DOCUMENTS

You may combine the Document with other documents released under this License, under the terms defined in section 4 above for modified versions, provided that you include in the combination all of the Invariant Sections of all of the original documents, unmodified, and list them all as Invariant Sections of your combined work in its license notice, and that you preserve all their Warranty Disclaimers.

The combined work need only contain one copy of this License, and multiple identical Invariant Sections may be replaced with a single copy. If there are multiple Invariant Sections with the same name but different contents, make the title of each such section unique by adding at the end of it, in parentheses, the name of the original author or publisher of that section if known, or else a unique number. Make the same adjustment to the section titles in the list of Invariant Sections in the license notice of the combined work.

In the combination, you must combine any sections Entitled "History" in the various original documents, forming one section Entitled "History"; likewise combine any sections Entitled "Acknowledgements", and any sections Entitled "Dedications". You must delete all sections Entitled "Endorsements."

6. COLLECTIONS OF DOCUMENTS

You may make a collection consisting of the Document and other documents released under this License, and replace the individual copies of this License in the various documents with a single copy that is included in the collection, provided that you follow the rules of this License for verbatim copying of each of the documents in all other respects.

You may extract a single document from such a collection, and distribute it individually under this License, provided you insert a copy of this License into the extracted document, and follow this License in all other respects regarding verbatim copying of that document.

7. AGGREGATION WITH INDEPENDENT WORKS

A compilation of the Document or its derivatives with other separate and independent documents or works, in or on a volume of a storage or distribution medium, is called an "aggregate" if the copyright resulting from the compilation is not used to limit the legal rights of the compilation's users beyond what the individual works permit. When the Document is included an aggregate, this License does not apply to the other works in the aggregate which are not themselves derivative works of the Document.

If the Cover Text requirement of section 3 is applicable to these copies of the Document, then if the Document is less than one half of the entire aggregate, the Document's Cover Texts may be placed on covers that bracket the Document within the aggregate, or the electronic equivalent of covers if the Document is in electronic form. Otherwise they must appear on printed covers that bracket the whole aggregate.

8. TRANSLATION

Translation is considered a kind of modification, so you may distribute translations of the Document under the terms of section 4. Replacing Invariant Sections with translations requires special permission from their copyright holders, but you may include translations of some or all Invariant Sections in addition to the original versions of these Invariant Sections. You may include a translation of this License, and all the license notices in the Document, and any Warrany Disclaimers, provided that you also include the original English version of this License and the original versions of those notices and disclaimers. In case of a disagreement between the translation and the original version of this License or a notice or disclaimer, the original version will prevail.

If a section in the Document is Entitled "Acknowledgements", "Dedications", or "History", the requirement (section 4) to Preserve its Title (section 1) will typically require changing the actual title.

9. TERMINATION

You may not copy, modify, sublicense, or distribute the Document except as expressly provided for under this License. Any other attempt to copy, modify, sublicense or distribute the Document is void, and will automatically terminate your rights under this License. However, parties who have received copies, or rights, from you under this License will not have their licenses terminated so long as such parties remain in full compliance.

10. FUTURE REVISIONS OF THIS LICENSE

The Free Software Foundation may publish new, revised versions of the GNU Free Documentation License from time to time. Such new versions will be similar in spirit to the present version, but may differ in detail to address new problems or concerns. See http://www.gnu.org/copyleft/.

Each version of the License is given a distinguishing version number. If the Document specifies that a particular numbered version of this License "or any later version" applies to it, you have the option of following the terms and conditions either of that specified version or of any later version that has been published (not as a draft) by the Free Software Foundation. If the Document does not specify a version number of this License, you may choose any version ever published (not as a draft) by the Free Software Foundation.

A.1 ADDENDUM: How to use this License for your documents

To use this License in a document you have written, include a copy of the License in the document and put the following copyright and license notices just after the title page:

```
Copyright (C)  year  your name.
Permission is granted to copy, distribute and/or modify this document
under the terms of the GNU Free Documentation License, Version 1.2
or any later version published by the Free Software Foundation;
with no Invariant Sections, no Front-Cover Texts, and no Back-Cover Texts.
A copy of the license is included in the section entitled ''GNU
Free Documentation License''.
```

If you have Invariant Sections, Front-Cover Texts and Back-Cover Texts, replace the "with...Texts." line with this:

```
with the Invariant Sections being list their titles, with
the Front-Cover Texts being list, and with the Back-Cover Texts
being list.
```

If you have Invariant Sections without Cover Texts, or some other combination of the three, merge those two alternatives to suit the situation.

If your document contains nontrivial examples of program code, we recommend releasing these examples in parallel under your choice of free software license, such as the GNU General Public License, to permit their use in free software.

Appendix B Binding Index

D

M

Q

R

S

T

X

Y

Z

Appendix C Concept Index

D

T

X

Z